The Ultimate
CHINESE
& ASIAN
Cookbook

The Ultimate
CHINESE
& ASIAN
Cookbook

Enticing stir-fries and sensational
aromatic dishes from the East

Consultant Editor: Linda Doeser

HERMES
HOUSE

This edition published by Hermes House
27 West 20th Street, New York, NY 10011

HERMES HOUSE books are available for bulk purchase for sales promotion
and for premium use. For details, write or call the sales director,
Hermes House, 27 West 20th Street, New York, NY 10011;
(800) 354-9657

Hermes House is an imprint of
Anness Publishing Inc.

ISBN 1 901289 09 5

Publisher: Joanna Lorenz
Project Editor: Linda Doeser
Copy Editor: Harriette Lanzer
Designer: Ian Sandom

Photography: Karl Adamson, Edward Allwright, David Armstrong, Steve Baxter, James Duncan,
Michelle Garrett, Amanda Heywood, Patrick McLeavey, Michael Michaels and Thomas Odulate
Styling: Madeleine Brehaut, Michelle Garrett, Maria Kelly, Blake Minton and Kirsty Rawlings
Food for Photography: Carla Capalbo, Kit Chan, Elizabeth Wolf-Cohen, Joanne Craig, Nicola
Fowler, Carole Handslip, Jane Hartshorn, Shehzad Husain, Wendy Lee, Lucy McKelvie, Annie
Nichols, Jane Stevenson and Steven Wheeler
Illustrations: Madeleine David

Printed and bound in Germany

CONTENTS

INTRODUCTION

Chinese and Asian cooking have become increasingly popular in the West with the proliferation of Chinese, Thai, Indonesian, Japanese and Balti restaurants. This superb collection of recipes now provides the opportunity for Western cooks to re-create the unique flavors and textures of the East in their own kitchens.

The cuisines of each country that have inspired these mouth-watering recipes have their own distinctive and special qualities: from the subtle spiciness of Thai cooking to the harmonious mixing of color, texture and flavor in Chinese stir-fries, from the fiery heat of Indonesian dishes to the almost painterly elegance of Japanese presentation. Yet they have many things in common, too – a careful blending of herbs and spices, a thoughtful combining of complementary ingredients and, of course, the widespread use of the wok. This multi-purpose pan, closely related to the karahi or Balti pan, is ideal for poaching, steaming and deep-frying, as well as stir-frying. Western cooks have been quick to recognize the ease and speed of wok cooking and so recipes that marry the best of East and West are also featured.

The book includes a basic introduction to taking care of and using a wok and a guide to other useful kitchen equipment. This is followed by notes on some of the more exotic ingredients, as well as standard Chinese and Asian sauces, spices and herbs. All the recipes are beautifully illustrated in color with easy-to-follow, step-by-step instructions. Hints and tips throughout the book advise on variations, best buys and ways of preparing some of the more unfamiliar ingredients.

Whether your tastes tend towards a full Chinese banquet, a satisfying curry for a midweek family supper, a quick and easy lunchtime treat or simply a different dessert, you will find just what you are looking for among the hundreds of recipes here.

INGREDIENTS

Bamboo shoots Mild-flavored, tender shoots of the young bamboo, widely available fresh, or sliced or halved in cans.

Basil Several different types of basil are used in Asian cooking. Thai cooks use two varieties, holy and sweet basil, but ordinary basil works well.

Bean curd See under Tofu.

Bean sprouts Shoots of the mung bean, usually available from supermarkets. They add a crisp texture to stir-fries.

Black bean sauce Made of salted black beans crushed and mixed with flour and spices (such as ginger, garlic or chili) to form a thickish paste. It is sold in jars or cans and, once opened, should be kept in the refrigerator.

Bok choy Also known as Pak choi, this is a leaf vegetable with long, smooth, milky white stems and dark green foliage.

Cardamom pods Available both as small green pods and as larger black pods containing seeds, they have a strong aromatic quality.

Cashews Whole cashews feature prominently in Chinese stir-fries, especially those with chicken.

Cassia bark A form of cinnamon, but with a more robust flavor.

Chili bean sauce Made from fermented bean paste mixed with hot chili and other seasonings. Sold in jars, chili bean sauces are quite mild, but some are very hot.

Chili oil Made from dried red chilies, garlic, onions, salt and vegetable oil, this is used more as a dip than as a cooking ingredient.

Chili sauce A very hot sauce made from chilies, vinegar, sugar and salt. Usually sold in bottles, it should be used sparingly. Tabasco sauce can be a substitute.

Chilies There is a wide range of fresh and dried chilies from which to choose. Generally, the larger the chili, the milder the flavor, but there are some exceptions, and the only way to gauge potency is by taste. Remove the seeds for a milder flavor. Whether using dried or fresh chilies, take care when preparing them, as their seeds and flesh can "burn": wash your hands immediately afterward or, better still, wear rubber gloves—and never rub your eyes.

Chinese cabbage Also known as Chinese leaves, two types are widely available. The most commonly seen variety has a pale green color and tightly wrapped elongated head, and about two-thirds of the cabbage is stem, which has a crunchy texture. The other type has a shorter and fatter head with curlier, pale yellow or green leaves, and white stems.

Chinese chives Better known as garlic chives, these are sometimes sold with their flowers.

Chinese five-spice powder This flavoring contains star anise, pepper, fennel, cloves and cinnamon.

Chinese pancakes Thin flour-and-water pancakes with no added seasonings or spices. They are available fresh or frozen.

Chinese rice wine Made from glutinous rice, this is also known as yellow wine—*huang jin* or *chiew*—because of its color. The best variety is called Shao Hsing or Shaoxing and comes from the southeast of China. Dry sherry may be used as a substitute.

Coconut milk and cream Coconut milk should not be confused with the "milk" or juice found inside a fresh coconut (though the latter makes a refreshing drink). The coconut milk used for cooking is produced from the white flesh of the nut. If left to stand, the thick part of the milk will rise to the surface like cream.

To make your own, break open a fresh coconut and remove the brown inner skin from the flesh. Grate sufficient flesh to measure 1⅔ cups. Place the grated flesh, together with 1¼ cups water, in a blender or food processor fitted with a metal blade and process for 1 minute. Strain the mixture through a strainer lined with cheesecloth into a bowl. Gather up the corners of the cheesecloth and squeeze out the liquid. The coconut milk is then ready to use, but you should stir it before use.
Coconut milk is also available in can.

Coriander Fresh coriander (cilantro) has a strong, pungent smell that combines well with other rich flavors. The white coriander root is used when the green coloring is not required. The seeds are also used, whole and ground.

Cornstarch paste To make cornstarch paste, mix 4 parts cornstarch with about 5 parts cold water until smooth.

Cumin Available as whole seeds and as a powder, cumin has a strong, slightly bitter flavor. It is used mainly in Indian recipes and in many other Asian dishes as well.

Curry paste Curry paste is traditionally made by pounding fresh herbs and spices in a mortar with a pestle. The two types of Thai curry paste, red and green, are made with red and green chilies, respectively. Other ingredients vary with individual cooks, but red curry paste typically contains ginger, shallots, garlic, coriander and cumin seeds and lime juice, as well as chilies. Herbs and flavorings in green curry paste usually include scallions, fresh cilantro, kaffir lime leaves, ginger, garlic and lemongrass. Making curry paste is time-consuming, but it tastes excellent and keeps well. Ready-made pastes, available in jars, are satisfactory substitutes.

Top shelf, left to right: *garlic, ginger, lemongrass, dried shrimp, Thai fish sauce, Szechuan peppercorns, sweet chili sauce, ground coriander, galangal, Chinese five-spice powder, fresh green chilies*

Middle shelf: *dried red chilies, peanuts (skins on), cardamom pods, cashew nuts (in jar), peanuts (skins off), kaffir lime leaves, tamarind, hoisin sauce, salted black beans, chili oil*

Bottom shelf, back row: *sake, rice vinegar, Chinese rice wine*

Bottom shelf, middle row: *sesame oil, mirin, peanut oil, fresh cilantro, cumin seeds*

Bottom shelf, front row: *basil, dried shrimp paste, red and green chilies, flaked coconut and creamed coconut, light soy sauce, oyster sauce, pieces of coconut, whole coconut*

Hoisin sauce A thick, dark brownish-red sauce that is sweet and spicy.

Kaffir lime leaves These are used rather like bay leaves, but to give an aromatic lime flavor to dishes. The fresh leaves are available from Asian food stores and can be frozen for future use.

Daikon A member of the radish family with a fresh, slightly peppery taste and white skin and flesh. Unlike other radishes, it is good when cooked, but should be salted and allowed to drain first, as it has a high water content. It is widely used in Chinese cooking and may be carved into an elaborate garnish.

Dashi Light Japanese broth, available in powder form. The flavor derives from kelp. Diluted vegetable broth made from a cube may be substituted.

Dried shrimp and shrimp paste Dried shrimp are tiny shrimp that are salted and dried. They are used as a seasoning for stir-fried dishes. First soak them in warm water until soft, then either process them in a blender or food processor or pound them in a mortar with a pestle. Shrimp paste, also known as *terasi*, is a dark, odorous paste made from fermented shrimp. Use sparingly.

Fish sauce The most commonly used flavoring in Thai food. Fish sauce (*nam pla*) is used in Thai cooking in the same way that soy sauce is used in Chinese dishes. It is made from salted anchovies and has a strong, salty flavor.

Galangal Fresh galangal, also known as *lengkuas*, tastes and looks a little like ginger with a pinkish tinge to its skin. Prepare it in the same way. It is also available dried and ground.

Garlic Garlic, together with ginger, is an indispensable ingredient in Asian cooking.

Ginger Fresh ginger has a sharp, distinctive flavor. Choose firm, plump pieces of fresh root with unwrinkled, shiny skins.

Gram flour Made from ground chickpeas, this flour has a unique flavor and is worth seeking out in Indian food stores.

Lemongrass Also known as citronella, lemongrass has a long, pale green stalk and a bulbous end similar to that of a scallion. Only the bottom five inches are used. It has a woody texture and an aromatic, lemony scent. Unless finely chopped, it is always removed before serving because it is so fibrous.

Lengkuas See under Galangal.

Mirin A mild, sweet Japanese rice wine used in cooking.

Miso A fermented bean paste that adds richness and flavor to Japanese soups.

Mushrooms Chinese shiitake mushrooms are used both fresh and dried to add texture and flavor to a dish. Wood ears are used in their dried form. All varieties of dried mushrooms need to be soaked in warm water for before use. Dried mushrooms are expensive, but a small quantity goes a long way.

Noodles: Cellophane noodles, also known as bean thread, transparent or glass noodles, are made from ground mung beans. Dried noodles must be soaked in hot water before cooking.

Egg noodles are made from wheat flour, egg and water. The dough is flattened and then shredded or extruded through a pasta machine to the required shape and thickness.

Rice noodles are made from ground rice and water. They range in thickness from very thin to wide ribbons and sheets. Dried ribbon rice noodles are usually sold tied together in bundles. Fresh rice noodles are also available. Rinse rice noodles in warm water and drain before use.

Rice vermicelli are thin, brittle noodles that look like white hair and are sold in large bundles. They cook almost instantly in hot liquid, provided the noodles are first soaked in warm water. They can also be deep-fried.

Somen noodles are delicate, thin, white Japanese noodles made from wheat flour. They are sold dried, usually tied in bundles held together with a paper band.

Udon noodles, also Japanese, are made of wheat flour and water. They are usually round but can also be flat and are available fresh, precooked or dried.

Nori Paper-thin sheets of Japanese seaweed.

Oyster sauce Made from oyster extract, this is used in many Asian fish dishes, soups and sauces.

Palm sugar Strongly flavored, hard brown sugar made from the sap of the coconut palm tree. It is available in Asian stores. If you have trouble finding it, use dark brown sugar instead.

Peanut oil This oil can be heated to a high temperature, making it perfect for stir-frying and deep-frying.

Peanuts Used to add flavor and a crunchy texture. The thin red skins must be removed before cooking: Immerse the peanuts in boiling water for a few minutes and then rub off the skins.

Red bean paste A reddish-brown paste made from puréed red beans and crystallized sugar. It is sold in cans.

Rice Long-grain rice is generally used for savory dishes. There are many high-quality varieties, coming from a range of countries. Basmati, which means "fragrant" in Hindi, is generally acknowledged as the king of rices. Thai jasmine rice is also fragrant and slightly sticky.

Rice vinegar There are two basic types of rice vinegar: Red vinegar is made from fermented rice and has a distinctive dark color and depth of flavor; white vinegar is stronger in flavor, as it is distilled from rice. If rice vinegar is unavailable, cider vinegar may be substituted.

Sake A strong, fortified rice wine from Japan.

Sesame oil This is used more for flavoring than for cooking. It is very intensely flavored, so only a little is required.

Dried noodles, pictured

1 ribbon noodles	7 cellophane noodles
2 somen noodles	8 rice sheets
3 udon noodles	9 rice vermicelli
4 soba noodles	10 egg noodles
5 egg ribbon noodles	11 rice ribbon noodles
6 medium egg noodles	

Soy sauce A major seasoning ingredient in Asian cooking, this is made from fermented soy beans combined with yeast, salt and sugar. Chinese soy sauce falls into two main categories: light and dark. Light soy sauce has more flavor than the sweeter dark soy sauce, which gives food a rich, reddish color.

Spring roll wrappers Paper-thin wrappers made from wheat or rice flour and water. Wheat wrappers are usually sold frozen and should be thawed and separated before use. Rice flour wrappers are dry and must be soaked before use.

Sweet potato The sweet richness of this red tuber marries well with the hot-and-sour flavors of Southeast Asia. In Japan the sweet potato is used to make delicious candies and sweetmeats.

Szechuan peppercorns Also known as *farchiew*, these aromatic red peppercorns are best used roasted and ground. They are not as hot as either white or black peppercorns, but do add a unique taste.

Tamari Japanese dark soy sauce with a mellow flavour. It is not so strong or concentrated as Chinese soy sauce.

Tamarind The brown, sticky pulp of the beanlike seedpod of the tamarind tree. It is used in Thai and Indonesian cooking to add tartness to recipes, much as Western cooks use vinegar or lemon juice. It is usually sold dried or pulped. The pulp is diluted with water and strained before use. Soak 1 ounce tamarind pulp in ⅔ cup warm water for about 10 minutes. Squeeze out as much tamarind juice as possible by pressing all the liquid through a strainer.

Terasi See under Dried Shrimp and shrimp paste.

Tofu This custardlike preparation of puréed and pressed soybeans, also known as bean curd, is high in protein. Plain tofu is bland in flavor but readily

absorbs the flavors of the food with which it is cooked. Tofu is also available smoked and marinated. Firm blocks of tofu are best suited to stir-frying.

Turmeric A member of the ginger family, turmeric is a rich, golden-colored root. If you are using the fresh root, wear rubber gloves when peeling it to avoid staining your skin. Turmeric is also available in powder form.

Wasabi This is an edible root that is used in Japanese cooking to make a condiment with a sharp, pungent and fiery flavor. It is very similar to horseradish and is available fresh, and in powder and paste form.

Water chestnuts Walnut-sized bulbs from an Asian water plant that look like sweet chestnuts. They are sold fresh by some Asian food stores, but are more readily available canned.

Top shelf, left to right: *fresh egg noodles, wonton wrappers, water chestnuts, cellophane noodles, gram flour, spring roll wrappers*
Middle shelf: *dried Chinese mushrooms, bok choy, tofu, dried egg noodles, Chinese pancakes*
Bottom shelf, at back: *rice; snow peas, baby corn, shallots, shiitake mushrooms (in basket); Chinese cabbage, rice vermicelli*
Bottom shelf, at front: *bamboo shoots, bean sprouts, wood ears (mushrooms), scallions, yard-long beans*

Wonton wrappers Small, paper-thin squares of wheat flour and egg dough.

Yard-long beans Long, thin beans similar to French beans but three or four times longer. Cut into smaller lengths and use just like ordinary green beans.

Yellow bean sauce A thick paste made from salted, fermented yellow soy beans, crushed with flour and sugar.

EQUIPMENT

You don't need special equipment to produce a Chinese or other Asian meal—you can even use a heavy-bottomed frying pan instead of a wok in many instances. However, the items listed below will make your Asian dishes easier and more pleasant to prepare.

Wok There are many different varieties of wok available. All are bowl-shaped, with gently sloping sides that allow the heat to spread rapidly and evenly over the surface. One that is about 14 inches in diameter is a useful size for most families, allowing adequate room for deep-frying, steaming and braising, as well as stir-frying.

Originally always made from cast iron, woks are now manufactured in a number of different metals. Cast iron remains very popular, as it is an excellent conductor of heat and develops a patina over a period of time that makes it virtually nonstick. Carbon steel is also a good choice, but stainless steel tends to scorch. Nonstick woks are available but are not really very efficient because they cannot withstand the high heat required for wok cooking. They are also expensive.

Woks may have an ear-shaped handle or two made from metal or wood, a single long handle or both. Wooden handles are safer.

Seasoning the wok New woks, apart from those with a nonstick lining, must be seasoned. Many need to be scrubbed first with a nonabrasive cleanser to remove the manufacturer's protective coating of oil. Once the oil has been removed, place the wok over low heat and add about 2 tablespoons vegetable oil. Rub the oil over the inside surface of the wok with a pad of paper towels. Heat the wok slowly for 10–15 minutes, then wipe off the oil with more paper towels. The paper will become black. Repeat this process of coating, heating and wiping several times until the paper comes out clean. Once the wok has been seasoned, it should not be scrubbed again. After use, just wash it in hot water without using any detergent, then wipe it completely dry before storage.

Wok accessories There is a range of accessories available to go with woks, but they are by no means essential.

Lid This is a useful addition, particularly if you want to use the wok for steaming and braising, as well as frying. Usually made of aluminum, it is a close-fitting, dome-shaped cover. Some woks are sold already supplied with matching lids. However, any snug-fitting, dome-shaped saucepan lid is an adequate substitute.

Stand This provides a secure base for the wok when it is used for steaming, braising or deep-frying and is a particularly useful accessory. Stands are always made of metal but vary in form, usually either a simple open-sided frame or a solid metal ring with holes punched around the sides.

Trivet This is essential for steaming to support the plate above the water level. Trivets are made of wood or metal.

Scoop This is a long-handled metal spatula, often with a wooden handle, used to toss ingredients during stir-frying. Any good, long-handled spoon can be used instead, although it does not have quite the same action.

Bamboo steamer This fits inside the wok, where it should rest safely perched on the sloping sides. Bamboo steamers range in size from small for dumplings and dim sum to those large enough to hold a whole fish.

Bamboo strainer This wide, flat metal strainer with a long bamboo handle makes lifting foods from steam or hot oil easier. A slotted metal spoon can also be used.

Other equipment Most equipment required for cooking the recipes in this book will be found in any kitchen. However, specialized tools are generally simple and inexpensive, especially if you seek out authentic implements from Asian stores.

A selection of cooking utensils, clockwise from top: *bamboo steamer, mortar and pestle, cutting board with cleaver, chef's knife and small paring knife, wok with lid and draining wire, wok scoop*

Cleaver No Chinese cook would be without one. This is an all-purpose cutting tool, available in various weights and sizes. It is easy to use and serves many purposes, from chopping up bones to precision cutting, such as deveining shrimp. It is a superb instrument for slicing vegetables thinly. It must be kept very sharp.

Mortar and pestle Usually made of earthenware or stone, this is extremely useful for grinding small amounts of spices and for pounding ingredients together to make pastes.

Food processor This is a quick and easy alternative to the mortar and pestle for grinding spices and making pastes. It can also be used for chopping and slicing vegetables.

COOKING TECHNIQUES

STIR-FRYING

This quick technique preserves the fresh flavor, color and texture of ingredients. Its success depends upon having everything you will need ready before starting to cook.

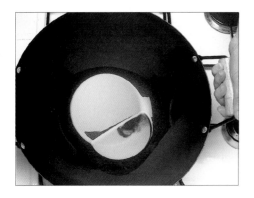

1 Heat an empty wok over high heat. This prevents food from sticking and will ensure an even heat. Add the oil and swirl it around so that it coats the base and halfway up the sides of the wok. It is important that the oil is hot when the food is added, so that it will start to cook immediately.

2 Add the ingredients in the order specified in the recipe. Aromatics (garlic, ginger, scallions) are usually added first: Do not wait for the oil to get so hot that it is almost smoking or they will burn and become bitter. Toss them in the oil for a few seconds. Next add the main ingredients that require longer cooking, such as dense vegetables or meat. Follow with the faster-cooking items. Toss the ingredients from the center of the wok to the sides using a wok scoop, long-handled spoon, or wooden spatula.

DEEP-FRYING

A wok is ideal for deep-frying, as it uses far less oil than a deep-fat fryer. Make sure that it is fully secure on its stand before adding the oil, and never leave the wok unattended.

1 Put the wok on a stand and half-fill with oil. Heat until the required temperature registers on a thermometer. Alternatively, test it by dropping in a small piece of food: If bubbles form all over the surface of the food, the oil is ready.

2 Carefully add the food to the oil using long wooden chopsticks or tongs, and move it around to prevent it from sticking. Use a wok scoop or slotted spoon to remove the food. Drain on paper towels before serving.

STEAMING

Steamed foods are cooked by a gentle moist heat, which must circulate freely in order for the food to cook. Steaming is increasingly popular with health-conscious cooks, as it preserves flavor and nutrients. It is perfect for vegetables, meat, poultry, and especially fish. The easiest way to steam food in a wok is by using a bamboo steamer.

USING A BAMBOO STEAMER

1 Put the wok on a stand. Pour in sufficient boiling water to come about 2 inches up the sides and bring back to the simmering point. Carefully put the bamboo steamer into the wok so that it rests securely against the sloping sides without touching the surface of the water.

2 Cover the steamer with its matching lid and cook for the time recommended in the recipe. Check the water level from time to time and add more boiling water if necessary.

USING A WOK AS A STEAMER

Put a trivet in the wok, then place the wok securely on its stand. Pour in sufficient boiling water to come just below the trivet. Carefully place a plate containing the food to be steamed on the trivet. Cover the wok with its lid, bring the water back to a boil, then lower the heat so that it is simmering gently. Steam for the time recommended in the recipe. Check the water level from time to time and add more boiling water if necessary.

SOUPS

The delicious soups in this chapter can be served as a first course, a light lunch or as part of a selection of main course dishes, as they usually do in China. Some familiar favorites include Corn and Crabmeat Soup, Hot-and-Sour Soup, Three-Delicacy Soup and Chicken Wonton Soup with Shrimp. For a change, why not try Pork and Pickled Mustard Greens Soup, Balinese Vegetable Soup or Hanoi Beef and Noodle Soup? There is even an unusual and satisfying Japanese breakfast soup, which will set up the whole family for the day ahead!

Basic Broth

This broth is used not only as the basis for soup making, but also for general cooking whenever liquid is required instead of plain water.

INGREDIENTS

Makes 10½ cups

1½ pounds chicken parts, skinned
1½ pounds pork spareribs
15 cups cold water
3–4 scallions, each tied into a knot
3–4 pieces fresh ginger, unpeeled and crushed
3–4 tablespoons Chinese rice wine or dry sherry

1 Trim off any excess fat from the chicken and spareribs and chop them into large pieces.

2 Place the chicken, spareribs and water in a large saucepan. Add the scallion knots and ginger.

3 Bring to a boil and, using a strainer, skim off the foam. Reduce the heat and simmer, uncovered, for 2–3 hours.

4 Strain the broth, discarding the chicken, pork, scallions and ginger, and return it to the pan. Add the rice wine or dry sherry and bring to a boil. Simmer for 2–3 minutes. Refrigerate the broth when cool. It will keep for up to 5 days. Alternatively, it can be frozen in small containers and defrosted when required.

Chicken Wonton Soup with Shrimp

This soup is a more luxurious version of the familiar, basic wonton soup and is almost a meal in itself.

INGREDIENTS

Serves 4

10 ounces boneless chicken
  breast, skinned
7 ounces jumbo shrimp, raw or cooked
1 teaspoon finely chopped fresh ginger
2 scallions, finely chopped
1 egg
2 teaspoons oyster sauce (optional)
1 packet wonton wrappers
1 tablespoon cornstarch paste
3¾ cups chicken broth
¼ cucumber, peeled and diced
salt and freshly ground black pepper
1 scallion, cut into strips
4 sprigs fresh cilantro and 1 tomato,
  skinned, seeded and diced, to garnish

1 Place the chicken breast, three-quarters of the shrimp, the ginger and scallions in a food processor and process for 2–3 minutes. Add the egg, oyster sauce, if using, and seasoning and process briefly. Set aside.

2 Place 8 wonton wrappers at a time on a surface, moisten the edges with cornstarch paste and place ½ teaspoon of the chicken mixture in the center of each. Fold them in half and pinch to seal. Simmer in salted water for 4 minutes.

3 Bring the chicken broth to a boil, add the remaining shrimp and the cucumber and simmer for 3–4 minutes. Add the filled wontons and simmer for 3–4 minutes to warm through. Garnish with the scallion, cilantro and diced tomato and serve hot.

Thai Chicken Soup

The subtle combination of herbs, spices and creamed coconut makes this satisfying soup a special treat.

INGREDIENTS

Serves 4

1 tablespoon vegetable oil
1 garlic clove, finely chopped
2 boneless chicken breasts
 (6 ounces each), skinned and chopped
½ teaspoon ground turmeric
¼ teaspoon hot chili powder
3 ounces creamed coconut
3¾ cups hot chicken broth
2 tablespoons lemon or lime juice
2 tablespoons crunchy peanut butter
12 ounces thread egg noodles, broken
 into small pieces
1 tablespoon finely chopped scallion
1 tablespoon chopped fresh cilantro
salt and freshly ground black pepper
2 tablespoons shredded coconut and
 ½ fresh red chili, seeded and finely
 chopped, to garnish

1 Heat the oil in a large pan and fry the garlic for 1 minute or until lightly golden. Add the chicken, turmeric and chili powder and stir-fry for another 3–4 minutes. Remove from heat.

2 Crumble the creamed coconut into the hot chicken broth and stir until dissolved. Pour into the pan with the chicken and add the lemon or lime juice, peanut butter and egg noodles.

3 Cover and simmer for about 15 minutes. Add the scallion and cilantro, then season well and cook for another 5 minutes.

4 Meanwhile, place the shredded coconut and chopped chili in a small frying pan and heat for 2–3 minutes, stirring frequently, until the coconut is lightly browned.

5 Serve the soup in bowls sprinkled with the fried coconut and chili.

Chinese Tofu and Lettuce Soup

This light, clear soup is brimful of nourishing, tasty vegetables.

INGREDIENTS

Serves 4

2 tablespoons peanut or sunflower oil

7 ounces smoked or marinated
firm tofu, cubed

3 scallions, sliced diagonally

2 garlic cloves, cut into thin strips

1 carrot, thinly sliced into rounds

4 cups vegetable broth

2 tablespoons soy sauce

1 tablespoon dry sherry or vermouth

1 teaspoon sugar

4 ounces romaine lettuce, shredded

salt and freshly ground black pepper

1 Heat the oil in a preheated wok, then stir-fry the tofu until browned. Drain and set aside on paper towels.

2 Add the scallions, garlic and carrot to the wok and stir-fry for 2 minutes. Pour in the broth, soy sauce, dry sherry or vermouth, sugar and lettuce. Heat through gently for 1 minute, season to taste and serve hot.

Crab and Egg Noodle Broth

This delicious broth is the ideal solution when you are hungry, time is short and you need a fast, nutritious and filling meal.

INGREDIENTS

Serves 4

3 ounces thin egg noodles
2 tablespoons unsalted butter
1 small bunch scallions, chopped
1 celery stalk, sliced
1 medium carrot, cut into sticks
5 cups chicken broth
4 tablespoons dry sherry
4 ounces white crabmeat, fresh or
  frozen
pinch of celery salt
pinch of cayenne pepper
2 teaspoons lemon juice
1 small bunch cilantro or flat-leaf
  parsley, roughly chopped, to garnish

1 Bring a large saucepan of salted water to a boil. Toss in the egg noodles and cook according to the instructions on the package. Cool under cold running water and leave immersed in water until required.

COOK'S TIP

Fresh and frozen crabmeat have a better flavor than canned crab, which tends to taste rather bland.

2 Heat the butter in another large pan, add the scallions, celery and carrot, cover and cook the vegetables over gentle heat for 3-4 minutes or until soft.

3 Add the chicken broth and dry sherry, bring to a boil and simmer for another 5 minutes.

4 Flake the crabmeat between your fingers onto a plate and remove any stray pieces of shell.

5 Drain the noodles and add to the broth together with the crabmeat. Season to taste with celery salt and cayenne pepper and stir in the lemon juice. Return to a simmer.

6 Ladle the broth into shallow soup plates, scatter with roughly chopped cilantro or parsley and serve immediately.

Cheat's Shark's Fin Soup

Shark's fin soup is a renowned delicacy. In this poor man's vegetarian version, cellophane noodles, cut into short lengths, mimic shark's fin needles.

INGREDIENTS

Serves 4–6

4 dried Chinese mushrooms
1½ tablespoons dried wood ears
4 ounces cellophane noodles
2 tablespoons vegetable oil
2 carrots, cut into fine strips
4 ounces canned bamboo shoots, rinsed, drained and cut into fine strips
4 cups vegetable broth
1 tablespoon soy sauce
1 tablespoon arrowroot or potato flour
2 tablespoons water
1 egg white, beaten (optional)
1 teaspoon sesame oil
salt and freshly ground black pepper
2 scallions, finely chopped, to garnish
Chinese red vinegar, to serve (optional)

1 Soak the mushrooms and wood ears separately in warm water for 20 minutes. Drain well. Remove and discard the stems from the mushrooms and slice the caps thinly. Cut the wood ears into fine strips, discarding any hard pieces. Soak the noodles in hot water until soft. Drain and cut into short lengths. Set aside until required.

2 Heat the oil in a large saucepan. Add the mushrooms, and stir-fry for 2 minutes. Add the wood ears, stir-fry for 2 minutes, then stir in the carrots, bamboo shoots and noodles.

3 Add the broth to the pan. Bring to a boil, reduce the heat, and simmer gently for 15–20 minutes. Season with salt, pepper and soy sauce.

4 Blend the arrowroot or potato flour with a little water. Pour into the soup, stirring constantly to prevent lumps from forming as the soup continues to simmer.

5 Remove the pan from the heat. Stir in the egg white, if using, so that it sets to form small threads in the hot soup. Stir in the sesame oil, then pour the soup into individual bowls. Sprinkle each portion with chopped scallions, and offer the Chinese red vinegar separately, if using.

Miso Breakfast Soup

Miso is a fermented bean paste that adds richness and flavor to many of Japan's favorite soups. It is available in health food and specialty stores. This soup provides a nourishing start to the day.

INGREDIENTS

Serves 4

3 shiitake mushrooms, fresh or dried
5 cups vegetable broth
4 tablespoons miso paste
4 ounces firm tofu, cut into large dice
1 scallion, green part only, sliced, to garnish

1 If using dried mushrooms, soak them in hot water for 3–4 minutes, then drain. Slice the mushrooms thinly and set aside.

2 Bring the broth to a boil in a large saucepan. Stir in the miso paste and mushrooms, lower the heat, and simmer for 5 minutes.

3 Ladle the broth into four soup bowls and divide the tofu among them. Sprinkle the scallion on top and serve immediately.

Noodle Soup with Pork and Szechuan Pickle

INGREDIENTS

Serves 4

4 cups chicken broth
12 ounces egg noodles
1 tablespoon dried shrimp, soaked
 in water
2 tablespoons vegetable oil
8 ounces lean pork, finely shredded
1 tablespoon yellow bean paste
1 tablespoon soy sauce
4 ounces Szechuan hot pickle, rinsed,
 drained and shredded
pinch of sugar
salt and freshly ground black pepper
2 scallions, finely sliced, to garnish

1 Bring the broth to a boil in a large saucepan. Add the noodles, and cook until almost tender. Drain the dried shrimp, rinse under cold water, drain again, and add to the broth. Lower the heat, and simmer for about 2 minutes more. Keep hot. Heat the oil in a frying pan or wok. Add the pork, and stir-fry over a high heat for about 3 minutes.

2 Add the bean paste and soy sauce to the pork. Stir-fry for 1 minute more. Add the hot pickle with a pinch of sugar. Stir-fry for 1 minute more.

3 Divide the noodles and soup among individual serving bowls. Spoon the pork mixture on top, then sprinkle with the scallions. Serve the dish at once.

Snapper, Tomato and Tamarind Noodle Soup

Tamarind gives this light, fragrant noodle soup a slightly sour taste.

INGREDIENTS

Serves 4

8 cups water
2¼ pounds red snapper (or other red
 fish such as bass)
1 onion, sliced
2 ounces tamarind pods
1 tablespoon fish sauce
1 tablespoon sugar
2 tablespoons vegetable oil
2 garlic cloves, finely chopped
2 lemon grass stalks, very
 finely chopped
4 ripe tomatoes, coarsely chopped
2 tablespoons yellow bean paste
8 ounces rice vermicelli, soaked in
 warm water until soft
4 ounces bean sprouts
8–10 basil or mint sprigs
¼ cup roasted peanuts, ground
salt and freshly ground black pepper

1 Bring the water to a boil in a saucepan. Lower the heat, and add the fish and onion, with ½ teaspoon salt. Simmer gently until the fish is cooked right through.

2 Remove the fish from the stock, and set aside. Add the tamarind, fish sauce and sugar to the stock. Cook for 5 minutes, then strain the stock into a large pitcher or bowl. Carefully remove all of the bones from the fish, keeping the flesh in big pieces.

3 Heat the oil in a large frying pan. Add the garlic and lemon grass, and fry for a few seconds. Stir in the tomatoes and bean paste. Cook gently for 5–7 minutes, until the tomatoes are soft. Add the stock, bring back to a simmer, and adjust the seasoning.

4 Drain the vermicelli. Plunge it into a saucepan of boiling water for a few minutes, drain, and divide among individual serving bowls. Add the bean sprouts, fish, basil or mint, and sprinkle the ground peanuts on top. Fill each bowl with the hot soup.

Beef Noodle Soup

A steaming bowl, packed with delicious flavors and a taste of the Orient, will be welcome on cold winter days.

Ingredients

Serves 4

¼ ounce dried porcini mushrooms
⅔ cup boiling water
6 scallions
2 medium carrots
12 ounces sirloin steak
about 2 tablespoons sunflower oil
1 garlic clove, crushed
1-inch piece fresh ginger, peeled and finely chopped
5 cups beef broth
3 tablespoons light soy sauce
4 tablespoons Chinese rice wine or dry sherry
3 ounces thin egg noodles
3 ounces spinach, shredded
salt and freshly ground black pepper

1 Break the mushrooms into small pieces, place in a bowl and pour the boiling water over them. Set aside to soak for 15 minutes.

2 Shred the scallions and carrots into fine 2-inch-long strips. Trim any fat off the steak and slice into thin strips.

3 Heat the oil in a large saucepan and brown the beef in batches, adding a little more oil if necessary. Remove the beef with a slotted spoon and set aside to drain on paper towels.

4 Add the garlic, ginger, scallions and carrots to the pan and stir-fry for 3 minutes.

5 Add the beef broth, the mushrooms and their soaking liquid, the soy sauce, rice wine or dry sherry and plenty of seasoning. Bring to a boil and simmer, covered, for 10 minutes.

6 Break up the noodles slightly and add to the pan with the spinach. Simmer gently for 5 minutes, or until the beef is tender. Adjust the seasoning before serving.

Pork and Noodle Broth with Shrimp

This delicately flavored Vietnamese soup is very quick and easy to make, but tastes really special.

INGREDIENTS

Serves 4–6

12 ounces pork chops or loins
8 ounces jumbo shrimp, raw or cooked
5 ounces thin egg noodles
1 tablespoon vegetable oil
2 teaspoons sesame oil
4 shallots or 1 medium onion, sliced
1 tablespoon finely sliced fresh
    ginger
1 garlic clove, crushed
1 teaspoon sugar
6¼ cups chicken broth
2 kaffir lime leaves
3 tablespoons fish sauce
juice of ½ lime
4 sprigs fresh cilantro and 2 scallions,
    green parts only, chopped,
    to garnish

1 If you are using pork chops, trim away any fat and the bones. Place the meat in the freezer for 30 minutes to firm, but not freeze it. Slice the pork thinly and set aside. Peel and devein the shrimp, if using raw shrimp.

2 Bring a large saucepan of salted water to a boil and simmer the noodles according to the instructions on the package. Drain and refresh in cold water. Set aside.

3 Heat the vegetable and sesame oils in a preheated wok, add the shallots or onion and stir-fry for 3–4 minutes, or until evenly browned. Remove from the wok and set aside.

4 Add the ginger, garlic, sugar and chicken broth to the wok and bring to a simmer. Add the lime leaves, fish sauce and lime juice. Add the pork, then simmer for 15 minutes. Add the shrimp and noodles and simmer for 3–4 minutes to heat through. Serve in shallow bowls, garnished with cilantro sprigs, the green parts of the scallions and the browned shallots or onion.

Hanoi Beef and Noodle Soup

Millions of North Vietnamese eat this fragrant soup for breakfast.

INGREDIENTS

Serves 4–6
1 onion
3–3½ pounds beef shank with bones
1 inch fresh ginger
1 star anise
1 bay leaf
2 whole cloves
½ teaspoon fennel seeds
1 piece of cassia bark or
   cinnamon stick
12 cups water
fish sauce, to taste
juice of 1 lime
5 ounces fillet steak
1 pound fresh flat rice noodles
salt and freshly ground black pepper

For the accompaniments
1 small red onion, sliced into rings
4 ounces bean sprouts
2 red chilies, seeded and sliced
2 scallions, finely sliced
handful of cilantro leaves

1 Cut the onion in half. Broil under a high heat, cut side up, until the exposed sides are caramelized, and deep brown. Set aside.

2 Cut the meat into large chunks, and then place with the bones in a large saucepan or stock pot. Add the caramelized onion with the ginger, star anise, bay leaf, cloves, fennel seeds and cassia bark or cinnamon stick.

3 Add the water, bring to a boil, reduce the heat, and simmer gently for 2–3 hours, skimming off the fat and scum from time to time.

4 Using a slotted spoon, remove the meat from the stock. When cool enough to handle, cut into small pieces, discarding the bones. Strain the stock, and return to the pan or stock pot together with the meat. Bring back to a boil, and season with the fish sauce and the lime juice.

5 Slice the fillet steak very thinly, and then chill until required. Place the accompaniments in separate bowls.

6 Cook the noodles in a large saucepan of boiling water until just tender. Drain, and divide among individual serving bowls. Arrange the thinly sliced steak over the noodles, and pour the hot stock on top. Serve, offering the accompaniments separately so that each person may garnish their soup as they like.

Tamarind Soup with Peanuts and Vegetables

Sayur Asam is a colorful and refreshing soup from Jakarta with more than a hint of sharpness.

INGREDIENTS

Serves 4 or 8 as part of a buffet

For the spice paste

5 shallots or 1 medium red
onion, sliced
3 garlic cloves, crushed
1 inch *laos,* peeled and sliced
1–2 fresh red chilies, seeded and sliced
3 tablespoons raw peanuts
1 teaspoon shrimp paste
5 cups well-flavored chicken or
vegetable broth
½ cup salted peanuts, lightly crushed
1–2 tablespoons dark brown sugar
1 teaspoon tamarind pulp, soaked in
5 tablespoons warm water for
15 minutes
salt

For the vegetables

1 chayote, thinly peeled, seeds
removed, flesh finely sliced
4 ounces green beans, trimmed and
finely sliced
⅓ cup corn kernels (optional)
handful green leaves, such as
watercress, arugula or Chinese
cabbage, finely shredded
1 fresh green chili, sliced, to garnish

1 Prepare the spice paste by grinding the shallots or onion, garlic, *laos,* chilies, raw peanuts and shrimp paste to a paste in a food processor or with a mortar and pestle.

2 Pour in some of the broth to moisten and then pour this mixture into a pan or wok, adding the rest of the broth. Cook for 15 minutes with the lightly crushed peanuts and sugar.

3 Strain the tamarind, discarding the seeds, and reserve the juice.

4 About 5 minutes before serving, add the chayote slices, beans and corn, if using, to the soup and cook fairly rapidly. At the last minute, add the greens or cabbage.

5 Add the tamarind juice and taste for seasoning. Serve, garnished with slices of green chili.

Corn and Chicken Soup

This popular, classic Chinese soup is delicious and extremely easy to make in a wok.

INGREDIENTS

Serves 4–6

1 boneless chicken breast (about 4 ounces), skinned and cubed
2 teaspoons light soy sauce
1 tablespoon Chinese rice wine or dry sherry
1 teaspoon cornstarch
¼ cup cold water
1 teaspoon sesame oil
2 tablespoons peanut oil
1 teaspoon grated fresh ginger
4 cups chicken stock
15-ounce can creamed corn
8-ounce can corn kernels
2 eggs, beaten
salt and ground black pepper
2–3 scallions, green parts only, cut into tiny rounds, to garnish

1 Grind the chicken in a food processor or blender, taking care not to overprocess. Transfer the chicken to a bowl and stir in the soy sauce, rice wine or sherry, cornstarch, water, sesame oil and seasoning. Cover and let sit for about 15 minutes to absorb the flavors.

2 Heat a wok over medium heat. Add the peanut oil and swirl it around. Add the ginger and stir-fry for a few seconds. Add the stock, creamed corn and corn kernels. Bring to just below boiling point.

3 Spoon about 6 tablespoons of the hot liquid into the chicken mixture and stir until it forms a smooth paste. Add to the wok. Slowly bring to a boil, stirring constantly, then simmer for 2–3 minutes, until cooked.

4 Pour the beaten eggs into the soup in a slow, steady stream, using a fork or chopsticks to stir the top of the soup in a figure-eight pattern. The egg should set in lacy threads. Serve immediately with the scallions sprinkled on top.

Chicken and Asparagus Soup

This is a very delicate soup, with chicken and asparagus simply and quickly prepared in a wok.

INGREDIENTS

Serves 4

1 boneless chicken breast (about
   5 ounces), skinned
1 teaspoon egg white
1 teaspoon cornstarch paste
½ bunch fresh asparagus (about 4 ounces)
3 cups chicken stock
salt and ground black pepper
fresh cilantro, to garnish

1 Cut the chicken into thin slices, each about the size of a postage stamp. Mix with a pinch of salt, then add the egg white and finally the cornstarch paste.

2 Discard the tough stems of the asparagus, and cut the tender spears diagonally into short lengths.

3 Bring the stock to a rolling boil in a wok. Add the asparagus, bring back to a boil and cook for 2 minutes.

4 Add the chicken, stir to separate and bring back to a boil again. Adjust the seasoning to taste. Serve hot, garnished with fresh cilantro leaves.

Corn and Crabmeat Soup

Surprisingly, this soup originated in the United States, but it has since been introduced into mainstream Chinese cooking. It is important that you make sure you use creamed corn in the recipe to achieve exactly the right consistency.

INGREDIENTS

Serves 4

4 ounces crabmeat
½ teaspoon finely chopped fresh ginger
2 egg whites
2 tablespoons milk
1 tablespoon cornstarch paste
2½ cups chicken stock
8-ounce can creamed corn
salt and ground black pepper
finely chopped scallions, to garnish

1 Flake the crabmeat roughly with chopsticks. Mix the crabmeat with the chopped ginger.

2 Beat the egg whites until frothy, add the milk and cornstarch paste and beat again until smooth. Blend with the crabmeat.

COOK'S TIP

The crabmeat can be replaced with chopped boneless chicken breast.

3 Bring the stock to a boil in a wok. Add the creamed corn and bring back to a boil again.

4 Stir in the crabmeat and egg white mixture, adjust the seasoning and simmer gently until cooked. Serve garnished with finely chopped scallions.

Hot-and-sour Soup

This surely must be the best-known and all-time favorite soup in Chinese restaurants throughout the world. It is fairly simple to make once you have all the necessary ingredients together.

INGREDIENTS

Serves 4

4–6 dried Chinese mushrooms, soaked in warm water for 30 minutes
4 ounces pork or chicken
8-ounce package fresh tofu
⅓ cup sliced bamboo shoots, drained
2½ cups chicken stock
1 tablespoon Chinese rice wine or dry sherry
1 tablespoon light soy sauce
1 tablespoon rice vinegar
salt and ground white pepper
1 tablespoon cornstarch paste

1 Squeeze the soaked mushrooms dry, then discard the hard stalks. Thinly shred the mushrooms, meat, tofu and bamboo shoots.

2 Bring the stock to a rolling boil in a wok and add the shredded ingredients. Bring back to a boil and simmer for about 1 minute.

3 Add the wine or sherry, soy sauce and vinegar and season. Bring back to a boil, then add the cornstarch paste, stir until thickened and serve.

Spinach and Tofu Soup

If fresh young spinach leaves are not available, watercress or lettuce can be used instead. Sorrel leaves may also be used as a substitute, but they have a stronger and slightly more bitter flavor than spinach.

INGREDIENTS

Serves 4
3-inch block fresh tofu
½ bunch spinach
3 cups chicken stock
1 tablespoon light soy sauce
salt and ground black pepper

1 Cut the tofu into 12 small pieces, each about ¼ inch thick. Wash the spinach leaves and cut them into small pieces.

2 Bring the stock to a rolling boil in a wok. Add the tofu and soy sauce, bring back to a boil and simmer for about 2 minutes.

3 Add the spinach and simmer for another minute. Skim the surface to make it clear, then adjust the seasoning and serve immediately.

COOK'S TIP

Fresh tofu is sold in cakes about 3 inches square in Asian food stores. Do not confuse it with fermented tofu, which is much stronger-tasting, quite salty and usually used as a condiment.

Sliced Fish and Cilantro Soup

It is not necessary to remove the skin from the fish; it helps to keep the flesh together when poached in the wok.

INGREDIENTS

Serves 4
8 ounces white fish fillets, such as lemon sole or flounder
1 tablespoon egg white
2 teaspoons cornstarch paste
3 cups chicken stock
1 tablespoon light soy sauce
½ cup chopped fresh cilantro
salt and ground black pepper

1 Cut the fish into slices, each about 1½ inches square. Mix with the egg white and cornstarch paste.

2 Bring the stock to a rolling boil in a wok and poach the fish slices for about 1 minute.

3 Add the soy sauce and chopped cilantro, adjust the seasoning and serve immediately.

Three-delicacy Soup

This delicious soup combines the three ingredients chicken, ham and shrimp.

INGREDIENTS

Serves 4
4 ounces boneless chicken breast
4 ounces honey-roast ham
4 ounces shelled shrimp
3 cups chicken stock
salt

COOK'S TIP

Fresh, uncooked shrimp impart the best flavor. If these are not available, you can use cooked shrimp. They must be added at the last stage to prevent over-cooking.

1 Thinly slice the chicken and ham into small pieces. Devein the shrimp and, if they are large, cut each in half lengthwise.

2 Bring the stock to a rolling boil in a wok. Add the chicken, ham and shrimp. Bring back to a boil, add salt and simmer for 1 minute. Serve the soup hot.

Lamb and Cucumber Soup

This is a variation on hot-and-sour soup, but it is even simpler to prepare

INGREDIENTS

Serves 4
8 ounces lamb steak
1 tablespoon light soy sauce
1 tablespoon Chinese rice wine or
 dry sherry
½ teaspoon sesame oil
3-inch piece cucumber
3 cups chicken stock
1 tablespoon rice vinegar
salt and ground white pepper

1 Trim off any excess fat from the lamb and discard. Thinly slice the lamb into small pieces. Put it in a shallow dish and add the soy sauce, rice wine or sherry and sesame oil. Set aside to marinate for 25–30 minutes. Discard the marinade.

2 Halve the cucumber piece lengthwise (do not peel), then cut it into thin slices diagonally.

3 Bring the stock to a rolling boil in a wok. Add the lamb and stir to separate. Return to a boil, then add the cucumber slices, vinegar and seasoning. Bring to a boil again, and serve immediately.

Wonton Soup

In China, wonton soup is served as a snack or dim sum rather than as a soup course during a large meal.

INGREDIENTS

Serves 4

6 ounces pork, not too lean, roughly chopped
8 medium shrimp, shelled and ground
1 teaspoon light brown sugar
1 tablespoon Chinese rice wine or dry sherry
2 tablespoons light soy sauce
1 teaspoon finely chopped scallion
1 teaspoon finely chopped fresh ginger
24 wonton wrappers
3 cups chicken stock
finely chopped scallions, to garnish

1 In a bowl, mix the chopped pork and ground shrimp with the sugar, rice wine or sherry, 1 tablespoon of the soy sauce, the scallions and chopped ginger. Blend well and set aside for 25–30 minutes for the flavors to blend.

2 Place 1 teaspoon of the filling in the center of each wonton wrapper.

3 Wet the edges of each wonton with a little water and press them together with your fingers to seal, then fold each wonton over.

4 To cook, bring the stock to a rolling boil in a wok, add the wontons and cook for 4–5 minutes. Add the remaining soy sauce and scallions, transfer to individual soup bowls and serve.

Seafood Laksa

For a special occasion, serve creamy rice noodles in a spicy coconut-flavored soup, topped with seafood. There is a fair amount of work involved in the preparation but you can make the soup base ahead.

INGREDIENTS

Serves 4
4 red chilies, seeded and
   coarsely chopped
1 onion, coarsely chopped
1 piece *blacan*, the size of a
   bouillon cube
1 lemon grass stalk, chopped
1 small piece fresh ginger,
   coarsely chopped
6 macadamia nuts or almonds
4 tablespoons vegetable oil
1 teaspoon paprika
1 teaspoon ground turmeric
2 cups broth or water
2½ cups coconut milk
fish sauce
12 jumbo shrimp, peeled and deveined
8 scallops
8 ounces prepared squid, cut into rings
12 ounces rice vermicelli, soaked in
   warm water until soft
salt and freshly ground black pepper
lime halves, to serve

For the garnish
¼ cucumber, cut into matchsticks
2 red chilies, seeded and finely sliced
2 tablespoons mint leaves
2 tablespoons fried shallots or onions

1 In a blender or food processor, process the chilies, onion, shrimp paste, lemon grass, ginger and nuts, until smooth in texture.

COOK'S TIP

Blacan is dried shrimp paste. It is sold in small blocks and you will find it in most oriental supermarkets.

2 Heat 3 tablespoons of the oil in a large saucepan. Add the chili paste, and fry for 6 minutes. Stir in the paprika and turmeric, and fry for about 2 minutes more.

3 Add the broth or water and the coconut milk to the pan. Bring to a boil, reduce the heat, and simmer gently for 15–20 minutes. Season to taste with fish sauce.

4 Season the seafood with salt and pepper. Heat the remaining oil in a frying pan, add the seafood, and fry quickly for 2–3 minutes until cooked.

5 Add the vermicelli to the soup, and heat through. Divide among individual serving bowls. Place the fried seafood on top, then garnish with the cucumber, chilies, mint and fried shallots or onions. Serve with the limes.

Chicken and Buckwheat Noodle Soup

Buckwheat or soba noodles are enjoyed widely throughout Japan. The simplest way of serving these noodles is in hot, seasoned broth. Almost any topping can be added; the variations are endless.

INGREDIENTS

Serves 4
8 ounces skinless, boneless
   chicken breast
½ cup soy sauce
1 tablespoon saké
4 cups chicken broth
2 pieces young leek, cut into
   1-inch pieces
6 ounces spinach leaves
11 ounces buckwheat or soba noodles
sesame seeds, toasted, to garnish

1 Slice the chicken diagonally into bite-size pieces. Combine the soy sauce and saké in a saucepan. Bring to a simmer. Add the chicken, and cook gently for about 3 minutes until it is tender. Keep hot.

2 Bring the stock to a boil in a saucepan. Add the leek. Simmer for 3 minutes, then add the spinach. Remove from the heat but keep warm.

3 Cook the noodles in a large saucepan of boiling water until just tender, following the manufacturer's directions on the package.

4 Drain the noodles, and divide among individual serving bowls. Ladle the hot soup into the bowls, then add a portion of chicken to each. Serve at once, sprinkled with sesame seeds.

COOK'S TIP

Homemade chicken stock makes a world of difference to noodle soup. Make a big batch of stock, use as much as you need, and freeze the rest until required. Put about 3–3½ pounds meaty chicken bones into a large saucepan, add 12 cups water, and slowly bring to a boil, skimming off any foam that rises to the top. Add 2 slices fresh ginger, 2 garlic cloves, 2 celery stalks, 4 scallions, a handful of cilantro stalks and about 10 peppercorns, crushed. Reduce the heat, and simmer the stock for about 2–2½ hours. Remove from the heat, and let cool, uncovered and undisturbed. Strain the stock into a clean bowl, leaving the last dregs behind as they tend to cloud the soup. Use as required, removing any fat that congeals on top.

Pork and Pickled Mustard Greens Soup

INGREDIENTS

Serves 4–6

8 ounces pickled mustard
    greens, soaked
2 ounces cellophane noodles, soaked
1 tablespoon vegetable oil
4 garlic cloves, finely sliced
4 cups chicken stock
1 pound pork ribs, cut into
    large chunks
2 tablespoons fish sauce
pinch of sugar
freshly ground black pepper
2 red chilies, seeded and finely sliced,
    to garnish

3 Heat the oil in a small frying pan, add the garlic and stir-fry until golden. Transfer the mixture to a bowl and set aside.

4 Put the stock in a saucepan, bring to a boil, then add the pork and simmer gently for 10–15 minutes.

5 Add the pickled mustard greens and cellophane noodles. Bring back to a boil. Season to taste with fish sauce, sugar and freshly ground black pepper. Serve hot, topped with the fried garlic and red chilies.

1 Cut the pickled mustard greens into bite-size pieces. Taste to check the seasoning. If they are too salty, then soak them for a little bit longer.

2 Drain the cellophane noodles and cut them into short lengths.

Clear Soup with Meatballs

INGREDIENTS

Serves 8

For the meatballs

6 ounces very finely ground beef
1 small onion, very finely chopped
1–2 garlic cloves, crushed
1 tablespoon cornstarch
a little egg white, lightly beaten
salt and freshly ground black pepper

For the soup

4–6 Chinese mushrooms, soaked in
   warm water for 30 minutes
2 tablespoons peanut oil
1 large onion, finely chopped
2 garlic cloves, finely crushed
½ inch fresh ginger root, bruised
8 cups beef or chicken broth, including
   strained soaking liquid from
   the mushrooms
2 tablespoons soy sauce
4 ounces spinach or Chinese
   cabbage, shredded

1 First prepare the meatballs. Mix the beef with the onion, garlic, cornstarch and seasoning in a food processor and then bind with sufficient egg white to make a firm mixture. With dampened hands, roll into tiny, bite-size balls and set aside.

2 Drain the mushrooms and reserve the soaking liquid to add to the broth. Trim off and discard the stalks. Slice the caps finely and set aside.

3 Heat a large saucepan or wok and add the oil. Fry the onion, garlic and ginger to bring out the flavor, but do not allow to brown.

4 When the onion is soft, pour in the broth. Bring to a boil, then stir in the soy sauce and mushroom slices and simmer for 10 minutes. Add the meatballs and cook for 10 minutes.

5 Just before serving, remove the ginger. Stir in the shredded spinach or Chinese cabbage. Heat through for 1 minute only: no longer or the leaves will be overcooked. Serve the soup immediately.

Balinese Vegetable Soup

Any seasonal vegetables can be used in *Sayur Oelih*.

INGREDIENTS

Serves 8

8 ounces green beans
5 cups boiling water
1²/₃ cups coconut milk
1 garlic clove
2 macadamia nuts or 4 almonds
½ teaspoon shrimp paste
2–3 teaspoons coriander seeds, dry-
    fried and ground
oil for frying
1 onion, finely sliced
2 *duan salam* or bay leaves
8 ounces bean sprouts
2 tablespoons lemon juice
salt

1 Remove the ends from the green beans and cut into small pieces. Cook the beans in the salted, boiling water for 3–4 minutes. Drain the beans and reserve the cooking water.

2 Spoon off 3–4 tablespoons of the cream from the top of the coconut milk and reserve it.

3 Grind the garlic, nuts, shrimp paste, and ground coriander together to a paste in a food processor or with a mortar and pestle.

4 Heat the oil in a wok or saucepan, and fry the onion until transparent. Remove and reserve. Fry the paste for 2 minutes without browning. Pour in the reserved vegetable water and coconut milk. Bring to a boil and add the *duan salam* or bay leaves. Cook, uncovered, for 15–20 minutes.

5 Just before serving, add the beans, fried onion, bean sprouts, reserved coconut cream and lemon juice. Taste for seasoning and adjust it, if necessary. Serve at once.

--- COOK'S TIP ---

Even in the East, cooks use canned coconut milk. Any leftovers can be chilled for 3–4 days or frozen immediately, then thawed before use.

Pumpkin and Coconut Soup

INGREDIENTS

Serves 4–6

2 garlic cloves, crushed
4 shallots, finely chopped
½ teaspoon shrimp paste
1 tablespoon dried shrimp, soaked for 10 minutes and drained
1 lemongrass stalk, chopped
2 green chilies, seeded
2½ cups chicken stock
1 pound pumpkin, cut into ¾-inch thick chunks
2½ cups coconut cream
2 tablespoons fish sauce
1 teaspoon sugar
4 ounces small cooked shelled shrimp
salt and freshly ground black pepper
2 red chilies, seeded and finely sliced, and 10–12 basil leaves, to garnish

1 Grind the garlic, shallots, shrimp paste, dried shrimp, lemongrass, green chilies and salt into a paste.

2 In a large saucepan, bring the chicken stock to a boil, add the ground paste and stir to dissolve.

3 Add the pumpkin and simmer for about 10–15 minutes, or until the pumpkin is tender.

4 Stir in the coconut cream, then bring back to a simmer. Add the fish sauce, sugar and ground black pepper to taste.

5 Add the shrimp and cook until they are heated through. Serve garnished with the sliced red chilies and basil leaves.

COOK'S TIP

Shrimp paste is used here to give a wonderful savory flavor.

Chiang Mai Noodle Soup

A signature dish of the city of Chiang Mai, this delicious noodle soup has Burmese origins and is the Thai equivalent of the Malaysian "Laksa."

INGREDIENTS

Serves 4–6

2½ cups unsweetened coconut milk
2 tablespoons red curry paste
1 teaspoon ground turmeric
1 pound chicken thighs, boned and cut into bite-size chunks
2½ cups chicken stock
4 tablespoons fish sauce
1 tablespoon dark soy sauce
juice of ½–1 lime
1 pound fresh egg noodles, blanched briefly in boiling water
salt and freshly ground black pepper

For the garnish

3 scallions, chopped
4 red chilies, chopped
4 shallots, chopped
4 tablespoons sliced pickled mustard greens, rinsed
2 tablespoons fried sliced garlic
cilantro leaves
4 fried noodle nests (optional)

1 In a large saucepan, add about one-third of the coconut milk and bring to a boil, stirring often with a wooden spoon until it separates.

2 Add the curry paste and ground turmeric, stir to mix completely and cook until fragrant.

3 Add the chicken and stir-fry for about 2 minutes, ensuring that all the chunks are coated with the paste.

4 Add the remaining coconut milk, chicken stock, fish sauce and soy sauce. Season with salt and freshly ground black pepper to taste. Simmer gently for 7–10 minutes. Remove from the heat and stir in the lime juice.

5 Reheat the noodles in boiling water, drain and divide between individual bowls. Divide the chicken between the bowls and ladle in the hot soup. Top each serving with a few of each of the garnishes.

Ginger, Chicken and Coconut Soup

This aromatic soup is rich with coconut milk and intensely flavored with galangal, lemongrass and kaffir lime leaves.

INGREDIENTS

Serves 4–6

3 cups unsweetened coconut milk
2 cups chicken stock
4 lemongrass stalks, bruised
 and chopped
1-inch piece galangal, thinly sliced
10 black peppercorns, crushed
10 kaffir lime leaves, torn
11 ounces boneless chicken, cut
 into thin strips
1½ cups button mushrooms
5 tablespoons canned baby corn
4 tablespoons lime juice
3 tablespoons fish sauce
2 red chilies, chopped, to garnish
chopped scallions, to garnish
cilantro leaves, to garnish

1 Bring the coconut milk and chicken stock to a boil. Add the lemongrass, galangal, peppercorns and half the kaffir lime leaves, reduce the heat and simmer gently for 10 minutes.

2 Strain the stock into a clean pan. Return to the heat, then add the chicken, button mushrooms and baby corn. Cook for about 5–7 minutes or until the chicken is cooked.

3 Stir in the lime juice, fish sauce to taste and the rest of the lime leaves. Serve hot, garnished with red chilies, scallions and cilantro.

Hot-and-sour Soup with Lemongrass

This classic Thai seafood soup – *Tom Yam Goong* – is probably the most popular and well-known soup from Thailand.

INGREDIENTS

Serves 4–6

1 pound jumbo shrimp
4 cups chicken stock or water
3 lemongrass stalks
10 kaffir lime leaves, torn in half
8-ounce can straw mushrooms, drained
3 tablespoons fish sauce
¼ cup lime juice
2 tablespoons chopped scallion
1 tablespoon cilantro leaves
4 red chilies, seeded and chopped
2 scallions, finely chopped

1 Shell and devein the shrimp and set aside. Rinse the shrimp shells and place in a large saucepan with the stock or water and bring to a boil.

2 Bruise the lemongrass stalks with the blunt edge of a chopping knife and add them to the stock, together with half the lime leaves. Simmer gently for 5–6 minutes, until the stalks change color and the stock is fragrant.

3 Strain the stock and return to the saucepan and reheat. Add the mushrooms and shrimp, then cook until the shrimp turn pink.

4 Stir in the fish sauce, lime juice, scallions, cilantro, red chilies and the rest of the lime leaves. Taste and adjust the seasoning. It should be sour, salty, spicy and hot.

APPETIZERS AND SNACKS

Recipes in this chapter range from robust, spicy and filling snacks to delicately flavored, melt-in-the-mouth morsels to tempt the taste buds. Many of the mouth-watering appetizers – a variety of spring rolls with spicy dipping sauces, dim sum, wontons and tempura – need no introduction, as they are long-established favorites in the West. Others are lesser known but just as tasty. Try Lacy Duck Egg Nets from Thailand, Spiced Honey Chicken Wings from China or Spicy Meat Patties with Coconut from Indonesia, for example.

Shrimp Crackers

These are a popular addition to many Chinese and other Far Eastern dishes and are often served before guests come to the table. Freshly cooked shrimp crackers are more delicious than the ready-to-eat variety.

INGREDIENTS

Serves 4–6
1¼ cups vegetable oil
2 ounces uncooked shrimp crackers
salt, to serve

1 Line a tray with paper towels. Heat the oil in a large wok until it begins to smoke. Reduce the heat to maintain a steady temperature. Drop 3 or 4 shrimp crackers into the oil.

2 After they swell up, remove them from the oil almost immediately, before they start to color. Transfer to the paper-lined tray to drain. Serve sprinkled with salt.

Hot Chili Shrimp

These can be prepared up to eight hours in advance and are delicious either grilled or barbecued.

INGREDIENTS

Serves 4–6
1 garlic clove, crushed
½-inch piece fresh ginger, finely
    chopped
1 small fresh red chili, seeded and
    chopped
2 teaspoons sugar
1 tablespoon light soy sauce
1 tablespoon vegetable oil
1 teaspoon sesame oil
juice of 1 lime
1½ pounds jumbo shrimp
6 ounces cherry tomatoes
½ cucumber, cut into chunks
salt
1 small bunch cilantro, roughly
    chopped, to garnish
lettuce leaves, to serve

1 Pound the garlic, ginger, chili and sugar to a paste in a mortar with a pestle. Add the soy sauce, vegetable and sesame oils, lime juice and salt to taste. Place the shrimp in a shallow dish and pour the marinade over them. Set aside to marinate for up to 8 hours. Soak some bamboo skewers.

2 Thread the shrimp, tomatoes and cucumber chunks onto bamboo skewers. Cook under a preheated broiler or on a grill for 3–4 minutes. Transfer to a serving dish, scatter the cilantro on top, and serve on a bed of lettuce.

Spring Rolls with Sweet Chili Dipping Sauce

Miniature spring rolls make a delicious appetizer or unusual finger food for serving at a party.

INGREDIENTS

Makes 20–24

1 ounce rice vermicelli noodles
peanut oil, for deep-frying
1 teaspoon grated fresh ginger
2 scallions, cut into fine strips
1 medium carrot, cut into fine strips
2 ounces snow peas, cut into fine strips
1 ounce young spinach leaves
2 ounces fresh bean sprouts
1 tablespoon chopped fresh mint
1 tablespoon chopped fresh cilantro
2 tablespoons fish sauce
20–24 spring roll wrappers, each
    5 inches square
1 egg white, lightly beaten

For the dipping sauce

¼ cup superfine sugar
¼ cup rice vinegar
2 tablespoons water
2 fresh red chilies, seeded and finely
    chopped

1 First make the dipping sauce. Place the sugar, vinegar and water in a small pan. Heat gently, stirring until the sugar dissolves, then boil rapidly until it forms a light syrup. Stir in the chilies and let cool.

2 Soak the noodles according to the package instructions, then rinse and drain well. Using scissors, snip the noodles into short lengths.

3 Heat 1 tablespoon of the oil in a preheated wok and swirl it around. Add the ginger and scallions and stir-fry for 15 seconds. Add the carrot and snow peas and stir-fry for 2–3 minutes. Add the spinach, bean sprouts, mint, cilantro, fish sauce and noodles and stir-fry for another minute. Set aside to cool.

4 Soften the spring roll wrappers, following the directions on the package. Take one spring roll wrapper and arrange it so that it faces you in a diamond shape. Place a spoonful of filling just below the center, then fold up the bottom point over the filling.

5 Fold in each side, then roll up tightly. Brush the end with beaten egg white to seal. Repeat until all the filling has been used up.

6 Half-fill a wok with oil and heat to 350°F. Deep-fry the spring rolls in batches for 3–4 minutes or until golden and crisp. Drain on paper towels. Serve hot with the sweet chili dipping sauce.

COOK'S TIP

You can cook the spring rolls 2–3 hours in advance, then reheat them on a foil-lined baking sheet at 400°F for about 10 minutes.

Crab Spring Rolls and Dipping Sauce

Chili and grated ginger add a hint of heat to these sensational treats. Serve them as an appetizer or with other Chinese dishes as part of a main course.

INGREDIENTS

Serves 4–6

1 tablespoon peanut oil
1 teaspoon sesame oil
1 garlic clove, crushed
1 fresh red chili, seeded and finely sliced
1 pound fresh stir-fry vegetables, such as bean sprouts and shredded carrots, bell peppers and snow peas
2 tablespoons chopped cilantro
1-inch piece fresh ginger, grated
1 tablespoon Chinese rice wine or dry sherry
1 tablespoon soy sauce
12 ounces fresh dressed crabmeat (brown and white meat)
12 spring roll wrappers
1 small egg, beaten
oil, for deep-frying
salt and freshly ground black pepper
lime wedges and fresh cilantro, to garnish

For the dipping sauce
1 onion, thinly sliced
oil, for deep-frying
1 fresh red chili, seeded and finely chopped
2 garlic cloves, crushed
4 tablespoons dark soy sauce
4 teaspoons lemon juice or 1–1½ tablespoons prepared tamarind juice
2 tablespoons hot water

1 First make the sauce. Spread the onion out on paper towels and let dry for 30 minutes. Then half-fill a wok with oil and heat to 375°F. Fry the onion in batches until crisp and golden, turning all the time. Drain on paper towels.

2 Combine the chili, garlic, soy sauce, lemon or tamarind juice and hot water in a bowl.

3 Stir in the onion and let stand for 30 minutes.

4 To make the spring rolls, heat the peanut and sesame oils in a clean, preheated wok. When hot, stir-fry the crushed garlic and chili for 1 minute. Add the vegetables, cilantro and ginger and stir-fry for 1 minute more. Drizzle with the rice wine or dry sherry and soy sauce. Allow the mixture to bubble up for 1 minute.

5 Using a slotted spoon, transfer the vegetables to a bowl. Set aside until cool, then stir in the crabmeat and season with salt and pepper.

6 Soften the spring roll wrappers, following the directions on the package. Place some of the filling on a wrapper, fold over the front edge and the sides, and roll up neatly, sealing the edges with a little beaten egg. Repeat with the remaining wrappers and filling.

7 Heat the oil for deep-frying in the wok and fry the spring rolls in batches, turning several times, until brown and crisp. Remove with a slotted spoon, drain on paper towels and keep hot while frying the remainder. Serve at once, garnished with lime wedges and cilantro, with the dipping sauce.

Mini Spring Rolls

Eat these irresistibly light and crisp rolls with your fingers. If you like slightly spicier food, sprinkle them with a little cayenne pepper before serving.

INGREDIENTS

Makes 20

1 green chili
½ cup vegetable oil
1 small onion, finely chopped
1 garlic clove, crushed
3 ounces cooked boneless chicken
   breast, skinned
1 small carrot, cut into short thin sticks
1 scallion, finely sliced
1 small red bell pepper, seeded and cut
   into short thin sticks
1 ounce bean sprouts
1 teaspoon sesame oil
4 large sheets phyllo pastry
1 small egg white, lightly beaten
chives to garnish (optional)
3 tablespoons light soy sauce, to serve

1 Carefully remove the seeds from the chili and chop finely, wearing rubber gloves to protect your hands, if necessary.

2 Heat 2 tablespoons of the vegetable oil in a preheated wok. Add the onion, garlic and chili and stir-fry for 1 minute.

3 Slice the chicken breast very thinly, then add to the wok and fry over high heat, stirring constantly, until browned.

4 Add the carrot, scallion and red bell pepper and stir-fry for 2 minutes. Add the bean sprouts, stir in the sesame oil, and let cool.

5 Cut each sheet of phyllo pastry into 5 short strips. Place a small amount of filling at one end of each strip, then fold in the long sides and roll up the pastry. Seal and glaze the rolls with the egg white, then chill, uncovered, for 15 minutes before frying.

6 Wipe the wok with paper towels, reheat it, and add the remaining vegetable oil. When the oil is hot, fry the rolls in batches until crisp and golden brown. Drain on paper towels and serve, garnished with chives, if using, and dipped in light soy sauce.

COOK'S TIP

Be careful to avoid touching your face or eyes when seeding and chopping chilies, because they are very potent and may cause burning and irritation to the skin. Try preparing chilies under running water.

Thai Spring Rolls

These crunchy spring rolls are as popular in Thai cuisine as they are in the Chinese. Thais fill their version with a garlic, pork and noodle filling.

INGREDIENTS

Makes about 24

4–6 dried Chinese mushrooms, soaked
2 ounces bean thread noodles, soaked
2 tablespoons vegetable oil
2 garlic cloves, chopped
2 red chilies, seeded and chopped
8 ounces ground pork
2 ounces chopped cooked shrimp
2 tablespoons fish sauce
1 teaspoon sugar
1 carrot, finely shredded
2 ounces bamboo shoots, chopped
¼ cup bean sprouts
2 scallions, chopped
1 tablespoon chopped cilantro
2 tablespoons flour
24 × 6-inch square spring roll wrappers
freshly ground black pepper
oil for frying

1 Drain and chop the mushrooms. Drain the noodles and cut into short lengths of about 2 inches.

2 Heat the oil in a wok or frying pan, add the garlic and chilies and fry for 30 seconds. Add the pork, stirring until the meat is browned.

3 Add the noodles, mushrooms and shrimp. Season with fish sauce, sugar and pepper. Turn into a bowl.

4 Mix in the carrot, bamboo shoots, bean sprouts, scallions and chopped cilantro for the filling.

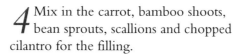

5 Put the flour in a small bowl and mix with a little water to make a paste. Place a spoonful of filling in the center of a spring roll wrapper.

6 Turn the bottom edge over to cover the filling, then fold in the left and right sides. Roll the wrapper up almost to the top edge. Brush the top edge with flour paste and seal. Repeat with the rest of the wrappers.

7 Heat the oil in a wok or deep-fat fryer. Slide in the spring rolls a few at a time and fry until crisp and golden brown. Remove with a slotted spoon and drain on paper towels. Serve hot with Thai sweet chili sauce to dip them into, if you like.

Chinese Crispy Spring Rolls

These dainty vegetarian stir-fried rolls are ideal served as appetizers or cocktail snacks. For a heartier version replace the mushrooms with chicken or pork, and substitute shrimp for the carrots.

INGREDIENTS

Makes about 40

1 cup bean sprouts
1 bunch scallions
2 carrots
⅔ cup bamboo shoots, sliced
1½ cups white mushrooms
3–4 tablespoons vegetable oil
1 teaspoon salt
1 teaspoon light brown sugar
1 tablespoon light soy sauce
1 tablespoon Chinese rice wine or
   dry sherry
about 40 spring roll wrappers
1 tablespoon cornstarch paste
flour, for dusting
oil, for deep-frying
soy sauce, to serve (optional)

1 Cut all the vegetables into thin shreds, roughly the same size and shape as the bean sprouts.

COOK'S TIP

To make cornstarch paste, mix 4 parts dry cornstarch with about 5 parts cold water until smooth.

2 Heat the oil in a wok and stir-fry the vegetables for about 1 minute. Add the salt, sugar, soy sauce and rice wine or sherry and stir-fry for 1½–2 minutes. Remove and drain the excess liquid, then let cool.

3 To make the spring rolls, cut each wrapper in half diagonally, then place about 1 tablespoon of the vegetable mixture one-third of the way down on the wrapper, with the triangle pointing away from you.

4 Lift the lower flap over the filling and roll it up once.

5 Fold in both ends and roll once more, then brush the upper edge with a little cornstarch paste, and roll into a neat package. Lightly dust a baking sheet with flour and place the spring rolls on the baking sheet with the flap side down.

6 To cook, heat the oil in a wok until hot, then reduce the heat to low. Deep-fry the spring rolls in batches (about 8–10 at a time) for 2–3 minutes, or until golden and crisp, then remove and drain. Serve the spring rolls hot with soy sauce, if desired.

Vietnamese Spring Rolls with Nuoc Cham Sauce

INGREDIENTS

Makes 25

6 dried Chinese mushrooms, soaked
   in hot water for 30 minutes
8 ounces lean ground pork
4 ounces uncooked shrimp, peeled,
   deveined and chopped
4 ounces white crabmeat, picked over
1 carrot, shredded
2 ounces cellophane noodles, soaked
   in water, drained and cut into
   short lengths
4 scallions, finely sliced
2 garlic cloves, finely chopped
2 tablespoons fish sauce
juice of 1 lime
freshly ground black pepper
25 x 4-inch Vietnamese rice sheets
oil for deep-frying
lettuce leaves, cucumber slices and
   cilantro leaves, to garnish

For the nuoc cham sauce
2 garlic cloves, finely chopped
2 tablespoons white wine vinegar
juice of 1 lime
2 tablespoons sugar
½ cup fish sauce
½ cup water
2 red chilies, seeded and chopped

1 Drain the mushrooms, squeezing out the excess moisture. Remove the stems, and thinly slice the caps into a bowl. Add the pork, shrimp, crabmeat, carrot, cellophane noodles, scallions and garlic.

2 Season with the fish sauce, lime juice and pepper. Set the mixture aside for about 30 minutes to allow the flavors to blend.

3 Meanwhile, make the nuoc cham sauce. Mix together the garlic, vinegar, lime juice, sugar, fish sauce, water and chilies in a serving bowl, then cover and set aside.

4 Assemble the spring rolls. Place a rice sheet on a flat surface, and brush with warm water until it is pliable. Place about 2 teaspoons of the filling near the edge of the rice sheet. Fold the sides over the filling, fold in the two ends, then roll up, sealing the ends of the roll with a little water. Make more rolls in the same way until all the filling is used up.

5 Heat the oil for deep-frying to 350°F or until a cube of dry bread added to the oil browns in about 30–45 seconds. Add the rolls, a few at a time, and fry until golden brown and crisp. Drain on paper towels. Serve the spring rolls hot, garnished with the lettuce, cucumber and cilantro. Offer the nuoc cham sauce separately.

Crab and Tofu Dumplings

These little crab- and ginger-flavored dumplings are usually served as a delicious side dish as part of a Japanese meal.

INGREDIENTS

Serves 4–6

4 ounces frozen white crabmeat,
   thawed
4 ounces firm tofu
1 egg yolk
2 tablespoons rice flour or wheat flour
2 tablespoons finely chopped scallion,
   green part only
¾-inch piece fresh ginger, grated
2 teaspoons light soy sauce
salt
vegetable oil, for deep-frying
2 ounces daikon, very finely grated,
   to serve

For the dipping sauce
½ cup vegetable broth
1 tablespoon sugar
3 tablespoons dark soy sauce

1 Squeeze as much moisture out of the crabmeat as you can. Press the tofu through a fine sieve with the back of a tablespoon. Combine the tofu and crabmeat in a bowl.

2 Add the egg yolk, rice or wheat flour, scallion, ginger and soy sauce and season to taste with salt. Combine thoroughly to form a light paste.

3 To make the dipping sauce, combine the broth, sugar and soy sauce in a serving bowl.

4 Line a tray with paper towels. Heat the vegetable oil in a wok or frying pan to 375°F. Meanwhile, shape the crab and tofu mixture into thumb-sized pieces. Fry in batches of three at a time for 1–2 minutes. Drain on the paper towels and serve with the sauce and daikon.

Dim Sum

Popular as a snack in China, these tiny dumplings are fast becoming fashionable in many restaurants in the West.

INGREDIENTS

Serves 4

For the dough
1¼ cups all-purpose flour
¼ cup boiling water
1½ tablespoons cold water
½ tablespoon vegetable oil

For the filling
3 ounces ground pork
3 tablespoons canned chopped
  bamboo shoots
½ tablespoon light soy sauce
1 teaspoon dry sherry
1 teaspoon light brown sugar
½ teaspoon sesame oil
1 teaspoon cornstarch
lettuce leaves such as iceberg or frisée,
  soy sauce, scallion curls, sliced fresh
  red chili and shrimp crackers,
  to serve

1 To make the dough, sift the flour into a bowl. Stir in the boiling water, then the cold water together with the oil. Mix to form a dough, turn out onto a lightly floured surface, and knead until smooth.

2 Divide the mixture into 16 equal pieces and shape into circles.

3 For the filling, mix together the pork, bamboo shoots, soy sauce, dry sherry, sugar and oil.

4 Add the cornstarch and stir well until thoroughly combined.

5 Place a little of the filling in the center of each dim sum circle. Pinch the edges of the dough together to form little "purses."

6 Line a steamer with a damp kitchen towel. Place the dim sum in the steamer and steam for 5–10 minutes. Arrange the lettuce leaves on four individual serving plates, top with the dim sum and serve with soy sauce, scallion curls, sliced red chili and shrimp crackers.

VARIATION

You can replace the pork with cooked, peeled shrimp. Sprinkle 1 tablespoon sesame seeds over the dim sum before cooking, if desired.

Pork Dumplings

These dumplings, when shallow-fried, make a good first course to a multicourse meal. They can also be steamed and served as a snack or poached in large quantities for a complete meal.

INGREDIENTS

Makes about 80–90
2½ cups all-purpose flour, plus extra
    for dusting
2 cups water
salt

For the filling

1 pound bok choy leaves or white
    cabbage
1 pound ground pork
1 tablespoon finely chopped scallions
1 teaspoon finely chopped fresh ginger
2 teaspoons salt
1 teaspoon light brown sugar
2 tablespoons light soy sauce
1 tablespoon Chinese rice wine or
    dry sherry
2 teaspoons sesame oil

For the dipping sauce

2 tablespoons red chili oil
1 tablespoon light soy sauce
1 teaspoon finely chopped garlic
1 tablespoon finely chopped scallions

2 For the filling, blanch the bok choy until soft. Drain and chop finely. Mix the bok choy with the pork, scallions, ginger, salt, sugar, soy sauce, wine or sherry and sesame oil.

3 Lightly dust a work surface with flour. Knead and roll the dough into a long sausage about 1 inch in diameter. Cut the sausage into 80–90 small pieces and flatten each piece with the palm of your hand.

1 Sift the flour into a bowl, then pour in the water and mix to a firm dough. Knead until smooth on a lightly floured surface, then cover with a damp cloth and set aside for 25–30 minutes.

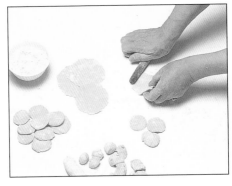

4 Using a rolling pin, roll out each piece into a thin pancake about 2½ inches in diameter.

5 Place about 1½ tablespoons of the filling in the center of each pancake and fold into a half-moon pouch.

6 Pinch the edges firmly so that the dumpling is tightly sealed.

7 Bring ⅔ cup salted water to a boil in a wok. Add the dumplings and poach for 2 minutes. Remove the wok from the heat and leave the dumplings in the water for another 15 minutes.

8 Make the dipping sauce by combining all the sauce ingredients in a bowl and mixing well. Serve in a small bowl with the dumplings.

Seafood Wontons with Cilantro Dressing

These tasty wontons resemble tortellini. Water chestnuts add a light crunch to the filling.

INGREDIENTS

Serves 4

8 ounces raw shrimp, peeled
  and deveined
4 ounces white crabmeat, picked over
4 canned water chestnuts, finely diced
1 scallion, finely chopped
1 small green chili, seeded and
  finely chopped
½ teaspoon grated fresh ginger
1 egg, separated
20–24 wonton wrappers
salt and freshly ground black pepper
cilantro leaves, to garnish

For the cilantro dressing

2 tablespoons rice vinegar
1 tablespoon chopped pickled ginger
6 tablespoons olive oil
1 tablespoon soy sauce
3 tablespoons chopped cilantro
2 tablespoons diced red bell pepper

1 Finely dice the shrimp, and place in a bowl. Add the crabmeat, water chestnuts, scallion, chili, ginger and egg white. Season with salt and pepper, and stir well.

2 Place a wonton wrapper on a board. Put about 1 teaspoon of the filling just above the center of the wrapper. With a pastry brush, moisten the edges of the wrapper with a little of the egg yolk. Bring the bottom of the wrapper up over the filling. Press gently to expel any air, then seal the wrapper neatly in a triangle.

3 For a more elaborate shape, bring the two side points up over the filling, overlap the points, and pinch the ends firmly together. Place the filled wontons on a large baking sheet, lined with wax paper, so that they do not stick together.

4 Half fill a large saucepan with water. Bring to simmering point. Add the filled wontons, a few at a time, and simmer for 2–3 minutes. The wontons will float to the surface. When ready, the wrappers will be translucent and the filling should be cooked. Remove the wontons with a large slotted spoon, drain them briefly, then spread them on trays. Keep warm while cooking the remaining wontons.

5 Make the cilantro dressing by whisking all the ingredients together in a bowl. Divide the wontons among serving dishes, drizzle with the dressing, and serve garnished with a handful of cilantro leaves.

Steamed Pork and Water Chestnut Wontons

Ginger and Chinese five-spice powder flavor this version of steamed dumplings—a favorite snack in many teahouses.

INGREDIENTS

Makes about 36

2 large Chinese cabbage leaves, plus extra for lining the steamer
2 scallions, finely chopped
½-inch piece fresh ginger, chopped
2 ounces canned water chestnuts, rinsed and finely chopped
8 ounces ground pork
½ teaspoon Chinese five-spice powder
1 tablespoon cornstarch
1 tablespoon light soy sauce
1 tablespoon Chinese rice wine or dry sherry
2 teaspoons sesame oil
generous pinch of superfine sugar
about 36 wonton wrappers, each 3 inches square
light soy sauce and hot chili oil, for dipping

1 Place the Chinese cabbage leaves one on top of the other. Cut them lengthwise into quarters and then across into thin shreds.

2 Place the shredded Chinese cabbage leaves in a bowl. Add the scallions, ginger, water chestnuts, pork, five-spice powder, cornstarch, soy sauce, rice wine or dry sherry, sesame oil and sugar and mix well.

3 Place a heaped teaspoon of the filling in the center of a wrapper. Lightly dampen the edges with water.

4 Lift the wrapper up around the filling, gathering it to form a "purse." Squeeze the wrapper firmly around the middle, then tap the bottom to make a flat base. The top should be open. Place the wonton on a tray and cover with a damp kitchen towel. Repeat until the filling is used up.

5 Line a steamer with cabbage leaves and steam the dumplings for 12–15 minutes, or until tender. Remove each batch from the steamer as soon they are cooked, cover with foil and keep warm. Serve hot with soy sauce and chili oil for dipping.

Seared Scallops with Wonton Crisps

Quick seared scallops with crisp vegetables in a lightly spiced sauce make a lovely appetizer.

INGREDIENTS

Serves 4
16 scallops, halved
oil for deep-frying
8 wonton wrappers
3 tablespoons olive oil
1 large carrot, cut into long thin strips
1 large leek, cut into long thin strips
juice of 1 lemon
juice of ½ orange
2 scallions, finely sliced
2 tablespoons cilantro leaves
salt and freshly ground black pepper

For the marinade
1 teaspoon Thai red curry paste
1 teaspoon grated fresh ginger
1 garlic clove, finely chopped
1 tablespoon soy sauce
1 tablespoon olive oil

1 Make the marinade by mixing all the ingredients in a bowl. Add the scallops, toss to coat, and let marinate for about 30 minutes.

2 Heat the oil in a large heavy-bottomed saucepan or deep-fryer, and deep-fry the wonton wrappers in small batches until crisp and golden.

3 When the wrappers are ready, drain them on paper towels. Set aside until required.

4 Heat half the olive oil in a large frying pan. Add the scallops, with the marinade, and sear over a high heat for about 1 minute or until golden, taking care not to overcook (they should feel firm to the touch but not rubbery). Using a slotted spoon, transfer the scallops to a plate.

5 Add the remaining olive oil to the pan. When hot, add the carrot and leek strips. Toss and turn the vegetables until they start to wilt and soften, but remain crisp. Season to taste with salt and pepper, stir in the lemon and orange juices, and add a little more soy sauce if needed.

6 Return the scallops to the pan, mix lightly with the vegetables, and heat for just long enough to warm through. Transfer to a bowl, and add the scallions and cilantro. To serve, sandwich a quarter of the mixture between two wonton crisps. Make three more "sandwiches" in the same way, and serve at once.

Wonton Flowers with Sweet-and-Sour Sauce

These melt-in-the-mouth, crisp dumplings make a delicious first course or snack—and take hardly any time at all to prepare.

INGREDIENTS

Serves 4–6
16–20 wonton wrappers
vegetable oil, for deep-frying

For the sauce
1 tablespoon vegetable oil
2 tablespoons light brown sugar
3 tablespoons rice vinegar
1 tablespoon light soy sauce
1 tablespoon ketchup
3–4 tablespoons broth or water
1 tablespoon cornstarch paste

1 Pinch the center of each wonton wrapper and twist it around to form a floral shape.

2 Heat the oil in a wok and deep-fry the floral wontons for 1–2 minutes, until crisp. Remove and drain on paper towels.

3 To make the sauce, heat the oil in a wok or frying pan and add the sugar, vinegar, soy sauce, ketchup and broth or water.

4 Stir in the cornstarch paste to thicken the sauce. Continue stirring until smooth. Pour a little sauce over the wontons and serve immediately with the remaining sauce.

Butterfly Shrimp

For best results, use uncooked jumbo shrimp in their shells for this deep-fried dish. Sold headless, they are about 3–4 inches long, and you should get 18–20 shrimp per pound.

INGREDIENTS

Serves 6–8

1 pound uncooked shrimp in their shells, heads removed
1 teaspoon ground Szechuan peppercorns
1 tablespoon light soy sauce
1 tablespoon Chinese rice wine or dry sherry
2 teaspoons cornstarch
2 eggs, lightly beaten
4–5 tablespoons bread crumbs
vegetable oil, for deep-frying
2–3 scallions, to garnish
lettuce leaves, to serve

1 Shell the shrimp but leave the tails on. Butterfly the shrimp, about three-quarters of the way through their length, leaving the tails still firmly attached.

2 Put the shrimp in a bowl with the pepper, soy sauce, rice wine or sherry and cornstarch and set aside to marinate for 10–15 minutes.

3 Pick up one shrimp at a time by the tail, and dip it in the beaten egg.

4 Roll the egg-covered shrimp in bread crumbs.

5 Heat the oil in a wok until medium-hot. Gently lower the shrimp into the oil.

6 Deep-fry the shrimp in batches until golden brown. Remove and drain. To serve, arrange the shrimp neatly on a bed of lettuce leaves. Garnish with scallions, either raw or after soaking for about 30 seconds in hot oil.

Deep-fried Squid with Spicy Salt and Pepper

This recipe is one of the specialities of the Cantonese school of cuisine. Southern China is famous for its seafood, often flavored with ginger.

INGREDIENTS

Serves 4

1 pound squid
1 teaspoon ginger juice (see
  Cook's Tip)
1 tablespoon Chinese rice wine or
  dry sherry
about 2½ cups boiling water
vegetable oil, for deep-frying
spicy salt and pepper (see index)
fresh cilantro leaves, to garnish

1 Clean the squid by discarding the head and the transparent backbone as well as the ink bag; peel off and discard the thin skin, then wash the squid and dry well on paper towels. Open up the squid and, using a sharp knife, score the inside of the flesh in a crisscross pattern.

2 Cut the squid into pieces, each about the size of a postage stamp. Marinate in a bowl with the ginger juice and rice wine or sherry for 25–30 minutes.

3 Blanch the squid in boiling water for a few seconds—each piece will curl up and the crisscross pattern will open out to resemble ears of corn. Remove and drain. Dry well.

4 Heat sufficient oil for deep-frying in a wok. Deep-fry the squid for 15–20 seconds, remove quickly and drain. Sprinkle with the spicy salt and pepper and serve garnished with fresh cilantro leaves.

COOK'S TIP

To make ginger juice, mix finely chopped or grated fresh ginger with an equal quantity of cold water and place in a piece of damp cheesecloth. Twist tightly to extract the juice. Alternatively, crush the ginger in a garlic press.

Quick-fried Shrimp with Hot Spices

These spicy shrimp are stir-fried in moments to make a wonderful appetizer. Don't forget that you will need to provide your guests with finger bowls.

INGREDIENTS

Serves 4

1 pound uncooked large shrimp
1-inch piece fresh ginger, grated
2 garlic cloves, crushed
1 teaspoon hot chili powder
1 teaspoon ground turmeric
2 teaspoons black mustard seeds
seeds from 4 green cardamom pods, crushed
4 tablespoons ghee or butter
1/2 cup coconut milk
salt and ground black pepper
2–3 tablespoons chopped fresh cilantro, to garnish
naan, to serve

1 Shell the shrimp carefully, leaving the tails attached.

2 Using a small, sharp knife, make a slit along the back of each shrimp and remove the dark vein. Rinse under cold running water, drain and pat dry.

3 Put the ginger, garlic, chili powder, turmeric, mustard seeds and cardamom seeds in a bowl. Add the shrimp and toss to coat completely with spice mixture.

4 Heat a wok until hot. Add the ghee or butter and swirl it around until foaming.

5 Add the marinated shrimp and stir-fry for 1–1½ minutes, until they are just turning pink.

6 Stir in the coconut milk and simmer for 3–4 minutes, until the shrimp are just cooked through. Season to taste with salt and pepper. Sprinkle the cilantro on top and serve immediately with naan.

Crab, Pork and Mushroom Spring Rolls

If you cannot obtain ground pork, use the meat from the equivalent weight of best-quality pork sausages. Filled spring rolls can be made in advance and kept in the refrigerator until they are ready for frying.

INGREDIENTS

Serves 4–6

1 ounce rice noodles
2 ounces shiitake mushrooms, fresh
 or dried
vegetable oil, for deep-frying
4 scallions, chopped
1 small carrot, grated
6 ounces ground pork
4 ounces white crabmeat
1 teaspoon fish sauce (optional)
12 frozen spring roll wrappers, defrosted
2 tablespoons cornstarch paste
salt and ground black pepper
1 head iceberg or Bibb lettuce,
 separated into leaves
1 bunch fresh mint or basil, coarsely
 chopped
1 bunch fresh cilantro leaves, coarsely
 chopped
½ cucumber, sliced

1 Bring a large saucepan of salted water to a boil, add the noodles and simmer for 8 minutes. Cut the noodles into finger-length pieces. If the mushrooms are dried, soak them in hot water for 10 minutes, then drain. Slice the mushrooms thinly.

2 To make the filling, heat 1 tablespoon of the oil in a wok or frying pan, add the scallions, carrot and pork and cook for 8–10 minutes. Remove from the heat, then add the crabmeat, fish sauce, if using, and seasoning. Add the noodles and mushrooms and set aside.

3 To fill the rolls, brush one spring roll wrapper at a time with the cornstarch paste, then place 1 teaspoon of the filling on the skin. Fold the edges toward the middle and roll evenly to make a neat cigar shape. The paste will help seal the wrapper.

4 Heat the oil for deep-frying in a wok or deep-fryer until hot. Fry the spring rolls, two or three at a time, for 6–8 minutes. Make sure the oil is not too hot, or the filling will not heat through. Arrange the lettuce leaves, mint or basil, cilantro and cucumber on a serving platter and top with the spring rolls.

Hot and Spicy Crab Claws

Crab claws are used to delicious effect in this quick stir-fried appetizer based on an Indonesian dish called *kepiting pedas*.

INGREDIENTS

Serves 4

12 fresh or frozen and thawed cooked
  crab claws
4 shallots, roughly chopped
2–4 fresh red chilies, seeded and
  roughly chopped
3 garlic cloves, roughly chopped
1 teaspoon grated fresh ginger
1/2 teaspoon ground coriander
3 tablespoons peanut oil
1/4 cup water
2 teaspoons sweet soy sauce
2–3 teaspoons lime juice
salt
fresh cilantro leaves, to garnish

1 Crack the crab claws with the back of a heavy knife to make eating them easier and set aside. In a mortar, pound the chopped shallots with the pestle until pulpy. Add the chilies, garlic, ginger and ground coriander and pound until the mixture forms a fairly coarse paste.

2 Heat the wok over medium heat. Add the oil and swirl it around. When it is hot, stir in the chili paste. Stir-fry for about 30 seconds. Increase the heat to high. Add the crab claws and stir-fry for another 3–4 minutes.

3 Stir in the water, sweet soy sauce, lime juice and salt to taste. Continue to stir-fry for 1–2 minutes. Serve immediately, garnished with fresh cilantro. The crab claws are eaten with the fingers, so it is helpful to provide finger bowls.

COOK'S TIP

If whole crab claws are unavailable, look for frozen ready-prepared crab claws. These are shelled, with just the tip of the claw attached to the whole meat. Stir-fry for about 2 minutes, until heated through.

Steamed Seafood Packages

Very neat and delicate, these make an excellent appetizer.

INGREDIENTS

Serves 4

8 ounces crab meat
2 ounces shelled shrimp, chopped
6 water chestnuts, chopped
2 tablespoons chopped bamboo shoots
1 tablespoon chopped scallions
1 teaspoon chopped ginger
1 tablespoon soy sauce
1 tablespoon fish sauce
12 rice sheets
banana leaves
oil for brushing
1 tablespoon soy sauce
2 scallions, shredded, to garnish
2 red chilies, seeded and sliced, and
   cilantro leaves, to garnish

1 Combine the crab meat, chopped shrimp, chestnuts, bamboo shoots, scallion and ginger in a bowl. Mix well, then add the soy sauce and fish sauce. Stir until blended.

2 Take a rice sheet and dip it in warm water. Place it on a flat surface and leave for a few seconds to soften.

COOK'S TIP

The seafood packages will spread out when steamed so be sure to space them well apart to prevent them sticking together.

3 Place a spoonful of the filling in the center of the sheet and fold into a square package. Repeat with the rest of the rice sheets and seafood mixture.

4 Line a steamer with banana leaves and brush them with oil. Put the packages, seam-side down, on the leaves and steam over high heat for 6–8 minutes, until the filling is cooked.

5 Transfer to a plate and garnish with the remaining ingredients.

Crisp-fried Crab Claws

INGREDIENTS

Serves 4

8 tablespoons rice flour
1 tablespoon cornstarch
1/2 teaspoon sugar
1 egg
4 tablespoons cold water
1 lemongrass stalk, finely chopped
2 garlic cloves, finely chopped
1 tablespoon chopped cilantro
1–2 red chilies, seeded and chopped
1 teaspoon fish sauce
oil for frying
12 half-shelled crab claws
freshly ground black pepper

For the chili vinegar dip

3 tablespoons sugar
1/2 cup water
1/2 cup red wine vinegar
1 tablespoon fish sauce
2–4 red chilies, seeded and chopped

1 To make the chili dip, put the sugar and water in a saucepan and bring to a boil, stirring, until the sugar dissolves. Lower the heat and simmer for 5–7 minutes. Stir in the rest of the ingredients and set aside.

2 Combine the rice flour, cornstarch and sugar in a large bowl. Beat the egg with the cold water, then stir the liquid into the flour mixture and mix well until it forms a light batter.

3 Add the lemongrass, garlic, cilantro, red chilies, fish sauce and freshly ground black pepper.

4 Heat the oil in a wok or deep-fat fryer. Pat dry the crab claws with paper towels and dip one at a time in the batter. Gently drop the battered claws in the hot oil, a few at a time. Fry until golden brown. Drain on paper towels. Serve hot with the chili vinegar dip.

Golden Wonton Pouches

These crisp pouches are delicious served as an appetizer or to accompany drinks at a party.

INGREDIENTS

Makes about 20

4 ounces ground pork
4 ounces crab meat
2–3 wood ears, soaked and chopped
1 tablespoon chopped cilantro
1 teaspoon chopped garlic
2 tablespoons chopped scallion
1 egg
1 tablespoon fish sauce
1 teaspoon soy sauce
pinch of sugar
20 wonton wrappers
20 chives, blanched (optional)
oil for deep-frying
freshly ground black pepper
plum or sweet chili sauce, to serve

1 In a mixing bowl, combine the pork, crab meat, wood ears, cilantro, garlic, scallions and egg. Mix thoroughly and season with fish sauce, soy sauce, sugar and freshly ground black pepper.

2 Take a wonton wrapper and place it on a flat surface. Put a heaped teaspoonful of filling in the center of the wrapper, then pull up the edges of the pastry around the filling.

3 Pinch together to seal. If you like, you can go a step further and tie it with a long chive. Repeat with the remaining pork mixture.

4 Heat the oil in a wok or deep-fat fryer. Fry the wontons in batches until they are crisp and golden brown. Drain on paper towels and serve immediately with either a plum or sweet chili sauce.

Rice Cakes with Spicy Dipping Sauce

Rice cakes are a classic Thai appetizer. They are easy to make and can be kept in an airtight box almost indefinitely.

INGREDIENTS

Serves 4–6
1 cup jasmine rice
1½ cups water
oil for frying and greasing

For the spicy dipping sauce
6–8 dried chilies
½ teaspoon salt
2 shallots, chopped
2 garlic cloves, chopped
4 cilantro roots
10 white peppercorns
1 cup unsweetened coconut milk
1 teaspoon shrimp paste
4 ounces ground pork
4 ounces cherry tomatoes, chopped
1 tablespoon fish sauce
1 tablespoon palm sugar
2 tablespoons tamarind juice
2 tablespoons coarsely chopped
  roasted peanuts
2 scallions, finely chopped

1 Stem the chilies and remove most of the seeds. Soak the chilies in warm water for 20 minutes. Drain and transfer to a mortar.

2 Add the salt and grind with a pestle until the chilies are crushed. Add the shallots, garlic, cilantro roots and peppercorns. Pound together until you have a coarse paste.

3 Pour the coconut milk into a saucepan and boil until it begins to separate. Add the pounded chili paste. Cook for 2–3 minutes, until it is fragrant. Stir in the shrimp paste. Cook for another minute.

4 Add the pork, stirring to break up any lumps. Cook for about 5–10 minutes. Add the tomatoes, fish sauce, palm sugar and tamarind juice. Simmer until the sauce thickens.

5 Stir in the chopped peanuts and scallions. Remove from the heat and set aside to cool.

6 Wash the rice in several changes of water. Put in a saucepan, add the water and cover with a tight-fitting lid. Bring to a boil, reduce the heat and simmer gently for about 15 minutes.

7 Remove the lid and fluff up the rice. Turn out on to a lightly greased tray and press down with the back of a large spoon. Set aside to dry out overnight in a very low oven, until it is completely dry and firm.

8 Remove the rice from the tray and break into bite-size pieces. Heat the oil in a wok or deep-fat fryer.

9 Deep-fry the rice cakes in batches for about 1 minute, until they puff up, taking care not to brown them too much. Remove and drain. Serve accompanied with the dipping sauce.

Fish Cakes with Cucumber Relish

These wonderful small fish cakes are a very familiar and popular appetizer. They are usually accompanied by Thai beer.

INGREDIENTS

Makes about 12

11 ounces white fish fillet, such as cod, cut into chunks
2 tablespoons red curry paste
1 egg
2 tablespoons fish sauce
1 teaspoon sugar
2 tablespoons cornstarch
3 kaffir lime leaves, shredded
1 tablespoon chopped cilantro
2 ounces green beans, finely sliced
oil for frying
Chinese mustard cress, to garnish

For the cucumber relish

4 tablespoons Thai coconut or rice vinegar
4 tablespoons water
4 tablespoons sugar
1 head pickled garlic
1 cucumber, quartered and sliced
4 shallots, finely sliced
1 tablespoon finely chopped ginger
2 red chilies, seeded and finely sliced

1 For the cucumber relish, bring the vinegar, water and sugar to a boil. Stir until the sugar dissolves, remove from the heat and cool.

2 Combine the rest of the relish ingredients together in a bowl and pour over the vinegar mixture.

3 Combine the fish, curry paste and egg in a food processor and process well. Transfer the mixture to a bowl, add the rest of the ingredients, except for the oil and garnish, and mix well.

4 Mold and shape the mixture into cakes about 2 inches in diameter and ¼ inch thick.

5 Heat the oil in a wok or deep-fat fryer. Fry the fish cakes, a few at a time, for about 4–5 minutes or until golden brown. Remove and drain on paper towels. Garnish with Chinese mustard cress and serve with the cucumber relish.

Vegetable Tempura

These deep-fried fritters are based on *kaki-age*, a Japanese dish that often incorporates fish and shrimp as well as vegetables.

INGREDIENTS

Serves 4

2 medium zucchini
½ medium eggplant
1 large carrot
½ small Spanish onion
1 egg
½ cup ice water
1 cup all-purpose flour
salt and ground black pepper
vegetable oil, for deep-frying
sea salt flakes, lemon slices and Japanese soy sauce (*shoyu*), to serve

1 Using a potato peeler, pare strips of peel from the zucchini and eggplant to give a striped effect.

2 Cut the zucchini, eggplant and carrot into strips about 4 inches long and ⅛ inch wide.

3 Put the zucchini, eggplant and carrot in a colander and sprinkle liberally with salt. Leave for about 30 minutes, then rinse thoroughly under cold running water. Drain well.

4 Thinly slice the onion from top to base, discarding the plump pieces in the middle. Separate the layers so that there are lots of fine, long strips. Mix all the vegetables together and season with salt and pepper.

5 Make the batter just before frying. Combine the egg and ice water in a bowl, then sift in the flour. Mix briefly with a fork or chopsticks. Do not overmix; the batter should remain lumpy. Add the vegetables to the batter and mix to combine.

6 Half-fill a wok with oil and heat to 350°F. Scoop up one heaped tablespoon of the mixture at a time and carefully lower it into the oil. Deep-fry in batches for about 3 minutes, or until golden brown and crisp. Drain on paper towels. Serve each portion with sea salt flakes, slices of lemon and a tiny bowl of Japanese soy sauce for dipping.

Spicy Spareribs

Fragrant with spices, this authentic Chinese dish makes a great—if slightly messy—appetizer to an informal meal.

INGREDIENTS

Serves 4

1½–2 pounds meaty pork spareribs
1 teaspoon Szechuan peppercorns
2 tablespoons sea salt
½ teaspoon Chinese five-spice powder
1½ tablespoons cornstarch
peanut oil, for deep-frying
cilantro sprigs, to garnish

For the marinade

2 tablespoons light soy sauce
1 teaspoon superfine sugar
1 tablespoon Chinese rice wine or
  dry sherry
freshly ground black pepper

1 Using a sharp, heavy cleaver, chop the spareribs into pieces about 2 inches long, or ask your butcher to do this for you. Place them in a shallow dish and set aside.

2 Heat a wok to medium heat. Add the Szechuan peppercorns and salt and dry-fry for about 3 minutes, stirring constantly, until the mixture colors slightly. Remove from the heat and stir in the five-spice powder. Set aside to cool.

3 Grind the cooled spice mixture to a fine powder in a mortar with a pestle.

4 Sprinkle 1 teaspoon of the spice powder over the spareribs and rub in well with your hands. To make the marinade, add all the ingredients and toss the ribs to coat thoroughly. Cover and marinate in the refrigerator for about 2 hours, turning occasionally.

5 Pour off any excess marinade from the spareribs. Sprinkle the ribs with the cornstarch and mix to coat evenly.

6 Half-fill a wok with oil and heat to 350°F. Deep-fry the spareribs in batches for 3 minutes, or until golden. Remove and set aside. When all the batches have been cooked, reheat the oil to 350°F and deep-fry the ribs for a second time for 1–2 minutes, or until crisp and thoroughly cooked. Drain on paper towels. Transfer the ribs to a warm serving platter and sprinkle with 1–1½ teaspoons of the remaining spice powder. Garnish with cilantro sprigs and serve immediately.

COOK'S TIP

Any leftover spice powder can be kept in a screw-top jar for several months. Use to rub on the flesh of duck, chicken or pork before cooking.

Deep-fried Ribs with Spicy Salt and Pepper

INGREDIENTS

Serves 4–6
10–12 pork spareribs (about 1½ pounds),
  excess fat trimmed
2–3 tablespoons flour
vegetable oil, for deep-frying
scallion tassels, to garnish (optional)

For the marinade
1 clove garlic, crushed
1 tablespoon light brown sugar
1 tablespoon light soy sauce
1 tablespoon dark soy sauce
2 tablespoons Chinese rice wine or
  dry sherry
½ teaspoon chili sauce
few drops of sesame oil

For the spicy salt and pepper
1 tablespoon salt
2 teaspoons ground Szechuan
  peppercorns
1 teaspoon five-spice powder

1 Chop each rib into three or four pieces, then mix with all the marinade ingredients and marinate for at least 2–3 hours.

— COOK'S TIP —

Ideally, each sparerib should be chopped into three or four bite-size pieces before or after deep-frying in a wok. If this is not possible, serve the ribs whole.

2 Coat the ribs with flour and deep-fry in medium-hot oil for 4–5 minutes, stirring to separate. Remove from the oil and drain.

3 Heat the oil to high and deep-fry the ribs again for about 1 minute or until the color is an even dark brown. Remove and drain.

4 To make the spicy salt and pepper, heat all the ingredients in a preheated dry wok for about 2 minutes over low heat, stirring constantly. Serve with the ribs. Garnish the dish with scallion tassels, if desired.

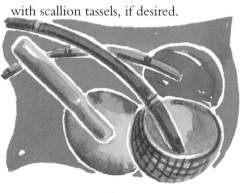

Lacy Duck Egg Nets

You can find duck eggs in good Asian supermarkets or order them direct from farms, but regular eggs are also good here. Thais have a special dispenser to make the net, but you can use a pastry bag fitted with a small nozzle or a squeeze bottle.

INGREDIENTS

Makes about 12–15

For the filling
4 cilantro roots
2 garlic cloves
10 white peppercorns
pinch of salt
3 tablespoons oil
1 small onion, finely chopped
4 ounces lean ground pork
3 ounces shelled shrimp, chopped
½ cup roasted peanuts, ground
1 teaspoon palm sugar
fish sauce, to taste

For the egg nets
6 duck eggs or jumbo hen eggs
cilantro leaves, to serve, plus extra
    to garnish
scallion tassels and sliced red chillies,
    to garnish

1 Using a mortar and pestle, grind the cilantro roots, garlic, white peppercorns and salt into a paste.

2 Heat 2 tablespoons of the oil, add the paste and fry until fragrant. Add the onion and cook until softened. Add the pork and shrimp and continue to stir-fry until the meat is cooked.

3 Add the peanuts, palm sugar, salt and fish sauce, to taste. Stir the mixture and continue to cook until it becomes a little sticky. Remove from the heat. Transfer the mixture to a bowl and set aside.

4 Break the eggs into a bowl, and beat with a fork. Grease a non-stick frying pan with the remaining oil and heat. Using a special dispenser or a suitable alternative, trail the eggs across the pan to make a net pattern, about 5 inches in diameter.

5 When the net is set, carefully remove it from the pan, and repeat until all the eggs have been used up.

6 To assemble, lay a net on a board, lay a few cilantro leaves on it and top with a spoonful of filling. Turn in the edges to make a neat square shape. Repeat with the rest of the nets. Arrange on a serving dish and garnish with the fresh cilantro leaves, scallion tassels and chilies.

Son-in-law Eggs

This fascinating name comes from a story about a prospective bridegroom who wanted to impress his future mother-in-law and devised a recipe from the only other dish he knew how to make – cooked eggs. The hard-cooked eggs are deep fried and then drenched with a sweet, piquant tamarind sauce.

INGREDIENTS

Serves 4–6
scant ½ cup palm sugar
5 tablespoons fish sauce
6 tablespoons tamarind juice
oil for frying
6 shallots, finely sliced
6 garlic cloves, finely sliced
6 red chilies, sliced
6 hard-cooked eggs, shelled
lettuce, to serve
sprigs of cilantro, to garnish

1 Combine the palm sugar, fish sauce and tamarind juice in a small saucepan. Bring to a boil, stirring until the sugar dissolves, then simmer for about 5 minutes.

2 Taste and add more palm sugar, fish sauce or tamarind juice, if necessary. It should be sweet, salty and slightly sour. Transfer the sauce to a bowl and set aside.

3 Heat the oil in a wok or deep-fat fryer. Meanwhile, heat a couple of spoonfuls of the oil in a frying pan and fry the shallots, garlic and chilies until golden brown. Transfer the mixture to a bowl and set aside.

4 Deep-fry the eggs in the oil for about 3–5 minutes, until golden brown. Remove and drain on paper towels. Cut the eggs in quarters and arrange on a bed of lettuce. Drizzle with the sauce and sprinkle over the shallots. Garnish with sprigs of cilantro.

Fried Clams with Chili and Yellow Bean Sauce

Seafood is abundant in Thailand, especially at all of the beach holiday resorts. This delicious dish, which is simple to prepare, is one of the favorites.

INGREDIENTS

Serves 4–6
2¼ pounds fresh clams
2 tablespoons vegetable oil
4 garlic cloves, finely chopped
1 tablespoon grated ginger
4 shallots, finely chopped
2 tablespoons yellow bean sauce
6 red chilies, seeded and chopped
1 tablespoon fish sauce,
pinch of sugar
handful of basil leaves, plus extra
    to garnish

1 Wash and scrub the clams. Heat the oil in a wok or large frying pan. Add the garlic and ginger and fry for 30 seconds, add the shallots and fry for another minute.

2 Add the clams. Using a fish slice or spatula, turn them a few times to coat with the oil. Add the yellow bean sauce and half the red chilies.

3 Continue to cook, stirring often, for about 5–7 minutes until all the clams open. You may need to add a splash of water. Adjust the seasoning with fish sauce and a little sugar.

4 Finally add the basil and transfer to individual bowls or a platter. Garnish with the remaining red chilies and basil leaves.

Pickled Sweet-and-Sour Cucumber

The "pickling" can be done in minutes rather than days—but the more time you have, the better the result.

INGREDIENTS

Serves 6–8
1 slender cucumber, about
    12 inches long
1 teaspoon salt
2 teaspoons superfine sugar
1 teaspoon rice vinegar
½ teaspoon red chili oil (optional)
few drops of sesame oil

1 Halve the unpeeled cucumber lengthwise. Scrape out the seeds and cut the cucumber into thick chunks.

2 In a bowl, sprinkle the cucumber chunks with the salt and mix well. Leave for at least 20–30 minutes—longer if possible—then pour the liquid off.

3 Mix the cucumber with the sugar, vinegar and chili oil, if using. Sprinkle with the sesame oil just before serving.

Hot-and-Sour Cabbage

This popular dish from Szechuan in western China can be served hot or cold.

INGREDIENTS

Serves 6–8
1 pound pale green or white cabbage
3–4 tablespoons vegetable oil
10–12 red Szechuan peppercorns
few whole dried red chilies
1 teaspoon salt
1 tablespoon light brown sugar
1 tablespoon light soy sauce
2 tablespoons rice vinegar
few drops of sesame oil

1 Cut the cabbage leaves into small pieces, each roughly 1 x ½ inch.

2 Heat the oil in a preheated wok until smoking, then add the peppercorns and chilies.

3 Add the cabbage to the wok and stir-fry for about 2 minutes. Add the salt and sugar, continue stirring for 1 minute more, then add the soy sauce, vinegar and sesame oil. Blend well and serve immediately.

Crispy "Seaweed"

Surprisingly, the very popular and rather exotic-sounding "seaweed" served in Chinese restaurants is, in fact, just ordinary spring greens.

INGREDIENTS

Serves 4

1 pound collards or spring greens
vegetable oil, for deep-frying
$^1/_2$ teaspoon salt
1 teaspoon superfine sugar
1 tablespoon ground fried fish, to garnish (optional)

1 Cut out the hard stalks in the center of each spring green leaf. Pile the leaves on top of each other, and roll into a tight sausage shape. Thinly cut the leaves into fine shreds. Spread them out to dry.

2 Heat the oil in a wok until hot. Deep-fry the shredded greens in batches, stirring to separate them.

3 Remove the greens with a slotted spoon as soon as they are crispy, but before they turn brown. Drain. Sprinkle the salt and sugar evenly all over the "seaweed," mix well, garnish with ground fish, if desired, and serve.

Sesame Seed Shrimp Toasts

Use uncooked shrimp for this dish, as cooked ones will tend to separate from the bread during cooking.

INGREDIENTS

Serves 4

8 ounces uncooked shrimp, shelled
1 tablespoon vegetable shortening
1 egg white, lightly beaten
1 teaspoon finely chopped scallions
$^1/_2$ teaspoon finely chopped fresh ginger
1 tablespoon Chinese rice wine or dry sherry
1 tablespoon cornstarch paste
1 cup white sesame seeds
6 large slices white bread
vegetable oil, for deep-frying
salt and ground black pepper

1 Chop the shrimp with the shortening to form a smooth paste. In a bowl, mix with all the other ingredients except the sesame seeds and bread.

2 Spread the sesame seeds evenly on a large plate or baking sheet; spread the shrimp paste thickly on one side of each slice of bread, then press, spread side down, onto the seeds.

3 Heat the oil in a wok until medium-hot; fry 2–3 slices of the sesame bread at a time, spread side down, for 2–3 minutes. Remove and drain. Cut each slice into six or eight fingers (without crusts).

Sweet Potato and Pumpkin Shrimp Cakes

Serve these fried cakes warm
with Thai fish sauce.

INGREDIENTS

Serves 4–6
1½ cups all-purpose flour
½ teaspoon salt
½ teaspoon active dry yeast
¾ cup warm water
1 egg, beaten
8 ounces uncooked shrimp, shelled
1 small sweet potato, peeled
   and grated
1 small wedge pumpkin (about 8
   ounces), peeled, seeded and grated
2 scallions, chopped
¼ cup water chestnuts, sliced
   and chopped
½ teaspoon chili sauce
1 clove garlic, crushed
juice of ½ lime
2–3 tablespoons vegetable oil
scallion tassel, to garnish

1 Sift the flour and salt into a mixing bowl and make a well in the center. Dissolve the yeast in the water, then pour into the well. Pour in the egg and leave for a few minutes, until bubbles appear. Mix to a batter.

2 Place the shelled shrimp in a saucepan and cover with water. Bring to a boil and simmer for 10–12 minutes. Drain, refresh in cold water and drain again. Roughly chop and set the shrimp aside.

3 Add the sweet potato and pumpkin to the batter, then add the scallions, water chestnuts, chili sauce, garlic, lime juice and shrimp. Heat a little oil in a wok or frying pan. Spoon in the batter in small heaps and fry until golden. Drain and serve, garnished with a scallion tassel.

Spicy Meat-filled Packages

In Indonesia the finest gossamer dough is made for *Martabak*. You can achieve equally good results using ready-made filo pastry or spring roll wrappers.

INGREDIENTS

Makes 16

1 pound lean ground beef
2 small onions, finely chopped
2 small leeks, very
    finely chopped
2 garlic cloves, crushed
2 teaspoons coriander seeds, dry-fried
    and ground
1 teaspoon cumin seeds, dry-fried
    and ground
1–2 teaspoons mild curry powder
2 eggs, beaten
1-pound package filo pastry
3–4 tablespoons sunflower oil
salt and freshly ground black pepper
light soy sauce, to serve

1 To make the filling, mix the meat with the onions, leeks, garlic, coriander, cumin, curry powder and seasoning. Turn into a heated wok, without oil, and stir constantly, until the meat has changed color and looks cooked, about 5 minutes.

2 Allow to cool and then mix in enough beaten egg to bind to a soft consistency. Any leftover egg can be used to seal the edges of the dough; otherwise, use milk.

3 Brush a sheet of filo with oil and lay another sheet on top. Cut the sheets in half. Place a large spoonful of the filling on each double piece of filo. Fold the sides to the middle so that the edges just overlap. Brush these edges with either beaten egg or milk and fold the other two sides to the middle in the same way, so that you now have a square package. Make sure that the package is as flat as possible, to speed cooking. Repeat with the other fifteen packages and place on a floured sheet of wax paper on a tray in the fridge.

4 Heat the remaining oil in a shallow pan and cook several packages at a time, depending on the size of the pan. Cook for 3 minutes on the first side and then turn them over and cook for another 2 minutes, or until heated through. Cook the remaining packages in the same way and serve hot, sprinkled with light soy sauce.

5 If preferred, these spicy packages can be cooked in a hot oven at 400°F for 20 minutes. Glaze with more beaten egg before baking for a rich, golden color.

Spicy Meat Patties with Coconut

Spicy meat patties, known as *Rempah*, with a hint of coconut, often feature as one of the delicious accompaniments in an Indonesian-style buffet.

INGREDIENTS

Makes 22

4 ounces freshly grated coconut, or
   dried coconut, soaked in
   4–6 tablespoons boiling water
12 ounces finely ground beef
½ teaspoon each coriander and cumin
   seeds, dry-fried
1 garlic clove, crushed
a little beaten egg
1–2 tablespoons flour
peanut oil for frying
salt
thin lemon or lime wedges, to serve

1 Mix the moistened coconut with the ground beef.

2 Grind the dry-fried coriander and cumin seeds with a mortar and pestle. Add the ground spices to the meat and coconut mixture together with the garlic, salt to taste, and sufficient beaten egg to bind.

3 Divide the meat into even-size portions, the size of a walnut, and form into patty shapes.

4 Dust with flour. Heat the oil and then fry the patties for 4–5 minutes until both sides are golden brown and cooked through. Serve with lemon or lime wedges, to squeeze over.

Corn Fritters

There is no doubt that freshly cooked corn is best for this recipe, called *Perkedel Jagung*. Do not add salt to the water, because this toughens the outer husk.

INGREDIENTS

Makes 20

2 fresh corn on the cob, or 12-ounce
   can corn kernels
2 macadamia nuts or 4 almonds
1 garlic clove
1 onion, quartered
½ inch fresh *laos*, peeled
   and sliced
1 teaspoon ground coriander
2–3 tablespoons oil
3 eggs, beaten
2 tablespoons dried coconut
2 scallions, finely shredded
a few celery leaves, finely
   shredded (optional)
salt

1 Cook the corn on the cob in boiling water for 7–8 minutes. Drain, cool slightly and, using a sharp knife, strip the kernels from the cob. If using canned corn kernels, drain well.

2 Grind the nuts, garlic, onion, *laos* and coriander to a fine paste in a food processor or mortar and pestle. Heat a little oil and fry the paste until it gives off a spicy aroma.

3 Add the fried spices to the beaten eggs with the coconut, scallions and celery leaves, if using. Add salt to taste with the corn kernels.

4 Heat the remaining oil in a shallow frying pan. Drop large spoonfuls of batter into the pan and cook for about 2–3 minutes until golden. Flip the fritters over with a metal spatula and cook until golden brown and crispy. Cook three or four fritters at a time.

Spiced Honey Chicken Wings

Be prepared to get very sticky when you eat these stir-fried chicken wings, as the best way to enjoy them is by eating them with your fingers. Provide individual finger bowls for your guests.

INGREDIENTS

Serves 4

1 red chili, finely chopped
1 teaspoon chili powder
1 teaspoon ground ginger
finely grated zest of 1 lime
12 chicken wings
$^1/_4$ cup sunflower oil
1 tablespoon fresh cilantro, chopped
2 tablespoons soy sauce
4 tablespoons honey
lime zest and fresh cilantro sprigs,
   to garnish (optional)

1 Combine the fresh chili, chili powder, ground ginger and lime rind. Rub the mixture into the chicken skins and let sit for at least 2 hours to let the flavors penetrate.

2 Heat a wok and add half the oil. When the oil is hot, add half the wings and stir-fry for 10 minutes, turning regularly, until crisp and golden. Drain on paper towels. Repeat with the remaining oil and chicken wings.

3 Add the cilantro to the hot wok and stir-fry for 30 seconds, then return the wings to the wok and stir-fry for 1 minute.

4 Stir in the soy sauce and honey, and stir-fry for 1 minute. Serve the chicken wings hot with the sauce drizzled over them. Garnish with lime zest and cilantro, if wished.

Pork Satay

Originating in Indonesia, satay are skewers of meat marinated with spices and grilled quickly over charcoal. It's street food at its best, prepared by vendors with portable grills who set up stalls at every street corner and market place. As well as pork, you can also make satay with chicken, beef or lamb. Serve with satay sauce and cucumber relish.

INGREDIENTS

Makes about 20

1 pound lean pork
1 teaspoon grated ginger
1 lemongrass stalk, finely chopped
3 garlic cloves, finely chopped
1 tablespoon medium curry paste
1 teaspoon ground cumin
1 teaspoon ground turmeric
4 tablespoons coconut cream
2 tablespoons fish sauce
1 teaspoon sugar
20 wooden satay skewers
oil for cooking

For the satay sauce

1 cup unsweetened coconut milk
2 tablespoons red curry paste
½ cup crunchy peanut butter
½ cup chicken stock
3 tablespoons brown sugar
2 tablespoons tamarind juice
1 tablespoon fish sauce
½ teaspoon salt

1 Cut the pork thinly into 2-inch strips. Mix together the ginger, lemongrass, garlic, medium curry paste, cumin, turmeric, coconut cream, fish sauce and sugar.

3 Meanwhile, make the sauce. Heat the coconut milk over a medium heat, then add the red curry paste, peanut butter, chicken stock and sugar.

4 Cook and stir until smooth, about 5–6 minutes. Add the tamarind juice, fish sauce and salt to taste.

5 Thread the meat onto skewers. Brush with oil and grill over charcoal or under a preheated broiler for 3–4 minutes on each side, turning occasionally, until cooked and golden brown. Serve with the satay sauce.

2 Pour over the pork and set aside to marinate for about 2 hours.

Bon-bon Chicken with Sesame Sauce

The chicken meat is tenderized by being beaten with a stick (called a *bon* in Chinese), hence the name for this very popular Szechuan dish.

INGREDIENTS

Serves 6–8
1 chicken (about 3 pounds)
5 cups water
1 tablespoon sesame oil
shredded cucumber, to garnish

For the sauce
2 tablespoons light soy sauce
1 teaspoon sugar
1 tablespoon finely chopped scallions
1 teaspoon red chili oil
$1/2$ teaspoon ground Szechuan peppercorns
1 teaspoon white sesame seeds
2 tablespoons tahini or 2 tablespoons peanut butter creamed with a little sesame oil

1 Clean the chicken well. Bring the water to a rolling boil in a wok and add the chicken. Reduce the heat, cover and cook for 40–45 minutes. Remove the chicken and immerse in cold water to cool.

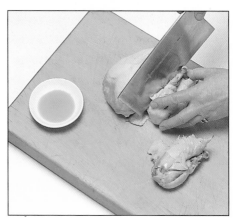

2 After at least 1 hour, remove the chicken and drain; dry well with paper towels and brush on a coating of sesame oil. Carve the meat off the legs, wings and breast and pull the meat off the rest of the bones.

3 On a flat surface, pound the meat with a rolling pin, then tear it into shreds with your fingers.

4 Place the meat in a dish with the shredded cucumber around the edge. In a bowl, combine all the sauce ingredients, keeping the scallions to garnish. Pour the sauce over the chicken, garnish and serve.

Barbecue-glazed Chicken Skewers

Known as *yakitori*, this appetizer is often served with predinner drinks in Japan.

INGREDIENTS

Makes 12 skewers and 8 wing pieces

4 chicken thighs, skinned
4 scallions, blanched and cut into short lengths
8 chicken wings
1 tablespoon grated daikon, to serve (optional)

For the sauce

4 tablespoons sake
5 tablespoons dark soy sauce
2 tablespoons tamari sauce
3 tablespoons sweet sherry
¼ cup sugar

1 Bone the chicken thighs and cut the meat into large dice. Thread the scallions and chicken onto 12 bamboo skewers.

2 To prepare the chicken wings, remove the tip at the first joint. Chop through the second joint, revealing the two narrow bones. Take hold of the bones with a clean cloth and pull, turning the meat around the bones inside out. Remove the smaller bone and set the meat aside.

3 To make the sauce, combine all the sauce ingredients in a stainless steel or enamel saucepan and simmer until reduced by two-thirds. Set aside to cool.

4 Cook the skewers of chicken and the wings under a preheated broiler without brushing on any oil. When juices begin to emerge from the chicken, baste liberally with the sauce. Cook the chicken on the skewers for another 3 minutes and cook the wings for another 5 minutes. Serve with grated daikon, if desired.

Lamb Satés

INGREDIENTS

Makes 25–30 skewers

2¼-pound leg of lamb, boned
3 garlic cloves, crushed
3–4 fresh chilies, seeded and ground, or
   1–2 teaspoons chili powder
4–6 tablespoons dark soy sauce
juice of 1 lemon
salt and freshly ground black pepper
oil for brushing

For the sauce

6 garlic cloves, crushed
2–3 fresh chilies, seeded and ground
6 tablespoons dark soy sauce
1½ tablespoons lemon juice
2 tablespoons boiling water

To serve

small onion pieces
cucumber wedges

1 Cut the lamb into thick slices and then into neat ½-inch cubes. Remove any pieces of gristle but do not trim off any of the fat because this keeps the *satés* moist during cooking and enhances the flavor.

—— VARIATION ——

Lamb neck fillet is now widely available in supermarkets and can be used instead of boned leg. Brush the lamb fillet with oil before grilling.

2 Blend the garlic, ground fresh chilies or chili powder, soy sauce, lemon juice and seasoning to a paste in a food processor or with a pestle and mortar. Pour over the lamb. Cover and set aside in a cool place for at least an hour. Soak wooden or bamboo skewers in water so that they won't burn during cooking.

3 Prepare the sauce. Put the garlic cloves into a bowl. Add the chilies, soy sauce, lemon juice and boiling water. Stir well.

4 Thread the meat onto the skewers. Brush with oil and cook under a broiler, turning often. Brush each *saté* with a little of the sauce and serve hot, with small pieces of onion and cucumber. Serve with the remaining sauce.

Chicken and Sticky Rice Balls

These balls can either be steamed or deep-fried. The fried versions are crunchy and are excellent for serving at cocktail parties.

INGREDIENTS

Makes about 30
1 pound ground chicken
1 egg
1 teaspoon tapioca flour
4 scallions, finely chopped
2 tablespoons chopped cilantro
2 tablespoons fish sauce
pinch of sugar
8 ounces cooked sticky rice
banana leaves
oil for brushing
freshly ground black pepper
1 small carrot, shredded, to garnish
1 red bell pepper, to garnish
chopped chives, to garnish
sweet chili sauce, to serve

1 In a mixing bowl, combine the ground chicken, egg, tapioca flour, scallions and cilantro. Mix well and season with fish sauce, sugar and freshly ground black pepper.

2 Spread the cooked sticky rice on a plate or flat tray.

3 Place a teaspoonful of the chicken mixture on the bed of rice. With damp hands, roll and shape the mixture in the rice to make a ball about the size of a walnut. Repeat with the rest of the chicken mixture.

COOK'S TIP

Sticky rice, also known as glutinous rice, has a very high gluten content. It is so called because the grains stick together when cooked. It can be eaten both as a savory and as a sweet dish.

4 Line a bamboo steamer with banana leaves and lightly brush them with oil. Place the chicken balls on the leaves, spacing well apart to prevent them sticking together. Steam over high heat for about 10 minutes or until cooked.

5 Remove and arrange on serving plates. Garnish with shredded carrots, strips of red pepper and chives. Serve with sweet chili sauce.

FISH AND SEAFOOD

*The many islands in the Pacific and the
long coastline of mainland China insure
an abundance of wonderful fish and
seafood recipes in the cuisines of Asia.
Whole fish and fillets are combined
with fragrant herbs and marinades and
then steamed, baked or fried quickly.
The different ways of preparing shrimp,
mussels, scallops, squid and other
seafood are almost endless, from the
subtly aromatic Pan-steamed Mussels
with Thai Herbs to the robust and spicy
Shrimp with Chayote in Turmeric
Sauce. All are highly nutritious
and utterly delicious.*

Steamed Fish with Ginger and Scallions

Firm and delicate fish steaks, such as salmon or turbot, can be cooked by this same method.

INGREDIENTS

Serves 4–6

1 sea bass, sea trout or red snapper, weighing about 1½ pounds, cleaned
½ teaspoon salt
1 tablespoon sesame oil
2–3 scallions, cut in half lengthwise
2 tablespoons light soy sauce
2 tablespoons Chinese rice wine or dry sherry
1 tablespoon fresh ginger, cut into fine strips
2 tablespoons vegetable oil
scallions, cut into fine strips, to garnish

1 Using a sharp knife, score both sides of the fish as far down as the bone with diagonal cuts about 1 inch apart. Rub the fish all over, inside and out, with salt and sesame oil.

2 Sprinkle the scallions over a heatproof platter and place the fish on top. Blend together the soy sauce and rice wine or dry sherry with the ginger and pour evenly all over the fish.

3 Place the platter in a very hot steamer (or inside a wok on a rack) and steam vigorously, covered, for 12–15 minutes.

4 Heat the vegetable oil until hot. Remove the platter from the steamer, place the scallions on top of the fish, then pour the hot oil along the whole length of the fish. Serve immediately.

Chinese-spiced Fish Fillets

INGREDIENTS

Serves 4

generous ½ cup all-purpose flour
1 teaspoon Chinese five-spice powder
8 skinless fillets of fish, such as flounder
   or lemon sole, about 2 pounds total
1 egg, lightly beaten
scant 1 cup fine fresh bread crumbs
peanut oil, for frying
2 tablespoons butter
4 scallions, cut diagonally into thin
   slices
12 ounces tomatoes, seeded and diced
2 tablespoons soy sauce
salt and freshly ground black pepper
red bell pepper strips and chives,
   to garnish

1 Sift the flour together with the
Chinese five-spice powder and salt
and pepper to taste onto a plate. Dip
the fish fillets first in the seasoned flour,
then in the beaten egg and finally in
bread crumbs.

2 Pour oil into a large frying pan to a
depth of ½ inch. Heat until it is
very hot and starting to sizzle. Add the
coated fillets, a few at a time, and fry
for 2–3 minutes on each side,
depending on their thickness, until just
cooked and golden brown. Do not
crowd the pan, or the temperature of
the oil will drop and the fish will
absorb too much of it.

3 Drain the fillets on paper towels,
then transfer to serving plates and
keep warm. Pour off all the oil from
the frying pan and wipe it out with
paper towels.

4 Cook the scallions and tomatoes in
the butter for 1 minute, then add
the soy sauce.

5 Spoon the tomato mixture over
the fish, garnish with red bell
pepper strips and chives and serve.

Whole Fish with Sweet-and-sour Sauce

INGREDIENTS

Serves 4

1 whole fish, such as red snapper or
    carp, about 2¼ pounds prepared
2–3 tablespoons cornstarch
oil for frying
salt and freshly ground black pepper
boiled rice, to serve

For the spice paste

2 garlic cloves
2 lemon grass stems
1 inch fresh *laos*
1 inch fresh ginger root
¾ inch fresh turmeric or
    ½ teaspoon ground turmeric
5 macadamia nuts or 10 almonds

For the sauce

1 tablespoon brown sugar
3 tablespoons cider vinegar
about 1½ cups water
2 lime leaves, torn
4 shallots, quartered
3 tomatoes, skinned and cut in wedges
3 scallions, finely shredded
1 fresh red chili, seeded and shredded

1 Wash and dry the fish thoroughly
and then sprinkle it inside and out
with salt. Set aside for 15 minutes,
while preparing the other ingredients.

2 Peel and crush the garlic cloves.
Use only the lower white part of
the lemon grass stems and slice thinly.
Peel and slice the fresh *laos*, the ginger
root and turmeric, if using. Grind the
nuts, garlic, lemon grass, *laos*, ginger
and turmeric to a fine paste in
a food processor or with a mortar
and pestle.

3 Scrape the paste into a bowl. Stir
in the brown sugar, cider vinegar,
seasoning to taste and the water. Add
the lime leaves.

4 Dust the fish with the cornstarch
and fry on both sides in hot oil for
about 8–9 minutes or until almost
cooked through. Drain the fish on
paper towels and transfer to a serving
dish. Keep warm.

5 Pour off most of the oil and then
pour in the spicy liquid and allow
to come to a boil. Reduce the heat and
cook for 3–4 minutes. Add the shallots
and tomatoes, followed a minute later
by the scallions and chili. Taste and
adjust the seasoning.

6 Pour the sauce over the fish. Serve
at once, with plenty of rice.

Sesame Baked Fish with a Hot Ginger Marinade

Although tropical varieties of fish are found increasingly frequently in supermarkets, Oriental food stores usually have a wider selection suitable for this Malaysian dish.

INGREDIENTS

Serves 4–6

2 red snapper, or monkfish, heads off, each weighing 12 ounces
2 tablespoons vegetable oil, plus extra for greasing
2 teaspoons sesame oil
2 tablespoons sesame seeds
1-inch piece fresh ginger, thinly sliced
2 garlic cloves, crushed
2 small fresh red chilies, seeded and finely chopped
4 shallots or 1 medium onion, halved and sliced
2 tablespoons water
½-inch square shrimp paste or 1 tablespoon fish sauce
2 teaspoons sugar
½ teaspoon cracked black pepper
juice of 2 limes
3–4 banana leaves (optional)

1 Clean and dry the fish well. Slash both sides of the fish deeply with a sharp knife.

2 To make the marinade, heat the vegetable and sesame oils in a preheated wok. Add the sesame seeds and fry until golden. Add the ginger, garlic, chilies and shallots or onion and stir-fry 1–2 minutes, or until softened. Add the water, shrimp paste or fish sauce, sugar, pepper and lime juice and simmer for 2–3 minutes. Remove from the heat and allow to cool.

COOK'S TIP

Banana leaves are available from Indian and Southeast Asian food stores.

---

3 If using banana leaves, remove and discard the central stems. Soften the leaves by dipping them in boiling water. To keep them supple, rub the surfaces with vegetable oil. Spread the sesame seed marinade over the fish, then wrap them separately in the banana leaves, secured with a skewer, or enclose them in foil. Set aside in a cool place to allow the flavors to mingle, for up to 3 hours.

4 Place the wrapped fish on a baking sheet and cook in a preheated oven at 350°F or on a glowing barbecue for 35–40 minutes. Serve hot.

Sea Bass with Chinese Chives

Chinese chives are widely available in Asian supermarkets but if you are unable to buy them, use half a large Spanish onion, finely sliced, instead.

INGREDIENTS

Serves 4

2 sea bass, about 1 pound total
1 tablespoon cornstarch
3 tablespoons vegetable oil
6 ounces Chinese chives
1 tablespoon Chinese rice wine or
    dry sherry
1 teaspoon superfine sugar
salt and freshly ground black pepper
Chinese chives with flower heads,
    to garnish

1 Remove the scales from the bass by scraping them with the back of a knife, working from the tail end toward the head end. Fillet the fish. Your fishmonger could do this for you.

2 Cut the fillets into large chunks and dust them lightly with cornstarch, salt and pepper.

3 Heat 2 tablespoons of the oil in a preheated wok. When the oil is hot, toss the chunks of fish in the wok briefly to seal, then set aside. Wipe out the wok with paper towels.

4 Cut the Chinese chives into 2-inch lengths and discard the flowers. Reheat the wok and add the remaining oil, then stir-fry the Chinese chives for 30 seconds. Add the fish and rice wine or dry sherry, then bring to a boil and stir in the sugar. Serve hot, garnished with some flowering Chinese chives.

Sizzling Chinese Steamed Fish

Steamed whole fish is very popular in China, where the wok is used as a steamer. In this recipe the fish is flavored with garlic, ginger and scallions cooked in sizzling hot oil.

INGREDIENTS

Serves 4

4 rainbow trout, about 9 ounces each
¼ teaspoon salt
½ teaspoon sugar
2 garlic cloves, finely chopped
1 tablespoon finely diced fresh ginger
5 scallions, cut into 2-inch lengths and
   then into fine strips
¼ cup peanut oil
1 teaspoon sesame oil
3 tablespoons light soy sauce
thread egg noodles and stir-fried
   vegetables, to serve

1 Make three diagonal slits on both sides of each fish and lay them on a heatproof plate. Place a small rack or trivet in a wok half-filled with water, cover and heat until just simmering.

2 Sprinkle the fish with the salt, sugar, garlic and ginger. Place the plate securely on the rack or trivet and cover. Steam gently for about 12 minutes, or until the flesh has turned pale pink and feels quite firm.

3 Turn off the heat, remove the lid and scatter the scallions over the fish. Replace the lid.

4 Heat the peanut and sesame oils in a small pan over high heat until just smoking, then quickly pour a quarter over the scallions on each of the fish—the scallions will sizzle and cook in the hot oil. Sprinkle the soy sauce over the top. Serve the fish and juices immediately with boiled noodles and stir-fried vegetables.

Salmon Teriyaki

Marinating the salmon makes it so wonderfully tender it just melts in the mouth; the crunchy condiment provides an excellent foil.

INGREDIENTS

Serves 4
1½ pounds salmon fillet
2 tablespoons sunflower oil
watercress, to garnish

For the teriyaki sauce
1 teaspoon superfine sugar
1 teaspoon dry white wine
1 teaspoon sake, rice wine or
  dry sherry
2 tablespoons dark soy sauce

For the condiment
2-inch piece fresh ginger, thinly sliced
pink food coloring (optional)
2 ounces daikon, grated

1 For the teriyaki sauce, combine the sugar, white wine, sake or rice wine or dry sherry and soy sauce, stirring until the sugar dissolves.

2 Remove the skin from the salmon using a very sharp filleting knife.

3 Cut the fillet into strips, then place in a nonmetallic dish. Pour the teriyaki sauce over the fish and set aside to marinate for 10–15 minutes.

4 To make the condiment, place the ginger in a bowl and add a little pink food coloring if you wish. Stir in the daikon.

5 Lift the salmon from the teriyaki sauce and drain.

6 Heat the oil in a preheated wok. Add the salmon in batches and stir-fry for 3–4 minutes, or until it is cooked. Transfer to serving plates, garnish with the watercress and serve with the daikon and ginger condiment.

Salt-grilled Mackerel

In Japan salt is applied to oily fish before cooking to draw out the flavors. Mackerel and snapper are the most popular choices for this treatment, known as *Shio-yaki* in Japanese. The fish develop a unique flavor and texture when treated with salt. The salt is washed away before cooking.

INGREDIENTS

Serves 2

2 small or 1 large mackerel or snapper, gutted and cleaned, with head on
2 tablespoons salt
1 medium carrot, shredded, to serve

For the soy-ginger dip
¼ cup dark soy sauce
2 tablespoons sugar
1-inch piece fresh ginger

For the Japanese horseradish
3 tablespoons wasabi powder
2 teaspoons water

1 To make the soy-ginger dip, put the soy sauce, sugar and ginger in a stainless steel saucepan. Bring to a boil, lower the heat and simmer for 2–3 minutes. Strain and set aside to cool. To make the Japanese horseradish, put the wasabi powder in a small bowl and stir in the water to make a stiff paste. Shape the mixture into a neat ball and set aside.

2 Rinse the fish under cold, running water and pat thoroughly dry with paper towels. Slash the fish several times on both sides, cutting down as far as the bone. Sprinkle the salt inside the fish and rub it well into the skin. Set aside on a plate for 40 minutes.

3 Wash the fish in plenty of cold water to remove all traces of salt. Shape the fish neatly and secure in position with two bamboo skewers inserted along the length of the body, one above and one below the eye.

4 Cook the fish under a preheated broiler or on a grill for 10 to 12 minutes, or until it is cooked, turning once. The skin can be basted with a little of the soy-ginger dip partway through cooking, if desired. Transfer the fish to a serving plate and arrange carrot, Japanese horseradish and soy-ginger dip decoratively around it.

COOK'S TIP

Wasabi is the ground root of an Asian type of horseradish. It is very sharp and aromatic and often served with raw fish and shellfish. In the West, it is usually available only as a powder, which has to be mixed with water to make a paste.

Fried Monkfish Coated with Rice Noodles

These marinated medallions of fish are coated in rice vermicelli and deep-fried – they taste as good as they look.

INGREDIENTS

Serves 4

1 pound monkfish
1 teaspoon grated fresh ginger
1 garlic clove, finely chopped
2 tablespoons soy sauce
6 ounces rice vermicelli
4 tablespoons cornstarch
2 eggs, beaten
salt and freshly ground black pepper
oil for deep-frying
banana leaves, to serve (optional)

For the dipping sauce

2 tablespoons soy sauce
2 tablespoons rice vinegar
1 tablespoon sugar
2 red chilies, thinly sliced
1 scallion, thinly sliced

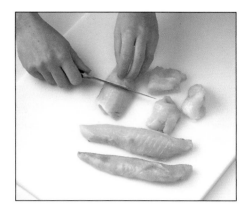

1 Trim the monkfish, and cut into 1-inch thick medallions. Place in a dish, and add the ginger, garlic and soy sauce. Mix lightly, and let marinate for 10 minutes.

2 Meanwhile, make the dipping sauce. Combine the soy sauce, vinegar and sugar in a small saucepan. Bring to a boil. Add salt and pepper to taste. Remove from the heat, add the chilies and scallion, and then set aside until required.

3 Using kitchen scissors, cut the noodles into 1½-inch lengths. Spread them out in a shallow bowl.

4 Lightly coat the fish medallions in cornstarch, dip in beaten egg, and cover with noodles, pressing them on to the fish so that they stick.

5 Deep-fry the coated fish in hot oil, two to three pieces at a time, until the noodle coating is fluffy, crisp and light golden brown. Drain, and serve hot on banana leaves, if you like, accompanied by the dipping sauce.

Fish with a Cashew-Ginger Marinade

To capture the sweet, spicy flavor of this Indonesian favorite, marinated fish are wrapped in foil before baking. When they are unwrapped at the table, their delicious aroma will make your mouth water.

INGREDIENTS

Serves 4

2½ pounds sea bass or halibut, scaled and cleaned
1¼ cups raw cashews
2 shallots or 1 small onion, finely chopped
½-inch piece fresh ginger, finely chopped
1 garlic clove, crushed
1 small fresh red chili, seeded and finely chopped
2 tablespoons vegetable oil
1 tablespoon shrimp paste
2 teaspoons sugar
2 tablespoons tamarind sauce
2 tablespoons ketchup
juice of 2 limes
salt

3 Cover both sides of each fish with the paste and set aside in the refrigerator for up to 8 hours to allow the flavors to mingle.

4 Wrap the fish in foil, securing the parcels carefully. Bake in a preheated oven at 350°F for 30–35 minutes.

1 Slash the fish 3 or 4 times on each side with a sharp knife. Set aside.

2 Grind the cashews, shallots or onion, ginger, garlic and chili to a fine paste in a mortar with a pestle or in a food processor. Add the vegetable oil, shrimp paste and sugar and season to taste with salt. Blend, then add the tamarind sauce, ketchup and lime juice and blend again.

Fish Balls with Chinese Greens

These tasty fish balls are steamed over a wok with a selection of green vegetables—bok choy is widely available.

INGREDIENTS

Serves 4
For the fish balls
1 pound white fish fillets, skinned, boned and cubed
3 scallions, chopped
1 slice bacon, chopped
1 tablespoon Chinese rice wine or dry sherry
2 tablespoons light soy sauce
1 egg white
fresh cilantro, to garnish

For the vegetables
1 small head bok choy
1 teaspoon cornstarch
1 tablespoon light soy sauce
$2/3$ cup fish stock
2 tablespoons peanut oil
2 garlic cloves, sliced
1-inch piece fresh ginger, cut into shreds
$1/2$ cup green beans
$3/4$ cup snow peas
3 scallions, sliced diagonally into 2–3-inch lengths
salt and ground black pepper

1 Put the fish, scallions, bacon, wine or sherry, soy sauce and egg white in a food processor and process until smooth. With wet hands, form the mixture into about 24 small balls.

2 Steam the fish balls in batches in a lightly greased bamboo steamer in a wok for 5–10 minutes, until cooked through and firm. Remove from the steamer and keep warm.

3 Meanwhile trim the bok choy, removing any discolored leaves or damaged stems, then tear into manageable pieces.

4 Combine the cornstarch, soy sauce and stock in a small bowl and set aside.

5 Heat a wok until hot, add the oil and swirl it around. Add the garlic and ginger and stir-fry for 2–3 minutes. Add the beans and stir-fry for 2–3 minutes, then add the snow peas, scallions and bok choy. Stir-fry for 2–3 minutes.

6 Add the sauce to the wok and cook, stirring, until it has thickened and the vegetables are tender but crisp. Taste and adjust the seasoning, if necessary. Garnish the fish balls with fresh cilantro and serve with the vegetables.

COOK'S TIP

You can replace the snow peas and green beans with broccoli florets. Blanch them before stir-frying.

Balti Fried Fish

Both freshwater and sea fish are widely eaten in Pakistan. The coastal city of Karachi is particularly famous for its delicious seafood.

INGREDIENTS

Serves 4–6

1½ pounds cod fillet
1 onion, sliced
1 tablespoon lemon juice
1 teaspoon salt
1 teaspoon garlic pulp
1 teaspoon crushed dried red chilies
1½ teaspoons garam masala
2 tablespoons chopped fresh cilantro
2 tomatoes
2 tablespoons cornstarch
⅔ cup corn oil
apricot chutney and paratha (optional), to serve

1 Skin the fish and cut it into small cubes. Place in a bowl and chill in the refrigerator.

2 In a bowl mix together the onion, lemon juice, salt, garlic pulp, crushed red chilies, garam masala and chopped cilantro. Set aside.

3 Place the tomatoes in boiling water for a few seconds. Remove with a slotted spoon and peel off the skins. Coarsely chop the tomatoes and add to the onion mixture.

4 Transfer the onion mixture to a food processor or blender and process for about 30 seconds.

5 Remove the fish from the fridge and add the onion mixture from the food processor or blender. Mix thoroughly.

6 Add the cornstarch and mix thoroughly again until the fish pieces are well coated.

7 Heat the oil in a preheated wok or frying pan. Lower the heat slightly and add the fish pieces, a few at a time. Cook, turning them gently with a slotted spoon, for about 5 minutes or until lightly browned.

8 Remove the fish with a slotted spoon and drain on kitchen paper. Keep warm while you cook the remaining fish pieces in the same way. Serve immediately with apricot chutney and paratha, if liked.

Thai Fish Stir-fry

This is a substantial dish, best served with crusty bread for mopping up all the spicy juices.

INGREDIENTS

Serves 4

1½ pounds mixed seafood, such as red snapper and cod, filleted and skinned, and raw shrimp
1¼ cups coconut milk
1 tablespoon vegetable oil
salt and ground black pepper
crusty bread, to serve

For the sauce

2 large red fresh chilies
1 onion, roughly chopped
2-inch piece fresh ginger, peeled and sliced
2-inch piece lemongrass, outer leaf discarded, roughly sliced
2-inch piece galangal, peeled and sliced
6 blanched almonds, chopped
½ teaspoon ground turmeric
½ teaspoon salt

1 Cut the filleted fish into large chunks. Peel the shrimp, keeping their tails intact.

COOK'S TIP

Galangal, also spelled galingale, is a rhizome from the same family as ginger, with a similar but milder flavor. It is peeled and sliced, chopped or grated in the same way as ginger. It is an important ingredient in Southeast Asian cooking, particularly in Indonesia, Malaysia and Thailand.

2 To make the sauce, carefully remove the seeds from the chilies and chop the flesh roughly. Put the chilies and the other sauce ingredients in a food processor or blender with 3 tablespoons of the coconut milk. Process until smooth.

3 Heat a wok, then add the oil. When the oil is hot, stir-fry the seafood for 2–3 minutes, then remove.

4 Add the sauce and the remaining coconut milk to the wok, then return the seafood. Bring to a boil, season well and serve with crusty bread.

Boemboe Bali of Fish

The island of Bali has wonderful fish, surrounded as it is by the sparkling blue sea. This simple fish "curry" is packed with many of the characteristic flavors associated with Indonesia.

INGREDIENTS

Serves 4–6

1½ pounds cod or haddock fillet
½ teaspoon shrimp paste
2 red or white onions
1 inch fresh ginger root, peeled
   and sliced
½ inch fresh *laos*, peeled and sliced, or
   1 teaspoon *laos* powder
2 garlic cloves
1–2 fresh red chilies, seeded, or
   1–2 teaspoons chili powder
6–8 tablespoons sunflower oil
1 tablespoon dark soy sauce
1 teaspoon tamarind pulp, soaked in
   2 tablespoons warm water
1 cup water
celery leaves or chopped fresh chili,
   to garnish
boiled rice, to serve

1 Skin the fish, remove any bones and then cut the flesh into bite-size pieces. Pat dry with paper towels and set aside.

2 Grind the shrimp paste, onions, ginger, *laos*, garlic and fresh red chilies, if using, to a paste in a food processor or with a mortar and pestle. Stir in the chili powder and *laos* powder, if using.

3 Heat 2 tablespoons of the oil and fry the spice mixture, stirring, until it gives off a rich aroma. Add the soy sauce. Strain the tamarind and add the juice and water. Cook for 2–3 minutes.

—— VARIATION ——

Substitute 1 pound cooked large shrimp. Add them 3 minutes before the end.

4 In a separate pan, fry the fish in the remaining oil for 2–3 minutes. Turn only once so that the pieces stay whole. Lift out with a slotted spoon and put into the sauce.

5 Cook the fish in the sauce for 3 minutes more and serve with boiled rice. Garnish the dish with feathery celery leaves or a little chopped fresh chili, if liked.

Fish Fillets in Spicy Coconut Sauce

Use fresh fish fillets to make this dish if you can, as they have much more flavor than frozen ones. However, if you are using frozen fillets, make sure that they are thawed before you begin to cook.

INGREDIENTS

Serves 4

2 tablespoons corn oil
1 teaspoon onion seeds
4 dried red chilies
3 garlic cloves, sliced
1 onion, sliced
2 tomatoes, sliced
2 tablespoons dry unsweetened coconut
1 teaspoon salt
1 teaspoon ground coriander
4 whitefish fillets, such as sole or
  flounder (each about 3 ounces)
$^2/_3$ cup water
1 tablespoon lime juice
1 tablespoon chopped fresh cilantro
cooked rice, to serve (optional)

1 Heat the oil in a wok. Lower the heat slightly and add the onion seeds, dried red chilies, garlic slices and onion. Cook for 3–4 minutes, stirring once or twice.

2 Add the tomatoes, coconut, salt and coriander and stir thoroughly.

3 Cut each fish fillet into three pieces. Drop the fish pieces into the mixture and turn them over gently until they are well coated.

4 Cook for 5–7 minutes, lowering the heat if necessary. Add the water, lime juice and fresh cilantro and cook for another 3–5 minutes, until the water has mostly evaporated. Serve immediately with rice, if desired.

— COOK'S TIP —

The Indian equivalent of the Chinese wok is the karahi. It is usually round-bottomed with two carrying handles. Like the wok, the karahi is traditionally made of cast iron in order to withstand the high temperatures and hot oil used in cooking. They are now made in a variety of different metals and are available in a range of sizes, including small ones for individual servings.

Braised Whole Fish in Chili and Garlic Sauce

This is a classic Szechuan recipe. When it is served in a restaurant, the fish's head and tail are usually discarded before cooking, and used in other dishes. A whole fish may be used, however, and always looks impressive, especially for special occasions and formal dinner parties.

INGREDIENTS

Serves 4–6

1 carp, bream, sea bass, trout, grouper or gray mullet (1½ pounds), cleaned
1 tablespoon light soy sauce
1 tablespoon Chinese rice wine or dry sherry
vegetable oil, for deep-frying

For the sauce
2 garlic cloves, finely chopped
2–3 scallions, finely chopped, with the white and green parts separated
1 teaspoon finely chopped fresh ginger
2 tablespoons chili bean sauce
1 tablespoon tomato paste
2 teaspoons light brown sugar
1 tablespoon rice vinegar
½ cup chicken stock
1 tablespoon cornstarch paste
few drops of sesame oil

1 Rinse and dry the fish well. Using a sharp knife, score both sides of the fish down to the bone with diagonal cuts about 1 inch apart. Rub both sides of the fish with the soy sauce and rice wine. Set aside for 10–15 minutes to marinate.

2 Heat sufficient oil for deep-frying in a wok. When it is hot, add the fish and fry for 3–4 minutes on both sides, until golden brown.

3 To make the sauce, pour away all but about 1 tablespoon of the oil. Push the fish to one side of the wok and add the garlic, the white part of the scallions, the ginger, chili bean sauce, tomato paste, sugar, vinegar and stock. Bring to a boil and braise the fish in the sauce for 4–5 minutes, turning it over once. Add the green part of the scallions. Stir in the cornstarch paste to thicken the sauce. Sprinkle with a little sesame oil and serve.

Indian Seafood with Vegetables

The spicy seafood is cooked separately and combined with vegetables at the last minute.

INGREDIENTS

Serves 4
For the seafood
8 ounces cod, or any other firm, white fish
8 ounces shelled cooked shrimp
6 crab sticks, halved lengthwise
1 tablespoon lemon juice
1 teaspoon ground coriander
1 teaspoon chili powder
1 teaspoon salt
1 teaspoon ground cumin
¼ cup cornstarch
⅔ cup corn oil

For the vegetables
⅔ cup corn oil
2 onions, chopped
1 teaspoon onion seeds
½ cauliflower, cut into florets
4 ounces green beans, cut into 1-inch lengths
1 cup canned corn
1 teaspoon shredded fresh ginger
1 teaspoon chili powder
1 teaspoon salt
4 fresh green chilies, sliced
2 tablespoons chopped fresh cilantro
lime slices, to garnish

1 Skin the fish and cut into small cubes. Put it in a mixing bowl with the shrimp and crab sticks.

COOK'S TIP

Raita makes a delicious accompaniment to this seafood dish. Whisk 1¼ cups plain yogurt, then whisk in ½ cup water. Stir in 1 teaspoon salt, 2 tablespoons chopped fresh cilantro and 1 finely chopped green chili. Garnish with slices of cucumber and 1 or 2 mint sprigs.

2 In a separate bowl, combine the lemon juice, ground coriander, chili powder, salt and ground cumin. Pour this over the seafood and combine thoroughly using your hands.

3 Sprinkle on the cornstarch and mix again until the seafood is well coated. Set aside in the refrigerator for about 1 hour to let the flavors develop fully.

4 To make the vegetable mixture, heat the oil in a preheated wok. Add the onions and the onion seeds and stir-fry until lightly browned.

5 Add the cauliflower, green beans, corn, ginger, chili powder, salt, green chilies and fresh cilantro. Stir-fry for 7–10 minutes over medium heat, making sure that the cauliflower florets retain their shape.

6 Spoon the fried vegetables around the edge of a shallow dish, leaving a space in the middle for the seafood, and keep warm.

7 Wash and dry the pan, then heat the oil to fry the seafood pieces. Fry the seafood pieces in two or three batches, until they turn golden brown. Remove with a slotted spoon and drain on paper towels.

8 Arrange each batch of seafood in the middle of the dish of vegetables and keep warm while you fry the remaining batches. Garnish with lime slices and serve immediately.

Braised Fish Fillet with Mushrooms

This is the Chinese stir-fried version of the French *filets de sole bonne femme* (sole cooked with mushrooms and wine sauce).

INGREDIENTS

Serves 4

1 pound lemon sole or flounder fillets
1 teaspoon salt
¹/₂ egg white
2 tablespoons cornstarch paste
about 2¹/₂ cups vegetable oil
1 tablespoon finely chopped scallions
¹/₂ teaspoon finely chopped fresh ginger
1¹/₂ cups white mushrooms, thinly sliced
1 teaspoon light brown sugar
1 tablespoon light soy sauce
2 tablespoons Chinese rice wine or dry sherry
1 tablespoon brandy
about ²/₃ cup stock
few drops of sesame oil

1 Trim off the soft bones along the edge of the fish, but leave the skin on. Cut each fillet into bite-size pieces. Mix the fish with a little salt, the egg white and about half of the cornstarch paste.

COOK'S TIP

You could substitute straw mushrooms, so called because they are grown on beds of rice straw. They have a subtle flavor and a slightly slippery texture.

2 Heat the oil in a preheated wok until medium-hot, add the fish, slice by slice, and stir gently so the pieces do not stick. Remove after about 1 minute and drain. Pour off the excess oil, leaving about 2 tablespoons in the wok.

3 Stir-fry the scallions, ginger and mushrooms for 1 minute. Add the sugar, soy sauce, rice wine or sherry, brandy and stock. Bring to a boil. Return the fish to the wok and braise for 1 minute. Stir in the remaining cornstarch paste to thicken the sauce, sprinkle with sesame oil and serve.

Shrimp Fu-yung

This is a very colorful dish that is simple to make in a wok. Most of the preparation can be done well in advance.

INGREDIENTS

Serves 4

3 eggs
1 tablespoon finely chopped scallion
3–4 tablespoons vegetable oil
8 ounces uncooked shrimp, shelled
2 teaspoons cornstarch paste
¹/₂ cup green peas
1 tablespoon Chinese rice wine or dry sherry
salt

1 Reserving 1 teaspoon of egg white, beat the eggs with a pinch of salt and a few pieces of the scallion. Heat a little oil in a preheated wok over medium heat. Add the egg mixture and stir to scramble. Remove the scrambled eggs and reserve.

2 Mix the shrimp with a little salt, the reserved egg white and the cornstarch paste. Stir-fry the peas in hot oil for 30 seconds Add the shrimp.

3 Add the remaining scallion. Stir-fry for 1 minute, then stir the mixture into the scrambled egg with the wine or sherry and serve.

Thai Fish Cakes

Bursting with flavors of chilies, lime and lemongrass, these little fish cakes make a wonderful appetizer or light lunch dish.

INGREDIENTS

Serves 4

1 pound cod or haddock fillet
3 scallions, sliced
1 lemongrass stalk, finely chopped
2 tablespoons chopped fresh cilantro
2 tablespoons Thai red curry paste
1 fresh green chili, seeded and chopped
2 teaspoons grated lime zest
1 tablespoon lime juice
2 tablespoons peanut oil
flour, for dusting
salt
crisp lettuce leaves, shredded
    scallions, fresh red chili slices, fresh
    cilantro sprigs and lime wedges,
    to serve

1 Cut the fish into chunks, then place them in a blender or food processor.

2 Add the scallions, lemongrass, cilantro, curry paste, green chili, lime zest and juice to the fish. Season with salt. Process until finely ground.

3 Using lightly floured hands, divide the mixture into 16 pieces and shape each one into a small cake about 1½ inches across. Place the fish cakes on a plate, cover with plastic wrap and chill for about 2 hours, until firm.

4 Heat a wok over high heat until hot. Add the oil and swirl it around. Fry the fish cakes, a few at a time, for 6–8 minutes, turning them over carefully until evenly browned. Drain each batch on paper towels and keep hot while you are cooking the remainder. Serve on a bed of crisp lettuce leaves with shredded scallions, red chili slices, fresh cilantro sprigs and lime wedges.

Sweet and Sour Fish

When fish is cooked in this way the skin becomes crispy on the outside, while the flesh remains moist and juicy inside. The sweet and sour sauce, with its colorful cherry tomatoes, complements the fish beautifully.

INGREDIENTS

Serves 4–6

1 large or 2 medium-size fish such as snapper or mullet, heads removed
2 tablespoons cornstarch
½ cup vegetable oil
1 tablespoon chopped garlic
1 tablespoon chopped fresh ginger
2 tablespoons chopped shallots
8 ounces cherry tomatoes
2 tablespoons red wine vinegar
2 tablespoons sugar
2 tablespoons tomato ketchup
1 tablespoon fish sauce
3 tablespoons water
salt and freshly ground black pepper
cilantro leaves and shredded scallions, to garnish

1 Thoroughly rinse and clean the fish. Score the skin diagonally on both sides of the fish.

2 Coat the fish lightly on both sides with 1 tablespoon cornstarch. Shake off any excess.

3 Heat the oil in a wok or large frying pan and slide the fish into the wok. Reduce the heat to medium and fry the fish for about 6–7 minutes, until crisp and brown on both sides.

4 Remove the fish with a spatula and place on a large platter.

5 Pour off all but 2 tablespoons of the oil and add the garlic, ginger and shallots. Fry until golden.

6 Add the cherry tomatoes and cook until they burst open. Stir in the vinegar, sugar, tomato ketchup and fish sauce. Simmer gently for 1–2 minutes and adjust the seasoning to taste.

7 Blend the remaining 1 tablespoon cornstarch with the water. Stir into the sauce and heat until it thickens. Pour the sauce over the fish and garnish with cilantro leaves and shredded scallions.

Spiced Salmon Stir-fry

Marinating the salmon allows all the flavors to develop, and the lime juice tenderizes the fish beautifully, so it needs very little stir-frying—be careful not to overcook it.

INGREDIENTS

Serves 4

4 salmon steaks (about 8 ounces each)
4 whole star anise
1 dried chili
2 lemongrass stalks, sliced
juice and finely grated zest of 3 limes
2 tablespoons honey
2 tablespoons peanut oil
salt and ground black pepper
lime wedges, to garnish

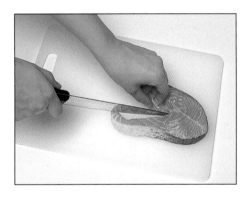

1 Remove the middle bone from each steak, using a very sharp filleting knife, to make two strips from each one.

2 Remove the skin by inserting the knife at the thin end of each piece of salmon and sliding it along under the flesh. Sprinkle 1 teaspoon salt on the cutting board to prevent the fish from slipping while you do this.

3 Roughly crush the star anise and chili in a mortar with a pestle. Place the salmon in a nonmetallic dish and add the star anise, lemongrass, lime juice and zest and honey. Season well with salt and pepper. Turn the salmon strips to coat. Cover and set in the refrigerator to marinate overnight.

4 Carefully drain the salmon, reserving the marinade, and pat dry with paper towels.

5 Heat a wok, then add the oil. When the oil is hot, add the salmon and stir-fry, stirring constantly, until cooked. Increase the heat, add the marinade and bring to a boil. Garnish with lime wedges and serve.

COOK'S TIP

Star anise contains the same oil as the more familiar Mediterranean spice anise or aniseed, but looks completely different. Its star-shaped pods are particularly attractive, so it is often used whole in Chinese cooking for its decorative effect. It is also becoming increasingly popular with Western cooks for the same reason. It is an essential ingredient in many classic Chinese recipes and is one of the spices that constitute five-spice powder. The flavor of star anise is very strong and licorice-tasting, with deeper undertones than its European counterpart.

Malaysian Fish Curry

Fish cooked in a wok full of coconut milk makes a mouthwatering curry.

INGREDIENTS

Serves 4–6

1½ pounds monkfish or red snapper fillet

3 tablespoons grated or dry unsweetened coconut

2 tablespoons vegetable oil

1-inch piece galangal or fresh ginger, peeled and thinly sliced

2 small red chilies, seeded and finely chopped

2 garlic cloves, crushed

2-inch piece lemongrass, shredded

1 piece shrimp paste (½ inch square), or 1 tablespoon fish sauce

14-ounce can coconut milk

2½ cups chicken stock

½ teaspoon ground turmeric

1 tablespoon sugar

juice of 1 lime or ½ lemon

salt

cilantro and lime slices, to garnish

1 Cut the fish into large chunks, season with salt and set aside.

COOK'S TIP

Sambal, a fiery hot relish, is traditionally served with this curry. Combine 2 skinned and chopped tomatoes, 1 finely chopped onion, 1 finely chopped green chili and 2 tablespoons lime juice. Season to taste with salt and pepper and sprinkle with 2 tablespoons grated coconut.

2 Dry-fry the coconut in a large wok until evenly brown. Add the oil, galangal or ginger, chilies, garlic and lemongrass and fry briefly. Stir in the shrimp paste. Strain the coconut milk through a strainer, reserving what remains in the strainer, then add to the wok.

3 Add the chicken stock, turmeric, sugar, a little salt and the lime or lemon juice. Simmer for 10 minutes. Add the fish and simmer for 6–8 minutes. Stir in the reserved part of the coconut milk and simmer to thicken. Garnish with cilantro and lime slices and serve.

Vinegar Fish

Fish cooked in a spicy mixture that includes chilies, ginger and vinegar is an Indonesian specialty. It is a method that lends itself particularly well to strong-flavored, oily fish, such as the mackerel used here.

INGREDIENTS

Serves 2–3

2–3 medium mackerel, filleted
2-3 fresh red chilies, seeded
4 macadamia nuts or 8 almonds
1 red onion, quartered
2 garlic cloves, crushed
½-inch piece fresh ginger, peeled and sliced
1 teaspoon ground turmeric
3 tablespoons vegetable oil
3 tablespoons wine vinegar
⅔ cup water
salt
deep-fried onions and finely chopped fresh chili, to garnish
plain cooked rice or coconut rice, to serve (optional)

1 Rinse the mackerel fillets in cold water and dry well on paper towels. Set aside.

—————— COOK'S TIP ——————

To make coconut rice, put ⅔ cup washed long-grain rice in a heavy saucepan with ½ teaspoon salt, a 2-inch piece of lemongrass and 1 ounce creamed coconut. Add 3 cups boiling water and stir once to prevent the grains from sticking together. Simmer over medium heat for 10–12 minutes. Remove the pan from the heat, cover and set aside for 5 minutes. Fluff the rice with a fork or chopsticks before serving.

2 Put the chilies, macadamia nuts or almonds, onion, garlic, ginger, turmeric and 1 tablespoon of the oil in a food processor and process to form a paste. Alternatively, pound them together in a mortar with a pestle to form a paste. Heat the remaining oil in a wok. When it is hot, add the paste and cook for 1–2 minutes without browning. Stir in the vinegar and water and season with salt to taste. Bring to a boil, then lower the heat.

3 Add the mackerel fillets to the sauce and simmer for 6–8 minutes, or until the fish is tender and cooked.

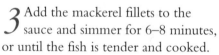

4 Transfer the fish to a warm serving dish. Bring the sauce to a boil and cook for 1 minute or until it has reduced slightly. Pour the sauce over the fish, garnish with deep-fried onions and chopped chili and serve with rice, if desired.

Fragrant Swordfish with Ginger and Lemongrass

Swordfish is a firm-textured, meaty fish that cooks well in a wok if it has been marinated as steaks rather than cut strips. It can be a little dry, but this is counteracted by the marinade. If you cannot get swordfish, use any variety of fresh tuna.

INGREDIENTS

Serves 4

1 kaffir lime leaf
3 tablespoons rock salt
5 tablespoons light brown sugar
4 swordfish steaks (about 8 ounces each)
1 lemongrass stalk, sliced
1-inch piece fresh ginger, cut into matchsticks
1 lime
1 tablespoon peanut oil
1 large ripe avocado, peeled and pitted
salt and ground black pepper

1 Bruise the lime leaf by crushing slightly, to release the flavor.

COOK'S TIP

Kaffir lime leaves are intensely aromatic, with a distinctive figure-eight shape. They are used extensively in Indonesian and Thai cooking. Thai cuisine also makes use of the rind of the lime from this tree.

2 To make the marinade, process the rock salt, brown sugar and lime leaf in a food processor or blender until thoroughly blended.

3 Place the swordfish steaks in a bowl. Sprinkle the marinade over them and add the lemongrass and ginger matchsticks. Set aside in the refrigerator for 3–4 hours to marinate.

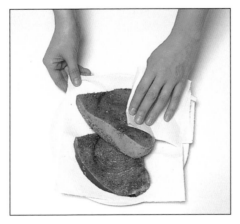

4 Rinse off the marinade and pat the fish dry with paper towels.

5 Peel the lime. Remove any excess pith from the peel. Cut the peel into very thin strips. Squeeze the juice from the fruit.

6 Heat a wok, then add the oil. When the oil is hot, add the lime rind and then the swordfish steaks. Stir-fry for 3–4 minutes. Add the lime juice. Remove the wok from the heat. Slice the avocado and add to the fish. Season to taste and serve.

Balti Shrimp in Hot Sauce

This sizzling shrimp dish is cooked in a fiery hot and spicy sauce. Not only does the sauce contain chili powder, it is further enhanced by the addition of ground green chilies and other spices.

INGREDIENTS

Serves 4

2 onions, coarsely chopped
2 tablespoons tomato paste
1 teaspoon ground coriander
¼ teaspoon turmeric
1 teaspoon chili powder
3 fresh green chilies
3 tablespoons chopped fresh cilantro
2 tablespoons lemon juice
1 teaspoon salt
3 tablespoons corn oil
16 peeled cooked jumbo shrimp

1 Put the onions, tomato paste, ground coriander, turmeric, chili powder, 2 of the green chilies, 2 tablespoons of the chopped cilantro, the lemon juice and salt into a food processor. Process for about 1 minute. If the mixture seems too thick, add a little water to loosen it. Chop the remaining chili and reserve for garnishing the dish.

2 Heat the oil in a preheated wok or frying pan. Lower the heat, add the spice mixture and fry for 3–5 minutes or until the sauce has thickened slightly.

3 Add the shrimp and stir-fry over medium heat until they are heated through, but not overcooked.

4 Transfer to a serving dish and garnish with the remaining chili and chopped fresh cilantro. Serve immediately.

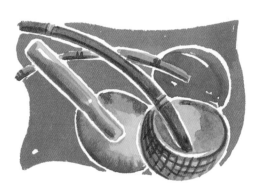

Battered Fish, Shrimp and Vegetables

This is a recipe for tempura, one of the few dishes that was brought to Japan from the West. The idea came from Spanish and Portuguese missionaries who settled in southern Japan in the late sixteenth century.

INGREDIENTS

Serves 4-6

1 sheet nori
8 large jumbo shrimp
6 ounces monkfish fillet, cut into fingers
1 small eggplant
4 scallions, trimmed
6 fresh shiitake mushrooms
vegetable oil, for deep-frying
flour, for dusting
salt
5 tablespoons soy or tamari sauce, to serve

For the batter

2 egg yolks
1¼ cups ice water
2 cups flour
½ teaspoon salt

1 Cut the nori into strips ½ inch wide and 2 inches long. Moisten one end of each strip with water and wrap it round the tail end of each shrimp. Skewer the shrimp along their length to straighten them. Skewer the fingers of monkfish and set aside.

2 Slice the eggplant into neat sections, sprinkle with salt and arrange in layers on a plate. Press lightly with your hand to expel the bitter juices, then leave for 20–30 minutes. Rinse thoroughly under cold water, dry well and thread onto bamboo skewers. Thread the scallions and shiitake mushrooms onto skewers.

3 Make the batter just before using. Beat together the egg yolks and half the ice water. Sift in the flour and salt and stir lightly with chopsticks without mixing to a dry paste. Add the remaining water and stir to make a smooth batter. Avoid overmixing.

4 Heat the oil to 350°F in a wok fitted with a wire draining rack. Dust the skewered vegetables and fish in flour. Dip them into the batter to coat, then fry, not more than three at a time, for 1–2 minutes, or until crisp and golden. Drain well, sprinkle with salt and drain on paper towels. Serve with soy or tamari sauce for dipping.

Green Shrimp Curry

A popular, fragrant, creamy curry
that takes very little time to
prepare. It can also be made with
thin strips of chicken meat.

INGREDIENTS

Serves 4–6
2 tablespoons vegetable oil
2 tablespoons green curry paste
1 pound jumbo shrimp, shelled
   and deveined
4 kaffir lime leaves, torn
1 lemongrass stalk, bruised
   and chopped
1 cup unsweetened coconut milk
2 tablespoons fish sauce
½ cucumber, seeded and cut into
   thin batons
10–15 basil leaves
4 green chilies, sliced, to garnish

1 Heat the oil in a frying pan. Add
the green curry paste and fry until
bubbling and fragrant.

2 Add the shrimp, kaffir lime leaves
and lemongrass. Fry for 1–2
minutes, until the shrimp are pink.

3 Stir in the coconut milk and bring
to a gentle boil. Simmer, stirring
occasionally, for about 5 minutes or
until the shrimp are tender.

4 Stir in the fish sauce, cucumber
and basil, then top with the sliced
green chilies and serve.

Shrimp Satés

For *Saté Udang*, jumbo shrimp look spectacular and taste wonderful. The spicy coconut marinade marries beautifully with the shrimp and is also excellent when used with firm cubes of monkfish or halibut and cooked in the same way.

INGREDIENTS

Makes 4 skewers
12 uncooked jumbo shrimp

For the marinade
¼ teaspoon shrimp paste
1 garlic clove, crushed
1 lemon grass stem, lower 2½ inches sliced, top reserved
3–4 macadamia nuts or 6–8 almonds
½ teaspoon chili powder
salt
oil for frying
8 tablespoons coconut milk
½ teaspoon tamarind pulp, soaked in 2 tablespoons water, then strained and juice reserved

To serve
Peanut Sauce
cucumber cubes (optional)
lemon wedges

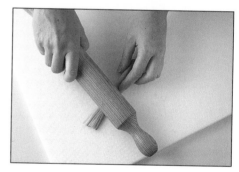

1 Remove the heads from the shrimp. Peel the shrimp and remove the black cord, if liked. Using a small sharp knife, make an incision along the underbody of each shrimp, without cutting it completely in half and open it up like a book. Thread 3 of the shrimp onto each skewer.

2 Make the marinade. Grind the shrimp paste, garlic, lemon grass slices, nuts, chili powder and a little salt to a paste in a food processor or with a mortar and pestle.

3 Fry the paste in oil for 1 minute. Add the coconut milk and tamarind juice. Simmer for 1 minute. Cool. Pour over the shrimp and leave for 1 hour.

4 Cook the shrimp under a hot broiler or on the barbecue grill for 3 minutes or until cooked through. Beat the top part of the lemon grass with the end of a rolling pin, to make it into a brush. Use this to brush the shrimp with the marinade during cooking.

5 Serve on a platter, with the Peanut Sauce, cucumber cubes, if using, and lemon wedges.

Shrimp with Chayote in Turmeric Sauce

This delicious, attractively colored dish is called *Gule Udang Dengan Labu Kuning.*

INGREDIENTS

Serves 4

1–2 chayotes or 2–3 zucchini
2 fresh red chilies, seeded
1 onion, quartered
¼ inch fresh *laos,* peeled
1 lemon grass stem, lower 2 inches
   sliced, top bruised
1 inch fresh turmeric, peeled
⅞ cup water
lemon juice
14-ounce can coconut milk
1 pound cooked, peeled shrimp
salt
red chili shreds, to garnish (optional)
boiled rice, to serve

1 Peel the chayotes, remove the seeds and cut into strips. If using zucchini, cut into 2-inch strips.

2 Grind the fresh red chilies, onion, sliced *laos,* sliced lemon grass and the fresh turmeric to a paste in a food processor or with a mortar and pestle. Add the water to the paste mixture, with a squeeze of lemon juice and salt to taste.

3 Pour into a pan. Add the top of the lemon grass stem. Bring to the boil and cook for 1–2 minutes. Add the chayote or zucchini pieces and cook for 2 minutes. Stir in the coconut milk. Taste and adjust the seasoning.

4 Stir in the shrimp and cook gently for 2–3 minutes. Remove the lemon grass stem. Garnish with shreds of chili, if using, and serve with rice.

Doedoeh of Fish

Haddock or cod fillet may be substituted in this recipe.

INGREDIENTS

Serves 6–8

2¼ pounds fresh mackerel
   fillets, skinned
2 tablespoons tamarind pulp, soaked in
   ⅞ cup water
1 onion
½ inch fresh *laos*
2 garlic cloves
1–2 fresh red chilies, seeded, or
   1 teaspoon chili powder
1 teaspoon ground coriander
1 teaspoon ground turmeric
½ teaspoon ground fennel seeds
1 tablespoon dark brown sugar
6–7 tablespoons oil
⅞ cup coconut cream
salt and freshly ground black pepper
fresh chili shreds, to garnish

1 Rinse the fish fillets in cold water and dry them well on paper towels. Put into a shallow dish and sprinkle with a little salt. Strain the tamarind and pour the juice over the fish fillets. Set aside for 30 minutes.

2 Quarter the onion, peel and slice the *laos* and peel the garlic. Grind the onion, *laos,* garlic and chilies or chili powder to a paste in a food processor or with a mortar and pestle. Add the ground coriander, turmeric, fennel seeds and sugar.

3 Heat half of the oil in a frying pan. Drain the fish fillets and fry for 5 minutes, or until cooked. Set aside.

4 Wipe out the pan and heat the remaining oil. Fry the spice paste, stirring constantly, until it gives off a spicy aroma. Do not let it brown. Add the coconut cream and simmer gently for a few minutes. Add the fish fillets and gently heat through.

5 Taste for seasoning and serve sprinkled with shredded chili.

Red and White Shrimp with Green Vegetables

The Chinese name for this dish is *Yuan Yang* shrimp. Pairs of mandarin ducks are also known as *yuan yang*, or love birds, because they are always seen together. They symbolize affection and happiness.

Ingredients

Serves 4–6

1 pound jumbo shrimp
½ egg white
1 tablespoon cornstarch paste
6 ounces snow peas
about 2½ cups vegetable oil
1 teaspoon light brown sugar
1 tablespoon finely chopped scallion
1 teaspoon finely chopped fresh ginger
1 tablespoon light soy sauce
1 tablespoon Chinese rice wine or
    dry sherry
1 teaspoon chili bean sauce
1 tablespoon tomato paste
salt

1 Peel and devein the shrimp and mix with the egg white, cornstarch paste and a pinch of salt. Trim the snow peas.

2 Heat 2–3 tablespoons of the oil in a preheated wok and stir-fry the snow peas for about 1 minute. Add the sugar and a little salt and continue stirring for 1 more minute. Remove and place in the center of a warmed serving platter.

3 Add the remaining oil to the wok and cook the shrimp for 1 minute. Remove and drain.

4 Pour off all but about 1 tablespoon of the oil. Add the scallion and ginger to the wok.

5 Return the shrimp to the wok and stir-fry for 1 minute, then add the soy sauce and rice wine or dry sherry. Blend the mixture thoroughly. Transfer half the shrimp to one end of the serving platter.

6 Add the chili bean sauce and tomato paste to the remaining shrimp in the wok, blend well and place the "red" shrimp at the other end of the platter. Serve.

Cook's Tip

All raw shrimp have an intestinal tract that runs just beneath the outside curve of the tail. The tract is not poisonous, but it can taste unpleasant. It is therefore best to remove it, or "devein." To do this, peel the shrimp, leaving the tail intact. Score each shrimp lightly along its length to expose the tract. Remove the tract with a small knife or Chinese cleaver.

Karahi Shrimp and Fenugreek

The black-eyed peas, shrimp and paneer in this dish mean that it is rich in protein. The combination of both ground and fresh fenugreek makes the dish very fragrant and delicious.

INGREDIENTS

Serves 4–6

¼ cup corn oil
2 onions, sliced
2 medium tomatoes, sliced
1½ teaspoons minced garlic
1 teaspoon chili powder
1 teaspoon grated fresh ginger
1 teaspoon ground cumin
1 teaspoon ground coriander
1 teaspoon salt
1 cup paneer (Indian cheese), cubed
1 teaspoon ground fenugreek
1 bunch fresh fenugreek leaves
4 ounces shelled cooked shrimp
2 fresh red chilies, sliced
2 tablespoons chopped fresh cilantro
¼ cup canned black-eyed peas, drained
1 tablespoon lemon juice

1 Heat the oil in a preheated wok. Lower the heat slightly and add the onions and tomatoes. Fry, stirring occasionally, for about 3 minutes.

2 Add the garlic, chili powder, ginger, ground cumin, ground coriander, salt, paneer and the ground and fresh fenugreek. Lower the heat and stir-fry for about 2 minutes.

3 Add the shrimp, red chilies, fresh cilantro and the black-eyed peas and mix well. Cook for another 3–5 minutes, stirring occasionally, until the shrimp are heated through.

4 Finally, sprinkle on the lemon juice and serve.

Spiced Shrimp with Coconut

This spicy dish is based on the traditional Indonesian dish *sambal goreng udang*. Sambals are pungent, very hot dishes popular throughout southern India and Southeast Asia.

INGREDIENTS

Serves 3–4

2–3 fresh red chilies, chopped
3 shallots, chopped
1 lemongrass stalk, chopped
2 garlic cloves, chopped
thin sliver of dried shrimp paste
½ teaspoon ground galangal
1 teaspoon ground turmeric
1 teaspoon ground coriander
1 tablespoon peanut oil
1 cup water
2 kaffir lime leaves
1 teaspoon light brown sugar
2 tomatoes, skinned, seeded and
    chopped
1 cup coconut milk
1½ pounds uncooked jumbo shrimp,
    shelled and deveined
squeeze of lemon juice
salt
shredded scallions and grated
    unsweetened coconut, to garnish

2 Heat a wok, add the oil and swirl it around. Add the spice paste and stir-fry for 2 minutes. Pour in the water and add the kaffir lime leaves, sugar and tomatoes. Simmer for 8–10 minutes, until most of the liquid has evaporated.

COOK'S TIP

Dried shrimp paste, widely used in Southeast Asian cooking, is available at Asian food stores.

1 In a mortar, pound together the chilies, shallots, lemongrass, garlic, shrimp paste, galangal, turmeric and coriander with a pestle until the mixture forms a paste.

3 Add the coconut milk and shrimp and cook gently, stirring, for 4 minutes, until the shrimp are pink. Season with lemon juice and salt to taste. Transfer the mixture to a warm serving dish, garnish with the scallions and grated coconut, and serve.

Paneer with Shrimp

Paneer (Indian cheese) makes an excellent substitute for red meat. In this recipe paneer is combined with jumbo shrimp to make a memorable stir-fry dish.

INGREDIENTS

Serves 4

12 cooked jumbo shrimp
6 ounces paneer (Indian cheese)
2 tablespoons tomato paste
¼ cup plain yogurt
1½ teaspoons garam masala
1 teaspoon chili powder
1 teaspoon minced garlic
1 teaspoon salt
2 teaspoons mango powder
1 teaspoon ground coriander
1 stick butter
1 tablespoon corn oil
3 fresh green chilies, chopped
3 tablespoons chopped fresh cilantro
⅔ cup light cream or half-and-half

1 Shell the shrimp and cube the paneer.

2 Combine the tomato paste, yogurt, garam masala, chili powder, garlic, salt, mango powder and ground coriander in a mixing bowl and set aside.

3 Melt the butter with the oil in a wok. Lower the heat slightly and stir-fry the paneer and shrimp for about 2 minutes. Remove with a slotted spoon and drain on paper towels. Set aside.

4 Pour the spice mixture into the butter and oil left in the pan and stir-fry for about 1 minute.

5 Add the paneer and shrimp, and cook for 7–10 minutes, stirring occasionally, until the shrimp are heated through.

6 Add the fresh chilies and most of the cilantro, and pour in the cream. Heat for about 2 minutes, garnish with the remaining fresh cilantro and serve.

COOK'S TIP

To make paneer at home, bring 4 cups milk to a boil over low heat. Add 2 tablespoons lemon juice and stir constantly and gently until the milk thickens and begins to curdle. Strain the curdled milk through a strainer lined with cheesecloth. Set aside under a heavy weight for 1½–2 hours to press to a flat shape about ½ inch thick.

Make the paneer a day before you plan to use it in a recipe; then it will be firmer and easier to handle. Cut and use as required; it will keep for about 1 week in the refrigerator.

Stir-fried Shrimp with Broccoli

This is a very colorful dish, highly nutritious and at the same time extremely delicious; furthermore, it is neither time-consuming nor difficult to prepare.

INGREDIENTS

Serves 4

6–8 ounces uncooked shrimp, shelled and deveined
1 teaspoon salt
1 tablespoon Chinese rice wine or dry sherry
1 tablespoon egg white
1 tablespoon cornstarch paste
8 ounces broccoli
about 1¼ cups vegetable oil
1 scallion, cut into short sections
1 teaspoon light brown sugar
about 2 tablespoons light fish stock or water
1 teaspoon light soy sauce
few drops of sesame oil

1 Cut each shrimp in half lengthwise. Mix with a pinch of salt and about 1 teaspoon of the wine or sherry, the egg white and cornstarch paste.

2 Cut the broccoli into florets; remove the rough skin from the stalks, then cut the stalks into even-size pieces.

3 Heat the oil in a preheated wok and stir-fry the shrimp for about 30 seconds. Remove with a slotted spoon and drain thoroughly.

4 Pour off the excess oil, leaving 2 tablespoons in the wok. Add the broccoli and scallion, stir-fry for about 2 minutes, then add the remaining salt and the sugar, followed by the shrimp and stock or water. Add the soy sauce and remaining wine or sherry. Blend well, then add the sesame oil and serve.

Stir-fried Shrimp with Tamarind

The sour, tangy flavor that is characteristic of many Thai dishes comes from tamarind. Fresh tamarind pods, from the tamarind tree, can sometimes be bought, but preparing them for cooking is a laborious process. The Thais prefer to use compressed blocks of tamarind paste, which is simply soaked in warm water and then strained.

INGREDIENTS

Serves 4–6

2 tablespoons tamarind paste
²/₃ cup boiling water
2 tablespoons vegetable oil
2 tablespoons chopped onion
2 tablespoons palm sugar
2 tablespoons chicken stock or water
1 tablespoon fish sauce
6 dried red chilies, fried
1 pound uncooked shelled shrimp
1 tablespoon fried chopped garlic
2 tablespoons fried sliced shallots
2 scallions, chopped, to garnish

1 Put the tamarind paste in a small bowl, pour over the boiling water and stir well to break up any lumps. Set aside for 30 minutes. Strain, pushing as much of the juice through as possible. Measure 6 tablespoons of the juice, which is the amount needed, and store the rest in the fridge. Heat the oil in a wok. Add the chopped onion and fry until golden brown.

2 Add the sugar, stock, fish sauce, dried chilies and the tamarind juice, stirring well until the sugar dissolves. Bring to a boil.

3 Add the shrimp, garlic and shallots. Stir-fry for about 3–4 minutes until the shrimp are cooked. Garnish with the chopped scallions.

Shrimp Satay

Serve this enticing and tasty dish with greens and jasmine rice.

INGREDIENTS

Serves 4–6

1 pound jumbo shrimp, shelled, tail ends left intact and deveined
½ bunch cilantro leaves, to garnish
4 red chilies, finely sliced and scallions, cut diagonally, to garnish

For the peanut sauce

3 tablespoons vegetable oil
1 tablespoon chopped garlic
1 small onion, chopped
3–4 red chilies, crushed and chopped
3 kaffir lime leaves, torn
1 lemongrass stalk, bruised and chopped
1 teaspoon medium curry paste
1 cup unsweetened coconut milk
½-inch cinnamon stick
⅓ cup crunchy peanut butter
3 tablespoons tamarind juice
2 tablespoons fish sauce
2 tablespoons palm sugar
juice of ½ lemon

1 To make the sauce, heat half the oil in a wok or large frying pan and add the garlic and onion. Cook for about 3–4 minutes, until it softens.

2 Add the chilies, kaffir lime leaves, lemongrass and curry paste. Cook for a further 2–3 minutes.

COOK'S TIP

Curry paste has a far superior, authentic flavor to powdered varieties. Once opened, it should be kept in the fridge and used within two months.

3 Stir in the coconut milk, cinnamon stick, peanut butter, tamarind juice, fish sauce, palm sugar and lemon juice.

4 Reduce the heat and simmer gently for 15–20 minutes until the sauce thickens, stirring occasionally to make sure that the sauce doesn't stick to the bottom of the pan.

5 Heat the rest of the oil in a wok or large frying pan. Add the shrimp and stir-fry for about 3–4 minutes, or until the shrimp turn pink and are slightly firm to the touch.

6 Mix the shrimp with the sauce. Serve garnished with cilantro leaves, red chilies and scallions.

Shrimp Curry with Quail Eggs

This luscious Indonesian recipe is characterized by the mix of flavors—galangal, chilies, turmeric and coconut milk.

INGREDIENTS

Serves 4

12 quail eggs
2 tablespoons vegetable oil
4 shallots or 1 medium onion, finely
 chopped
1-inch piece fresh galangal or ginger,
 chopped
2 garlic cloves, crushed
2-inch piece lemongrass, shredded
1–2 small, fresh red chilies, seeded and
 finely chopped
½ teaspoon ground turmeric
½-inch square shrimp paste or
 1 tablespoon fish sauce
2 pounds jumbo shrimp, peeled and
 deveined
1⅔ cups coconut milk
1¼ cups chicken broth
4 ounces Chinese cabbage, roughly
 shredded
2 teaspoons sugar
salt
2 scallions, green parts only, cut into
 fine strips, and 2 tablespoons
 shredded fresh coconut, to garnish

1 Put the quail eggs in a saucepan, cover with water and boil for 8 minutes. Refresh in cold water, peel by dipping in cold water to release the shells and set aside.

2 Heat the oil in a preheated wok. Add the shallots or onion, galangal or ginger and garlic and stir-fry for 1 minute, or until soft but not colored. Add the lemongrass, chilies, turmeric and shrimp paste or fish sauce and stir-fry for 1 minute.

3 Add the shrimp to the wok and stir-fry for 1 minute. Strain the coconut milk and add the thin liquid to the wok, together with the chicken broth. Add the Chinese cabbage and sugar and season to taste with salt. Bring to a boil, reduce the heat and simmer for 6 to 8 minutes.

4 Turn the curry out onto a serving dish. Halve the quail eggs and toss them in the sauce. Scatter the scallions and shredded coconut on top and serve immediately.

COOK'S TIP

Quail eggs are available from specialty grocers and delicatessens. If you cannot find them, use hen eggs—one hen egg is the equivalent of four quail eggs.

Balti Shrimp and Vegetables in Thick Sauce

Tender shrimp, crunchy vegetables and a thick curry sauce combine to produce a dish rich in flavor and texture.

INGREDIENTS

Serves 4

3 tablespoons corn oil
1 teaspoon mixed fenugreek, mustard and onion seeds
2 curry leaves
½ medium cauliflower, cut into florets
8 baby carrots, halved lengthwise
6 new potatoes, thickly sliced
½ cup frozen peas
2 medium onions, sliced
2 tablespoons tomato purée
1½ teaspoons chili powder
1 teaspoon ground coriander
1 teaspoon ginger pulp
1 teaspoon garlic pulp
1 teaspoon salt
2 tablespoons lemon juice
1 pound peeled cooked shrimp
2 tablespoons chopped fresh cilantro
1 fresh red chili, seeded and sliced
½ cup light cream

1 Heat the oil in a preheated wok or frying pan. Lower the heat slightly and add the fenugreek, mustard and onion seeds and the curry leaves.

2 Add the cauliflower, carrots, potatoes and peas, increase the heat and stir-fry until the vegetables are cooked. Remove from the wok or frying pan with a slotted spoon and drain on kitchen paper.

3 Add the onions to the oil left in the wok or frying pan and fry over medium heat until golden brown.

4 Meanwhile, mix together the tomato purée, chili powder, ground coriander, ginger pulp, garlic pulp, salt and lemon juice. When the onions are cooked, pour the spice paste over them.

5 Lower the heat, add the shrimp to the wok or frying pan and stir-fry for about 5 minutes or until heated through.

6 Return the fried vegetables to the wok or frying pan and mix together thoroughly.

7 Add the chopped fresh cilantro and red chili to the wok or frying pan and pour on the cream. Bring to a boil and serve immediately.

— COOK'S TIP —

Monkfish is an excellent alternative to the shrimp used in this recipe, as it is a firm-fleshed fish that will not break up when fried. Cut the monkfish into chunks, add to the onion and spice mixture at Step 5 and stir-fry over low heat for 5–7 minutes or until cooked through.

Lemon Grass Shrimp on Crisp Noodle Cake

INGREDIENTS

Serves 4

11 ounces thin egg noodles
4 tablespoons vegetable oil
1¼ pounds raw jumbo shrimp, peeled and deveined
½ teaspoon ground coriander
1 tablespoon ground turmeric
2 garlic cloves, finely chopped
2 slices fresh ginger, finely chopped
2 lemon grass stalks, finely chopped
2 shallots, finely chopped
1 tablespoon tomato paste
1 cup coconut cream
4–6 kaffir lime leaves (optional)
1–2 tablespoons fresh lime juice
1–2 tablespoons fish sauce
1 cucumber, peeled, seeded and cut into 2-inch batons
1 tomato, seeded and cut into strips
2 red chilies, seeded and finely sliced
salt and freshly ground black pepper
2 scallions, finely sliced, and a few cilantro sprigs, to garnish

1 Cook the egg noodles in a saucepan of boiling water until just tender. Drain, rinse under cold running water, and drain well.

2 Heat 1 tablespoon of the oil in a large frying pan. Add the noodles, distributing them evenly, and fry for 4–5 minutes until crisp and golden. Turn the noodle cake over, and fry the other side. Alternatively, make four individual cakes. Keep hot.

3 In a bowl, toss the shrimp with the ground coriander, turmeric, garlic, ginger and lemon grass. Add salt and pepper to taste.

4 Heat the remaining oil in a large frying pan. Add the shallots, fry for 1 minute, then add the shrimp, and fry for 2 minutes more. Using a slotted spoon, remove the shrimp.

5 Stir the tomato paste and coconut cream into the mixture remaining in the pan. Stir in lime juice to taste, and season with the fish sauce. Bring the sauce to a simmer, return the shrimp to the sauce, then add the kaffir lime leaves, if using, and the cucumber. Simmer gently until the shrimp is cooked, and the sauce is reduced to a nice coating consistency.

6 Add the tomato, stir until just warmed through, then add the chilies. Serve on top of the crisp noodle cake(s), garnished with sliced scallions and cilantro sprigs.

Gingered Seafood Stir-fry

This cornucopia of scallops, shrimp and squid in an aromatic sauce makes a refreshing summer supper, served with plenty of crusty bread to mop up the juices—together with a glass of chilled dry white wine. It would also make a great dinner-party appetizer for four people.

INGREDIENTS

Serves 2

1 tablespoon sunflower oil
1 teaspoon sesame oil
1-inch piece fresh ginger, finely
    chopped
1 bunch scallions, sliced
1 red bell pepper, seeded and finely
    chopped
4 ounces bay scallops
8 jumbo shrimp, peeled
4 ounces squid rings
1 tablespoon lime juice
1 tablespoon light soy sauce
4 tablespoons coconut milk
salt and freshly ground black pepper
mixed salad greens and lime slices,
    to serve

1 Heat the sunflower and sesame oils in a preheated wok or large frying pan and cook the ginger and scallions for 2–3 minutes, or until golden. Stir in the red bell pepper and cook for another 3 minutes.

2 Add the scallops, shrimp and squid rings and cook over medium heat for about 3 minutes, or until the seafood is just cooked.

3 Stir in the lime juice, soy sauce and coconut milk. Simmer, uncovered, for 2 minutes, or until the juices begin to thicken slightly.

4 Season well. Arrange the salad greens on two serving plates and spoon the seafood mixture with the juices on top. Serve with lime slices for squeezing over the seafood.

Chili Shrimp

This delightful, spicy combination makes a lovely, light main course for a casual supper. Serve with rice, noodles or even freshly cooked pasta and a leafy green salad.

INGREDIENTS

Serves 3–4

3 tablespoons olive oil
2 shallots, chopped
2 garlic cloves, chopped
1 fresh red chili, chopped
1 pound ripe tomatoes, skinned, seeded
  and chopped
1 tablespoon tomato paste
1 bay leaf
1 thyme sprig
6 tablespoons dry white wine
1 pound cooked jumbo shrimp, peeled
salt and freshly ground black pepper
roughly torn basil leaves, to garnish

1 Heat the oil in a pan, then add the shallots, garlic and chili and stir-fry until the garlic starts to brown.

2 Add the tomatoes, tomato paste, bay leaf, thyme, wine and seasoning. Bring to a boil, then reduce the heat and cook gently for about 10 minutes, stirring occasionally, until the sauce has thickened. Discard the herbs.

3 Stir the shrimp into the sauce and heat through for a few minutes. Taste and adjust the seasoning. Scatter the basil leaves on top and serve at once.

----- COOK'S TIP -----

For a milder flavor, remove all the seeds from the chili.

Scallops with Ginger

Scallops are of course at their best fresh, but are available frozen throughout the year. Rich and creamy, this dish is very simple to make and utterly scrumptious.

INGREDIENTS

Serves 4

8–12 scallops
3 tablespoons butter
1-inch piece fresh ginger, finely
  chopped
1 bunch scallions, sliced diagonally
4 tablespoons white vermouth
1 cup crème fraîche or half-and-half
salt and freshly ground black pepper
chopped fresh parsley, to garnish

1 Remove the tough muscle opposite the coral on each scallop. Separate the coral and cut the white part of the scallop in half horizontally.

2 Melt the butter in a frying pan. Add the scallops, including the corals, and sauté for about 2 minutes, or until lightly browned. Take care not to overcook the scallops, as this will make them tough.

3 Lift out the scallops with a slotted spoon and transfer to a warmed serving dish. Keep warm.

4 Add the ginger and scallions to the pan and stir-fry for 2 minutes. Pour in the vermouth and allow to bubble until it has almost evaporated. Stir in the crème fraîche or half-and-half and cook for a few minutes, until the sauce has thickened. Season to taste.

5 Pour the sauce over the scallops, sprinkle with parsley and serve immediately.

Scallops with Ginger Relish

Buy scallops in their shells to be absolutely sure of their freshness; your fishmonger will open them for you if you find this difficult. Remember to ask for the shells, which make excellent and attractive serving dishes. Queen scallops are particularly prized for their delicate-tasting coral, or roe.

INGREDIENTS

Serves 4
8 king or queen scallops
4 whole star anise
2 tablespoons unsalted butter
salt and ground white pepper
fresh chervil sprigs and whole star
 anise, to garnish

For the relish
¹/₂ cucumber, peeled
salt, for sprinkling
2-inch piece fresh ginger, peeled
2 teaspoons superfine sugar
3 tablespoons rice wine vinegar
2 teaspoons ginger syrup, strained from
 a jar of preserved ginger
sesame seeds, to garnish

1 To make the relish, halve the cucumber lengthwise, scoop out the seeds with a teaspoon and discard.

2 Cut the cucumber into 1-inch pieces, place in a colander and sprinkle liberally with salt. Set aside for 30 minutes.

3 Open the scallop shells, detach the scallops and remove the edible parts. Cut each scallop into two or three slices and reserve the coral. Coarsely grind the star anise in a mortar with a pestle.

4 Place the scallop slices and coral in a bowl, sprinkle the star anise on top and season with salt and pepper. Set aside to marinate for about 1 hour.

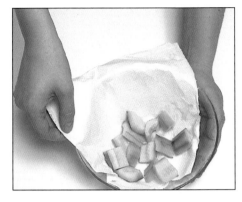

5 Rinse the cucumber under cold water, drain well and pat dry with paper towels. Cut the ginger into thin julienne strips and mix with the cucumber, sugar, vinegar and ginger syrup. Cover and chill until needed.

6 Heat a wok and add the butter. When the butter is hot, add the scallop slices and coral and stir-fry for 2–3 minutes. Garnish with sprigs of chervil and whole star anise, and serve with the cucumber relish, sprinkled with sesame seeds.

COOK'S TIP

To prepare scallops, hold flat side up and insert a strong knife between the shells to cut through the muscle. Separate the two shells. Slide the knife blade underneath the scallop in the bottom shell to cut the second muscle. Remove the scallop and separate the edible parts—the white muscle and orange coral, or roe. The skirt can be used for making fish stock, but the other parts should be discarded.

Baked Fish in Banana Leaves

Fish that is prepared in this way is particularly succulent and flavorful. Fillets are used here rather than whole fish – easier for those who don't like to mess around with bones. It is a great dish for outdoor barbecues.

INGREDIENTS

Serves 4

1 cup unsweetened coconut milk
2 tablespoons red curry paste
3 tablespoons fish sauce
2 tablespoons superfine sugar
5 kaffir lime leaves, torn
4 x 6-ounce fish fillets, such as snapper
6 ounces mixed vegetables, such as carrots or leeks, finely shredded
4 banana leaves, or aluminum foil
2 tablespoons shredded scallions and 2 red chilies, finely sliced, to garnish

1 Combine the coconut milk, curry paste, fish sauce, sugar and kaffir lime leaves in a shallow dish.

2 Marinate the fish in this mixture for about 15–30 minutes. Preheat the oven to 400°F.

3 Mix the vegetables together and lay a portion on top of a banana leaf or piece of foil. Place a piece of fish on top with a little of its marinade.

4 Wrap the fish up by turning in the sides and ends of the leaf and secure with toothpicks. Repeat with the rest of the leaves and the fish.

5 Bake in the hot oven for 20–25 minutes or until the fish is cooked. Alternatively, cook under the broiler or on the barbecue. Just before serving, garnish the fish with a sprinkling of scallions and sliced red chilies.

Stir-fried Scallops with Asparagus

Asparagus is extremely popular among the Chinese Thai. The combination of garlic and black pepper gives this dish its spiciness. You can substitute the scallops with shrimp or other firm fish.

INGREDIENTS

Serves 4–6

4 tablespoons vegetable oil
1 bunch asparagus, cut into 2-inch lengths
4 garlic cloves, finely chopped
2 shallots, finely chopped
1 pound scallops, cleaned
2 tablespoons fish sauce
½ teaspoon coarsely ground black pepper
½ cup unsweetened coconut milk
cilantro leaves, to garnish

1 Heat half the oil in a wok or large frying pan. Add the asparagus and stir-fry for about 2 minutes. Transfer the asparagus to a plate and set aside.

2 Add the rest of the oil, garlic and shallots to the same wok and fry until fragrant. Add the scallops and cook for another 1–2 minutes.

3 Return the asparagus to the wok. Add the fish sauce, black pepper and coconut milk.

4 Stir and cook for about another 3–4 minutes or until the scallops and asparagus are cooked. Garnish with the cilantro leaves.

Spiced Scallops in their Shells

Scallops are excellent steamed. When served with this spicy sauce, they make a delicious, yet simple, appetizer for four people or a light lunch for two. Each person spoons sauce onto the scallops before eating them.

INGREDIENTS

Serves 2

8 scallops, shelled (ask the fishmonger to reserve the cupped side of 4 shells)
2 slices fresh ginger, shredded
½ garlic clove, shredded
2 scallions, green parts only, cut into fine strips
salt and freshly ground black pepper

For the sauce

1 garlic clove, crushed
1 tablespoon grated fresh ginger
2 scallions, white parts only, chopped
1–2 fresh green chilies, seeded and finely chopped
1 tablespoon light soy sauce
1 tablespoon dark soy sauce
2 teaspoons sesame oil

1 Remove the dark beardlike fringe and tough muscle from the scallops.

2 Place 2 scallops in each shell. Season lightly with salt and pepper, then scatter the ginger, garlic and scallions on top. Place the shells in a bamboo steamer in a wok and steam for about 6 minutes, or until the scallops look opaque (you may have to do this in batches).

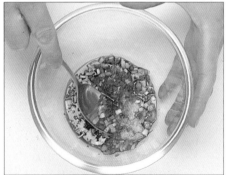

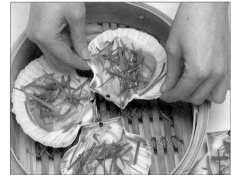

3 Meanwhile, make the sauce. Mix together the garlic, ginger, scallions, chilies, soy sauces and sesame oil and pour into a small serving bowl.

4 Carefully remove each shell from the steamer, taking care not to spill the juices, and arrange them on a serving plate with the sauce bowl in the center. Serve at once.

Lemongrass-and-Basil-scented Mussels

The classic Thai flavorings of lemongrass and basil are used in this fragrant dish.

INGREDIENTS

Serves 4

4–4½ pounds fresh mussels in
  their shells
2 lemongrass stalks
5–6 fresh basil sprigs
2-inch piece fresh ginger, finely chopped
2 shallots, finely chopped
⅔ cup fish broth

1 Scrub the mussels under cold running water, scraping off any barnacles with a small, sharp knife. Pull or cut off the hairy "beards." Discard any mussels with damaged shells and any that remain open when they are sharply tapped.

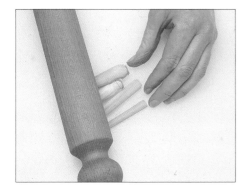

2 Cut each lemongrass stalk in half and bruise with a rolling pin.

3 Pull the basil leaves off the stems and roughly chop half of them. Reserve the remainder.

4 Put the mussels, lemongrass, chopped basil, shallots, ginger and broth in a wok. Bring to a boil, cover and simmer for 5 minutes. Discard the lemongrass and any mussels that remain closed, scatter the reserved basil leaves on top, and serve immediately.

Pineapple Curry with Shrimp and Mussels

The delicate sweet-and-sour flavor of this curry comes from the pineapple and, although it seems an odd combination, it is rather delicious. Use the freshest shellfish that you can find.

INGREDIENTS

Serves 4–6
2¹⁄₂ cups unsweetened coconut milk
2 tablespoons red curry paste
2 tablespoons fish sauce
1 tablespoon sugar
8 ounces jumbo shrimp, shelled
  and deveined
1 pound mussels, cleaned and
  beards removed
6 ounces fresh pineapple, finely crushed
  or chopped
5 kaffir lime leaves, torn
2 red chilies, chopped, and cilantro
  leaves, to garnish

1 In a large saucepan, bring half the coconut milk to a boil and heat, stirring, until it separates.

2 Add the red curry paste and cook until fragrant. Add the fish sauce and sugar and continue to cook for a few moments.

3 Stir in the rest of the coconut milk and bring back to a boil. Add the jumbo shrimp, mussels, pineapple and kaffir lime leaves.

4 Reheat until boiling and then simmer for 3–5 minutes, until the shrimp are cooked and the mussels have opened. Remove any mussels that have not opened and discard. Serve garnished with chopped red chilies and cilantro leaves.

Curried Shrimp in Coconut Milk

A curry-like dish where the shrimp are cooked in a spicy coconut gravy.

INGREDIENTS

Serves 4–6
2¹⁄₂ cups unsweetened coconut milk
2 tablespoons yellow curry paste
  (see Cook's Tip)
1 tablespoon fish sauce
¹⁄₂ teaspoon salt
1 teaspoon sugar
1 pound jumbo shrimp, shelled, tails
  left intact and deveined
8 ounces cherry tomatoes
juice of ¹⁄₂ lime, to serve
2 red chilies, cut into strips, and
  cilantro leaves, to garnish

1 Put half the coconut milk into a pan or wok and bring to a boil.

2 Add the yellow curry paste to the coconut milk, stir until it disperses, then simmer for about 10 minutes.

3 Add the fish sauce, salt, sugar and remaining coconut milk. Simmer for another 5 minutes.

4 Add the shrimp and cherry tomatoes. Simmer very gently for about 5 minutes until the shrimp are pink and tender.

5 Serve sprinkled with lime juice and garnished with chilies and cilantro.

COOK'S TIP

To make yellow curry paste, process 6–8 yellow chilies, 1 chopped lemongrass stalk, 4 peeled shallots, 4 garlic cloves, 1 tablespoon peeled chopped fresh ginger, 1 teaspoon coriander seeds, 1 teaspoon mustard powder, 1 teaspoon salt, ¹⁄₂ teaspoon ground cinnamon, 1 tablespoon light brown sugar and 2 tablespoons oil in a blender or food processor. When a paste forms, transfer to a jar and keep in the fridge.

Baked Crab with Scallions and Ginger

This recipe is far less complicated than it looks and will delight the eye as much as the taste buds.

INGREDIENTS

Serves 4

1 large or 2 medium crabs, about
  1½ pounds total
2 tablespoons Chinese rice wine or
  dry sherry
1 egg, lightly beaten
1 tablespoon cornstarch
3–4 tablespoons vegetable oil
1 tablespoon finely chopped
  fresh ginger
3–4 scallions, cut into short lengths
2 tablespoons soy sauce
1 teaspoon light brown sugar
about 5 tablespoons broth
few drops of sesame oil

1 Cut the crab in half from the underbelly. Break off the claws and crack them with the back of a cleaver. Discard the legs and crack the shell, breaking it into several pieces. Discard the feathery gills and the sac. Put the pieces of crab in a bowl.

2 Combine the rice wine or dry sherry, egg and cornstarch and pour over the crab. Marinate for 10–15 minutes.

3 Heat the oil in a preheated wok. Add the crab pieces, ginger and scallions and stir-fry for 2 to 3 minutes.

4 Add the soy sauce, sugar and broth and blend well. Bring to a boil, reduce the heat, cover and braise for 3–4 minutes, or until it is cooked. Transfer the crab to a serving dish, sprinkle with the sesame oil and serve.

COOK'S TIP

For the very best flavor, buy a live crab and cook it yourself. However, if you prefer to buy a cooked crab, look for one that feels heavy for its size. This is an indication that it has fully grown into its shell and that there will be plenty of meat. Male crabs have larger claws and so will yield a greater proportion of white meat. However, females—identifiable by a broader, less pointed tail flap—may contain coral, which many people regard as a delicacy.

Pan-steamed Mussels with Thai Herbs

Another simple dish to prepare. The lemongrass adds a refreshing tang to the mussels.

INGREDIENTS

Serves 4–6
2¼ pounds mussels, cleaned and
 beards removed
2 lemongrass stalks, finely chopped
4 shallots, chopped
4 kaffir lime leaves, coarsely torn
2 red chilies, sliced
1 tablespoon fish sauce
2 tablespoons lime juice
2 scallions, chopped, to garnish
cilantro leaves, to garnish

1 Place all the ingredients, except for the scallions and cilantro, in a large saucepan and stir thoroughly.

2 Cover and steam for 5–7 minutes, shaking the saucepan occasionally, until the mussels open. Discard any mussels that remain closed.

3 Transfer the cooked mussels to a serving platter.

4 Garnish the mussels with chopped scallions and cilantro leaves. Serve the dish immediately.

Chili Crabs

It is possible to find variations on *Kepitang Pedas* all over Asia. It will be memorable whether you eat it in simple surroundings or in an elegant restaurant.

INGREDIENTS

Serves 4

2 cooked crabs, about 1½ pounds
½ teaspoon shrimp paste
2 garlic cloves
2 fresh red chilies, seeded, or
   1 teaspoon chopped chili from a jar
½ inch fresh ginger root, peeled
   and sliced
4 tablespoons sunflower oil
1¼ cups tomato ketchup
1 tablespoon dark brown sugar
½ cup warm water
4 scallions, chopped, to garnish
cucumber chunks and hot toast,
   to serve (optional)

1 Remove the large claws of one crab and turn onto its back with the head facing away from you. Use your thumbs to push the body up from the main shell. Discard the stomach sac and "dead men's fingers," i.e. lungs and any green matter. Leave the creamy brown meat in the shell and cut the shell in half with a cleaver or heavy knife. Cut the body section in half and crack the claws with a sharp blow from a hammer or cleaver. Avoid splintering the claws. Repeat with the other crab.

2 Grind the shrimp paste, garlic, chilies and ginger in a food processor or with a mortar and pestle.

3 Heat a wok and add the oil. Fry the spice paste, stirring it constantly, without browning.

4 Stir in the tomato ketchup, sugar and water and mix the sauce well. When just boiling, add all the crab pieces and toss in the sauce until well-coated and hot. Serve in a large bowl, sprinkled with the spring onions. Place in the center of the table for everyone to help themselves. Accompany this finger-licking dish with cool cucumber chunks and hot toast for mopping up the sauce, if you like.

Baked Lobster with Black Beans

The term "baked," as used on most Chinese restaurant menus, is not strictly correct—"pot-roasted" or "pan-baked" is more accurate.

INGREDIENTS

Serves 4–6

1 large or 2 medium lobsters, about 1¾ pounds total
vegetable oil, for deep-frying
1 garlic clove, finely chopped
1 teaspoon finely chopped fresh ginger
2–3 scallions, chopped
2 tablespoons black bean sauce
2 tablespoons Chinese rice wine or dry sherry
½ cup broth
fresh cilantro leaves, to garnish

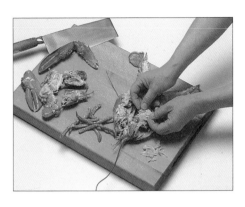

1 Starting from the head, cut the lobster in half lengthwise. Discard the legs, remove the claws and crack them with the back of a cleaver. Discard the feathery lungs and intestine. Cut each half into 4–5 pieces.

2 Heat the oil in a preheated wok and deep-fry the lobster pieces for about 2 minutes, or until the shells turn bright orange. Remove the pieces from the wok and drain on paper towels.

3 Pour off the excess oil, leaving about 1 tablespoon in the wok. Add the garlic, ginger, scallions and black bean sauce and stir-fry for 1 minute.

4 Add the lobster pieces to the sauce and blend well. Add the rice wine or dry sherry and broth, bring to a boil, cover and cook for 2–3 minutes. Serve garnished with cilantro leaves.

COOK'S TIP

Ideally, buy live lobsters and cook them yourself. Ready-cooked ones have usually been boiled for far too long and have lost much of their delicate flavor and texture.

Ragout of Shellfish with Sweet-Scented Basil

Green curry paste, so called because it is made with green chilies, is an essential part of Thai cuisine. It can be used to accompany many other dishes and will keep for up to three weeks in the refrigerator. Ready-made curry pastes are available, but they are not as full of flavor as the homemade variety.

INGREDIENTS

Serves 4–6

1 pound mussels in their shells

¼ cup water

8 ounces medium squid

1⅔ cups coconut milk

1¼ cups chicken or vegetable broth

12 ounces monkfish or red snapper, skinned

5 ounces raw or cooked jumbo shrimp, peeled and deveined

4 scallops, shelled and sliced

3 ounces green beans, trimmed and cooked

2 ounces canned bamboo shoots, drained

1 tomato, skinned, seeded and roughly chopped

4 sprigs large-leaf basil, torn, to garnish

boiled rice, to serve

For the green curry paste

2 teaspoons coriander seeds

½ teaspoon caraway or cumin seeds

3–4 medium fresh green chilies, finely chopped

4 teaspoons sugar

2 teaspoons salt

3-inch piece lemongrass

¾-inch piece fresh galangal or ginger, peeled and finely chopped

3 garlic cloves, crushed

4 shallots or 1 medium onion, finely chopped

¾-inch square shrimp paste

2 ounces fresh cilantro leaves, finely chopped

3 tablespoons finely chopped fresh basil

½ teaspoon grated nutmeg

2 tablespoons vegetable oil

1 Scrub the mussels in cold running water and pull off the "beards." Discard any that do not shut when sharply tapped. Put them in a saucepan with the water, cover and cook for 6–8 minutes. Discard any mussels that remain closed and remove three-quarters of the mussels from their shells. Set aside. Strain the cooking liquid and set aside.

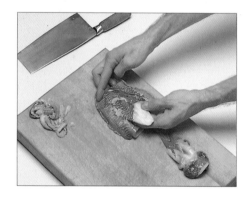

2 To prepare the squid, trim off the tentacles and discard the gut. Remove the cuttle shell from inside the body and rub off the skin. Cut the body open and score in a crisscross pattern with a sharp knife. Cut into strips and set aside.

3 To make the green curry paste, dry-fry the coriander and caraway or cumin seeds in a wok. Grind the chilies with the sugar and salt in a mortar with a pestle or in a food processor. Add the coriander and caraway or cumin seeds, lemongrass, galangal or ginger, garlic and shallots or onion and grind. Add the shrimp paste, fresh cilantro, chopped basil, nutmeg and oil and combine thoroughly.

4 Strain the coconut milk and pour the thin liquid into a wok with the chicken or vegetable broth and the reserved cooking liquid from the mussels. Reserve the thick part of the coconut milk. Add 4–5 tablespoons of the green curry paste to the wok and bring the mixture to a boil. Boil rapidly for a few minutes, until the liquid has reduced completely.

5 Add the thick part of the coconut milk, then add the squid and monkfish or red snapper. Simmer for 15–20 minutes. Then add the shrimp, scallops, mussels, beans, bamboo shoots and tomato. Simmer for 2–3 minutes, or until cooked through. Transfer to a warmed serving dish, garnish with torn basil leaves and serve immediately with boiled rice.

Vietnamese Stuffed Squid

The smaller the squid, the sweeter the dish will taste. Be very careful not to overcook the flesh, as it becomes tough extremely quickly.

INGREDIENTS

Serves 4
8 small squid
2 ounces cellophane noodles
2 tablespoons peanut oil
2 scallions, finely chopped
8 shiitake mushrooms, halved if large
9 ounces ground pork
1 garlic clove, chopped
2 tablespoons fish sauce
1 teaspoon superfine sugar
1 tablespoon finely chopped fresh
    cilantro
1 teaspoon lemon juice
salt and freshly ground black pepper

1 Cut off the tentacles of the squid just below the eye. Remove the transparent "quill" from inside the body and rub off the skin on the outside. Wash thoroughly in cold water and set aside.

2 Bring a saucepan of water to a boil and add the noodles. Remove from the heat and set aside to soak for 20 minutes.

3 Heat 1 tablespoon of the oil in a preheated wok and stir-fry the scallions, shiitake mushrooms, pork and garlic for 4 minutes, or until the meat is golden.

4 Drain the noodles and add to the wok, with the fish sauce, sugar, cilantro, lemon juice and salt and pepper to taste.

5 Stuff the squid with the mixture and secure with toothpicks or satay sticks. Arrange the squid in an ovenproof dish, drizzle with the remaining oil, and prick each squid twice. Bake in a preheated oven at 400°F for 10 minutes. Serve hot.

Stir-fried Five-Spice Squid

Squid is perfect for stir-frying, as it should be cooked quickly. The spicy sauce makes the ideal accompaniment.

INGREDIENTS

Serves 6

1 pound small squid, cleaned
3 tablespoons oil
1-inch piece fresh ginger, grated
1 garlic clove, crushed
8 scallions, cut diagonally into
    1-inch lengths
1 red bell pepper, seeded and cut into
    strips
1 fresh green chili, seeded and sliced
6 mushrooms, sliced
1 teaspoon Chinese five-spice powder
2 tablespoons black bean sauce
2 tablespoons soy sauce
1 teaspoon sugar
1 tablespoon Chinese rice wine or
    dry sherry

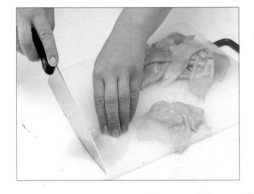

1 Rinse the squid and pull away and discard the outer skin. Dry on paper towels. Slit the squid open and score the inside into diamonds with a sharp knife. Cut the squid into strips.

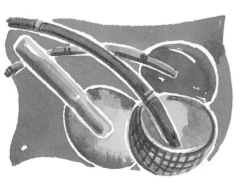

2 Heat the oil in a preheated wok. Stir-fry the squid quickly. Remove the squid strips from the wok with a slotted spoon and set aside. Add the ginger, garlic, scallions, red bell pepper, chili and mushrooms to the oil remaining in the wok and stir-fry for 2 minutes.

3 Return the squid to the wok and stir in the five-spice powder. Stir in the black bean sauce, soy sauce, sugar and rice wine or dry sherry. Bring to a boil and cook, stirring, for 1 minute. Serve immediately.

Clay Pot of Chili Squid and Noodles

INGREDIENTS

Serves 4

1½ pounds fresh squid
2 tablespoons vegetable oil
3 slices fresh ginger,
  finely shredded
2 garlic cloves, finely chopped
1 red onion, finely sliced
1 carrot, finely sliced
1 celery stalk, diagonally sliced
2 ounces sugar snap peas,
  ends removed
1 teaspoon sugar
1 tablespoon chili bean paste
½ teaspoon chili powder
3 ounces cellophane noodles, soaked
  in hot water until soft
½ cup chicken broth
  or water
1 tablespoon soy sauce
1 tablespoon oyster sauce
1 teaspoon sesame oil
pinch of salt
cilantro leaves, to garnish

1 Prepare the squid. Holding the body in one hand, gently pull away the head and tentacles. Discard the head; trim and reserve the tentacles. Remove the transparent "quill" from inside the body of the squid. Peel off the brown skin on the outside of the body. Rub a little salt into the squid, and wash thoroughly under cold running water. Cut the body of the squid into rings or split it open lengthwise, score crisscross patterns on the inside of the body, and cut it into 2-inch x 1½-inch pieces.

2 Heat the oil in a large clay pot or flameproof casserole. Add the ginger, garlic and onion, and fry for 1–2 minutes. Add the squid, carrot, celery and peas. Fry until the squid curls up. Season with salt and sugar, and stir in the chili bean paste and powder. Transfer the mixture to a bowl, and set aside until required.

3 Drain the soaked noodles, and add them to the clay pot or casserole. Stir in the broth or water, soy sauce and oyster sauce. Cover, and cook over a medium heat for about 10 minutes or until the noodles are tender.

4 Return the squid and vegetables to the pot. Cover, and cook for about 5–6 minutes more, until all the flavors are combined. Season to taste.

5 Just before serving, drizzle with the sesame oil, and sprinkle with the cilantro leaves.

COOK'S TIP

These noodles have a smooth, light texture that readily absorbs the other flavors in the dish. To vary the flavor, the vegetables can be altered according to what is available.

Squid with Bell Pepper and Black Bean Sauce

This dish is a product of the Cantonese school. It makes an attractive meal that is just as delicious as it looks.

INGREDIENTS

Serves 4

12–14 ounces squid
1 medium green bell pepper, cored
3–4 tablespoons vegetable oil
1 garlic clove, finely chopped
½ teaspoon finely chopped fresh ginger
1 tablespoon finely chopped scallion
1 teaspoon salt
1 tablespoon black bean sauce
1 tablespoon Chinese rice wine or
　dry sherry
few drops of sesame oil

1 To clean the squid, cut off the tentacles just below the eye. Remove the "quill" from inside the body. Peel off and discard the skin, then wash the squid and dry well. Cut open the squid and score the inside of the flesh in a crisscross pattern.

2 Cut the squid into pieces each about the size of an oblong postage stamp. Blanch the squid in a pan of boiling water for a few seconds. Remove and drain. Dry well.

3 Cut the green bell pepper into small triangular pieces. Heat the oil in a preheated wok and stir-fry the bell pepper for about 1 minute.

4 Add the garlic, ginger, scallion, salt and squid, then stir for 1 minute. Add the black bean sauce, rice wine or dry sherry and sesame oil and serve.

Spicy Fish

If you make *Ikan Kecap* a day· ahead, put it straight onto a serving dish after cooking and then pour over the sauce, cover and chill until required.

INGREDIENTS

Serves 3–4
1 pound fish fillets, such as mackerel, cod or haddock
2 tablespoons flour
peanut oil for frying
1 onion, coarsely chopped
1 small garlic clove, crushed
1½ inches fresh ginger root, peeled and grated
1–2 fresh red chilies, seeded and sliced
½ teaspoon shrimp paste
4 tablespoons water
juice of ½ lemon
1 tablespoon brown sugar
2 tablespoons dark soy sauce
salt
roughly torn lettuce leaves, to serve

1 Rinse the fish fillets under cold water and dry well on absorbent paper towels. Cut into serving portions and remove any bones.

2 Season the flour with salt and use it to dust the fish. Heat the oil in a frying pan and fry the fish on both sides for 3–4 minutes, or until cooked. Lift onto a plate and set aside.

3 Rinse out and dry the pan. Heat a little more oil and fry the onion, garlic, ginger and chilies just to bring out the flavor. Do not brown.

4 Blend the shrimp paste with a little water, to make a paste. Add it to the onion mixture, with a little extra water if necessary. Cook for 2 minutes and then stir in the lemon juice, brown sugar and soy sauce.

5 Pour over the fish and serve, hot or cold, with roughly torn lettuce.

COOK'S TIP

For a buffet dish cut the fish into bite-size pieces or serving portions.

Squid from Madura

This squid dish, *Cumi Cumi Madura*, is popular in Indonesia. It is quite usual to be invited into the restaurant kitchen and given a warm welcome.

INGREDIENTS

Serves 2–3
1 pound cleaned and drained squid, body cut in strips, tentacles left whole
3 garlic cloves
¼ teaspoon ground nutmeg
1 bunch of scallions
4 tablespoons sunflower oil
1 cup water
1 tablespoon dark soy sauce
salt and freshly ground black pepper
1 lime, cut in wedges (optional)
boiled rice, to serve

1 Squeeze out and discard the little central "bone" from each tentacle. Heat a wok, toss in the squid and stir-fry for 1 minute. Remove the squid.

2 Crush the garlic with the nutmeg and some salt and pepper. Trim the roots from the scallions, cut the white part into small pieces, slice the green part and then set aside.

3 Heat the wok, add the oil and fry the white part of the scallions. Stir in the garlic paste and the squid.

4 Rinse out the garlic paste container with the water and soy sauce and add to the pan. Half-cover and simmer for 4–5 minutes. Add the scallion tops, toss lightly and serve at once, with lime, if using, and rice.

MEAT

Satisfying beef curries, quick and easy stir-fried steak, fragrant lamb dishes and, of course, sweet-and-sour pork – the range of Chinese and Asian meat recipes is immense, offering something special for all tastes and budgets. The recipes in this chapter include inexpensive and easy-to-prepare weekday family meals, such as Balti Lamb Tikka and Pork and Vegetable Stir-fry, as well as impressive and unusual dinner party dishes, such as Beef and Vegetables in Table-top Broth and Braised Birthday Noodles with Hoisin Lamb.

Lemongrass Pork

Chilies and lemongrass flavor this simple stir-fry, while peanuts add crunch.

INGREDIENTS

Serves 4

1½ pounds boneless loin of pork
2 lemongrass stalks, finely chopped
4 scallions, thinly sliced
1 teaspoon salt
12 black peppercorns, coarsely crushed
2 tablespoons peanut oil
2 garlic cloves, chopped
2 fresh red chilies, seeded and chopped
1 teaspoon light brown sugar
2 tablespoons fish sauce, or to taste
¼ cup roasted unsalted peanuts, chopped
salt and ground black pepper
fresh cilantro leaves, to garnish
rice noodles, to serve

1 Trim any excess fat from the pork. Cut the meat across into ¼-inch thick slices, then cut each slice into ¼-inch strips. Put the pork into a bowl with the lemongrass, scallions, salt and crushed peppercorns. Mix well, then cover and let marinate for 30 minutes.

2 Heat a wok until hot, add the oil and swirl it around. Add the pork mixture and stir-fry for 3 minutes.

3 Add the garlic and chilies and stir-fry for another 5–8 minutes over medium heat, until the pork no longer looks pink.

4 Add the sugar, fish sauce and chopped peanuts and toss to mix. Taste and adjust the seasoning, if necessary. Serve immediately, garnished with roughly torn cilantro leaves, on a bed of rice noodles.

Stir-fried Pork with Lychees

Crispy pieces of pork with fleshy lychees make an unusual stir-fry that is ideal for a dinner party.

INGREDIENTS

Serves 4

1 pound fatty pork, such as pork belly
2 tablespoons hoisin sauce
4 scallions, sliced
6 heavy lychees, peeled, pitted and cut into slivers
salt and ground black pepper
lychees and fresh parsley sprigs, to garnish

1 Using a cleaver or sharp knife, cut the pork into bite-sized pieces.

2 Pour the hoisin sauce over the pork and marinate for 30 minutes.

3 Heat a wok, then add the pork and stir-fry for 5 minutes, until crisp and golden. Add the scallions and stir-fry for another 2 minutes.

4 Scatter the lychee slivers over the pork, and season well with salt and pepper. Garnish with fresh lychees and parsley, and serve.

— COOK'S TIP —

If you cannot buy fresh lychees, this dish can be made with drained canned lychees.

Savory Pork Ribs with Snake Beans

This is a rich and pungent dish. If snake beans are hard to find, you can substitute fine green beans or wax beans.

INGREDIENTS

Serves 4–6

1½ pounds pork spare ribs or boneless
   pork loin
2 tablespoons vegetable oil
½ cup water
1 tablespoon palm sugar
1 tablespoon fish sauce
5 ounces snake beans, cut into
   2-inch lengths
2 kaffir lime leaves, finely sliced
2 red chilies, finely sliced, to garnish

For the chili paste

3 dried red chilies, seeded and soaked
4 shallots, chopped
4 garlic cloves, chopped
1 teaspoon chopped galangal
1 lemongrass stalk, chopped
6 black peppercorns
1 teaspoon shrimp paste
2 tablespoons dried shrimp, rinsed

1 Put all the ingredients for the chili paste in a mortar and grind together with a pestle until it forms a thick paste.

2 Slice and chop the spare ribs (or pork loin) into 1½-inch lengths.

3 Heat the oil in a wok or frying pan. Add the pork and fry for about 5 minutes, until lightly browned.

4 Stir in the chili paste and continue to cook for another 5 minutes, stirring constantly to keep the paste from sticking to the pan.

5 Add the water, cover and simmer for 7–10 minutes, or until the spare ribs are tender. Season with palm sugar and fish sauce.

6 Mix in the snake beans and kaffir lime leaves and fry until the beans are cooked. Serve garnished with sliced red chilies.

Thai Sweet-and-sour Pork

Sweet and sour is traditionally a Chinese creation, but the Thais do it very well. This version has an altogether fresher and cleaner flavor and it makes a good one-dish meal with rice.

INGREDIENTS

Serves 4

12 ounces lean pork
2 tablespoons vegetable oil
4 garlic cloves, finely sliced
1 small red onion, sliced
2 tablespoons fish sauce
1 tablespoon sugar
1 red bell pepper, seeded and diced
½ cucumber, seeded and sliced
2 plum tomatoes, cut into wedges
4 ounces pineapple, cut into
   small chunks
freshly ground black pepper
2 scallions, cut into short lengths
cilantro leaves and shredded scallions,
   to garnish

1 Slice the pork into thin strips. Heat the oil in a wok or large frying pan.

2 Add the garlic and fry until golden, then add the pork and stir-fry for about 4–5 minutes. Add the onion.

3 Season with fish sauce, sugar and freshly ground black pepper. Stir and cook for 3–4 minutes, or until the pork is cooked.

4 Add the rest of the vegetables, the pineapple and scallions. You may need to add a few tablespoons of water. Continue to stir-fry for about another 3–4 minutes. Serve hot, garnished with cilantro leaves and scallions.

Pork Chow Mein

A perfect speedy meal, this family favorite is flavored with sesame oil for an authentic Asian taste.

INGREDIENTS

Serves 4

6 ounces medium egg noodles
12 ounces pork fillet
2 tablespoons sunflower oil
1 tablespoon sesame oil
2 garlic cloves, crushed
8 scallions, sliced
1 red bell pepper, seeded and roughly
   chopped
1 green bell pepper, seeded and roughly
   chopped
2 tablespoons dark soy sauce
3 tablespoons Chinese rice wine or
   dry sherry
6 ounces bean sprouts
3 tablespoons chopped flat-leaf parsley
1 tablespoon toasted sesame seeds

1 Soak the noodles according to the package instructions. Drain well.

2 Thinly slice the pork fillet. Heat the sunflower oil in a preheated wok or large frying pan and cook the pork over high heat until golden brown and cooked through.

3 Add the sesame oil to the wok or frying pan, with the garlic, scallions and bell peppers. Cook over high heat for 3–4 minutes, or until the vegetables are beginning to soften.

4 Reduce the heat slightly and stir in the noodles, with the soy sauce and rice wine or dry sherry. Stir-fry for 2 minutes. Add the bean sprouts and cook for another 1–2 minutes. If the noodles begin to stick, add a splash of water. Stir in the parsley and serve sprinkled with the sesame seeds.

Pork with Eggs and Mushrooms

Traditionally, this stir-fried dish is served as a filling wrapped in thin pancakes, but it can also be served on its own with plain rice.

INGREDIENTS

Serves 4
½ cup dried Chinese mushrooms
6–8 ounces pork fillet
1 head bok choy
½ cup drained bamboo shoots
2 scallions
3 eggs
1 teaspoon salt
¼ cup vegetable oil
1 tablespoon light soy sauce
1 tablespoon Chinese rice wine or
    dry sherry
few drops of sesame oil

1 Rinse the mushrooms thoroughly in cold water and then soak in warm water for 30 minutes. Rinse thoroughly again and discard the hard stalks, if any. Dry the mushrooms and shred thinly.

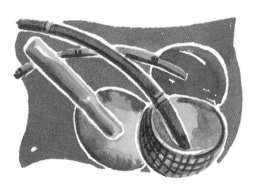

2 Cut the pork fillet into matchstick-size shreds and set to one side. Thinly shred the bok choy, bamboo shoots and scallions.

3 Beat the eggs with a pinch of salt. Heat a little oil in a wok, add the eggs and lightly scramble, but do not make too dry. Remove from the wok.

4 Heat the remaining oil in the wok and stir-fry the pork for about 1 minute or until the color changes.

5 Add the vegetables to the wok and stir-fry for 1 minute. Add the remaining salt, the soy sauce and wine or sherry. Stir for 1 more minute before adding the scrambled eggs. Break up the eggs and blend well. Sprinkle with sesame oil and serve.

COOK'S TIP

Chinese fungi grow on trees and are valued more for their unusual texture than their flavor—often they have very little flavor at all. Wood ears are the most frequently used in authentic Chinese cooking, especially in stir-fries with meat or fish. They are available dried at Asian food stores and should be well rinsed, then soaked in warm water for 30 minutes and rinsed again before use. Other types of dried mushrooms and fungi are also available at Asian stores.

Hot-and-Sour Pork

This tasty dish is cooked in the oven and uses less oil than a stir-fry. Trim all visible fat from the pork before cooking, for a healthy, low-fat recipe.

INGREDIENTS

Serves 4

12 ounces pork fillet
1 teaspoon sunflower oil
1-inch piece fresh ginger, grated
1 fresh red chili, seeded and
 finely chopped
1 teaspoon Chinese five-spice powder
1 tablespoon sherry vinegar
1 tablespoon soy sauce
1 can (8 ounces) pineapple chunks in
 natural juice
¾ cup chicken broth
4 teaspoons cornstarch
1 tablespoon water
1 green bell pepper, seeded and sliced
4 ounces baby corn, halved
salt and freshly ground black pepper
sprig of flat-leaf parsley, to garnish
boiled rice, to serve

1 Trim away any visible fat from the pork and cut into ½-inch-thick slices using a sharp knife.

2 Brush the sunflower oil over the base of a flameproof casserole. Heat over medium heat, then fry the pork for about 2 minutes on each side, or until lightly browned.

3 Blend together the ginger, chili, Chinese five-spice powder, sherry vinegar and soy sauce.

4 Drain the pineapple chunks, reserving the juice. Make the broth up to 1¼ cups by adding the reserved juice, mix together with the spices and pour over the pork.

5 Slowly bring the chicken broth to a boil. Blend the cornstarch with the water and gradually stir into the pork. Add the green bell pepper and baby corn and season to taste.

6 Cover and cook in a preheated oven at 325°F for 30 minutes, or until the pork is tender. Stir in the pineapple and cook for another 5 minutes. Garnish with flat-leaf parsley and serve with boiled rice.

COOK'S TIP

Chinese five-spice powder is available from Asian food stores and some large supermarkets. However, if you cannot find it, you can create your own by combining equal quantities of cinnamon, cloves, Szechuan peppercorns, fennel seeds and ground star anise or anise seeds.

Chinese Sweet-and-Sour Pork

Sweet-and-sour pork must be one of the most popular dishes served in Chinese restaurants throughout the Western world. Unfortunately, it is often spoiled by cooks who use too much ketchup in the sauce. Here is a classic recipe from Canton, the city of its origin.

INGREDIENTS

Serves 4

12 ounces lean pork
¼ teaspoon salt
½ teaspoon ground Szechuan
   peppercorns
1 tablespoon Chinese rice wine or
   dry sherry
1 can (4 ounces) bamboo shoots
2 tablespoons all-purpose flour
1 egg, lightly beaten
vegetable oil, for deep-frying

For the sauce
1 tablespoon vegetable oil
1 garlic clove, finely chopped
1 scallion, cut into short sections
1 green bell pepper, seeded and diced
1 fresh red chili, seeded and cut into
   fine strips
1 tablespoon light soy sauce
2 tablespoons light brown sugar
2–3 tablespoons rice vinegar
1 tablespoon tomato paste
about ½ cup Basic Broth or water

1 Cut the pork into small bite-sized cubes and place in a shallow dish. Add the salt, peppercorns and rice wine or dry sherry and marinate for 15–20 minutes.

2 Drain the bamboo shoots and cut them into small cubes the same size as the pork.

3 Dust the pork with flour, dip in the beaten egg and coat with more flour. Heat the oil in a preheated wok and deep-fry the pork in moderately hot oil for 3–4 minutes, stirring to separate the pieces. Remove and drain.

4 Reheat the oil until hot, return the pork to the wok and add the bamboo shoots. Fry for about 1 minute, or until the pork is golden. Remove and drain well.

5 To make the sauce, heat the oil in a clean wok or frying pan and add the garlic, scallion, green bell pepper and red chili. Stir-fry for 30–40 seconds, then add the soy sauce, sugar, rice vinegar, tomato paste and broth or water. Bring to a boil, then add the pork and bamboo shoots. Heat through and stir to mix, then serve.

Pork and Vegetable Stir-fry

A quick and easy stir-fry of pork and a mixture of vegetables, this makes an excellent family lunch or supper dish.

INGREDIENTS

Serves 4

8 ounces can pineapple chunks
1 tablespoon cornstarch
2 tablespoons light soy sauce
1 tablespoon Chinese rice wine or
  dry sherry
1 tablespoon light brown sugar
1 tablespoon white wine vinegar
1 teaspoon Chinese five-spice powder
2 teaspoons olive oil
1 red onion, sliced
1 garlic clove, crushed
1 fresh red chili, seeded and chopped
1-inch piece fresh ginger
12 ounces lean pork tenderloin, cut
  into thin strips
3 medium carrots, cut into short thin
  sticks
1 red bell pepper, seeded and sliced
6 ounces snow peas, halved
4 ounces bean sprouts
1 can (7 ounces) corn kernels
2 tablespoons chopped fresh cilantro
salt
1 tablespoon toasted sesame seeds,
  to garnish

1 Drain the pineapple, reserving the juice. To make the sauce mixture: blend, in a small bowl, the cornstarch with the reserved pineapple juice. Add the soy sauce, rice wine or dry sherry, sugar, vinegar and five-spice powder, stir to mix and set aside.

2 Heat the oil in a preheated wok or large, nonstick frying pan. Add the onion, garlic, chili and ginger and stir-fry for 30 seconds. Add the pork and stir-fry for 2–3 minutes.

3 Add the carrots to the wok with the red bell pepper and stir-fry for 2–3 minutes. Add the snow peas, bean sprouts and corn and stir-fry for 1–2 minutes.

4 Pour in the sauce mixture and the reserved pineapple and stir-fry until the sauce thickens. Reduce the heat and stir-fry for another 1–2 minutes. Stir in the cilantro and season to taste. Sprinkle with sesame seeds and serve immediately.

Sweet-and-Sour Pork and Shrimp Soup

This main-course soup has a rich, sour flavor.

INGREDIENTS

Serves 4–6

8 ounces jumbo shrimp, raw or
   cooked, peeled
2 tablespoons tamarind sauce
juice of 2 limes
12 ounces lean pork, diced
1 small green guava, peeled, halved
   and seeded
1 small underripe mango, peeled,
   pitted and chopped
6¼ cups chicken broth
1 tablespoon fish sauce or soy sauce
10 ounces sweet potato, peeled and cut
   into even-sized pieces
8 ounces unripe tomatoes, quartered
4 ounces green beans, halved
1 star fruit, thickly sliced
3 ounces green cabbage, shredded
salt and freshly ground black pepper
lime wedges, to garnish

1 Devein the shrimp and set aside. Put the tamarind sauce and lime juice in a saucepan.

2 Add the pork, guava and mango to the pan and pour in the broth. Add the fish sauce or soy sauce, bring to a boil, reduce the heat and simmer for 30 minutes.

3 Add the remaining fruit and vegetables and the shrimp and simmer for another 10–15 minutes. Season to taste. Transfer to a serving dish and garnish with lime wedges.

Savory Pork Pies

This recipe from the Philippines is a legacy of sixteenth-century Spanish colonialism, with a unique Eastern touch.

INGREDIENTS

Serves 6

1 tablespoon vegetable oil
1 medium onion, chopped
1 garlic clove, crushed
1 teaspoon chopped fresh thyme
4 ounces ground pork
1 teaspoon paprika
1 hard-cooked egg, chopped
1 medium gherkin, chopped
2 tablespoons chopped fresh parsley
12 ounces frozen pastry, thawed
salt and freshly ground black pepper
vegetable oil, for deep-frying

1 To make the filling, heat the oil in a saucepan, add the onions, garlic and thyme and fry for 3–4 minutes. Add the pork and paprika and stir-fry until the meat is evenly browned. Season and turn the mixture out into a bowl. Set aside to cool. Add the hard-cooked egg, gherkin and parsley.

2 Lightly knead the pastry on a floured surface, then roll out to a 15-inch square. Cut out 12 circles, 5 inches in diameter. Place 1 tablespoon of the filling on each circle, moisten the edges with a little water, fold over into a half-moon shape and press the edges together to seal.

3 Heat the vegetable oil in a deep-fryer to 385°F. Deep-fry the pies, 3 at a time, for 1–2 minutes, or until golden brown. Drain on paper towels and keep warm while you fry the remaining pies. Serve warm.

Lion's Head Casserole

The name of this dish—*shi zi tou* in Chinese—derives from the rather strange idea that the meatballs look like a lion's head and the Chinese cabbage resembles its mane.

INGREDIENTS

Serves 4–6

1 pound ground pork
2 teaspoons finely chopped scallion
1 teaspoon finely chopped fresh ginger
2 ounces mushrooms, chopped
2 ounces cooked jumbo shrimp, peeled, or crabmeat, finely chopped
1 tablespoon light soy sauce
1 teaspoon light brown sugar
1 tablespoon Chinese rice wine or dry sherry
1 tablespoon cornstarch
1½ pounds Chinese cabbage

3–4 tablespoons vegetable oil
1 teaspoon salt
1¼ cups broth or water

1 Combine the pork, scallion, ginger, mushrooms, shrimp or crabmeat, soy sauce, sugar, rice wine or dry sherry and cornstarch. Shape the mixture into 4–6 meatballs.

2 Cut the Chinese cabbage into large pieces, all about the same size.

3 Heat the oil in a preheated wok or large frying pan. Add the Chinese cabbage and salt and stir-fry for 2–3 minutes. Add the meatballs and the broth or water, bring to a boil, cover and simmer gently for 30–45 minutes. Serve immediately.

Stir-fried Pork with Vegetables

This dish is a perfect example of the Chinese way of balancing and harmonizing colours, flavors and textures.

INGREDIENTS

Serves 4

4 ounces firm tomatoes, skinned
6 ounces zucchini
1 scallion
8 ounces pork fillet, thinly sliced
1 tablespoon light soy sauce
1 teaspoon light brown sugar
1 teaspoon Chinese rice wine or dry sherry
2 teaspoons cornstarch paste
4 tablespoons vegetable oil
1 teaspoon salt (optional)
broth or water, if necessary

1 Cut the tomatoes and zucchini into wedges. Slice the scallion. Put the pork in a bowl with 1 teaspoon of the soy sauce, the sugar, rice wine or dry sherry and cornstarch paste. Set aside to marinate.

2 Heat the oil in a preheated wok and stir-fry the pork for 1 minute, or until it colors. Remove with a slotted spoon, set aside and keep warm.

3 Add the vegetables to the wok and stir-fry for 2 minutes. Add the salt, the pork and a little broth or water, if necessary, and stir-fry for 1 minute. Add the remaining soy sauce, mix well and serve.

Stuffed Green Bell Peppers

Stuffed bell peppers are given a different treatment here—they are deep-fried in a wok and served with a tangy sauce.

INGREDIENTS

Serves 4

8–10 ounces ground pork
4–6 water chestnuts, finely chopped
2 scallions, finely chopped
½ teaspoon finely chopped fresh ginger
1 tablespoon light soy sauce
1 tablespoon Chinese rice wine or
  dry sherry
3–4 green bell peppers
1 tablespoon cornstarch
vegetable oil, for deep-frying

For the sauce

2 teaspoons light soy sauce
1 teaspoon light brown sugar
1–2 fresh hot chilies, finely
  chopped (optional)
about 5 tablespoons stock or water

1 Combine the ground pork, water chestnuts, scallions, ginger, soy sauce and wine or sherry in a bowl.

— COOK'S TIP —

You could substitute ground beef or lamb for the ground pork used in this recipe.

2 Halve or quarter the bell peppers, discarding the seeds. Stuff the sections with the pork mixture and sprinkle with a little cornstarch.

3 Heat the oil in a preheated wok and deep-fry the stuffed bell peppers, with the meat sides down, for 2–3 minutes. Remove and drain.

4 Pour off the excess oil, then return the stuffed bell peppers to the wok with the meat sides up. Add the sauce ingredients, shaking the wok gently to make sure they do not stick to the bottom, and braise for 2–3 minutes. Lift the stuffed peppers on to a serving dish, meat sides up, and pour the sauce over them.

Stir-fried Pork with Vegetables

This is a basic recipe for stir-frying any meat with any vegetables, according to seasonal availability and preference.

INGREDIENTS

Serves 4

8 ounces pork loin
1 tablespoon light soy sauce
1 teaspoon light brown sugar
1 teaspoon Chinese rice wine or
  dry sherry
2 teaspoons cornstarch paste
4 ounces snow peas
1½ cups white mushrooms
1 carrot
1 scallion
¼ cup vegetable oil
1 teaspoon salt
stock (optional)
few drops of sesame oil

1 Cut the pork into thin slices, each about the size of a postage stamp. Marinate with about 1 teaspoon of the soy sauce, and the sugar, wine or sherry and cornstarch paste.

2 Trim the snow peas. Thinly slice the mushrooms. Cut the carrot into pieces roughly the same size as the pork. Cut the scallion into short sections.

3 Heat the oil in a preheated wok and stir-fry the pork for about 1 minute or until its color changes. Remove with a slotted spoon and keep warm while you cook the vegetables.

4 Add the vegetables to the wok and stir-fry for about 2 minutes. Add the salt and the partly cooked pork, and a little stock if necessary. Continue cooking and stirring for about 1 minute, then add the remaining soy sauce and blend well. Sprinkle with the sesame oil and serve.

Fragrant Thai Meatballs

INGREDIENTS

Serves 4–6

1 pound lean ground pork or beef
1 tablespoon chopped garlic
1 lemongrass stalk, finely chopped
4 scallions, finely chopped
1 tablespoon chopped fresh cilantro
2 tablespoons red curry paste
1 tablespoon lemon juice
1 tablespoon fish sauce
1 egg
rice flour for dusting
oil for frying
salt and freshly ground black pepper
sprigs of cilantro, to garnish

For the peanut sauce
1 tablespoon vegetable oil
1 tablespoon red curry paste
2 tablespoons crunchy peanut butter
1 tablespoon palm sugar
1 tablespoon lemon juice
1 cup unsweetened coconut milk

1 To make the peanut sauce, heat the oil in a small saucepan, add the curry paste and fry for 1 minute.

2 Stir in the rest of the ingredients and bring to a boil. Lower the heat and simmer for 5 minutes, until the sauce thickens.

3 To make the meatballs, combine all the ingredients except the rice flour, oil and cilantro, and season. Mix everything together thoroughly.

4 Roll and shape the meat into small balls about the size of a walnut. Dust the meatballs with rice flour.

5 Heat the oil in a wok until hot and deep fry the meatballs in batches until nicely browned and cooked through. Drain on paper towels. Serve garnished with sprigs of cilantro and accompanied by the peanut sauce.

Stuffed Thai Omelet

INGREDIENTS

Serves 4

2 tablespoons vegetable oil
2 garlic cloves, finely chopped
1 small onion, finely chopped
8 ounces ground pork
2 tablespoons fish sauce
1 teaspoon sugar
freshly ground black pepper
2 tomatoes, peeled and chopped
1 tablespoon chopped fresh cilantro

For the omelet
5–6 eggs
1 tablespoon fish sauce
2 tablespoons vegetable oil
sprigs of cilantro and red chilies, sliced,
    to garnish

1 First heat the oil in a wok or frying pan. Add the garlic and onion and fry for 3–4 minutes, until softened. Stir in the pork and fry for about 7–10 minutes, until lightly browned.

2 Add the fish sauce, sugar, freshly ground pepper and tomatoes. Stir to combine and simmer until the sauce thickens slightly. Mix in the chopped fresh cilantro.

3 To make the omelets, whisk together the eggs and fish sauce.

4 Heat 1 tablespoon of the oil in an omelet pan or wok. Add half the beaten egg and tilt the pan to spread the egg into a thin even sheet.

5 When set, spoon half the filling over the center of the omelet. Fold in opposite sides; first the top and bottom, then the right and left sides to make a neat square package.

6 Slide out on to a warm serving dish, folded-side down. Repeat with the rest of the oil, eggs and filling. Serve garnished with sprigs of cilantro and red chilies.

Spicy Meat Fritters

INGREDIENTS

Makes 30

1 pound potatoes, boiled and drained
1 pound lean ground beef
1 onion, quartered
1 bunch scallions, chopped
3 garlic cloves, crushed
1 teaspoon ground nutmeg
1 tablespoon coriander seeds, dry-fried
  and ground
2 teaspoons cumin seeds, dry-fried
  and ground
4 eggs, beaten
oil for shallow-frying
salt and freshly ground black pepper

1 While the potatoes are still warm, mash them in the pan until they are well broken up. Add to the ground beef and mix well together.

2 Finely chop the onion, scallions and garlic. Add to the meat with the ground nutmeg, coriander and cumin. Stir in enough beaten egg to give a soft consistency which can be formed into fritters. Season to taste.

3 Heat the oil in a large frying pan. Using a dessertspoon, scoop out 6–8 oval-shaped fritters and drop them into the hot oil. Allow to set, so that they keep their shape (this will take about 3 minutes) and then turn over and cook for another minute.

4 Drain well on paper towels and keep warm while cooking the remaining fritters.

Barbecued Pork Spareribs

INGREDIENTS

Serves 4

2 ¼ pounds pork spareribs
1 onion
2 garlic cloves
1 inch fresh ginger root
⅓ cup dark soy sauce
1–2 fresh red chilies, seeded
  and chopped
1 teaspoon tamarind pulp, soaked in
  ⅓ cup water
1–2 tablespoons dark brown sugar
2 tablespoons peanut oil
salt and freshly ground black pepper

1 Wipe the pork ribs and place them in a wok, wide frying pan or large flameproof casserole.

2 Finely chop the onion, crush the garlic and peel and slice the ginger. Blend the soy sauce, onion, garlic, ginger and chopped chilies together to a paste in a food processor or with a mortar and pestle. Strain the tamarind and reserve the juice. Add the tamarind juice, brown sugar, oil and seasoning to taste to the onion mixture and mix well together.

3 Pour the sauce over the ribs and toss well to coat. Bring to a boil and then simmer, uncovered and stirring frequently, for 30 minutes. Add extra water if necessary.

4 Put the ribs on a rack in a roasting pan, place under a preheated broiler, on a barbecue grill or in the oven at 400°F. Continue cooking until the ribs are tender, about 20 minutes, depending on the thickness of the ribs. Baste the ribs with the sauce and turn them over from time to time.

Peking Beef and Bell Pepper Stir-fry

This quick and easy stir-fry is perfect for today's busy cook and tastes superb.

INGREDIENTS

Serves 4

12 ounces sirloin steak, sliced into strips
2 tablespoons soy sauce
2 tablespoons medium sherry
1 tablespoon cornstarch
1 teaspoon light brown sugar
1 tablespoon sunflower oil
1 tablespoon sesame oil
1 garlic clove, finely chopped
1 tablespoon grated fresh ginger
1 red bell pepper, seeded and sliced
1 yellow bell pepper, seeded and sliced
4 ounces sugar snap peas
4 scallions, cut into 2-inch lengths
2 tablespoons oyster sauce
4 tablespoons water
cooked noodles, to serve

1 In a bowl, mix together the steak strips, soy sauce, sherry, cornstarch, and brown sugar. Cover and marinate for 30 minutes.

2 Heat the sunflower and sesame oils in a preheated wok or large frying pan. Add the garlic and ginger and stir-fry for about 30 seconds. Add the bell peppers, sugar snap peas and scallions and stir-fry for 3 minutes.

3 Add the beef, together with the marinade juices, to the wok or frying pan and stir-fry for another 3–4 minutes. Pour in the oyster sauce and water and stir until the sauce has thickened slightly. Serve immediately with cooked noodles.

Stir-fried Beef and Broccoli

This spicy beef may be served with noodles or on a bed of boiled rice for a speedy and low-calorie Chinese meal.

INGREDIENTS

Serves 4

12 ounces sirloin steak
1 tablespoon cornstarch
1 teaspoon sesame oil
12 ounces broccoli, cut into small
    florets
4 scallions, sliced diagonally
1 medium carrot, cut into short thin
    sticks
1 garlic clove, crushed
1-inch piece fresh ginger, cut into very
    fine strips
½ cup beef broth
2 tablespoons soy sauce
2 tablespoons dry sherry
2 teaspoons light brown sugar
scallion tassels, to garnish (optional)
noodles or rice, to serve

1 Trim the beef and cut into thin slices across the grain. Cut each slice into thin strips. Toss in the cornstarch to coat thoroughly.

2 Heat the sesame oil in a preheated wok or large nonstick frying pan. Add the beef strips and stir-fry for 3 minutes. Remove and set aside.

3 Add the broccoli, scallions, carrot, garlic, ginger and broth to the wok or frying pan. Cover and simmer for 3 minutes. Uncover and cook, stirring, until the broth has reduced entirely.

4 Combine the soy sauce, dry sherry and brown sugar together and add to the wok or frying pan with the beef. Cook for 2–3 minutes or until it is cooked, stirring continuously. Spoon into a warmed serving dish and garnish with scallion tassels, if desired. Serve on a bed of noodles or rice.

COOK'S TIP

To make scallion tassels, trim the bulb base, then cut the green shoot so that the onion is 3 inches long. Shred to within 1 inch of the base and put into ice water for 1 hour.

Beef Stir-fry with Crisp Parsnips

Wonderful crisp shreds of parsnip add extra crunchiness to this unusual stir-fry—a great supper dish to share with friends.

INGREDIENTS

Serves 4

12 ounces parsnips
1 pound sirloin steak
1 pound trimmed leeks
2 red bell peppers, seeded
12 ounces zucchini
6 tablespoons vegetable oil
2 garlic cloves, crushed
3 tablespoons hoisin sauce
salt and freshly ground black pepper

2 Cut the steak into thin strips. Split the leeks in half lengthwise and thickly slice at an angle. Roughly chop the bell peppers and thinly slice the zucchini.

5 Stir-fry the garlic, leeks, bell peppers and zucchini for about 10 minutes, or until golden brown and beginning to soften but still retaining a little bite. Season the mixture well.

1 Peel the parsnips and cut in half lengthwise. Place the halves flat surface down on a cutting board and cut them into thin strips. Finely shred each piece. Rinse in cold water and drain thoroughly. Dry the parsnips on paper towels, if necessary.

3 Heat the oil in a preheated wok or large frying pan. Fry the parsnips until crisp and golden. You may need to do this in batches, adding a little more oil if necessary. Remove with a slotted spoon and drain on paper towels.

6 Return the meat to the pan with the hoisin sauce. Stir-fry for 2–3 minutes, or until piping hot. Adjust the seasoning and serve with the crisp parsnips piled on top.

4 Stir-fry the steak in the wok or frying pan until golden and cooked through. You may need to do this in batches, adding more oil if necessary. Remove and drain on paper towels.

Beef with Cantonese Oyster Sauce

This is a classic Cantonese recipe in which any combination of vegetables can be used. Broccoli may be used instead of snow peas, bamboo shoots instead of baby corn, and white or black mushrooms instead of straw mushrooms, for example.

INGREDIENTS

Serves 4
10–12 ounces sirloin steak
1 teaspoon light brown sugar
1 tablespoon light soy sauce
2 teaspoons Chinese rice wine or dry sherry
2 teaspoons cornstarch paste
4 ounces snow peas
4 ounces baby corn
4 ounces straw mushrooms
1 scallion
1¼ cups vegetable oil
few small pieces of fresh ginger
½ teaspoon salt
2 tablespoons oyster sauce

1 Cut the beef into thin strips. Place in a bowl and add the sugar, soy sauce, rice wine or dry sherry and cornstarch paste. Mix well and marinate for 25–30 minutes.

2 Trim the snow peas and cut the baby corn in half. If using canned straw mushrooms, drain them. If the straw mushrooms are large, cut them in half, but leave whole if they are small. Cut the scallion into short sections.

3 Heat the oil in a preheated wok and stir-fry the beef until the color changes. Remove with a slotted spoon and drain.

4 Pour off the excess oil, leaving about 2 tablespoons in the wok, then add the scallion, ginger and vegetables. Stir-fry for about 2 minutes with the salt, then add the beef and the oyster sauce. Blend well and serve.

Beef Strips with Orange and Ginger

Stir-frying is one of the best ways to cook with the minimum of fat. This recipe is ideal for people trying to lose weight, those requiring a low-fat and low-cholesterol diet or, in fact, anyone who wants to eat healthfully.

INGREDIENTS

Serves 4

1 pound lean sirloin steak, cut into thin
   strips
finely grated rind and juice of 1 orange
1 tablespoon light soy sauce
1 teaspoon cornstarch
1-inch piece fresh ginger, chopped
2 teaspoons sesame oil
1 large carrot, cut into short thin sticks
2 scallions, thinly sliced
rice noodles or boiled rice, to serve

1 Place the steak strips in a bowl and sprinkle with the orange rind and juice. Marinate for about 30 minutes.

2 Drain the liquid from the steak and reserve it. Combine the steak, soy sauce, cornstarch and ginger.

3 Heat the oil in a preheated wok or large frying pan, then add the steak and stir-fry for 1 minute, or until lightly colored. Add the carrot and stir-fry for another 2–3 minutes.

4 Stir in the scallions and reserved marinade liquid. Cook, stirring constantly, until boiling and thickened. Serve hot with rice noodles or plain boiled rice.

Thick Beef Curry in Sweet Peanut Sauce

This curry is deliciously rich and thicker than most other Thai curries. Serve it with boiled jasmine rice and salted duck's eggs, if you like.

INGREDIENTS

Serves 4–6
2½ cups unsweetened coconut milk
3 tablespoons red curry paste
3 tablespoons fish sauce
2 tablespoons palm sugar
2 lemongrass stalks, bruised
1 pound sirloin steak, cut into
   thin strips
¾ cup roasted ground peanuts
2 red chilies, sliced
·5 kaffir lime leaves, torn
salt and freshly ground black pepper
2 salted eggs, to serve
10–15 Thai basil leaves, to garnish

1 Put half the coconut milk into a heavy-bottomed saucepan and heat, stirring, until it boils and separates.

2 Add the red curry paste and cook until fragrant. Add the fish sauce, palm sugar and lemongrass.

COOK'S TIP

If you don't have the time to make your own red curry paste, you can buy a ready-made Thai curry paste. There is a wide range available in most supermarkets.

3 Continue to cook until the color deepens. Add the rest of the coconut milk. Bring back to a boil.

4 Add the beef and ground peanuts. Stir and cook for 8–10 minutes or until most of the liquid has evaporated.

5 Add the chilies and kaffir lime leaves. Adjust the seasoning to taste. Serve with salted eggs and garnish with Thai basil leaves.

Sizzling Steak

This Malaysian method of sizzling richly marinated meat on a cast-iron grill can be applied with equal success to sliced chicken or pork.

INGREDIENTS

Serves 4–6

1 garlic clove, crushed
1-inch piece fresh ginger, finely chopped
2 teaspoons black peppercorns
1 tablespoon sugar
2 tablespoons tamarind sauce
3 tablespoons dark soy sauce
1 tablespoon oyster sauce
4 slices sirloin steak, each about 7 ounces
vegetable oil, for brushing
shredded scallions and carrot, to garnish

For the dipping sauce
5 tablespoons beef broth
2 tablespoons ketchup
1 teaspoon chili sauce
juice of 1 lime

2 Heat a cast-iron grill over high heat until very hot. Scrape the marinade from the meat into a saucepan and reserve. Brush the meat with oil and grill for 2 minutes on each side for rare and 3–4 minutes on each side for medium, depending on thickness.

3 Meanwhile, make the sauce. Add the beef broth, ketchup, chili sauce and lime juice to the marinade. Set over low heat and simmer to heat through. Garnish the steak with scallions and carrot and serve. Pass the dipping sauce separately.

1 Pound together the garlic, ginger, peppercorns, sugar and tamarind sauce in a mortar with a pestle. Mix in the soy sauce and oyster sauce, then spoon over the steaks. Marinate in the refrigerator for up to 8 hours.

Sesame Steak

Toasted sesame seeds bring their distinctive smoky aroma to this scrumptious Asian marinade.

INGREDIENTS

Serves 4

1 pound sirloin steak
2 tablespoons sesame seeds
1 tablespoon sesame oil
2 tablespoons vegetable oil
4 ounces small mushrooms, quartered
1 large green bell pepper, seeded and
    cut into strips
4 scallions, chopped diagonally
boiled rice, to serve

For the marinade

2 teaspoons cornstarch
2 tablespoons Chinese rice wine or
    dry sherry
1 tablespoon lemon juice
1 tablespoon soy sauce
few drops of Tabasco sauce
1-inch piece fresh ginger, grated
1 garlic clove, crushed

1 Trim the steak and cut into thin strips about ½ x 2 inch.

2 Make the marinade. In a bowl, blend the cornstarch with the rice wine or dry sherry, then stir in the lemon juice, soy sauce, Tabasco sauce, ginger and garlic. Stir in the steak strips, cover and leave in a cool place for 3–4 hours.

3 Place the sesame seeds in a wok or large frying pan and dry-fry over moderate heat, shaking the pan, until the seeds are golden. Set aside.

4 Heat the sesame and vegetable oils in the wok or frying pan. Drain the steak, reserving the marinade, and stir-fry a few pieces at a time until browned. Remove with a slotted spoon.

5 Add the mushrooms and green bell pepper and stir-fry for 2–3 minutes. Add the scallions and cook for 1 minute more.

6 Return the steak to the wok or frying pan, together with the reserved marinade, and stir over a moderate heat for a further 2 minutes, or until the ingredients are evenly coated with glaze. Sprinkle the sesame seeds on top and serve immediately with boiled rice.

COOK'S TIP

This marinade would also be good with pork or chicken.

Stir-fried Beef with Snow Peas

The crisp texture and fresh taste of snow peas perfectly complement the melt-in-the-mouth tenderness of the steak, all served in a richly aromatic sauce.

INGREDIENTS

Serves 4

1 pound sirloin steak
3 tablespoons soy sauce
2 tablespoons Chinese rice wine or dry sherry
1 tablespoon light brown sugar
½ teaspoon cornstarch
1 tablespoon vegetable oil
1 tablespoon finely chopped fresh ginger
1 tablespoon finely chopped garlic
8 ounces snow peas

1 Cut the steak into even-sized, very thin strips.

2 Combine the soy sauce, rice wine or dry sherry, sugar and cornstarch. Mix well and set aside.

3 Heat the oil in a preheated wok. Add the ginger and garlic and stir-fry for 30 seconds. Add the steak and stir-fry for 2 minutes, or until evenly browned.

4 Add the snow peas and stir-fry for another 3 minutes.

5 Stir the soy sauce mixture until smooth, then add to the wok. Bring to a boil, stirring constantly, lower the heat and simmer until the sauce is thick and smooth. Serve immediately.

Braised Beef in a Rich Peanut Sauce

Like many dishes brought to the Philippines by the Spanish, this slow-cooking stew, renamed *Kari Kari*, retains much of its original charm, while at the same time it has acquired a uniquely Asian flavor. Rice and peanuts are used to thicken the juices, yielding a rich, glossy sauce.

INGREDIENTS

Serves 4–6

2 pounds chuck steak
2 tablespoons vegetable oil
1 tablespoon annatto seeds
2 medium onions, chopped
2 garlic cloves, crushed
10 ounces celery root or rutabaga roughly chopped
2 cups beef broth
12 ounces new potatoes, peeled and cut into large dice
1 tablespoon fish or anchovy sauce
2 tablespoons tamarind sauce
2 teaspoons sugar
1 bay leaf
1 fresh thyme sprig
3 tablespoons long-grain rice
½ cup peanuts or 2 tablespoons peanut butter
1 tablespoon white wine vinegar
salt and freshly ground black pepper

1 Cut the beef into 1-inch cubes and set aside. Heat the oil in a flameproof casserole, add the annatto seeds and stir until the oil is dark red in color. Remove the seeds with a slotted spoon and discard.

2 Add the onions, garlic and celery root or rutabaga to the casserole and fry for 3–5 minutes, or until softened but not colored. Add the beef and fry until lightly and evenly browned. Add the broth, potatoes, fish or anchovy sauce, tamarind sauce, sugar, bay leaf and thyme. Bring to a simmer, cover and cook for 2 hours.

3 Meanwhile, place the rice in a bowl, cover with cold water and set aside for 30 minutes. Roast the peanuts, if using, under a preheated broiler for 2 minutes. Remove and rub off the skins with a clean kitchen towel. Drain the rice and grind with the peanuts or peanut butter in a mortar with a pestle or in a food processor.

4 When the beef is tender, add 4 tablespoons of the cooking liquid to the rice and nut mixture. Blend until smooth, then stir into the casserole. Simmer gently, uncovered, for 15–20 minutes, or until thickened. Stir in the wine vinegar and season to taste.

COOK'S TIP

Annatto seeds have little flavor, although they are edible. They are used to color oil or shortening to a rich reddish-orange shade. If you cannot find them, substitute 1 teaspoon paprika and a pinch of turmeric, adding these to the casserole with the beef.

Beef and Vegetables in a Tabletop Broth

In Japanese, this dish is called *Shabu Shabu*, which refers to the swishing sound made as wafer-thin slices of beef, tofu and vegetables cook in a special broth. This is a delicious and easy all-in-one main course for a dinner party.

INGREDIENTS

Serves 4–6
1 pound sirloin steak, trimmed
7½ cups water
½ packet instant dashi powder or
  ½ vegetable bouillon cube
2 large carrots
6 scallions, sliced
5 ounces Chinese cabbage, roughly
  chopped
8 ounces daikon, cut into thin strips
1 can (4 ounces) bamboo shoots,
  drained and sliced (optional)
6 ounces firm tofu, cut into large dice
10 shiitake mushrooms, fresh or dried
salt
10 ounces udon noodles, cooked,
  to serve

For the sesame dipping sauce
2 ounces sesame seeds or 2 tablespoons
  tahini paste
½ cup instant dashi broth or vegetable
  broth
4 tablespoons dark soy sauce
2 teaspoons sugar
2 tablespoons sake (optional)
2 teaspoons wasabi powder (optional)

For the ponzu dipping sauce
3 tablespoons lemon juice
1 tablespoon rice vinegar or white
  wine vinegar
3 tablespoons dark soy sauce
1 tablespoon tamari sauce
1 tablespoon mirin or 1 teaspoon sugar
¼ teaspoon instant dashi powder or
  ¼ vegetable bouillon cube

1 Place the beef in the freezer for 30 minutes, or until firm but not frozen. Slice it very thinly using a cleaver or large, sharp knife. Arrange it decoratively on a serving plate, cover and set aside. Bring the water to a boil in a Japanese *donabe*, a fondue pot or any other covered flameproof casserole with an unglazed outside. Stir in the *dashi* powder or bouillon cube, cover and simmer for 8–10 minutes. Transfer the container to a heat source (its own stand or a hot plate) at the dining table.

2 Meanwhile, prepare the vegetables and bring a saucepan of lightly salted water to a boil. With a paring knife, cut a series of grooves along the length of the carrots, then slice thinly. Blanch the carrots, scallions, Chinese cabbage and daikon, separately, for 2–3 minutes each and drain thoroughly. Arrange the vegetables decoratively on serving plates, together with the bamboo shoots and tofu. If using dried shiitake mushrooms, put them in a bowl, cover with hot water and soak for 3–4 minutes, then drain. Slice the mushrooms.

3 To make the sesame dipping sauce, dry-fry the sesame seeds, if using, in a heavy frying pan over medium heat. Grind them in a mortar with a pestle or in a food processor.

4 Combine the ground sesame seeds or tahini paste, broth, soy sauce, sugar, sake and wasabi powder, if using. Combine thoroughly and pour into a shallow dish.

5 To make the ponzu dipping sauce, put all the ingredients in a screw-top jar and shake vigorously. Pour into a shallow dish.

6 To serve, arrange the plates of vegetables and dishes of sauce around the *donabe*, fondue pot or flameproof casserole, and provide your guests with chopsticks and individual bowls so that they can help themselves to what they want, cook it in the broth and then serve themselves. Toward the end of the meal, each guest can take a portion of noodles and ladle a little stock over them before eating.

COOK'S TIP

Tahini paste is a purée of toasted sesame seeds that is used mainly in Greek, Turkish and some Middle Eastern cooking. It makes a quick alternative to using sesame seeds in this recipe and is readily available from large supermarkets and delicatessens.

Sukiyaki Beef

This Japanese dish, with its mixture of meat, vegetables, noodles and tofu, is a meal in itself. If you want to do it properly, eat the meal with chopsticks and then use a spoon to collect the broth.

INGREDIENTS

Serves 4

1 pound thick sirloin steak
7 ounces Japanese rice noodles
1 tablespoon shredded suet
7 ounces firm tofu, cut into cubes
8 shiitake mushrooms, hard stems trimmed
2 medium leeks, sliced into 1-inch lengths
3½ ounces baby spinach, to serve

For the broth

1 tablespoon superfine sugar
6 tablespoons sake, Chinese rice wine or dry sherry
3 tablespoons dark soy sauce
½ cup water

1 Cut the steak into thin slices using a cleaver or sharp knife.

2 Blanch the noodles in boiling water for 2 minutes. Drain thoroughly and set aside.

3 Make the broth: combine the sugar, sake, rice wine or dry sherry, soy sauce and water.

4 Melt the shortening in a preheated wok. Add the steak and stir-fry for 2–3 minutes, or until cooked through but still pink.

5 Pour the broth over the beef.

6 Add the tofu, mushrooms and leeks and cook for 4 minutes, or until the leeks are tender. Serve a selection of the different ingredients, together with a few baby spinach leaves, to each person.

Beef Saté with Hot Mango Dip

Aromatic beef is served with a spicy fruit sauce. Just add salad greens and plain boiled rice for the perfect balance of flavors and textures.

INGREDIENTS

Serves 4

1 pound sirloin steak
1 tablespoon coriander seeds
1 teaspoon cumin seeds
½ cup raw cashews
1 tablespoon vegetable oil
2 shallots or 1 small onion, finely
   chopped
½-inch piece fresh ginger, finely
   chopped
1 garlic clove, crushed
2 tablespoons tamarind sauce
2 tablespoons dark soy sauce
2 teaspoons sugar
1 teaspoon rice vinegar or white
   wine vinegar
salad greens, to serve

For the hot mango dip

1 ripe mango
1–2 small fresh red chilies, seeded and
   finely chopped
1 tablespoon fish sauce
juice of 1 lime
2 teaspoons sugar
2 tablespoons chopped fresh cilantro
salt

1 Slice the beef into long, narrow strips and thread, zigzag style, onto 12 bamboo skewers. Put them on a flat plate and set aside.

2 Dry-fry coriander seeds, cumin seeds and cashews in a preheated wok until evenly brown. Transfer to a mortar and crush with a pestle, or crush finely in a food processor. Combine the crushed spices and nuts, vegetable oil, shallots or onion, ginger, garlic, tamarind sauce, soy sauce, sugar and vinegar. Spoon this mixture over the beef and marinate for up to 8 hours.

3 Cook the steak skewers under a preheated broiler for 6–8 minutes, turning occasionally to ensure an even color.

4 Meanwhile, make the mango dip. Peel the mango and cut the flesh from the pit. Place in a food processor with the chilies, fish sauce, lime juice and sugar and process until smooth. Stir in the cilantro and season with salt to taste. Serve the skewers on a bed of greens; serve the sauce on the side.

Green Beef Curry with Thai Eggplant

This is a very quick curry so be sure to use good quality meat.

INGREDIENTS

Serves 4–6

3 tablespoons vegetable oil
3 tablespoons green curry paste
2½ cups unsweetened coconut milk
1 pound boneless sirloin steak
4 kaffir lime leaves, torn
1–2 tablespoons fish sauce
1 teaspoon palm sugar
5 ounces small Thai eggplant, halved
a small handful of Thai basil
2 green chilies, to garnish

For the green curry paste

15 hot green chilies
2 lemongrass stalks, chopped
3 shallots, sliced
2 garlic cloves
1 tablespoon chopped galangal
4 kaffir lime leaves, chopped
½ teaspoon grated kaffir lime rind
1 teaspoon chopped cilantro root
6 black peppercorns
1 teaspoon coriander seeds, roasted
1 teaspoon cumin seeds, roasted
1 tablespoon sugar
1 teaspoon salt
1 teaspoon shrimp paste (optional)

1 To make the green curry paste, combine all the ingredients except the oil. Pound using a mortar and pestle or process in a food processor until smooth. Add about 2 tablespoons of the oil, a little at a time, blending well. Keep in a jar in the fridge until required.

2 Heat the remaining oil in a large pan. Add 3 tablespoons of the curry paste and fry until fragrant.

3 Stir in half the coconut milk, a little at a time. Cook for about 5–6 minutes, until an oily sheen appears.

4 Cut the beef into long thin slices and add to the saucepan with the kaffir lime leaves, fish sauce, sugar and eggplant. Cook for 2–3 minutes, then stir in the remaining coconut milk.

5 Bring back to a simmer and cook until the meat and eggplant are tender. Stir in the Thai basil just before serving. Finely shred the green chilies and use as a garnish.

Asian Beef

This sumptuous stir-fried beef melts in the mouth, and is perfectly complemented by the delicious crunchy relish.

INGREDIENTS

Serves 4
1 pound sirloin steak
1 tablespoon sunflower oil
4 whole radishes, to garnish

For the marinade
2 garlic cloves, crushed
¼ cup dark soy sauce
2 tablespoons dry sherry
2 teaspoons dark brown sugar

For the relish
6 radishes
4-inch piece cucumber
1-inch piece preserved ginger

1 Cut the beef into thin strips. Place in a bowl.

2 To make the marinade, combine the garlic, soy sauce, sherry and sugar in another bowl. Pour it over the beef and let marinate overnight in the refrigerator.

3 To make the relish, chop the radishes and cucumber into short matchsticks, then cut the ginger into small matchsticks. Combine thoroughly in a bowl.

4 Heat a wok, then add the oil. When the oil is hot, add the meat and the marinade and stir-fry for 3–4 minutes. Serve with the relish, and garnish with a whole radish on each plate.

COOK'S TIP

Dark soy sauce has a stronger, more robust flavour than light soy sauce. It is particularly useful for imparting a rich, dark colour to meat dishes.

Chili Beef with Basil

This is a dish for chili lovers! It is very easy to prepare—all you need is a wok.

INGREDIENTS

Serves 2

about 6 tablespoons peanut oil
16–20 large fresh whole basil leaves
10 ounces sirloin steak
2 tablespoons fish sauce
1 teaspoon dark brown sugar
1–2 fresh red chilies, sliced into rings
3 garlic cloves, chopped
1 teaspoon chopped fresh ginger
1 shallot, thinly sliced
2 tablespoons finely chopped fresh basil
squeeze of lemon juice
salt and ground black pepper
Thai jasmine rice, to serve
 (see index)

1 Heat the oil in a wok and, when hot, add the whole basil leaves and fry for about 1 minute, until crisp and golden. Drain on paper towels. Remove the wok from the heat and pour off all but 2 tablespoons of the oil.

COOK'S TIP

Although not as familiar to Western cooks, Thai fish sauce is as widely used in Thai cooking as soy sauce is in Chinese cuisine. In fact, they are not dissimilar in appearance and taste. Called *nam pla*, Thai fish sauce is available at Asian food stores and some supermarkets, but if you cannot get it, soy sauce is an adequate substitute.

2 Cut the steak across the grain into thin strips. Combine the fish sauce and sugar in a bowl. Add the beef, mix well, then let marinate for about 30 minutes.

3 Reheat the oil until hot, add the chilies, garlic, ginger and shallot and stir-fry for 30 seconds. Add the beef and chopped basil, then stir-fry for about 3 minutes. Flavor with lemon juice and salt and pepper to taste.

4 Transfer to a warmed serving plate, scatter the fried whole basil leaves on top to garnish and serve immediately with Thai jasmine rice.

Spicy Meatballs

Serve *Pergedel Djawa* with either a *sambal* or spicy sauce.

INGREDIENTS

Makes 24

1 large onion, roughly chopped
1–2 fresh red chilies, seeded
  and chopped
2 garlic cloves, crushed
¼ teaspoon shrimp paste, prepared
1 tablespoon coriander seeds
1 teaspoon cumin seeds
1 pound lean ground beef
2 teaspoons dark soy sauce
1 teaspoon dark brown sugar
juice of ½ lemon
a little beaten egg
oil for shallow-frying
salt and freshly ground black pepper
fresh cilantro sprigs, to garnish

1 Put the onion, chilies, garlic and shrimp paste in a food processor. Process but do not over-chop or the onion will become too wet and spoil the consistency of the meatballs. Dry-fry the coriander and cumin seeds in a preheated pan for about 1 minute, to release the aroma. Do not brown. Grind with a mortar and pestle.

2 Put the meat in a large bowl. Stir in the onion mixture. Add the ground coriander and cumin, soy sauce, seasoning, sugar and lemon juice. Bind with a little beaten egg and shape into small, even-size balls.

3 Chill the meatballs briefly to firm them, if necessary. Fry in shallow oil, turning often, until cooked through and browned. This will take 4–5 minutes, depending on their size.

4 Remove from the pan, drain on paper towels and serve, garnished with cilantro sprigs.

Sizzling Beef with Celery Root Straw

Crisp celery root matchsticks look like fine pieces of straw when stir-fried, and they have a mild flavor that is quite delicious.

INGREDIENTS

Serves 4

1 pound celery root
²⁄₃ cup vegetable oil
1 red bell pepper
6 scallions
1 pound sirloin steak
¹⁄₄ cup beef stock
2 tablespoons sherry vinegar
2 teaspoons Worcestershire sauce
2 teaspoons tomato paste
salt and ground black pepper

1 Peel the celery root and then cut into fine matchsticks, using a cleaver.

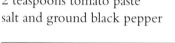

2 Heat a wok, then add two-thirds of the oil. When the oil is hot, fry the celery root matchsticks in batches until golden brown and crispy. Drain well on paper towels.

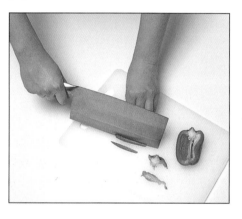

3 Halve, core and seed the red bell pepper, then slice each half horizontally into 1-inch lengths. Slice the scallions diagonally into 1-inch lengths.

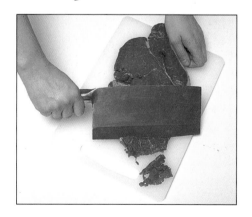

4 Chop the beef into thin strips, across the grain of meat.

5 Heat the wok again and add the remaining oil. When the oil is hot, stir-fry the chopped red bell pepper and scallions for 2–3 minutes.

6 Add the beef strips and stir-fry for another 3–4 minutes, until browned. Add the stock, vinegar, Worcestershire sauce and tomato paste. Season to taste and serve with the celery root straw.

COOK'S TIP

Avoid buying very large celery roots, as they tend to be woody or otherwise unpleasant in texture. Since it is a rather unwieldy vegetable, celery root is easier to peel if you cut it into more or less even-size slices first. Then peel each slice individually using a very sharp knife. They need to be peeled quite thickly to obtain a neat edge. You can then easily cut the slices into thin strips.

Stir-fried Beef in Oyster Sauce

Another simple but delicious recipe. In Thailand, fresh straw mushrooms are readily available, but oyster mushrooms make a good substitute. To make the dish even more interesting, use several types of mushroom.

INGREDIENTS

Serves 4–6

1 pound round steak
2 tablespoons soy sauce
1 tablespoon cornstarch
3 tablespoons vegetable oil
1 tablespoon chopped garlic
1 tablespoon chopped fresh ginger
8 ounces mixed mushrooms, such as
  shiitake, oyster and straw
2 tablespoons oyster sauce
1 teaspoon sugar
4 scallions, cut into short lengths
freshly ground black pepper
2 red chilies, cut into strips, to garnish

1 Slice the beef, on the diagonal, into long thin strips. Mix together the soy sauce and cornstarch in a large bowl, stir in the beef and let marinate for 1–2 hours.

—— COOK'S TIP ——

Made from extracts of oysters, oyster sauce is velvety smooth and has a savory sweet and meaty taste. There are several types available; buy the best you can afford.

2 Heat half the oil in a wok or frying pan. Add the garlic and ginger and fry until fragrant. Stir in the beef. Stir to separate the strips, let them color and cook for 1–2 minutes. Remove from the pan and set aside.

3 Heat the remaining oil in the wok. Add the shiitake, oyster and straw mushrooms. Cook until tender.

4 Return the beef to the wok with the mushrooms. Add the oyster sauce, sugar and freshly ground black pepper to taste. Mix well.

5 Add the scallions and mix together well. Serve garnished with strips of red chili.

Dry-fried Shredded Beef

Dry-frying is a unique Szechuan cooking method in which the main ingredient is first stir-fried slowly over low heat until dry, then finished off quickly with a mixture of other ingredients over high heat.

INGREDIENTS

Serves 4

1 pound flank steak
1 large or 2 small carrots
2–3 celery stalks
2 tablespoons sesame oil
1 tablespoon Chinese rice wine or
   dry sherry
1 tablespoon chili bean sauce
1 tablespoon light soy sauce
1 garlic clove, finely chopped
1 teaspoon light brown sugar
2–3 scallions, finely chopped
½ teaspoon finely chopped fresh ginger
ground Szechuan pepper

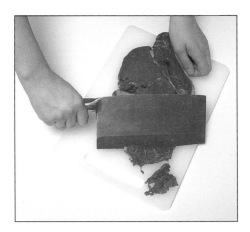

1 Cut the steak into matchstick-sized strips. Thinly shred the carrots and celery sticks.

2 Heat the sesame oil in a preheated wok (it will smoke very quickly). Reduce the heat and stir-fry the beef shreds with the rice wine or sherry, until the color changes.

3 Pour off the excess liquid and reserve. Continue stirring until the meat is absolutely dry.

4 Add the chili bean sauce, soy sauce, garlic and sugar. Blend well, then add the carrot and celery shreds. Increase the heat to high and add the scallions, ginger and the reserved liquid. Continue stirring, and when all the juice has evaporated, season with Szechuan pepper and serve.

Beef and Eggplant Curry

INGREDIENTS

Serves 6

½ cup sunflower oil
2 onions, thinly sliced
1 inch fresh ginger root, sliced and
    cut in matchsticks
1 garlic clove, crushed
2 fresh red chilies, seeded and very
    finely sliced
1 inch fresh turmeric, peeled and
    crushed, or 1 teaspoon
    ground turmeric
1 lemon grass stem, lower part finely
    sliced, top bruised
1½ pounds braising steak, cut in even-
    size strips
14 fluid-ounce can coconut milk
1¼ cups water
1 eggplant, sliced and patted dry
1 teaspoon tamarind pulp, soaked in
    4 tablespoons warm water
salt and freshly ground black pepper
finely sliced chili, (optional) and
    Deep-fried Onions, to garnish
boiled rice, to serve

1 Heat half the oil and fry the
onions, ginger and garlic until they
give off a rich aroma. Add the chilies,
turmeric and the lower part of the
lemon grass. Push to one side and then
turn up the heat and add the steak,
stirring until the meat changes color.

COOK'S TIP

If you want to make this curry, *Gulai
Terung Dengan Daging,* ahead, prepare to
the end of step 2 and finish later.

2 Add the coconut milk, water,
lemon grass top and seasoning to
taste. Cover and simmer gently for
1½ hours, or until the meat is tender.

3 Towards the end of the cooking
time heat the remaining oil in a
frying pan. Fry the eggplant slices until
brown on both sides.

4 Add the browned eggplant slices to
the beef curry and cook for
another 15 minutes. Stir gently from
time to time. Strain the tamarind and
stir the juice into the curry. Taste and
adjust the seasoning. Put into a warm
serving dish. Garnish with the sliced
chili, if using, and Deep-fried Onions,
and serve with boiled rice.

Braised Birthday Noodles with Hoisin Lamb

In China, the egg symbolizes continuity and fertility so it is frequently included in birthday dishes. The noodles traditionally served at birthday celebrations are left long: it is considered bad luck to cut them as this might shorten one's life.

INGREDIENTS

Serves 4

12 ounces thick egg noodles
2¼ pounds lamb cutlets
2 tablespoons vegetable oil
4 ounces fine green beans, ends
　removed and blanched
salt and freshly ground black pepper
2 hard-boiled eggs, halved, and
　2 scallions, finely chopped, to garnish

For the marinade
2 garlic cloves, crushed
2 teaspoons grated fresh ginger
2 tablespoons soy sauce
2 tablespoons rice wine
1–2 dried red chilies
2 tablespoons vegetable oil

For the sauce
1 tablespoon cornstarch
2 tablespoons soy sauce
2 tablespoons rice wine
grated rind and juice of ½ orange
1 tablespoon hoisin sauce
1 tablespoon wine vinegar
1 teaspoon light brown sugar

1 Bring a large saucepan of water to a boil. Add the noodles, and cook for 2 minutes only. Drain, rinse under cold water, and drain again. Set aside.

2 Cut the lamb into 2-inch thick medallions. Mix the ingredients for the marinade in a large, shallow dish. Add the lamb, and marinate for at least 4 hours or overnight.

3 Heat the oil in a heavy-bottomed saucepan or flameproof casserole. Fry the lamb for 5 minutes until browned. Add just enough water to cover the meat. Bring to a boil, skim, then reduce the heat, and simmer for 40 minutes or until the meat is tender, adding more water as necessary.

4 Make the sauce. Blend the cornstarch with the remaining ingredients in a bowl. Stir into the lamb, and mix well without breaking up the meat.

5 Add the noodles to the lamb with the beans. Simmer gently until both the noodles and the beans are cooked. Add salt and pepper to taste. Divide the noodles, lamb and beans among four large bowls, garnish each portion with half a hard-cooked egg, sprinkle with scallions and serve.

Spiced Lamb with Spinach

INGREDIENTS

Serves 3–4

3 tablespoons vegetable oil

1¼ pounds boneless lean lamb, cut into 1-inch cubes

1 onion, chopped

3 garlic cloves, finely chopped

½-inch piece fresh ginger, finely chopped

6 black peppercorns

4 whole cloves

1 bay leaf

3 green cardamom pods, crushed

1 teaspoon ground cumin

1 teaspoon ground coriander

generous pinch of cayenne pepper

⅔ cup water

2 tomatoes, peeled, seeded and chopped

1 teaspoon salt

1 bunch fresh spinach, trimmed, washed and finely chopped

1 teaspoon garam masala

crisp-fried onions and fresh cilantro sprigs, to garnish

naan or spiced basmati rice, to serve

1 Heat a wok until hot. Add 2 tablespoons of the oil and swirl it around. When hot, stir-fry the lamb in batches until evenly browned. Remove the lamb and set aside. Add the remaining oil, onion, garlic and ginger and stir-fry for 2–3 minutes.

2 Add the peppercorns, cloves, bay leaf, cardamom pods, cumin, ground coriander and cayenne pepper. Stir-fry for 30–45 seconds. Return the lamb and add the water, tomatoes and salt and bring to a boil. Simmer, covered, over very low heat for about 1 hour, stirring occasionally, until the meat is cooked and tender.

3 Increase the heat, then gradually add the spinach to the lamb, stirring to mix. Keep stirring and cooking until the spinach wilts completely and most, but not all, of the liquid has evaporated and you are left with a thick green sauce. Stir in the garam masala. Garnish with crisp-fried onions and cilantro sprigs. Serve with naan or spiced basmati rice.

Stir-fried Sweet-and-sour Chicken

Lemon and honey make a classical stir-fry combination in sweet dishes. This lamb recipe shows how well they work together in savory dishes, too. Serve with a fresh mixed salad to complete this delicious dish.

INGREDIENTS

Serves 4

1 pound boneless lean lamb
1 tablespoon peanut oil
6 ounces snow peas, trimmed
3 scallions, sliced
2 tablespoons honey
juice of ½ lemon
2 tablespoons chopped fresh cilantro
1 tablespoon sesame seeds
salt and ground black pepper
fresh cilantro sprigs, to garnish

1 Using a cleaver, cut the lamb into thin strips.

—— COOK'S TIP ——

This recipe would work just as well made with pork or chicken instead of lamb. You could substitute chopped fresh basil for the cilantro if using chicken.

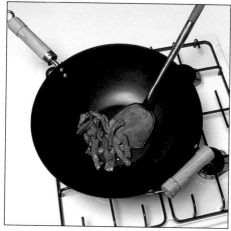

2 Heat a wok, then add the oil. When the oil is hot, stir-fry the lamb until browned all over. Remove from the wok and keep warm.

3 Add the snow peas and scallions to the hot wok and stir-fry for about 30 seconds.

4 Return the lamb to the wok and add the honey, lemon juice, chopped cilantro and sesame seeds and season well. Mix thoroughly, bring to a boil, then let bubble for 1 minute, until the lamb is completely coated in the honey mixture. Serve garnished with cilantro sprigs.

Lamb Tikka

One of the best ways of tenderizing meat is to marinate it in papaya, which must be unripe or it will lend too much sweetness to what should be a savory dish. Papaya, also known as pawpaw, is readily available at most large supermarkets.

INGREDIENTS

Serves 4

1½ pounds lean lamb, cubed
1 unripe papaya
3 tablespoons plain yogurt
1 teaspoon grated fresh ginger
1 teaspoon chili powder
1 teaspoon finely chopped garlic
¼ teaspoon ground turmeric
2 teaspoons ground coriander
1 teaspoon ground cumin
2 tablespoons lemon juice
1 tablespoon chopped fresh cilantro,
   plus extra to garnish
¼ teaspoon red food coloring
1¼ cups corn oil
salt
lemon wedges and onion rings,
   to garnish
raita and naan, to serve (optional)

1 Place the cubed lamb in a large mixing bowl. Peel the papaya, cut it in half and scoop out the seeds. Cut the flesh into cubes, place in a food processor or blender and blend until it is pulped, adding about 1 tablespoon water, if necessary.

COOK'S TIP

A good-quality meat tenderizer, available at supermarkets, can be used in place of the papaya. However, the meat will need a longer marinating time and should ideally be left to tenderize overnight.

2 Pour about 2 tablespoons of the papaya pulp over the lamb cubes and rub it in well with your fingers. Set aside to marinate for at least 3 hours.

3 Meanwhile, combine the yogurt, ginger, chili powder, garlic, turmeric, coriander, cumin, lemon juice, fresh cilantro, red food coloring and 2 tablespoons of the oil. Season with salt and set aside.

4 Spoon the spicy yogurt mixture over the lamb and combine well.

5 Heat the remaining oil in a wok. When it is hot, lower the heat slightly and add the lamb cubes, a few at a time. Deep-fry the batches of lamb for 5–7 minutes or until the lamb is cooked and tender. Transfer each batch to a warmed serving dish and keep it warm while you cook the next batch.

6 When all the batches of lamb have been cooked, garnish with the lemon wedges, onion rings and fresh cilantro. Serve with raita and naan, if you wish.

Paper-thin Lamb with Scallions

Scallions lend a delicious flavor to the lamb in this simple supper dish.

INGREDIENTS

Serves 3–4

1 pound lamb neck fillet
2 tablespoons Chinese rice wine or dry sherry
2 teaspoons light soy sauce
½ teaspoon roasted and ground Szechuan peppercorns
½ teaspoon salt
½ teaspoon dark brown sugar
4 teaspoons dark soy sauce
1 tablespoon sesame oil
2 tablespoons peanut oil
2 garlic cloves, thinly sliced
2 bunches scallions, cut into 3-inch lengths
2 tablespoons chopped fresh cilantro

1 Wrap the lamb and place in the freezer for about 1 hour, until just frozen. Cut the meat across the grain into paper-thin slices. Put the lamb slices in a bowl, add 2 teaspoons of the rice wine or dry sherry, the light soy sauce and ground Szechuan peppercorns. Mix well and set aside to marinate for 15–30 minutes.

COOK'S TIP

Some large supermarkets sell very thinly sliced lean lamb ready for stir-frying, which makes this dish even quicker to prepare.

2 Make the sauce: combine the remaining rice wine or dry sherry, salt, sugar, soy sauce and 2 teaspoons of the sesame oil in a bowl. Set aside.

3 Heat the groundnut oil in a preheated wok. Add the garlic and let it sizzle for a few seconds, then add the lamb. Stir-fry for about 1 minute, or until the lamb is no longer pink. Pour in the sauce and stir briefly to mix.

4 Add the scallions and cilantro and stir-fry for 15–20 seconds, or until the scallions just wilt. The finished dish should be slightly dry in appearance. Serve at once, sprinkled with the remaining sesame oil.

Minted Lamb Stir-fry

Lamb and mint have a long-established partnership that works particularly well in this full-flavored stir-fry. Serve with plenty of crusty bread.

INGREDIENTS

Serves 2

10 ounces lamb neck fillet
2 tablespoons sunflower oil
2 teaspoons sesame oil
1 onion, roughly chopped
2 garlic cloves, crushed
1 fresh red chili, seeded and
    finely chopped
3 ounces green beans, halved
8 ounces fresh spinach
2 tablespoons oyster sauce
2 tablespoons fish sauce
1 tablespoon lemon juice
1 teaspoon superfine sugar
3 tablespoons chopped fresh mint
salt and freshly ground black pepper
fresh mint sprigs, to garnish
crusty bread, to serve

1 Trim the lamb of any excess fat and cut into thin slices. Heat the sunflower and sesame oils in a preheated wok or large frying pan and stir-fry the lamb over high heat until browned. Remove with a slotted spoon and drain on paper towels.

2 Add the onion, garlic and chili to the wok and cook for 2–3 minutes. Add the green beans to the wok and stir-fry for 3 minutes.

3 Stir in the spinach with the browned lamb, oyster sauce, fish sauce, lemon juice and sugar. Stir-fry for another 3–4 minutes, or until the lamb is cooked through.

4 Sprinkle with the chopped mint, season to taste and garnish with mint sprigs. Serve piping hot, with plenty of crusty bread to mop up all the juices.

Stir-fried Lamb with Scallions

This is a classic Beijing "meat and vegetables" recipe, in which the lamb can be replaced with either beef or pork, and the scallions by other strongly flavored vegetables, such as leeks or onions.

INGREDIENTS

Serves 4
12–14 ounces leg of lamb fillet
1 teaspoon light brown sugar
1 tablespoon light soy sauce
1 tablespoon Chinese rice wine or
   dry sherry
2 teaspoons cornstarch paste
½ ounce dried wood ears
6–8 scallions
1¼ cups vegetable oil
few small pieces of fresh ginger
2 tablespoons yellow bean sauce
few drops of sesame oil

2 Heat the oil in a preheated wok and stir-fry the lamb for about 1 minute, or until the color changes. Remove with a slotted spoon, drain and set aside.

3 Pour off all but about 1 tablespoon of the oil from the wok, then add the scallions, ginger, wood ears and yellow bean sauce. Blend well, then add the meat and stir for about 1 minute. Sprinkle with the sesame oil and serve.

1 Slice the lamb thinly and place in a shallow dish. Combine the sugar, soy sauce, rice wine or dry sherry and cornstarch paste, pour over the lamb and marinate for 30–45 minutes. Soak the wood ears in water for 25–30 minutes, then drain and cut into small pieces. Finely chop the scallions.

Five-Spice Lamb

This mouthwatering and aromatic lamb dish is perfect for an informal supper party.

INGREDIENTS

Serves 4

2 tablespoons oil, plus more if needed
3–3½ pounds leg of lamb, boned
    and cubed
1 onion, chopped
2 teaspoons grated fresh ginger
1 garlic clove, crushed
1 teaspoon Chinese five-spice powder
2 tablespoons hoisin sauce
1 tablespoon light soy sauce
1¼ cups tomato paste
1 cup lamb or beef broth
1 red bell pepper, seeded and diced
1 yellow bell pepper, seeded and diced
2 tablespoons chopped fresh cilantro
1 tablespoon sesame seeds, toasted
salt and freshly ground black pepper
boiled rice, to serve

1 Heat the oil in a flameproof casserole and brown the lamb in batches over high heat. Remove and set aside.

2 Add the onion, ginger and garlic to the casserole with a little more oil, if necessary, and cook for about 5 minutes, until softened.

3 Return the lamb to the casserole. Stir in the five-spice powder, hoisin and soy sauces, tomato paste, broth and seasoning. Bring to a boil, cover and cook in a preheated oven at 325°F for 1¼ hours.

4 Remove the casserole from the oven, stir in the bell peppers, then cover and return to the oven for another 15 minutes, or until the lamb is cooked and very tender.

5 Sprinkle with the cilantro and sesame seeds. Serve hot with rice.

Balti Minced Lamb Koftas with Vegetables

These koftas look most attractive served on their bed of mixed fresh vegetables, especially if you make them quite small.

INGREDIENTS

Serves 4

1 pound lean ground lamb
1 teaspoon garam masala
1 teaspoon ground cumin
1 teaspoon ground coriander
1 teaspoon garlic pulp
1 teaspoon chili powder
1 teaspoon salt
1 tablespoon chopped fresh cilantro
1 small onion, finely diced
⅔ cup corn oil

For the vegetables

3 tablespoons corn oil
1 bunch scallions, coarsely chopped
½ large red pepper, seeded and chopped
½ large green pepper, seeded and chopped
6 ounces corn kernels
8 ounces canned lima beans, drained
½ small cauliflower, cut into florets
4 fresh green chilies, chopped

For the garnish

1 teaspoon chopped fresh mint
fresh cilantro sprigs
1 tablespoon shredded fresh ginger root
½ lime, thinly sliced
1 tablespoon lemon juice

1 Put the ground lamb into a food processor or blender and process for about 1 minute.

2 Transfer the lamb to a bowl and add the garam masala, ground cumin, ground coriander, garlic pulp, chili powder, salt, fresh cilantro and onion. Mix thoroughly using your fingers. Cover the bowl and set aside in the refrigerator.

3 Heat the oil for the vegetables in a preheated wok or frying pan. Add the scallions and stir-fry for about 2 minutes.

4 Add the red and green peppers, corn, lima beans, cauliflower and green chilies and stir-fry over high heat for about 2 minutes. Set the wok or frying pan aside.

5 Remove the kofta mixture from the refrigerator. Using your hands, roll small pieces of the mixture into portions about the size of golf balls. The mixture will make 12–16 koftas.

6 Heat the oil for the koftas in a frying pan. Lower the heat and add the koftas, a few at a time. Shallow fry each batch, turning the koftas, until they are evenly browned. Remove from the oil with a slotted spoon and drain on kitchen paper.

7 Return the wok or frying pan with the vegetables to medium heat and add the cooked koftas. Stir the mixture gently for about 5 minutes, or until heated through.

8 Transfer to a serving dish and garnish with the mint, cilantro, shredded ginger and lime slices. Just before serving, sprinkle on the lemon juice.

POULTRY

The versatility of chicken has never been so apparent – stir-fried with ginger, baked with spices, braised in coconut milk and even barbecued Thai-style – and, of course, this chapter also includes mouth-watering recipes for other types of poultry. Some dishes are familiar favorites, such as Indonesian-style Satay Chicken and Peking Duck, while others offer new and exciting combinations of ingredients. Try Chili Duck with Crab and Cashew Sauce, Sweet-and-sour Duck with Mango, Khara Masala or Baby Chicken in Tamarind Sauce.

Chicken Curry with Rice Vermicelli

Lemon grass gives this South East Asian curry a wonderful lemony flavor and fragrance.

INGREDIENTS

Serves 4
1 chicken, about 3–3½ pounds
8 ounces sweet potatoes
4 tablespoons vegetable oil
1 onion, finely sliced
3 garlic cloves, crushed
2–3 tablespoons Thai curry powder
1 teaspoon sugar
2 teaspoons fish sauce
2½ cups coconut milk
1 lemon grass stalk, cut in half
12 ounces rice vermicelli, soaked in hot water until soft
1 lemon, cut into wedges, to serve

For the garnish
4 ounces bean sprouts
2 scallions, finely sliced diagonally
2 red chilies, seeded and finely sliced
8–10 mint leaves

1 Remove the skin from the chicken. Cut the flesh into small pieces, and set aside. Peel the sweet potatoes, and cut them into chunks, about the size of the chicken pieces.

2 Heat half the oil in a large saucepan. Add the onion and garlic, and fry until the onion softens.

3 Add the chicken pieces, and stir-fry until they change color. Stir in the curry powder. Season with salt and sugar, and mix thoroughly. Then stir in the fish sauce.

4 Pour in the coconut milk, and add the lemon grass. Cook over a low heat for 15 minutes.

5 Meanwhile, heat the remaining oil in a large frying pan. Fry the sweet potatoes until lightly golden. Using a slotted spoon, add them to the chicken. Cook for 10–15 minutes more, or until both the chicken and sweet potatoes are tender.

6 Drain the rice vermicelli, and cook it in a saucepan of boiling water for 3–5 minutes. Drain well. Place in shallow bowls with the chicken curry. Garnish with the bean sprouts, scallions, chilies and mint leaves, and serve with lemon wedges.

Gingered Chicken Noodles

A blend of ginger, spice and coconut milk flavors this delicious supper dish, which is made in minutes. For a real Asian touch, add a little fish sauce to taste, just before serving.

INGREDIENTS

Serves 4

12 ounces boneless chicken breasts,
  skinned
8 ounces zucchini
10 ounces eggplant
2 tablespoons vegetable oil
2-inch piece fresh ginger, chopped
6 scallions, sliced
2 teaspoons Thai green curry paste
1⅔ cups coconut milk
2 cups chicken broth
4 ounces medium egg noodles
3 tablespoons chopped fresh cilantro
1 tablespoon lemon juice
salt and freshly ground black pepper
chopped fresh cilantro, to garnish

1 Cut the chicken into bite-sized pieces. Halve the zucchini lengthwise and roughly chop them. Roughly chop the eggplant.

2 Heat the oil in a large saucepan and cook the chicken until golden. Remove with a slotted spoon and drain on paper towels.

3 Add a little more oil, if necessary, and cook the ginger and scallions for 3 minutes. Add the zucchini and cook for 2–3 minutes, or until they are beginning to turn golden. Stir in the Thai curry paste and cook for 1 minute.

4 Add the coconut milk, broth, eggplant and chicken and simmer for 10 minutes. Add the noodles and cook for another 5 minutes, or until the chicken is cooked and the noodles are tender. Stir in the cilantro and lemon juice and season to taste. Serve immediately garnished with chopped fresh cilantro.

Spicy Chicken Stir-fry

The chicken is marinated in an aromatic blend of spices and stir-fried with crisp vegetables. If you find it too spicy, serve with a spoonful of sour cream or yogurt. It's delicious hot or cold.

INGREDIENTS

Serves 4

½ teaspoon ground turmeric
½ teaspoon ground ginger
1 teaspoon salt
1 teaspoon freshly ground black pepper
2 teaspoons ground cumin
1 tablespoon ground coriander
1 tablespoon superfine sugar
1 pound skinless, boneless chicken breasts
1 bunch scallions
4 celery stalks
2 red bell peppers, seeded
1 yellow bell pepper, seeded
6 ounces zucchini
6 ounces snow peas or sugar snap peas
sunflower oil, for frying
1 tablespoon lime juice
1 tablespoon honey

1 Combine the turmeric, ginger, salt, pepper, cumin, coriander and sugar in a bowl and mix well.

2 Cut the chicken into bite-sized strips. Add to the spice mixture and stir to coat the chicken pieces thoroughly. Set aside.

3 Prepare the vegetables. Cut the scallions, celery and bell peppers into thin 2-inch-long strips. Cut the zucchini at a slight angle into thin rounds and trim the snow peas or sugar snap peas.

4 Heat 2 tablespoons of oil in a preheated wok or large frying pan. Stir-fry the chicken in batches until cooked through and golden brown, adding a little more oil if necessary. Remove from the pan and keep warm.

5 Add a little more oil to the pan and cook the scallions, celery, bell peppers and zucchini over medium heat for 8–10 minutes, or until beginning to soften and turn golden. Add the snow peas or sugar snap peas and cook for another 2 minutes.

6 Return the chicken to the pan, with the lime juice and honey. Cook for 2 minutes. Serve immediately.

Spicy Clay-Pot Chicken

Clay-pot cooking stems from the practice of burying a glazed pot in the embers of an open fire. The heat surrounds the base and keeps the liquid inside at a slow simmer, similar to the way a modern-day casserole works.

INGREDIENTS

Serves 4–6

3–3½ pounds chicken
3 tablespoons freshly shredded coconut
2 tablespoons vegetable oil
2 shallots or 1 small onion, finely
　chopped
2 garlic cloves, crushed
2-inch piece lemongrass
1-inch piece galangal or fresh ginger,
　thinly sliced
2 small fresh green chilies, seeded and
　finely chopped
½-inch square shrimp paste or
　1 tablespoon fish sauce
1⅔ cups canned coconut milk
1¼ cups chicken broth
2 kaffir lime leaves (optional)
1 tablespoon sugar
1 tablespoon rice vinegar or white
　wine vinegar
2 ripe tomatoes, to garnish
2 tablespoons chopped cilantro leaves,
　to garnish

1 To separate the chicken, remove the legs and wings with a chopping knife. Skin the pieces, divide the drumsticks from the thighs and, using a pair of kitchen scissors, remove the lower part of the chicken, leaving the breast piece. Remove as many of the bones as you can, to make the dish easier to eat. Cut the breast piece into four pieces and set aside.

2 Dry-fry the coconut in a large wok until evenly brown. Add the vegetable oil, shallots or onion, garlic, lemongrass, galangal or ginger, chilies and shrimp paste or fish sauce. Fry briefly to release the flavors. Add the chicken pieces to the wok and brown evenly with the spices for 2–3 minutes.

3 Strain the coconut milk and reserve the thick part. Add the thin part to the wok, together with the chicken broth, lime leaves, if using, sugar and vinegar. Transfer to a ceramic casserole, cover and bake in a preheated oven at 350°F for 50–55 minutes, or until the chicken is tender. Stir in the thick part of the coconut milk and return to the oven for 5–10 minutes to simmer and thicken.

4 Place the tomatoes in a bowl and cover with boiling water to loosen and remove the skins. Halve the tomatoes, discard the seeds and cut into large dice. Add the tomatoes to the finished dish, scatter the chopped cilantro on top, and serve.

Green Curry Coconut Chicken

The recipe given here for green curry paste takes time to make properly. Pork, shrimp and fish can all be used instead of chicken, but cooking times must be adjusted accordingly.

INGREDIENTS

Serves 4–6
2½ pounds chicken
2½ cups coconut milk
1¾ cups chicken broth
2 kaffir lime leaves
12 ounces sweet potatoes, roughly chopped
12 ounces winter squash, seeded and roughly chopped
4 ounces green beans, halved
1 small bunch fresh cilantro, shredded, to garnish

For the green curry paste
2 teaspoons coriander seeds
½ teaspoon caraway or cumin seeds
3–4 medium fresh green chilies, finely chopped
4 teaspoons sugar
2 teaspoons salt
3-inch piece lemongrass
¾-inch piece galangal or fresh ginger, finely chopped
3 garlic cloves, crushed
4 shallots or 1 medium onion, finely chopped
¾-inch square shrimp paste
3 tablespoons finely chopped fresh cilantro
3 tablespoons finely chopped fresh mint
½ teaspoon ground nutmeg
2 tablespoons vegetable oil

1 To prepare the chicken, remove the legs, then separate the thighs from the drumsticks. Separate the lower part of the chicken carcass by cutting through the rib section with kitchen scissors. Divide the breast part in half down the middle, then chop each half in two. Remove the skin from all the pieces and discard.

2 Strain the coconut milk into a bowl, reserving the thick part. Place the chicken in a stainless steel or enamel saucepan and pour in the thin part of the coconut milk and the broth. Add the lime leaves and simmer, uncovered, for 40 minutes. Remove the chicken from the saucepan and allow to cool. Reserve the cooking liquid. Remove the cooled meat from the bone and set aside.

3 To make the curry paste, dry-fry the coriander seeds and caraway or cumin seeds in a large wok. Grind the chilies with the sugar and salt in a mortar with a pestle to make a smooth paste. Combine the seeds from the large wok with the chili paste, the lemongrass, galangal or ginger, garlic and shallots or onion, then grind until smooth. Add the shrimp paste, cilantro, mint, nutmeg and vegetable oil.

4 Place 1 cup of the reserved cooking liquid in a large wok. Add 4–5 tablespoons of the curry paste according to taste. Boil rapidly until the liquid has reduced completely. Add the remaining cooking liquid, chicken meat, sweet potatoes, squash and green beans. Simmer for 10–15 minutes, or until the potatoes are cooked. Stir in the thick part of the coconut milk and simmer gently to thicken. Serve garnished with cilantro.

Chicken Cooked in Coconut Milk

Traditionally, the chicken pieces would be part-cooked by frying, but roasting in the oven is a better option. *Ayam Opor* is an unusual recipe in that the sauce is white as it does not contain chilies or turmeric, unlike many other Indonesian dishes. The dish is usually served with crisp deep-fried onions.

INGREDIENTS

Serves 4

3–3½-pound chicken or
  4 chicken quarters
4 garlic cloves
1 onion, sliced
4 macadamia nuts or 8 almonds
1 tablespoon coriander seeds, dry-fried,
  or 1 teaspoon ground coriander
3 tablespoons oil
1 inch fresh *galangal*, peeled
  and bruised
2 lemon grass stems, fleshy part bruised
3 lime leaves
2 bay leaves
1 teaspoon sugar
2½ cups coconut milk
salt
boiled rice and deep-fried onions,
  to serve

1 Preheat the oven to 375°F. Cut the chicken into four or eight pieces. Season with salt. Put in an oiled roasting pan and cook in the oven for 25–30 minutes. Meanwhile, prepare the sauce.

2 Grind the garlic, onion, nuts and coriander to a fine paste in a food processor or with a mortar and pestle. Heat the oil and fry the paste to bring out the flavor. Do not allow it to brown.

3 Add the part-cooked chicken pieces to a wok together with the *laos*, lemon grass, lime and bay leaves, sugar, coconut milk and salt to taste. Mix well to coat in the sauce.

4 Bring to a boil and then reduce the heat and simmer gently for 30–40 minutes, uncovered, until the chicken is tender and the coconut sauce is reduced and thickened. Stir the mixture occasionally during cooking.

5 Just before serving remove the bruised *galangal* and lemongrass. Serve with boiled rice sprinkled with crisp deep-fried onions.

Chicken Teriyaki

A simple bowl of boiled rice is the ideal accompaniment to this subtle Japanese chicken dish.

INGREDIENTS

Serves 4

1 pound skinless, boneless chicken breasts
orange segments and mustard and watercress, to garnish

For the marinade

1 teaspoon sugar
1 tablespoon sake
1 tablespoon dry sherry
2 tablespoons dark soy sauce
grated rind of 1 orange

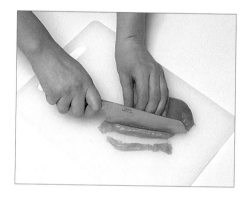

1 Slice the chicken into long, thin strips using a cleaver or sharp knife.

2 To make the marinade, combine all the marinade ingredients in a bowl.

3 Place the chicken in a separate bowl, pour the marinade over it and marinate for 15 minutes.

4 Add the chicken and the marinade to a preheated wok and stir-fry for 4–5 minutes, or until it is cooked. Serve garnished with orange segments and mustard and watercress.

Shredded Chicken with Celery

The tender chicken breast contrasts with the crunchy texture of the celery, and the red chilies add color and flavor.

INGREDIENTS

Serves 4
10 ounces skinless, boneless chicken
  breasts
1 teaspoon salt
½ egg white, lightly beaten
2 teaspoons cornstarch paste
2 cups vegetable oil
1 celery heart, cut into fine strips
1–2 fresh red chilies, seeded and cut
  into fine strips
1 scallion, cut into fine strips
few strips of fresh ginger, cut into
  fine strips
1 teaspoon light brown sugar
1 tablespoon Chinese rice wine or
  dry sherry
few drops of sesame oil

1 Using a sharp knife, thinly shred the chicken. In a bowl, mix together a pinch of the salt, the egg white and the cornstarch paste. Stir in the chicken.

2 Heat the oil in a preheated wok, add the chicken and stir to separate the shreds. When the chicken turns white, remove with a strainer and drain. Keep warm.

3 Pour off all but 2 tablespoons of the oil. Add the celery, chilies, scallion and ginger to the wok and stir-fry for 1 minute. Add the chicken, remaining salt, sugar and rice wine or dry sherry. Cook for 1 minute, then add the sesame oil. Serve hot.

Chicken with Chinese Vegetables

This dish makes an excellent family main course served with rice or noodles, but can also be combined with a selection of other dishes to serve as part of a dinner party menu.

INGREDIENTS

Serves 4
8-10 ounces skinless, boneless chicken
  breasts
1 teaspoon salt
½ egg white, lightly beaten
2 teaspoons cornstarch paste
4 tablespoons vegetable oil
6–8 small dried shiitake mushrooms,
  soaked in hot water
4 ounces canned sliced bamboo shoots
4 ounces snow peas

1 scallion, cut into short sections
few small pieces of fresh ginger
1 teaspoon light brown sugar
1 tablespoon light soy sauce
1 tablespoon Chinese rice wine or
  dry sherry
few drops of sesame oil

1 Cut the chicken into thin slices, each about the size of an oblong postage stamp. Place in a bowl and mix with a pinch of the salt, the egg white and the cornstarch paste.

2 Heat the oil in a preheated wok, add the chicken and stir-fry over medium heat for about 30 seconds, then remove with a slotted spoon and keep warm.

3 Add the vegetables and ginger to the wok and stir-fry over high heat for about 1 minute. Add the remaining salt, sugar and chicken. Blend, then add the soy sauce and rice wine or dry sherry. Stir for another minute. Sprinkle with the sesame oil and serve.

Fu-yung Chicken

Because the egg whites mixed with milk are deep-fried in a wok, some imaginative cooks call this dish "Deep-fried Milk"!

INGREDIENTS

Serves 4

1 boneless chicken breast (about 6 ounces), skinned
1 teaspoon salt
4 egg whites, lightly beaten
1 tablespoon cornstarch paste
2 tablespoons milk
vegetable oil, for deep-frying
1 lettuce heart, separated into leaves
about ½ cup stock
1 tablespoon Chinese rice wine or dry sherry
1 tablespoon green peas
few drops of sesame oil
1 teaspoon diced ham, to garnish

1 Finely mince the chicken meat, then mix with a pinch of the salt, the egg whites, cornstarch paste and milk. Blend well until smooth.

2 Heat the oil in a very hot wok, but before the oil gets too hot, gently spoon the chicken and egg white mixture into the oil in batches. Do not stir, otherwise it will scatter. Stir the oil from the bottom of the wok so that the egg whites will rise to the surface. Remove as soon as the color turns bright white. Drain.

3 Pour off the excess oil, leaving about 1 tablespoon in the wok. Stir-fry the lettuce leaves with the remaining salt for 1 minute, add the stock and bring to a boil.

4 Add the chicken to the wok with the wine or sherry and peas, and blend well. Sprinkle with sesame oil, garnish with diced ham and serve.

Szechuan Chicken

A wok is the ideal cooking pot for this stir-fried chicken dish. The flavors emerge wonderfully and the chicken is fresh and crisp.

INGREDIENTS

Serves 4

2 chicken thighs (about 12 ounces total), boned and skinned
$\frac{1}{4}$ teaspoon salt
$\frac{1}{2}$ egg white, lightly beaten
2 teaspoons cornstarch paste
1 green bell pepper
$\frac{1}{4}$ cup vegetable oil
3–4 dried red chilies, soaked in water for 10 minutes
1 scallion, cut into short sections
few small pieces of fresh ginger, peeled
1 tablespoon sweet bean paste or hoisin sauce
1 teaspoon chili bean paste
1 tablespoon Chinese rice wine or dry sherry
$\frac{2}{3}$ cup roasted cashews
few drops of sesame oil

1 Cut the chicken meat into small cubes, each about the size of a sugar cube. Combine the chicken, salt, egg white and cornstarch paste in a bowl.

2 Seed the bell pepper and cut it into cubes about the same size as the chicken.

3 Heat the oil in a preheated wok. Stir-fry the chicken cubes for about 1 minute or until the color changes. Remove from the wok with a slotted spoon and keep warm.

4 Add the bell pepper, chilies, scallion and ginger and stir-fry for about 1 minute. Then add the chicken, sweet bean paste, chili bean paste and wine or sherry. Blend well and cook for 1 more minute. Add the cashews and sesame oil. Serve hot.

Indonesian-style Satay Chicken

Satay traditionally forms part of a *rijsttafel*—literally, rice table—a vast feast of as many as 40 different dishes served with a large bowl of plain rice. However, for the less ambitious, creamy coconut satay makes these chicken pieces a mouthwatering dish to present at the table at any time of day.

INGREDIENTS

Serves 4

$\frac{1}{2}$ cup raw peanuts
3 tablespoons vegetable oil
1 small onion, finely chopped
1-inch piece fresh ginger, peeled and finely chopped
1 garlic clove, crushed
4 chicken thighs (about 1$\frac{1}{2}$ pounds), skinned and cut into cubes
4 ounces creamed coconut, roughly chopped
1 tablespoon chili sauce
$\frac{1}{4}$ cup crunchy peanut butter
1 teaspoon dark brown sugar
$\frac{2}{3}$ cup milk
$\frac{1}{4}$ teaspoon salt

1 Shell the peanuts and remove the skins by rubbing them between the palms of the hands. Put them in a small bowl, add just enough water to cover and soak for 1 minute. Drain the nuts and cut them into slivers.

2 Heat the wok and add 1 teaspoon of the oil. When the oil is hot, stir-fry the peanuts for 1 minute, until crisp and golden. Remove with a slotted spoon and drain on paper towels.

3 Add the remaining oil to the hot wok. When the oil is hot, add the onion, ginger and garlic and stir-fry for 2–3 minutes, until softened but not browned. Remove with a slotted spoon and drain on paper towels.

— COOK'S TIP —

Soak bamboo skewers in cold water for at least 2 hours, or preferably overnight, so that they do not char when the threaded chicken is kept warm in the oven.

4 Add the chicken pieces to the wok and stir-fry for 3–4 minutes, until crisp and golden on all sides. Thread onto presoaked bamboo skewers and keep warm.

5 Add the creamed coconut to the hot wok in small pieces and stir-fry until melted. Add the chili sauce, peanut butter and ginger mixture and simmer for 2 minutes. Stir in the sugar, milk and salt, and simmer for another 3 minutes. Serve the skewered chicken hot, with a dish of the hot dipping sauce sprinkled with the roasted peanuts.

Hot Chili Chicken

A tantalizing mixture of lemongrass and ginger provides the flavoring for this chicken feast. The ingredients are gently simmered in a wok to achieve a superb final product.

INGREDIENTS

Serves 4–6

3 chicken legs (thighs and drumsticks)
1 tablespoon vegetable oil
³⁄₄-inch piece fresh ginger, peeled and finely chopped
1 garlic clove, crushed
1 small red chili, seeded and finely chopped
2-inch piece lemongrass, shredded
²⁄₃ cup chicken stock
1 tablespoon fish sauce (optional)
2 teaspoons sugar
¹⁄₂ teaspoon salt
juice of ¹⁄₂ lemon
¹⁄₂ cup raw peanuts
2 scallions, shredded
rind of 1 mandarin orange or satsuma, shredded
2 tablespoons chopped fresh mint, to garnish
rice or rice noodles, to serve

1 With the heel of the knife, chop through the narrow end of the drumsticks. Remove the jointed parts of the drumsticks and thigh bones, then remove the skin.

2 Heat the oil in a large preheated wok. Add the chicken, ginger, garlic, chili and lemongrass and cook for 3–4 minutes. Add the chicken stock, fish sauce, if using, sugar, salt and lemon juice. Lower the heat, cover and simmer for 30–35 minutes.

3 To prepare the peanuts for the topping, broil or roast them under steady heat until evenly brown, 2–3 minutes. Turn the nuts out onto a dish towel and rub briskly to loosen the skins.

4 Serve the chicken scattered with roasted peanuts, shredded scallions and the rind of the mandarin orange. Garnish with mint and serve with rice or rice noodles.

COOK'S TIP

This dish can also be prepared using duck legs. Be sure to remove the jointed parts of the drumsticks and thigh bones to make the meat easier to eat with chopsticks.

Stir-fried Chicken with Basil and Chilies

This quick and easy chicken dish is an excellent introduction to Thai cuisine. Deep-frying the basil adds another dimension to this dish. Thai basil, which is sometimes known as Holy basil, has a unique, pungent flavor that is both spicy and sharp. The dull leaves have serrated edges.

INGREDIENTS

Serves 4–6

3 tablespoons vegetable oil
4 garlic cloves, sliced
2–4 red chilies, seeded
   and chopped
1 pound chicken, cut into
   bite-size pieces
2–3 tablespoons fish sauce
2 teaspoons dark soy sauce
1 teaspoon sugar
10–12 Thai basil leaves
2 red chilies, finely sliced and 20 Thai
   basil leaves, deep-fried (optional),
   to garnish

1 Heat the oil in a wok or large frying pan and swirl it around.

COOK'S TIP

To deep-fry Thai basil leaves, make sure that the leaves are completely dry. Deep-fry in hot oil for about 30–40 seconds, lift out and drain on paper towels.

2 Add the garlic and chilies and stir-fry until golden.

3 Add the chicken and stir-fry until it changes color.

4 Season with fish sauce, soy sauce and sugar. Continue to stir-fry for 3–4 minutes, or until the chicken is cooked. Stir in the fresh Thai basil leaves. Garnish with sliced chilies and the deep-fried basil, if using.

Chicken and Cashew Stir-fry

Hoisin sauce lends a sweet yet slightly hot note to this chicken stir-fry, while cashews add a pleasing contrast of texture.

INGREDIENTS

Serves 4

$^{1}/_{2}$ cup cashews
1 red bell pepper
1 pound boneless chicken breasts
3 tablespoons peanut oil
4 garlic cloves, finely chopped
2 tablespoons Chinese rice wine or
    dry sherry
3 tablespoons hoisin sauce
2 teaspoons sesame oil
5–6 scallions, green part only, cut into
    1-inch lengths

2 Cut the red bell pepper in half and remove the seeds. Slice into thin strips. Skin the chicken fillet and cut into thin finger-length strips.

4 Add the rice wine or sherry and hoisin sauce. Continue to stir-fry until the chicken is tender and all the ingredients are evenly glazed.

1 Heat a wok until hot, add the cashews and dry-fry over low to medium heat for 1–2 minutes, until golden brown. Remove and set aside.

3 Heat the wok again until hot, add the oil and swirl it around. Add the garlic and let it sizzle in the oil for a few seconds. Add the bell pepper and chicken and stir-fry for 2 minutes.

5 Stir in the sesame oil, toasted cashews and scallions. Serve immediately.

COOK'S TIP

Use blanched almonds instead of cashews, if you prefer. For a slightly less sweet taste, you could substitute light soy sauce for the hoisin sauce.

Chicken, Ham and Broccoli Stir-fry

The charmingly poetic Chinese name for this pretty and colorful dish—*jin hua yi shu ji*—means "golden flower and jade tree chicken." It is a marvelous cold-buffet-style stir-fry to serve on any occasion.

INGREDIENTS

Serves 6–8
1 chicken (about 3 pounds)
2 scallions
2–3 1-inch pieces fresh ginger
1 tablespoon salt
8 ounces honey-roasted ham
1 bunch broccoli
3 tablespoons vegetable oil
1 teaspoon light brown sugar
2 teaspoons cornstarch

1 Place the chicken in a large pan and cover it with cold water. Add the scallions, ginger and about 2 teaspoons of the salt. Bring to a boil, then reduce the heat and simmer for 10–15 minutes under a tightly fitting lid. Turn off the heat and let the chicken cook itself in the hot water for at least 4–5 hours; do not lift the lid, as this will let out the residual heat.

2 Remove the chicken from the pan, reserving the liquid, and carefully cut the meat away from the bones, keeping the skin on. Slice both the chicken and ham into pieces the size of a matchbox and arrange the meats in alternating layers on a plate.

3 Cut the broccoli into small florets and stir-fry in the hot oil with the remaining salt and the sugar for 2–3 minutes. Arrange the broccoli between the rows of chicken and ham and around the edge of the plate, making a border for the meat.

4 Heat 2 tablespoons of the chicken stock and thicken it with the cornstarch. Stir until smooth, then pour it evenly all over the chicken and ham to form a thin coat of transparent jelly. Let cool before serving.

Stir-fried Sweet-and-sour Chicken

This all-in-one stir-fry has a Southeast Asian influence. It is ideal for today's cook, who is so often short of time.

INGREDIENTS

Serves 4

1 package (10 ounces) Chinese egg noodles
2 tablespoons vegetable oil
3 scallions, chopped
1 garlic clove, crushed
1-inch piece fresh ginger, peeled and grated
1 teaspoon hot paprika
1 teaspoon ground coriander
3 chicken breasts, boned and sliced
4 ounces sugar-snap peas, trimmed
1 cup baby corn, halved
1¹/₂ cups bean sprouts
1 tablespoon cornstarch
3 tablespoons soy sauce
3 tablespoons lemon juice
1 tablespoon sugar
salt
3 tablespoons chopped fresh cilantro or scallion tops, to garnish

1 Bring a large saucepan of salted water to a boil. Add the noodles and cook according to the package instructions if using dried noodles. If using fresh egg noodles, cook for just a few minutes, stirring occasionally to separate. Drain thoroughly, cover and keep warm.

2 Heat the oil in a preheated wok. Add the scallions and cook over gentle heat. Mix in the garlic, ginger, paprika, coriander and chicken, then stir-fry for 3–4 minutes.

3 Add the peas, baby corn and bean sprouts, cover and cook briefly. Add the noodles.

4 Combine the cornstarch, soy sauce, lemon juice and sugar in a small bowl. Add to the wok and simmer briefly to thicken. Serve immediately, garnished with chopped cilantro or scallion tops.

COOK'S TIP

Large wok lids are cumbersome and can be difficult to store in a small kitchen. Instead of using a lid, you can set a circle of waxed paper against the food surface to keep the cooking juices in.

Indian Chicken with Lentils

This is rather an unusual combination of flavors, but it is certainly worth trying! The mango powder gives a delicious, tangy flavor to this spicy dish.

INGREDIENTS

Serves 4–6

¾ cup split yellow lentils
¼ cup corn oil
2 medium leeks, chopped
6 large dried red chilies
4 curry leaves
1 teaspoon mustard seeds
2 teaspoons mango powder
2 medium tomatoes, chopped
½ teaspoon chili powder
1 teaspoon ground coriander
1 pound boneless chicken breasts, skinned and cubed
salt
1 tablespoon chopped fresh cilantro, to garnish
paratha, to serve

1 Put the lentils in a strainer and wash carefully under plenty of cold running water.

2 Put the lentils in a saucepan and add just enough water to cover. Bring to a boil and cook for 10 minutes or until they are soft but not mushy. Drain thoroughly, transfer to a bowl and set aside.

3 Heat the oil in a preheated wok until hot. Lower the heat and add the leeks, dried red chilies, curry leaves and mustard seeds and stir-fry gently for 2–3 minutes.

4 Add the mango powder, tomatoes, chili powder, ground coriander and chicken. Season with salt and stir-fry for 7–10 minutes.

--- COOK'S TIP ---

Split yellow lentils, known as chana dhal, are available at Asian stores. However, if you cannot get them, split yellow peas are a good substitute.

5 Mix in the cooked lentils and fry for another 2 minutes or until the chicken is cooked through.

6 Garnish with fresh cilantro and serve immediately with paratha.

Aromatic Chicken from Madura

Magadip is best cooked ahead so that the flavors permeate the chicken flesh making it even more delicious. A cool cucumber salad is a good accompaniment.

INGREDIENTS

Serves 4

3–3½-pound chicken, cut in quarters,
   or 4 chicken quarters
1 teaspoon sugar
2 tablespoons coriander seeds
2 teaspoons cumin seeds
6 whole cloves
½ teaspoon ground nutmeg
½ teaspoon ground turmeric
1 small onion
1 inch fresh ginger root, peeled
   and sliced
1¼ cups chicken broth or water
salt and freshly ground black pepper
boiled rice and Deep-fried Onions,
   to serve

1 Cut each chicken quarter in half to obtain eight pieces. Place in a flameproof casserole, sprinkle with sugar and salt and toss together. This helps release the juices in the chicken. Use the backbone and any remaining carcass to make chicken stock for use later in the recipe, if you like.

— COOK'S TIP —

Add a large piece of bruised ginger and a small onion to the chicken stock to ensure a good flavor.

2 Dry-fry the coriander, cumin and whole cloves until the spices give off a good aroma. Add the nutmeg and turmeric and heat briefly. Grind in a processor or with a mortar and pestle.

3 If using a processor, put in the onion and ginger until finely chopped. Otherwise, finely chop the onion and ginger and pound to a paste with a mortar and pestle. Add the spices and broth or water and mix well.

4 Pour over the chicken in the flameproof casserole. Cover with a lid and cook over a gentle heat until the chicken pieces are really tender, about 45–50 minutes.

5 Serve portions of the chicken, with the sauce, on boiled rice, sprinkled with crisp Deep-fried Onions.

Chicken with Turmeric

INGREDIENTS

Serves 4

3–3½-pound chicken, cut in 8 pieces,
  or 4 chicken quarters, each halved
1 tablespoon sugar
3 macadamia nuts or 6 almonds
2 garlic cloves, crushed
1 large onion, quartered
1 inch fresh *laos*, peeled and sliced, or
  1 teaspoon *laos* powder
1–2 lemon grass stems, lower 2 inches
  sliced, top bruised
½ teaspoon shrimp paste
1½ inches fresh turmeric, peeled and
  sliced, or 1 tablespoon
  ground turmeric
1 tablespoon tamarind pulp, soaked in
  ⅔ cup warm water
4–6 tablespoons oil
1⅔ cup coconut milk
salt and freshly ground black pepper
Deep-fried Onions, to garnish

1 Rub the chicken joints with a little sugar and set them aside.

2 Grind the nuts and garlic in a food processor with the onion, *laos*, sliced lemon grass, shrimp paste, and turmeric. Alternatively, pound the ingredients to a paste with a mortar and pestle. Strain the tamarind pulp and reserve the juice.

3 Heat the oil in a wok and cook the paste, without browning, until it gives off a spicy aroma. Add the pieces of chicken and toss well in the spices. Add the strained tamarind juice. Spoon the coconut cream off the top of the milk and set it to one side.

4 Add the coconut milk to the pan. Cover and cook for 45 minutes, or until the chicken is tender.

5 Just before serving, stir in the coconut cream while bringing to a boil. Season and serve at once, garnished with Deep-fried Onions.

Spiced Chicken Stir-fry

INGREDIENTS

Serves 4

3–3½-pound chicken, cut in 8 pieces
1 teaspoon each salt and freshly ground
  black pepper
2 garlic cloves, crushed
⅝ cup sunflower oil

For the sauce

2 tablespoons butter
2 tablespoons sunflower oil
1 onion, sliced
4 garlic cloves, crushed
2 large, ripe beefsteak tomatoes, sliced
  and chopped, or 14-ounce can
  chopped tomatoes with chili, drained
2½ cups water
¼ cup dark soy sauce
salt and freshly ground black pepper
sliced fresh red chili, to garnish
Deep-fried Onions, to
  garnish (optional)
boiled rice, to serve

1 Preheat the oven to 375°F. Make two slashes in the fleshy part of each chicken piece. Rub well with the salt, pepper and garlic. Drizzle with a little of the oil and bake for about 30 minutes, or shallow-fry in hot oil for 12–15 minutes, until brown.

2 To make the sauce, heat the butter and oil in a wok and fry the onion and garlic until soft. Add the tomatoes, water, soy sauce and seasoning. Boil briskly for 5 minutes to reduce the sauce and concentrate the flavor.

3 Add the chicken to the sauce in the wok. Turn the chicken pieces over in the sauce to coat them well. Continue cooking slowly for about 20 minutes until the chicken pieces are tender. Stir the mixture occasionally.

4 Arrange the chicken on a warm serving platter and garnish with the sliced chili and Deep-fried Onions, if using. Serve with boiled rice.

Stir-fried Chicken with Pineapple

INGREDIENTS

Serves 4–6

1¼ pounds boneless, skinless chicken
  breasts, thinly sliced at an angle
2 tablespoons cornstarch
4 tablespoons sunflower oil
1 garlic clove, crushed
2 inches fresh ginger root, peeled and
  cut in matchsticks
1 small onion, thinly sliced
1 fresh pineapple, peeled, cored and
  cubed, or 15-ounce can pineapple
  chunks in natural juice
2 tablespoons dark soy sauce or
  1 tablespoon *kecap manis*
6–8 scallions, white bulbs left whole,
  green tops sliced
salt and freshly ground black pepper

1 Toss the strips of chicken in the cornstarch with a little seasoning. Fry in hot oil until tender.

2 Lift out of the wok or frying pan and keep warm. Reheat the oil and fry the garlic, ginger and onion until soft, but not browned. Add the fresh pineapple and ½ cup water, or the canned pineapple pieces together with their juice.

3 Stir in the soy sauce or *kecap manis* and return the chicken to the pan to heat through.

4 Taste and adjust the seasoning. Stir in the whole scallion bulbs and half of the sliced green tops. Toss well together and then turn the chicken stir-fry onto a serving platter. Serve garnished with the remaining sliced green scallions.

Soy-braised Chicken

As the chicken is braised in the wok, so the spicy ginger sauce releases its flavor into the meat to create a succulent dish. Enjoy it hot or cold.

INGREDIENTS

Serves 6–8
1 chicken (about 3 pounds)
1 tablespoon ground Szechuan
   peppercorns
2 tablespoons grated fresh ginger
3 tablespoons light soy sauce
2 tablespoons dark soy sauce
3 tablespoons Chinese rice wine or
   dry sherry
1 tablespoon light brown sugar
vegetable oil, for deep-frying
about 2¹⁄₂ cups stock or water
2 teaspoons salt
2 tablespoons sugar
lettuce leaves, to serve

1 Rub the chicken inside and out with the ground pepper and fresh ginger. Marinate the chicken with the soy sauces, wine or sherry and sugar for 3 hours, turning it several times.

COOK'S TIP

Any sauce that is left over can be stored, covered, in the refrigerator to be used again and again.

2 Heat the oil in a preheated wok, remove the chicken from the marinade and deep-fry for 5–6 minutes or until brown all over. Remove and drain.

3 Pour off the excess oil from the wok, add the marinade with the stock, salt and sugar and bring to a boil. Return the chicken, and cover and braise in the sauce for 35–40 minutes, turning once or twice.

4 Remove the chicken from the wok and let it cool down a little before chopping it into approximately 30 bite-size pieces. Arrange on a bed of lettuce leaves, then pour some of the sauce over the chicken and serve.

Chicken with Spices and Soy Sauce

A very simple recipe, called *Ayam Kecap,* which will often appear as one of the dishes on a Padang restaurant menu. Any leftovers taste equally good when reheated the following day.

INGREDIENTS

Serves 4

3–3½-pound chicken, jointed and cut
   in 16 pieces
3 onions, sliced
about 4 cups water
3 garlic cloves, crushed
3–4 fresh red chilies, seeded and sliced,
   or 1 tablespoon chili powder
3–4 tablespoons oil
½ teaspoon ground nutmeg
6 whole cloves
1 teaspoon tamarind pulp, soaked in
   3 tablespoons warm water
2–3 tablespoons dark or light
   soy sauce
salt
fresh red chili shreds, to garnish
boiled rice, to serve

3 When the chicken has cooked for about 20 minutes, lift it out of the stock in the pan with a slotted spoon. Transfer the chicken to the pan with the spicy paste mixture. Toss all together over a fairly high heat so that the spices can permeate the chicken pieces. Reserve 1¼ cups of the chicken stock to add to the pan later.

5 Taste and adjust the seasoning and cook, uncovered, for another 25–35 minutes, until the chicken pieces are tender.

6 Serve the chicken in a bowl, topped with shredded chili, and eat with boiled rice.

1 Prepare the chicken and place the pieces in a large pan with one of the onions. Pour over enough water to just cover. Bring to a boil and then reduce the heat and simmer gently for 20 minutes.

2 Grind the remaining onions, with the garlic and chilies, to a fine paste in a food processor or with a mortar and pestle. Heat a little of the oil in a wok or frying pan and cook the paste to bring out the flavor, but do not allow to brown.

4 Stir in the nutmeg and cloves. Strain the tamarind and add the tamarind juice and the soy sauce to the chicken. Cook for 2–3 minutes more, then add the reserved stock.

COOK'S TIP

Dark soy sauce is thicker and more salty than light. Adding the dark variety will give a deeper color to the chicken.

Thai Stir-fry Chicken Curry

Here chicken and potatoes are simmered in a wok filled with coconut milk, one of the essential ingredients of Thai cuisine. The end result is a superb, flavorful curry.

INGREDIENTS

Serves 4

1 onion
1 tablespoon peanut oil
1²⁄₃ cups coconut milk
2 tablespoons red curry paste
2 tablespoons fish sauce
1 tablespoon light brown sugar
8 ounces tiny new potatoes
1 pound boneless chicken breasts, skinned and cut into chunks
1 tablespoon lime juice
2 tablespoons chopped fresh mint
1 tablespoon chopped fresh basil
salt and ground black pepper
2 kaffir lime leaves, shredded, and 1–2 fresh red chilies, seeded and finely shredded, to garnish

1 Cut the onion into wedges, using a sharp knife.

COOK'S TIP

You can use boneless chicken thighs instead of breasts. Simply skin them, cut the flesh into chunks and cook in the coconut milk with the potatoes.

2 Heat a wok until hot, add the oil and swirl it around. Add the onion and stir-fry for 3–4 minutes.

3 Pour in the coconut milk, then bring to a boil, stirring. Stir in the curry paste, fish sauce and sugar.

4 Add the potatoes and seasoning, cover and simmer gently for about 20 minutes.

5 Add the chicken chunks, cover and cook over low heat for another 10–15 minutes, until the chicken and potatoes are tender.

6 Stir in the lime juice, chopped mint and basil. Serve immediately, sprinkled with the shredded kaffir lime leaves and red chilies.

Khara Masala Chicken

Whole spices—*khara*—are used in this recipe, giving it a wonderfully rich flavor. This is a dry dish, so it is best served with raita and paratha.

INGREDIENTS

Serves 4

3 curry leaves
¼ teaspoon mustard seeds
¼ teaspoon fennel seeds
¼ teaspoon onion seeds
½ teaspoon crushed dried red chilies
½ teaspoon white cumin seeds
¼ teaspoon fenugreek seeds
½ teaspoon crushed pomegranate seeds
1 teaspoon salt
1 teaspoon shredded fresh ginger
3 garlic cloves, sliced
¼ cup corn oil
4 fresh green chilies, slit
1 large onion, sliced
1 medium tomato, sliced
4 chicken breasts (about 1½ pounds), skinned, boned and cubed
1 tablespoon chopped fresh cilantro, to garnish

2 Add the shredded ginger and garlic cloves to the bowl.

3 Heat the oil in a preheated wok. When the oil is hot, add the spice mixture, then the green chilies.

1 Combine the curry leaves, mustard seeds, fennel seeds, onion seeds, crushed red chilies, cumin seeds, fenugreek seeds and crushed pomegranate seeds in a large bowl. Add the salt.

4 Add the onion to the wok and stir-fry over medium heat for 5–7 minutes.

5 Add the tomato and chicken pieces to the wok and cook over medium heat for about 7 minutes or until the chicken is cooked through and the sauce has reduced slightly.

6 Stir the mixture over the heat for another 3–5 minutes, then garnish with the chopped fresh cilantro and serve immediately.

Chicken Pot

This nourishing main course combines meat with beans in a spicy sauce.

INGREDIENTS

Serves 4–6

1¼ cups dried navy beans
3 chicken legs
1 tablespoon vegetable oil
12 ounces lean pork, diced
1 chorizo, sliced (optional)
1 small carrot, peeled and
   roughly chopped
1 onion, roughly chopped
8 cups water
1 garlic clove, crushed
2 tablespoons tomato paste
1 bay leaf
2 chicken bouillon cubes
12 ounces sweet potatoes or new
   potatoes, peeled and cubed
2 teaspoons chili sauce
2 tablespoons white wine vinegar
3 firm tomatoes, skinned, seeded
   and chopped
1 head bok choy, shredded
salt and ground black pepper
3 scallions, shredded, to garnish
cooked rice, to serve

1 Put the beans in a bowl, cover with plenty of cold water and set aside to soak for 8 hours or overnight.

2 Separate the chicken drumsticks from the thighs. Chop off the narrow end of each drumstick and discard.

3 Heat the vegetable oil in a preheated wok, add the chicken, pork, sliced chorizo, if using, carrot and onion, then brown evenly.

4 Drain the beans and add to the wok with the fresh water, the garlic, tomato paste and bay leaf and stir to mix. Bring to a boil, lower the heat and simmer for 2 hours, until the beans are almost tender.

5 Crumble the bouillon cubes into the wok, add the sweet or new potatoes and the chili sauce, then simmer for 15–20 minutes, until the potatoes are cooked.

6 Add the vinegar, tomatoes and bok choy to the wok, then simmer for 1–2 minutes. Season to taste with salt and pepper. Garnish with the scallions and serve with the rice.

----- COOK'S TIP -----

This dish is intended to provide enough liquid to be served as a soup for the first course, rather like a French *pot-au-feu*. This is followed by a main course of the meat and vegetables, served with rice.

Baby Chicken in Tamarind Sauce

The tamarind in this recipe gives the dish a sweet and sour flavor; this is also quite hot.

INGREDIENTS

Serves 4–6
¼ cup ketchup
1 tablespoon tamarind paste
¼ cup water
1½ teaspoons chili powder
1½ teaspoons salt
1 tablespoon sugar
1½ teaspoons grated fresh ginger
1½ teaspoons crushed garlic
2 tablespoons dry, unsweetened coconut
2 tablespoons sesame seeds
1 teaspoon poppy seeds
1 teaspoon ground cumin
1½ teaspoons ground coriander
1 baby chicken (1 pound), skinned and cut into 6–8 pieces
5 tablespoons corn oil
½ cup curry leaves
½ teaspoon onion seeds
3 large dried red chilies
½ teaspoon fenugreek seeds
10–12 cherry tomatoes
3 tablespoons chopped fresh cilantro
2 fresh green chilies, chopped

2 Add the chili powder, salt, sugar, ginger, garlic, coconut, sesame seeds, poppy seeds, ground cumin and ground coriander to the mixture.

3 Add the chicken pieces to the bowl and stir until they are well coated with the spice mixture. Set aside.

4 Heat the oil in a preheated wok. When it is hot, add the curry leaves, onion seeds, dried red chilies and fenugreek seeds and fry for 1 minute.

1 Put the ketchup, tamarind paste and water in a large mixing bowl and blend with a fork.

5 Lower the heat to medium and add the chicken pieces, together with their sauce, 2 or 3 pieces at a time. When all the chicken has been added to the wok, stir to mix well.

6 Simmer gently for 12–15 minutes or until the chicken is thoroughly cooked through.

7 Add the tomatoes, fresh cilantro and green chilies to the wok and serve immediately.

Thai-style Chicken Livers

Chicken liver is a good source of iron and is a popular meat, especially in the north-east. Serve this dish as an appetizer with salad, or as part of a main course with jasmine rice.

INGREDIENTS

Serves 4–6

3 tablespoons vegetable oil
1 pound chicken livers, trimmed
4 shallots, chopped
2 garlic cloves, chopped
1 tablespoon roasted ground rice
3 tablespoons fish sauce
3 tablespoons lime juice
1 teaspoon sugar
2 lemongrass stalks, bruised
   and finely chopped
2 tablespoons chopped cilantro
10–12 mint leaves, to garnish

1 Heat the oil in a wok or large frying pan. Add the livers and fry over medium-high heat for about 4 minutes, until the liver is golden brown and cooked, but still pink inside.

2 Move the liver to one side of the pan and add the shallots and garlic. Fry for about 1–2 minutes.

3 Add the roasted ground rice, fish sauce, lime juice, sugar, lemongrass and cilantro. Stir to combine. Remove from the heat and serve garnished with mint leaves.

Barbecued Chicken

Barbecued chicken is served almost everywhere in Thailand, from roadside stalls to sports stadiums and beaches.

INGREDIENTS

Serves 4–6

1 chicken, about 3–3½ pounds, cut
   into 8–10 pieces
2 limes, cut into wedges and 2 red
   chilies, finely sliced, to garnish

For the marinade

2 lemongrass stalks, chopped
1-inch piece fresh ginger
6 garlic cloves
4 shallots
½ bunch cilantro roots
1 tablespoon palm sugar
½ cup unsweetened coconut milk
2 tablespoons fish sauce
2 tablespoons soy sauce

1 To make the marinade, put all the ingredients into a food processor and process until smooth.

2 Put the chicken pieces in a dish and pour over the marinade. Set aside in a cool place to marinate for at least 4 hours or overnight.

3 Barbecue the chicken over glowing coals, or place on a rack over a baking pan and bake at 400°F for about 20–30 minutes, or until the chicken is cooked and golden brown. Turn the pieces occasionally and brush them with the marinade.

4 Garnish with lime wedges and finely sliced red chilies.

Duck and Ginger Chop Suey

Chicken can also be used in this recipe, but duck gives a richer contrast of flavors.

INGREDIENTS

Serves 4

2 duck breasts, about 6 ounces each
3 tablespoons sunflower oil
1 small egg, lightly beaten
1 garlic clove
6 ounces bean sprouts
2 slices fresh ginger, cut into thin sticks
2 teaspoons oyster sauce
2 scallions, cut into thin sticks
salt and freshly ground black pepper

For the marinade

1 tablespoon honey
2 teaspoons Chinese rice wine or
  dry sherry
2 teaspoons light soy sauce
2 teaspoons dark soy sauce

1 Remove the fat and skin from the duck, cut the breasts into strips and place in a bowl. To make the marinade, combine all the marinade ingredients together, pour over the duck, cover, and marinate overnight in the refrigerator.

2 The next day, make the omelet. Heat a small frying pan and add 1 tablespoon of the oil. When the oil is hot, pour in the egg and swirl around to make an omelet. Once cooked, leave it to cool and then cut into strips. Drain the duck and discard the marinade.

3 Bruise the garlic with the flat side of a knife. Heat 2 teaspoons of the oil in a preheated wok. When the oil is hot, add the garlic and fry for 30 seconds, pressing it to release the flavor. Discard. Add the bean sprouts with seasoning and stir-fry for 30 seconds. Transfer to a heated dish, draining off any liquid.

4 Heat the remaining oil in a preheated wok. When the oil is hot, stir-fry the duck for 3 minutes, until cooked. Add the ginger and oyster sauce and stir-fry for another 2 minutes. Add the bean sprouts, egg strips and scallions, stir-fry briefly and serve.

Mandarin Sesame Duck

Duck is a high-fat meat, but it is possible to get rid of a considerable proportion of the fat by cooking it in this way. (If you remove the skin completely, the meat can be dry.) For a special occasion, duck breasts are an excellent choice, but they are more expensive than legs.

INGREDIENTS

Serves 4

4 duck legs or boneless breasts
2 tablespoons light soy sauce
3 tablespoons honey
1 tablespoon sesame seeds
4 mandarin oranges
1 teaspoon cornstarch
salt and freshly ground black pepper
mixed vegetables, to serve

1 Prick the duck skin all over. If using breasts, slash the skin diagonally at intervals with a small, sharp knife.

2 Place the duck on a rack in a roasting pan and roast for 1 hour in a preheated oven at 350°F. Combine 1 tablespoon of the soy sauce with 2 tablespoons of the honey and brush over the duck. Sprinkle with sesame seeds. Roast for 15–20 minutes, or until golden brown.

3 Meanwhile, grate the rind from one mandarin and squeeze the juice from that one plus one other. Combine the rind, juice and cornstarch, then stir in the remaining soy sauce and honey. Heat, stirring, until thickened and clear. Season to taste. Peel and slice the remaining mandarins. Serve the duck with the mandarin slices, sauce and mixed vegetables.

Peking Duck

This has to be the *pièce de résistance* of any Chinese banquet. It is not too difficult to prepare and cook at home—the secret is to use duckling with a low fat content. Also, make sure that the skin of the duck is absolutely dry before you start to cook—the drier the skin, the crispier the duck.

INGREDIENTS

Serves 6–8

5–5¼ pounds oven-ready duckling
2 tablespoons honey, dissolved in
⅔ cup warm water

For the duck sauce

2 tablespoons sesame oil
6–8 tablespoons yellow bean sauce,
crushed
2–3 tablespoons light brown sugar

To serve

20–24 Thin Pancakes
6–8 scallions, thinly shredded
½ cucumber, thinly shredded

COOK'S TIP

If preferred, serve Peking Duck with plum sauce in place of the duck sauce. Plum sauce is available from Asian stores and larger supermarkets. Duck sauce can also be bought ready-made.

1 Remove any feather studs and any lumps of fat from inside the vent of the duck. Plunge the duck into a saucepan of boiling water for 2–3 minutes to seal the pores. This will make the skin airtight, thus preventing the fat from escaping during cooking. Remove the duck and drain well, then dry thoroughly.

2 Brush the duck all over with the dissolved honey, then hang the bird up in a cool place for at least 4–5 hours.

3 Place the duck, breast side up, on a rack in a roasting pan and cook in a preheated oven at 400°F for 1½–1¾ hours without either basting or turning.

4 Meanwhile, make the duck sauce. Heat the sesame oil in a small saucepan. Add the crushed yellow bean sauce and the light brown sugar. Stir until smooth and allow to cool.

5 To serve, peel off the crispy duck skin in small slices using a sharp carving knife or cleaver, then carve the juicy meat in thin strips. Arrange the skin and meat on separate serving plates.

6 Open a pancake on each plate and spread about 1 teaspoon of the chosen sauce in the middle, with a few strips of shredded scallion and cucumber. Top with 2–3 slices each of duck skin and meat. Roll up and eat.

Crispy and Aromatic Duck

Because this dish is often served with pancakes, scallions, cucumber and duck sauce, many people mistakenly think this is Peking Duck. This recipe, however, uses quite a different cooking method. The result is just as crispy but the delightful aroma makes this dish particularly distinctive. Plum sauce may be substituted for the duck sauce.

INGREDIENTS

Serves 6–8
4–5¼ pounds oven-ready duckling
2 teaspoons salt
5–6 whole star anise
1 tablespoon Szechuan peppercorns
1 teaspoon cloves
2–3 cinnamon sticks
3–4 scallions
3–4 slices fresh ginger, unpeeled
5–6 tablespoons Chinese rice wine or
    dry sherry
vegetable oil, for deep-frying

To serve
lettuce leaves
20–24 Thin Pancakes
½ cup duck sauce
6–8 scallions, cut into fine strips
½ cucumber, cut into fine strips

1 Remove the wings from the duck. Split the body in half down the length of the backbone.

2 Rub salt all over the two duck halves, taking care to rub it in well.

3 Place the duck in a dish with the star anise, peppercorns, cloves, cinnamon, scallions, ginger and rice wine or dry sherry and marinate for at least 4–6 hours.

4 Place the duck with the marinade in a steamer positioned in a wok partly filled with boiling water and steam vigorously for 3–4 hours (longer if possible). Remove the duck from the cooking liquid and let cool for at least 5–6 hours. The duck must be completely cool and dry or the skin will not become crispy.

5 Heat the oil in a preheated wok until smoking, place the duck pieces in the oil, skin side down, and deep-fry for 5–6 minutes, or until crisp and brown, turning just once at the very last moment.

6 Remove, drain, take the meat off the bone and place on a bed of lettuce leaves. To serve, wrap a portion of duck in each pancake with a little sauce, scallions and cucumber. Eat with your fingers.

Chili Duck with Crab and Cashew Sauce

This spicy dish would be delicious served with Thai rice, which is slightly aromatic.

INGREDIENTS

Serves 4–6

6 pounds duck
5 cups water
2 kaffir lime leaves
1½ teaspoons salt
2–3 small fresh red chilies, seeded and
    finely chopped
5 teaspoons sugar
2 tablespoons coriander seeds
1 teaspoon caraway seeds
1 cup raw cashews, chopped
3-inch piece lemongrass
1-inch piece galangal or fresh ginger,
    finely chopped
2 garlic cloves, crushed
4 shallots or 1 medium onion, finely
    chopped
¾-inch square shrimp paste
1 ounce cilantro white root or stem,
    finely chopped
6 ounces frozen white crabmeat,
    thawed
2 ounces creamed coconut
1 small bunch fresh cilantro, chopped,
    to garnish
boiled rice, to serve

1 Remove the legs from the duck, separate the thighs from the drumsticks and chop each thigh and drumstick into two pieces. Trim away the lower half of the duck with kitchen scissors. Cut the breast piece in half down the middle, then chop each half into four pieces.

2 Put the duck flesh and bones in a large saucepan and cover with the water. Add the lime leaves and 1 teaspoon of the salt, bring to a boil and simmer for 30–45 minutes, or until the meat is tender. Discard the duck bones. Skim off the fat from the broth and set the broth aside.

3 Grind together the chilies, sugar and remaining salt in a mortar with a pestle or in a food processor. Dry-fry the coriander seeds, caraway seeds and cashews in a preheated wok for 1–2 minutes to release their flavor. Add the seeds and nuts to the chili mixture, together with the lemongrass, galangal or ginger, garlic and shallots or onion and reduce to a smooth paste. Add the shrimp paste and cilantro root or stem and mix well.

4 Add 1 cup of the reserved broth and blend to make a thin paste.

5 Pour the spice mixture into the saucepan with the duck and mix thoroughly. Bring to a boil, lower the heat and simmer for 20–25 minutes.

6 Add the crabmeat and creamed coconut and simmer briefly to heat through. Turn out onto a warmed serving dish, garnish with the chopped cilantro and accompany with boiled rice.

Balinese Spiced Duck

There is a delightful hotel on the beach at Sanur which cooks this delicious duck dish perfectly.

INGREDIENTS

Serves 4
8 duck portions, fat trimmed
 and reserved
¹/₄ cup dried coconut
³/₄ cup coconut milk
salt and freshly ground black pepper
Deep-fried Onions and salad leaves or
 fresh herb sprigs, to garnish

For the spice paste
1 small onion or 4–6 shallots, sliced
2 garlic cloves, sliced
½ inch fresh ginger root, peeled
 and sliced
½ inch fresh *laos*, peeled and sliced
1 inch fresh turmeric or
 ½ teaspoon ground turmeric
1–2 red chilies, seeded and sliced
4 macadamia nuts or 8 almonds
1 teaspoon coriander seeds, dry-fried

1 Place the duck fat trimmings in a heated frying pan, and render the fat over a low heat. Reserve the fat.

2 Dry-fry the dried coconut in a preheated pan until crisp and brown in color.

3 To make the spice paste, blend the onion or shallots, garlic, ginger, *laos*, fresh or ground turmeric, chilies, nuts and coriander seeds to a paste in a food processor or with a mortar and pestle.

4 Spread the spice paste over the duck portions and let marinate in a cool place for 3–4 hours. Preheat the oven to 325°F. Shake off and reserve the spice paste, then transfer the duck breasts to an oiled roasting pan. Cover with a double layer of foil and cook the duck breasts in the preheated oven for 2 hours.

5 Turn the oven temperature up to 375°F. Heat the reserved duck fat in a pan, add the spice paste and fry for 1–2 minutes. Stir in the coconut milk and simmer for 2 minutes. Discard the duck juices then cover the duck with the spice mixture and sprinkle with the toasted coconut. Cook in the oven for 20–30 minutes.

6 Arrange the duck on a warm serving platter and sprinkle with the Deep-fried Onions. Season to taste and serve with the salad leaves or fresh herb sprigs of your choice.

Duck with Chinese Mushrooms and Ginger

Ducks are often seen, comically herded in single file, along the water channels between the rice paddies throughout the country. The substantial Chinese population in Indonesia is particularly fond of duck and the delicious ingredients in this recipe give it an oriental flavor.

INGREDIENTS

Serves 4

5½-pound duck
1 teaspoon sugar
¼ cup light soy sauce
2 garlic cloves, crushed
8 dried Chinese mushrooms, soaked in 1½ cups warm water for 15 minutes
1 onion, sliced
2 inches fresh ginger root, sliced and cut in matchsticks
7 ounces baby corn
3–4 scallions, white bulbs left whole, green tops sliced
1–2 tablespoons cornstarch, mixed to a paste with 4 tablespoons water
salt and freshly ground black pepper
boiled rice, to serve

1 Cut the duck along the breast, open it up and cut along each side of the backbone. Use the backbone, wings and giblets to make a stock, to use later in the recipe. Any trimmings of fat can be rendered in a frying pan, to use later in the recipe. Cut each leg and each breast in half. Place in a bowl, rub with the sugar and then pour over the soy sauce and garlic.

2 Strain the mushrooms, reserving the soaking liquid. Trim and discard the stalks.

3 Fry the onion and ginger in the duck fat, in a frying pan, until they give off a good aroma. Push to one side. Lift the duck pieces out of the soy sauce and fry them until browned. Add the mushrooms and reserved liquid.

4 Add 2½ cups of the duck stock or water to the browned duck pieces. Season, cover and cook over a gentle heat for about 1 hour, or until the duck is tender.

5 Add the corn and the white part of the scallions and cook for another 10 minutes. Remove from the heat and add the corn paste. Return to the heat and bring to a boil, stirring. Cook for about 1 minute until glossy. Sprinkle with the sliced scallion tops and serve with boiled rice.

VARIATION

Replace the corn with chopped celery and slices of drained, canned water chestnuts.

Sweet-and-sour Duck with Mango

Mango adds natural sweetness to this colorful stir-fry. Crispy deep-fried noodles make the perfect accompaniment.

INGREDIENTS

Serves 4

3 duck breasts (8–12 ounces total)
3 tablespoons dark soy sauce
1 tablespoon Chinese rice wine or
    dry sherry
1 teaspoon sesame oil
1 teaspoon five-spice powder
1 tablespoon brown sugar
2 teaspoons cornstarch
3 tablespoons Chinese rice vinegar
1 tablespoon ketchup
1 mango, not too ripe
3 baby eggplants
1 red onion
1 carrot
¼ cup peanut oil
1 garlic clove, sliced
1-inch piece fresh ginger, cut into shreds
3 ounces sugar-snap peas

1 Thinly slice the duck breasts and place in a bowl. Combine 1 tablespoon of the soy sauce with the rice wine or sherry, sesame oil and five-spice powder. Pour it over the duck, cover and let marinate for 1–2 hours. In a separate bowl, blend the sugar, cornstarch, rice vinegar, ketchup and remaining soy sauce. Set aside.

2 Peel the mango, slice the flesh from the pit, then cut into thick strips. Slice the eggplants, onion and carrot into similar-size pieces.

3 Heat a wok until hot, add 2 tablespoons of the oil and swirl it around. Drain the duck, reserving the marinade. Stir-fry the duck slices over high heat until the fat is crisp and golden. Remove and keep warm. Add 1 tablespoon of the oil to the wok and stir-fry the eggplants for 3 minutes until golden.

4 Add the remaining oil and fry the onion, garlic, ginger and carrot for 2–3 minutes, then add the sugar-snap peas and stir-fry for another 2 minutes.

5 Add the mango and return the duck with the sauce and reserved marinade to the wok. Cook, stirring, until the sauce thickens slightly. Serve immediately.

COOK'S TIP

If baby eggplants are not available, use the smallest eggplants you can find. Sprinkle with salt after slicing and set aside in a colander for the bitter juices to drain off. Rinse thoroughly before cooking.

Stir-fried Turkey with Broccoli and Mushrooms

This is a very easy, tasty supper dish that works well with chicken too.

INGREDIENTS

Serves 4

4 ounces broccoli florets
4 scallions
1 teaspoon cornstarch
3 tablespoons oyster sauce
1 tablespoon dark soy sauce
1/2 cup chicken stock
2 teaspoons lemon juice
3 tablespoons peanut oil
1 pound turkey cutlets, cut into
   1/4 x 2-inch strips
1 small onion, chopped
2 garlic cloves, crushed
2 teaspoons grated fresh ginger
1 cup fresh shiitake mushrooms, sliced
1 cup baby corn, halved lengthwise
1 tablespoon sesame oil
salt and ground black pepper
egg noodles, to serve

1 Divide the broccoli florets into smaller sprigs and cut the stalks into thin diagonal slices.

2 Finely chop the white parts of the scallions and slice the green parts into thin shreds.

3 In a bowl, combine the cornstarch, oyster sauce, soy sauce, stock and lemon juice. Set aside.

4 Heat 2 tablespoons of the peanut oil in a preheated wok. Add the turkey and stir-fry for 2 minutes, until golden and crisp at the edges. Remove from the wok and keep warm.

5 Add the remaining peanut oil to the wok and stir-fry the chopped onion, garlic and ginger over medium heat for about 1 minute. Increase the heat to high, add the broccoli, mushrooms and corn and stir-fry for 2 minutes.

6 Return the turkey to the wok, then add the sauce with the chopped scallion and seasoning. Cook, stirring, for about 1 minute, until the sauce has thickened. Stir in the sesame oil. Serve immediately on a bed of egg noodles with the finely shredded scallion scattered on top.

COOK'S TIP

Cook fresh egg noodles in salted boiling water, stirring occasionally to prevent them from sticking. They are ready within a few minutes. Follow the package instructions for cooking dried egg noodles.

Stir-fried Turkey with Snow Peas

Turkey is often a rather disappointing meat with a bland flavor. Here it is enlivened with a delicious marinade and combined with crunchy nuts to provide contrasting textures.

INGREDIENTS

Serves 4

2 tablespoons sesame oil
6 tablespoons lemon juice
1 garlic clove, crushed
½-inch piece fresh ginger, grated
1 teaspoon honey
1 pound turkey fillets, skinned and cut into strips
4 ounces snow peas
2 tablespoons peanut oil
2 ounces cashews
6 scallions, cut into strips
1 can (8 ounces) water chestnuts, drained and thinly sliced
salt
saffron rice, to serve

3 Drain the marinade from the turkey strips and reserve the marinade. Heat the peanut oil in a preheated wok or large frying pan, add the cashews and stir-fry for 1–2 minutes, or until golden brown. Remove the cashews from the wok or frying pan using a slotted spoon, and set aside.

4 Add the turkey to the wok or frying pan and stir-fry for 3–4 minutes, or until golden brown. Add the scallions, snow peas, water chestnuts and reserved marinade. Cook for a few minutes, until the turkey is tender and the sauce is bubbling and hot. Stir in the cashews and serve with saffron rice.

1 Combine the sesame oil, lemon juice, garlic, ginger and honey in a shallow, nonmetallic dish. Add the turkey and mix well. Cover and marinate for 3–4 hours.

2 Blanch the snow peas in boiling salted water for 1 minute. Drain, refresh under cold running water and set aside.

Honey-glazed Quail with a Five-Spice Marinade

Although the quail is a relatively small bird—four to five ounces—it is surprisingly meaty. One bird is usually sufficient for one serving.

INGREDIENTS

Serves 4

4 oven-ready quail
2 pieces star anise
2 teaspoons ground cinnamon
2 teaspoons fennel seeds
2 teaspoons ground Szechuan or
  Chinese pepper
pinch of ground cloves
1 small onion, finely chopped
1 garlic clove, crushed
4 tablespoons honey
2 tablespoons dark soy sauce
2 scallions, roughly chopped, finely
  grated rind of 1 mandarin orange or
  satsuma and radish and carrot
  "flowers," to garnish
banana leaves, to serve

1 Remove the backbones from the quail by cutting down either side with a pair of kitchen scissors.

2 Flatten the birds with the palm of your hand and secure each one with two bamboo skewers.

3 Grind together the star anise, cinnamon, fennel seeds, pepper and cloves in a mortar with a pestle. Add the onion, garlic, honey and soy sauce and mix well.

4 Place the quail on a flat dish, cover with the spice mixture and marinate for at least 8 hours.

5 Cook the quail under a preheated broiler or on a grill for 7–8 minutes on each side, basting from time to time with the marinade.

6 Arrange the quail on a bed of banana leaves and garnish with the scallions, orange or satsuma rind and radish and carrot "flowers."

VEGETABLES

Unusual ways of preparing familiar vegetables, as well as dishes using more exotic ingredients, can spice up Western grills and roasts or form part of a Chinese meal. Stir-frying is an especially good way of cooking vegetables without losing flavor, texture, color and valuable nutrients. There are recipes for all tastes: palate-tingling Bok Choi with Lime Dressing, Cooked Vegetable Gado-Gado with its colorful, crunchy mix of ingredients, Chinese Garlic Mushrooms, the perfect vegetarian snack, and even Chinese-style Brussels sprouts!

Stir-fried Bok Choy with Mushrooms

You can use fresh button mushrooms in this recipe if you prefer them, or if fresh or canned straw mushrooms are not available.

INGREDIENTS

Serves 4

1½ cups fresh straw mushrooms or 12-ounce can straw mushrooms, drained
¼ cup vegetable oil
1 head bok choy, cut into strips
1 teaspoon salt
1 teaspoon light brown sugar
1 tablespoon cornstarch paste
½ cup milk

1 Cut the mushrooms in half lengthwise. Heat half the oil, stir-fry the bok choy for 2 minutes, then add half the salt and half the sugar. Stir for 1 minute.

2 Transfer the bok choy to a warm serving dish. Add the mushrooms to the wok and stir-fry for 1 minute. Add the remaining salt and sugar, cook for 1 minute, then thicken with the cornstarch paste and milk. Serve with the bok choy.

COOK'S TIP

The Chinese approach to cooking illustrates the same overall desire for harmony and balance that characterizes their ancient philosophy. Recipes for stir-fried vegetables are not simply an arbitrary combination of whatever is at hand—they should balance and complement each other in both color and texture. The delicious slipperiness of straw mushrooms complements the crunchier texture of the bok choy, so it is best to use them if at all possible. Canned straw mushrooms are available at Asian food stores. Do not overcook, or the harmony and balance will be lost.

Stir-fried Bean Sprouts

This is an easy way to cook up some tasty bean sprouts in a wok. It is not necessary to trim them. Simply rinse in a bowl of cold water and discard any husks that float to the surface.

INGREDIENTS

Serves 4
2–3 scallions
3 tablespoons vegetable oil
2 cups bean sprouts
1 teaspoon salt
½ teaspoon light brown sugar
few drops of sesame oil (optional)

1 Cut the scallions into short sections about the same length as the bean sprouts.

2 Heat the oil in a wok and stir-fry the bean sprouts and scallions for about 1 minute. Add the salt and sugar and continue stirring for 1 minute. Sprinkle with the sesame oil, if using, and serve. Do not overcook, or the bean sprouts will become soggy.

COOK'S TIP

Fresh and canned bean sprouts are readily available, but they can easily be grown at home for a constant and completely fresh supply. Scatter mung beans on several layers of damp paper towels on a small plate. Keep moist in a fairly warm place, and the beans will sprout in a few days.

Braised Chinese Vegetables

The original recipe calls for no fewer than 18 different ingredients to represent the 18 Buddhas (*lo han*). Later, this was reduced to eight, but nowadays anything between four and six items is regarded as quite sufficient to put in a wok.

INGREDIENTS

Serves 4

¼ cup dried Chinese mushrooms
1 cup straw mushrooms
½ cup sliced bamboo shoots, drained
2 ounces snow peas
3-inch block fresh tofu
6 ounces bok choy leaves
3–4 tablespoons vegetable oil
1 teaspoon salt
½ teaspoon light brown sugar
1 tablespoon light soy sauce
few drops of sesame oil

1 Soak the Chinese mushrooms in warm water for 30 minutes, then rinse and discard the hard stalks, if any. Cut the straw mushrooms in half lengthwise if they are large; keep them whole if they are small. Rinse and drain the bamboo-shoot slices. Trim the snow peas. Cut the tofu into about 12 small pieces. Cut the bok choy into small pieces about the same size as the snow peas.

2 Harden the tofu pieces by placing them in a wok of boiling water for about 2 minutes. Remove and drain.

3 Discard the water and heat the oil in the wok, a saucepan or a flameproof casserole. Lightly brown the tofu pieces on both sides. Remove with a slotted spoon and keep warm.

4 Stir-fry all the vegetables in the wok for 1½ minutes, then add the tofu, salt, sugar and soy sauce. Continue stirring for 1 minute, then cover and braise for 2–3 minutes. Sprinkle with sesame oil and serve.

Eggplant in Spicy Sauce

Eggplant is given a royal treatment in this recipe, where it is stir-fried with seasonings more commonly associated with fish cooking.

INGREDIENTS

Serves 4

1 pound eggplants
3–4 dried red chilies, soaked in water
  for 10 minutes
vegetable oil, for deep-frying
1 garlic clove, finely chopped
1 teaspoon finely chopped fresh ginger
1 teaspoon finely chopped scallion,
  white part only
4 ounces lean pork, thinly shredded
  (optional)
1 tablespoon light soy sauce
1 tablespoon light brown sugar
1 tablespoon chili bean sauce
1 tablespoon Chinese rice wine or
  dry sherry
1 tablespoon rice vinegar
2 teaspoons cornstarch paste,
1 teaspoon finely chopped scallions,
  green part only, to garnish
few drops of sesame oil

1 Cut the eggplants into short strips the size of french fries—the skin can either be peeled off or left on, whichever you prefer. Cut the soaked red chilies into two or three small pieces and discard the seeds.

2 Heat the oil in a preheated wok and deep-fry the eggplant strips for 3–4 minutes or until limp. Remove and drain.

3 Pour off the excess oil, leaving about 1 tablespoon in the wok. Add the garlic, ginger, white scallions and chilies, stir a few times, then add the pork, if using. Stir-fry the meat for about 1 minute or until it becomes pale, almost white, in color. Add all the seasonings, then increase the heat and bring the mixture to a boil.

4 Add the eggplants to the wok, blend well and braise for 30–40 seconds, then thicken the sauce with the cornstarch paste, stirring until smooth. Garnish with the green scallions and sprinkle with sesame oil.

COOK'S TIP

Soaking dried chilies in water will reduce their spicy flavor. If you prefer a milder chili taste, soak for longer than the recommended 10 minutes.

Szechuan Spicy Tofu

The meat used in this popular wok recipe can be omitted to create a purely vegetarian dish, if you prefer.

INGREDIENTS

Serves 4

3-inch block fresh tofu
1 leek
3 tablespoons vegetable oil
4 ounces ground beef
1 tablespoon black bean sauce
1 tablespoon light soy sauce
1 teaspoon chili bean sauce
1 tablespoon Chinese rice wine or
   dry sherry
3–4 tablespoons stock or water
2 teaspoons cornstarch paste
ground Szechuan peppercorns, to taste
few drops of sesame oil

1 Cut the tofu into ½-inch square cubes. Fill a wok with boiling water, add the tofu cubes and bring back to a boil. Cook for 2–3 minutes to harden. Remove and drain. Cut the leek into short sections.

2 Empty the wok. Preheat and add the oil. When hot, stir-fry the ground beef until the color changes, then add the leek and black bean sauce. Add the tofu with the soy sauce, chili bean sauce and wine or sherry. Stir gently for 1 minute.

3 Add the stock or water, bring to a boil and braise for 2-3 minutes.

4 Stir in the cornstarch paste and cook, stirring, until thickened. Season with ground Szechuan pepper, sprinkle with the sesame oil and serve immediately.

Karahi Shredded Cabbage with Cumin

This cabbage is only lightly spiced and makes a good accompaniment to most other Indian dishes.

INGREDIENTS

Serves 4
1 tablespoon corn oil
4 tablespoons butter
½ teaspoon crushed coriander seeds
½ teaspoon white cumin seeds
6 dried red chilies
1 small Savoy cabbage, shredded
12 snow peas
3 fresh red chilies, seeded and sliced
12 ears baby corn
salt
1 ounce slivered almonds, toasted, and
    1 tablespoon chopped fresh cilantro
    (optional), to garnish

1 Heat the oil and butter in a preheated wok and, when the butter has melted, add the crushed coriander seeds, cumin seeds and dried red chilies.

2 Add the shredded cabbage and snow peas to the wok and stir-fry for about 5 minutes.

3 Add the fresh red chilies, baby corn and salt and stir-fry for a further 3 minutes.

4 Garnish the cabbage with toasted almonds and fresh cilantro, if using, and serve hot.

—— COOK'S TIP ——

Unlike many parts of the Indian sub-continent, Pakistan, where this dish originates, is generally a meat-eating nation. Vegetable dishes are, therefore, usually cooked as side dishes, rather than as a main dish, much in the way they are in the West. Consequently, this delicious, slightly spicy treatment of cabbage would go as well with a traditional Western roast as it would with an Indian curry or stir-fry.

Spicy Indian Potatoes

Potatoes often are an integral part of an Indian meal. Rice is not always served, or it may be served in addition to potatoes, which are frequently treated as just another vegetable rather than as a staple.

INGREDIENTS

Serves 4

3 tablespoons corn oil
½ teaspoon white cumin seeds
3 curry leaves
1 teaspoon crushed dried red chilies
½ teaspoon mixed onion, mustard and
  fenugreek seeds
½ teaspoon fennel seeds
3 garlic cloves, thinly sliced
½ teaspoon shredded fresh ginger
2 medium onions, sliced
6 new potatoes, cut into ¼-inch slices
1 tablespoon chopped fresh cilantro
1 fresh red chili, seeded and sliced
1 fresh green chili, seeded and sliced

1 Heat the oil in a preheated wok. When hot, lower the heat and add the cumin seeds, curry leaves, dried red chilies, onion, mustard and fenugreek seeds, fennel seeds, garlic and ginger. Stir-fry for about 1 minute, then add the onions and fry for 5 minutes or until the onions are golden brown.

2 Add the potatoes, cilantro and fresh red and green chilies to the wok and mix well. Cover tightly with a lid or foil, making sure the foil does not touch the food. Cook over very low heat for about 7 minutes or until the potatoes are tender.

3 Remove the lid or foil and serve in the traditional manner—straight from the pot.

Okra with Green Mango and Lentils

If you like okra, you will love this tangy and spicy dish.

INGREDIENTS

Serves 4

½ cup yellow lentils
3 tablespoons corn oil
½ teaspoon onion seeds
2 medium onions, sliced
½ teaspoon ground fenugreek
1 teaspoon grated fresh ginger
1 teaspoon crushed garlic
1½ teaspoon chili powder
¼ teaspoon ground turmeric
1 teaspoon ground coriander
1 unripe mango, peeled and pitted
1 pound okra, chopped
2 fresh red chilies, seeded and sliced
2 tablespoons chopped fresh cilantro
1 tomato, sliced

1 Wash the lentils thoroughly and put in a saucepan with just enough water to cover. Bring to a boil and cook until soft but not mushy. Drain and set aside.

2 Heat the oil in a preheated wok. Add the onion seeds and fry until they begin to pop. Add the onions and fry until they are golden brown. Lower the heat and add the ground fenugreek, ginger, garlic, chili powder, ground turmeric and ground coriander.

3 Slice the mango, then add with the okra. Stir well and add the red chilies and fresh cilantro. Stir-fry for about 3 minutes or until the okra is well cooked. Stir in the cooked lentils and sliced tomato, then cook for another 3 minutes. Serve immediately.

Crispy Cabbage

This makes a wonderful accompaniment to meat or vegetable dishes—just a couple spoonfuls add a crunchy texture to a meal. It goes especially well with shrimp dishes.

INGREDIENTS

Serves 4
4 juniper berries
1 large Savoy cabbage
¼ cup vegetable oil
1 clove garlic, crushed
1 teaspoon superfine sugar
1 teaspoon salt

1 Finely crush the juniper berries in a mortar with a pestle.

2 Finely shred the cabbage.

3 Heat a wok, then add the oil. When the oil is hot, stir-fry the garlic for 1 minute. Add the cabbage and stir-fry for 3–4 minutes, until crispy. Remove from the wok and pat dry with paper towels.

4 Reheat the wok and return the cabbage to it. Add the sugar, salt and crushed juniper berries and toss the cabbage until well coated and thoroughly mixed with the flavorings. Serve either hot or cold.

Stir-fried Greens

Quail's eggs look very attractive in *Chah Kang Kung*, but you can substitute some baby corn, halved at an angle.

INGREDIENTS

Serves 4

2 bunches spinach or chard or 1 head Chinese cabbage
3 garlic cloves, crushed
2 inches fresh ginger root, peeled and cut in matchsticks
3–4 tablespoons peanut oil
14 ounces boneless, skinless chicken breast, or pork loin, or a mixture of both, very finely sliced
12 quail's eggs, hard-boiled and shelled
1 fresh red chili, seeded and shredded
2–3 tablespoons oyster sauce
1 tablespoon brown sugar
2 teaspoons cornstarch, mixed with ¼ cup cold water
salt

COOK'S TIP

As with all stir-fries, don't start cooking until you have prepared all the ingredients and arranged them to hand. Cut everything into small, even-size pieces so the food can be cooked very quickly and all the colors and flavors preserved.

1 Wash the chosen leaves well and shake them dry. Strip the tender leaves from the stems and tear them into pieces. Discard the lower, tougher part of the stems and slice the remainder evenly.

2 Fry the garlic and ginger in the hot oil, without browning, for a minute. Add the chicken and/or pork and keep stirring it in the wok until the meat changes color. When the meat looks cooked, add the sliced stems first and cook them quickly; then add the torn leaves, quail's eggs and chili. Spoon in the oyster sauce and a little boiling water, if necessary. Cover and cook for 1–2 minutes only.

3 Remove the lid, stir and add sugar and salt to taste. Stir in the cornstarch and water mixture and toss thoroughly. Cook until the mixture is well coated in a glossy sauce.

4 Serve immediately, while still very hot and the colors are bright and glowingly jewel-like.

Water Spinach with Brown Bean Sauce

Water spinach, often known as Siamese watercress, is a green vegetable with arrowhead-shaped leaves. If you can't find it, use spinach, watercress, *bok choy* or even broccoli, and adjust the cooking time accordingly. There are excellent variations to this recipe using black bean sauce, instead of brown bean sauce.

INGREDIENTS

Serves 4–6
1 bunch water spinach, about
  2¼ pounds in weight
3 tablespoons vegetable oil
1 tablespoon chopped garlic
1 tablespoon brown bean sauce
2 tablespoons fish sauce
1 tablespoon sugar
freshly ground black pepper

1 Trim and discard the bottom coarse, woody end of the water spinach. Cut the remaining part into 2-inch lengths, keeping the leaves separate from the stems.

2 Heat the oil in a wok or large frying pan. When it starts to smoke, add the chopped garlic and toss for 10 seconds.

3 Add the stem part of the water spinach, let it sizzle and cook for 1 minute, then add the leafy parts.

4 Stir in the brown bean sauce, fish sauce, sugar and pepper. Toss and turn over the spinach until it begins to wilt, about 3–4 minutes. Transfer to a serving dish and serve immediately.

Mixed Vegetables in Coconut Milk

A most delicious way of cooking vegetables. If you don't like highly spiced food, use fewer red chili peppers.

INGREDIENTS

Serves 4–6
1 pound mixed vegetables, such as
  eggplant, baby canned corn, carrots,
  snake beans and patty pan squash
8 red chilies, seeded
2 lemongrass stalks, chopped
4 kaffir lime leaves, torn
2 tablespoons vegetable oil
1 cup unsweetened coconut milk
2 tablespoons fish sauce
a pinch of salt
15–20 Thai basil leaves, to garnish

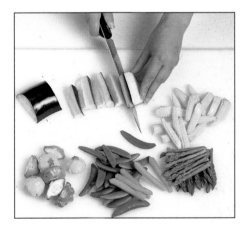

1 Cut the vegetables into similar size shapes using a sharp knife.

2 Put the red chilies, lemongrass and kaffir lime leaves in a mortar and grind together with a pestle.

3 Heat the oil in a wok or large deep frying pan. Add the chili mixture and fry for 2–3 minutes.

4 Stir in the coconut milk and bring to a boil. Add the vegetables and cook for about 5 minutes, or until they are tender. Season with the fish sauce and salt, and garnish with basil leaves.

Szechuan Eggplants

INGREDIENTS

Serves 4

2 small eggplants
1 teaspoon salt
3 dried red chilies
peanut oil, for deep-frying
3–4 garlic cloves, finely chopped
½-inch piece fresh ginger, finely
  chopped
4 scallions, chopped and white and
  green parts separated
1 tablespoon Chinese rice wine or
  dry sherry
1 tablespoon light soy sauce
1 teaspoon sugar
¼ teaspoon ground roasted
  Szechuan peppercorns
1 tablespoon rice vinegar
1 teaspoon sesame oil

1 Trim the eggplants and cut into strips about 1½ inches wide and 3 inches long. Place the eggplants in a colander and sprinkle with the salt. Let sit for 30 minutes, then rinse them thoroughly under cold running water. Pat dry with paper towels.

2 Meanwhile, soak the chilies in warm water for 15 minutes. Drain, then cut each chili into three or four pieces, discarding the seeds.

3 Half-fill a wok with oil and heat to 350°F. Deep-fry the eggplants, in batches if necessary, until golden brown. Drain on paper towels. Pour off most of the oil from the wok. Reheat the oil and add the garlic, ginger and white part of the scallions.

4 Stir-fry for 30 seconds. Add the eggplants and toss, then add the wine or sherry, soy sauce, sugar, ground peppercorns and vinegar. Stir-fry for 1–2 minutes. Sprinkle on the sesame oil and scallion greens.

Root Vegetables with Spiced Salt

All kinds of root vegetables can be finely sliced and deep fried to make "chips." Serve as an accompaniment to an Asian-style meal or simply by themselves as much tastier nibbles than store-bought snacks with predinner drinks.

INGREDIENTS

Serves 4–6
1 carrot
2 parsnips
2 raw beets
1 sweet potato
peanut oil, for deep-frying
¼ teaspoon chili powder
1 teaspoon sea salt flakes

1 Peel the carrot, parsnips, beets and sweet potato. Slice the carrot and parsnips into long, thin ribbons. Cut the beets and sweet potato into thin rounds. Pat dry with paper towels.

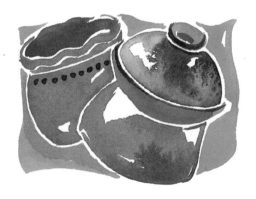

2 Half-fill a wok with oil and heat to 350°F. Add the vegetable slices in batches and deep-fry for 2–3 minutes, until golden and crisp. Remove and drain on paper towels.

3 Place the chili powder and sea salt flakes in a mortar and grind them together with a pestle to form a coarse powder.

4 Pile the vegetable "chips" on a serving plate and sprinkle with the spiced salt.

COOK'S TIP

To save time, you can slice the vegetables using a mandoline, blender or food processor with a thin slicing disc attached.

Spiced Cauliflower Braise

A delicious vegetable stew, known as *Sambal Kol Kembang,* which combines coconut milk with spices and is perfect as a vegetarian main course or as part of a buffet.

INGREDIENTS

Serves 4

1 cauliflower
2 medium or 1 large tomato(es)
1 onion, chopped
2 garlic cloves, crushed
1 fresh green chili, seeded
½ tablespoon ground turmeric
½ teaspoon shrimp paste
2 tablespoons sunflower oil
14-fluid ounce can coconut milk
1 cup water
1 teaspoon sugar
1 teaspoon tamarind pulp, soaked in
   3 tablespoons warm water
salt

1 Trim the stalk from the cauliflower and divide into tiny florets. Skin the tomato(es) if liked. Chop the flesh into ½–1-inch pieces.

2 Grind the chopped onion, garlic, green chili, ground turmeric and shrimp paste together to a paste in a food processor or with a mortar and pestle. Heat the sunflower oil in a wok or large frying pan and fry the spice paste to bring out the aromatic flavors, without allowing it to brown.

3 Add the cauliflower florets and toss well to coat in the spices. Stir in the coconut milk, water, sugar and salt to taste. Simmer for 5 minutes. Strain the tamarind and reserve the juice.

4 Add the tamarind juice and chopped tomatoes to the pan then cook for 2–3 minutes only. Taste for check the seasoning and serve.

Spicy Scrambled Eggs

This is a lovely way to liven up scrambled eggs. When making *Orak Arik*, prepare all the ingredients ahead so that the vegetables retain all their crunch and color.

INGREDIENTS

Serves 4

2 tablespoons sunflower oil
1 onion, finely sliced
8 ounces Chinese cabbage, finely sliced
   or cut in diamonds
7-ounce can corn kernels
1 small fresh red chili, seeded and finely
   sliced (optional)
2 tablespoons water
2 eggs, beaten
salt and freshly ground black pepper
Deep-fried Onions, to garnish

1 Heat a wok, add the oil and fry the onion, until soft but not browned.

2 Add the Chinese cabbage and toss well together. Add the corn, chili and water. Cover with a lid and cook for 2 minutes.

3 Remove the lid and stir in the beaten eggs and the seasoning. Stir constantly until the eggs are creamy and just set. Serve on warmed plates, sprinkled with crisp Deep-fried Onions.

Spiced Coconut Mushrooms

Here is a simple and delicious way to cook mushrooms. They can be served with almost any Asian meal, as well as with traditional Western grilled or roasted meats and poultry.

INGREDIENTS

Serves 4

2 tablespoons peanut oil
2 garlic cloves, finely chopped
2 fresh red chilies, seeded and sliced into rings
3 shallots, finely chopped
2 cups Crimini mushrooms, thickly sliced
$^2/_3$ cup coconut milk
2 tablespoons chopped fresh cilantro
salt and ground black pepper

1 Heat a wok until hot, add the oil and swirl it around the wok. Add the garlic and chilies, then stir-fry for a few seconds.

— COOK'S TIP —

Use snipped fresh chives instead of chopped fresh cilantro, if desired.

2 Add the shallots and stir-fry for 2–3 minutes, until softened. Add the mushrooms and stir-fry for 3 minutes.

3 Pour in the coconut milk and bring to a boil. Boil rapidly over high heat until the liquid has reduced by about half and coats the mushrooms. Season to taste with salt and pepper.

4 Sprinkle the chopped cilantro on top and toss the mushrooms gently to mix. Serve immediately.

Mixed Vegetable Pickle

If you can obtain fresh turmeric, it makes such a difference to the color and appearance of *Acar Campur*. You can use almost any vegetable, bearing in mind that you need a balance of textures, flavors and colors.

INGREDIENTS

Makes 2–3 11-ounce jars
1 fresh red chili, seeded and sliced
1 onion, quartered
2 garlic cloves, crushed
½ teaspoon shrimp paste
4 macadamia nuts or 8 almonds
1 inch fresh turmeric, peeled and
   sliced, or 1 teaspoon ground turmeric
¼ cup sunflower oil
2 cups white vinegar
1 cup water
3–6 tablespoons granulated sugar
3 carrots
8 ounces green beans
1 small cauliflower
1 cucumber
8 ounces white cabbage
¾ cup dry-roasted peanuts,
   roughly crushed
salt

1 Place the chili, onion, garlic, shrimp paste, nuts and turmeric in a food processor and blend to a paste, or pound in a mortar with a pestle.

2 Heat the oil and stir-fry the paste to release the aroma. Add the vinegar, water, sugar and salt. Bring to a boil. Simmer for 10 minutes.

3 Cut the carrots into flower shapes. Cut the green beans into short, neat lengths. Separate the cauliflower into neat, bite-size florets. Peel and seed the cucumber and cut the flesh in neat, bite-size pieces. Cut the cabbage in neat, bite-size pieces.

4 Blanch each vegetable separately, in a large pan of boiling water, for 1 minute. Transfer to a colander and rinse with cold water, to halt the cooking. Drain well.

COOK'S TIP

This pickle is even better if you make it a few days ahead.

5 Add the vegetables to the sauce. Slowly bring to a boil and allow to cook for 5–10 minutes. Do not overcook – the vegetables should still be crunchy.

6 Add the peanuts and cool. Spoon into clean jars with lids.

Black Bean and Vegetable Stir-fry

The secret of a quick stir-fry is proper preparation of all the ingredients first. It is important that the ingredients are added to the wok in the right order, so that the larger or thicker pieces have a longer cooking time than the smaller pieces—even if this is a difference of only a fraction of an inch and a few seconds!

INGREDIENTS

Serves 4
1¹/₂ cups scallions
8 ounces button mushrooms
1 red bell pepper
1 green bell pepper
2 large carrots
¹/₂ cup sesame oil
2 garlic cloves, crushed
¹/₄ cup black bean sauce
6 tablespoons warm water
1 cup bean sprouts
salt and ground black pepper

1 Thinly slice the scallions and button mushrooms.

2 Cut both the bell peppers in half, remove the seeds and slice the flesh into thin strips.

3 Cut the carrots in half. Cut each half into thin strips lengthwise. Stack the slices and cut through them to make very fine strips.

4 Heat the oil in a large preheated wok until very hot. Add the scallions and garlic and stir-fry for 30 seconds.

5 Add the mushrooms, bell peppers and carrots. Stir-fry for 5–6 minutes over high heat, until the vegetables are just beginning to soften.

6 Mix the black bean sauce with the water. Add to the wok and cook for 3–4 minutes. Stir in the bean sprouts and cook for 1 more minute, until all the vegetables are coated in the sauce. Season to taste, then serve immediately.

COOK'S TIP

Black bean sauce is made from salted black beans—which have a very distinctive flavor—that have been crushed and mixed with a variety of spices, such as ginger and chili. It is quite a thick paste and readily available in jars, bottles and cans at large supermarkets and Asian food stores. Store in the refrigerator after opening.

Stir-fried Spinach with Garlic and Sesame Seeds

The sesame seeds add a crunchy texture that contrasts well with the wilted spinach in this easy vegetable dish.

INGREDIENTS

Serves 2
½ bunch fresh spinach, washed
1½ tablespoons sesame seeds
2 tablespoons peanut oil
¼ teaspoon sea salt
2–3 garlic cloves, sliced

COOK'S TIP

Take care when adding the spinach to the hot oil, as it will spit furiously.

1 Shake the spinach to get rid of any excess water, then remove the stalks and discard any yellow or damaged leaves. Lay several spinach leaves one on top of another, roll up tightly and cut horizontally into wide strips. Repeat with the remaining leaves.

2 Heat a wok to medium heat, add the sesame seeds and dry-fry, stirring constantly, for 1–2 minutes, until golden brown. Transfer to a small bowl and set aside.

3 Add the oil to the wok and swirl it around. When hot, add the salt, spinach and garlic and stir-fry for 2 minutes, until the spinach just wilts and the leaves are coated in oil.

4 Sprinkle the dry-fried sesame seeds on top and toss well. Serve immediately.

Bok Choy with Oyster Sauce

Here, bok choy is prepared in a very simple way—stir-fried and served with oyster sauce. This Cantonese combination makes a simple, quickly prepared and tasty accompaniment to Asian or Western seafood dishes. Vegetarians may prefer to substitute light soy or hoisin sauce for the oyster sauce used in this recipe.

INGREDIENTS

Serves 3–4
1 head bok choy
2 tablespoons peanut oil
1–2 tablespoons oyster sauce

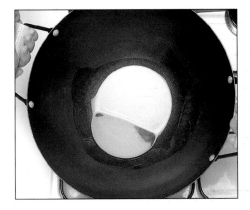

1 Trim the bok choy and tear into manageable pieces.

2 Heat a wok until hot, add the oil and swirl it around.

3 Add the bok choy and stir-fry for 2–3 minutes, until it has wilted a little.

4 Add the oyster sauce and continue to stir-fry for a few more seconds, until the bok choy is cooked but still slightly crisp. Serve immediately.

COOK'S TIP

You can replace the bok choy with Chinese flowering cabbage, which is also known by its Cantonese name *choi sam*. It has bright green leaves and tiny yellow flowers, which are eaten along with the leaves and stalks. It is available at Asian supermarkets.

Tofu Stir-fry

The tofu has a pleasant creamy texture, which contrasts delightfully with the crunchy stir-fried vegetables. Make sure you buy firm tofu that is easy to cut neatly.

INGREDIENTS

Serves 2–4

4 ounces white cabbage
2 fresh green chilies
8-ounce package fresh firm tofu
3 tablespoons vegetable oil
2 garlic cloves, crushed
3 scallions, chopped
6 ounces green beans, trimmed
1 cup baby corn, halved
½ cup bean sprouts
3 tablespoons smooth peanut butter
1½ tablespoons dark soy sauce
1¼ cups coconut milk

1 Shred the cabbage. Carefully remove the seeds from the chilies and chop finely.

2 Using a sharp knife, cut the tofu into thin strips.

3 Heat a wok, then add 2 tablespoons of the oil. When the oil is hot, add the tofu, stir-fry for 3 minutes and remove. Set aside. Wipe out the wok with paper towels.

4 Add the remaining oil to the wok. When it is hot, add the garlic, scallions and chilies and stir-fry for 1 minute. Then add the green beans, corn and bean sprouts and stir-fry for 2 more minutes.

5 Add the peanut butter and soy sauce to the wok. Stir well to coat the vegetables. Add the tofu to the vegetables in the wok.

6 Pour the coconut milk over the vegetables, simmer for 3 minutes and serve immediately.

COOK'S TIP

There are literally hundreds of varieties of chili. Generally speaking, dark green chilies are hotter than paler green ones, which are, in turn, hotter and less sweet than red chilies—but this is not a hard-and-fast rule and it is possible to be fooled by an unfamiliar variety. The "heat factor" of chilies is measured in Scoville units, with bell peppers at 0, at the bottom of the scale, and Mexican habanero chilies at 300,000, the hottest, at the top. Most Asian recipes call for medium to hot chilies. Some Indonesian and Thai dishes can be very fiery, but Chinese recipes tend to use fairly mild fresh green or red chilies.

Cooked Vegetable Gado-Gado

Instead of putting everything on a large platter, you can serve individual servings of this salad. It is a perfect recipe for lunchtime or informal gatherings.

INGREDIENTS

Serves 6

8 ounces waxy potatoes, cooked
1 pound mixed cabbage, spinach and
    bean sprouts, in equal proportions,
    rinsed and shredded
½ cucumber, cut in wedges, salted and
    set aside for 15 minutes
2–3 eggs, hard-boiled and shelled
4 ounces fresh bean curd
oil for frying
6–8 large Shrimp Crackers
lemon juice
Deep-fried Onions, to garnish
Peanut Sauce, to serve

1 Cube the potatoes and set aside. Bring a large pan of salted water to a boil. Plunge one type of raw vegetable at a time into the pan for just a few seconds to blanch. Lift out the vegetables with a large slotted spoon or sieve and run under very cold water, or plunge them into iced water and set aside 2 minutes. Drain thoroughly. Blanch all the vegetables, except the cucumber, in this way.

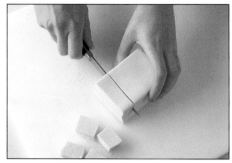

2 Rinse the cucumber pieces and drain them well. Cut the eggs in quarters. Cut the bean curd into cubes.

3 Fry the bean curd in hot oil in a wok until crisp on both sides. Lift out and drain on paper towels.

4 Add more oil to the pan and then deep-fry the Shrimp Crackers one or two at a time. Reserve them on a tray lined with paper towels.

5 Arrange all the cooked vegetables attractively on a platter, with the cucumber, hard-boiled eggs and bean curd. Scatter with the lemon juice and Deep-fried Onions at the last minute.

6 Serve with the prepared Peanut Sauce and hand round the fried Shrimp Crackers separately.

Spicy Zucchini Fritters with Thai Salsa

The Thai salsa goes just as well with plain stir-fried salmon strips or stir-fried beef as it does with these zucchini fritters.

INGREDIENTS

Serves 2–4

2 teaspoons cumin seeds
2 teaspoons coriander seeds
1 pound zucchini
1 cup gram flour
½ teaspoon baking soda
salt and ground black pepper
½ cup peanut oil
fresh mint sprigs, to garnish

For the Thai salsa

½ cucumber, diced
3 scallions, chopped
6 radishes, cubed
2 tablespoons chopped fresh mint
1-inch piece fresh ginger, peeled
  and grated
3 tablespoons lime juice
2 tablespoons superfine sugar
3 garlic cloves, crushed

1 Heat a wok, then dry-fry the cumin and coriander seeds. Cool them, then grind well, using a mortar and pestle.

COOK'S TIP

You can substitute daikon, also known as mooli or white radish, for the round radishes in the salsa.

2 Cut the zucchini into 3-inch sticks. Place in a bowl.

3 Process the flour, baking soda, spices and salt and pepper in a food processor or blender. Add 1 cup warm water with 1 tablespoon of the peanut oil and process again.

4 Coat the zucchini in the batter, then let stand for 10 minutes.

5 To make the salsa, combine the cucumber, scallions, radishes, mint, ginger and lime juice in a bowl. Stir in the sugar and garlic.

6 Heat the wok, then add the remaining oil. When the oil is hot, stir-fry the zucchini in batches. Drain well on paper towels, then serve hot with the Thai salsa, garnished with fresh mint sprigs.

Spiced Vegetables with Coconut

This spicy and substantial stir-fry could be served as an appetizer, or as a vegetarian main course for two. Eat it with spoons and forks, and provide hunks of whole-grain bread for mopping up the delicious coconut milk.

Ingredients

Serves 2–4
1 fresh red chili
1 fennel bulb
2 large carrots
6 celery stalks
2 tablespoons peanut oil
1-inch piece fresh ginger, peeled
 and grated
1 garlic clove, crushed
3 scallions, sliced
14-ounce can thin coconut milk
1 tablespoon chopped fresh cilantro
salt and ground black pepper
fresh cilantro sprigs, to garnish

Cook's Tip

When buying fennel, look for well-rounded bulbs; flatter ones are immature and will not have developed their full aniseed-like flavor. The bulbs should be white with overlapping ridged layers. Avoid any that look damaged or bruised. The fennel should be dry, but not desiccated.

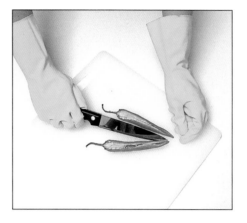

1 Halve, seed and finely chop the chili.

2 Thinly slice the carrots and the celery stalks on the diagonal.

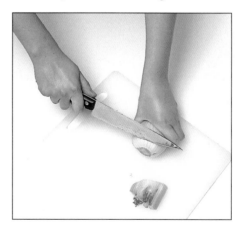

3 Trim the fennel bulb and slice roughly, using a sharp knife.

4 Heat a wok, then add the peanut oil. When the oil is hot, add the chili, fennel, carrots, celery, ginger, garlic and scallions and stir-fry for 2 minutes.

5 Stir in the coconut milk with a large spoon and bring to a boil.

6 Stir in the chopped cilantro and salt and pepper, and serve garnished with cilantro sprigs.

Bok Choy and Mushroom Stir-fry

Try to buy all the varieties of mushroom for this dish—wild oyster and shiitake mushrooms have particularly distinctive, delicate flavors that work well when stir-fried.

INGREDIENTS

Serves 4

4 dried black Chinese mushrooms
⅔ cup hot water
1 head bok choy
½ cup oyster mushrooms, preferably wild
½ cup shiitake mushrooms
1 tablespoon vegetable oil
1 garlic clove, crushed
2 tablespoons oyster sauce

1 Soak the black Chinese mushrooms in the hot water for 30 minutes to soften. Drain, and discard the tough stalks.

COOK'S TIP

Bok choy, also called pok choi and Chinese white cabbage, is an attractive member of the cabbage family, with long, smooth, white stems and dark green leaves. It has a pleasant flavor that does not in any way resemble that of cabbage.

2 Tear the bok choy into bite-size pieces with your fingers.

3 Halve any large oyster and shiitake mushrooms, using a sharp knife.

4 Heat a wok, then add the oil. When the oil is hot, stir-fry the garlic until softened but not colored.

5 Add the bok choy to the wok and stir-fry for 1 minute. Mix in all the mushrooms and stir-fry for 1 minute.

6 Add the oyster sauce, toss well and serve immediately.

Red-cooked Tofu with Chinese Mushrooms

"Red-cooked" is a term applied to Chinese dishes cooked with a dark soy sauce. This tasty dish can be served as either a side dish or a main course.

INGREDIENTS

Serves 4

8-ounce package fresh firm tofu
3 tablespoons dark soy sauce
2 tablespoons Chinese rice wine or
  dry sherry
2 teaspoons dark brown sugar
1 garlic clove, crushed
1 tablespoon grated fresh ginger
½ teaspoon five-spice powder
pinch of ground roasted Szechuan
  peppercorns
6 dried black Chinese mushrooms
1 teaspoon cornstarch
2 tablespoons peanut oil
5–6 scallions, sliced into 1-inch lengths,
  white and green parts separated
small fresh basil leaves, to garnish
rice noodles, to serve

2 Meanwhile, soak the dried black mushrooms in warm water for 30 minutes, until soft. Drain, reserving 6 tablespoons of the soaking liquid. Squeeze out any excess liquid from the mushrooms, remove the tough stalks and slice the caps. In a small bowl, blend the cornstarch with the reserved marinade and mushroom soaking liquid.

4 Add the mushrooms and white parts of the scallions to the wok and stir-fry for 2 minutes. Pour in the reserved marinade and stir for 1 minute, until thickened.

1 Drain the tofu, pat dry with paper towels and cut into 1-inch cubes. Place in a shallow dish. In a small bowl, combine the soy sauce, rice wine or sherry, sugar, garlic, ginger, five-spice powder and Szechuan peppercorns. Pour the marinade over the tofu, toss well and let marinate for about 30 minutes. Drain, reserving the marinade.

3 Heat a wok until hot, add the oil and swirl it around. Add the tofu and stir-fry for 2–3 minutes, until evenly golden. Remove from the wok and set aside.

5 Return the tofu to the wok with the green parts of the scallions. Simmer gently for 1–2 minutes. Scatter the basil leaves on top and serve immediately with rice noodles.

Pancakes with Stir-fried Vegetables

To serve, each person spreads a little hoisin sauce over a pancake, adds a helping of the filling from the wok and rolls up the pancake.

INGREDIENTS

Serves 4

3 eggs
2 tablespoons water
¼ cup peanut oil
¼ cup dried black Chinese mushrooms
¼ cup dried wood ear mushrooms
2 teaspoons cornstarch
2 tablespoons light soy sauce
2 tablespoons Chinese rice wine or
    dry sherry
2 teaspoons sesame oil
2 garlic cloves, finely chopped
½-inch piece fresh ginger, cut into
    thin shreds
½ cup canned sliced bamboo shoots,
    drained and rinsed
½ cup bean sprouts
4 scallions, finely shredded
salt and ground black pepper
fresh cilantro, to garnish
Chinese pancakes and hoisin sauce,
    to serve

1 Whisk the eggs, water and seasoning in a small bowl. Heat 1 tablespoon of the peanut oil in a wok and swirl it around. Pour in the eggs, then tilt the wok so that they spread into an even layer. Continue to cook over high heat for about 2 minutes, until set. Turn onto a board and, when cool, roll up the omelet and cut into thin strips. Wipe the wok clean.

COOK'S TIP

Chinese pancakes are available at Asian supermarkets. Reheat them in a bamboo steamer for 2–3 minutes just before serving.

2 Meanwhile, put the black Chinese mushrooms and wood ear mushrooms in separate bowls. Pour in enough warm water to cover, then let soak for 30 minutes, until soft. Drain the mushrooms, reserving their soaking liquid. Squeeze the excess liquid from each of them.

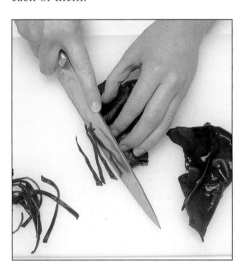

3 Remove the tough stalks and thinly slice the black mushrooms. Finely shred the wood ears. Set aside. Strain the reserved soaking liquid through cheesecloth into a bowl; reserve ½ cup of the liquid. In a bowl, blend the cornstarch with the reserved liquid, soy sauce, rice wine or sherry and sesame oil.

4 Heat the wok over medium heat, add the remaining peanut oil and swirl it around. Add the wood ears and black mushrooms and stir-fry for about 2 minutes. Add the garlic, ginger, bamboo shoots and bean sprouts and stir-fry for 1–2 minutes.

5 Pour in the cornstarch mixture and cook, stirring, for 1 minute, until thickened. Add the scallions and omelet strips and toss gently. Adjust the seasoning, adding more soy sauce, if needed. Serve immediately with the Chinese pancakes, garnished with cilantro, and accompanied by the hoisin sauce.

Stir-fried Vegetables with Cilantro Omelet

A wok is the ideal utensil for cooking an omelet, as the heat is evenly distributed over the wide surface. This is a great supper dish for vegetarians. The glaze is intended to give the vegetables an appealing shine and does not constitute a sauce.

INGREDIENTS

Serves 3–4

For the omelet

2 eggs
2 tablespoons water
3 tablespoons chopped fresh cilantro
salt and ground black pepper
1 tablespoon peanut oil

For the glazed vegetables

1 tablespoon cornstarch
2 tablespoons Chinese rice wine or
  dry sherry
1 tablespoon sweet chili sauce
½ cup vegetable stock
2 tablespoons peanut oil
1 teaspoon grated fresh ginger
6–8 scallions, sliced
4 ounces snow peas
1 yellow bell pepper, seeded and sliced
½ cup fresh shiitake or button
  mushrooms
½ cup canned water chestnuts, drained
  and rinsed
½ cup bean sprouts
½ small head bok choy, roughly
  shredded

COOK'S TIP

Vary the combination of vegetables used according to availability and taste, but make sure that you slice or chop them to approximately the same size and thickness.

1 To make the omelet, whisk the eggs, water, cilantro and seasoning in a small bowl. Heat the oil in a wok. Pour in the eggs, then tilt the wok so that the mixture spreads in an even layer. Cook over high heat until the edges are slightly crisp.

2 Flip the omelet over with a spatula and cook the other side for about 30 seconds until lightly browned. Turn the omelet onto a board and let cool. When cool, roll up loosely and cut into thin slices. Wipe the wok clean.

3 In a bowl, blend the cornstarch, wine or sherry, chili sauce and stock to make the glaze. Set aside.

4 Heat the wok until hot, add the oil and swirl it around. Add the ginger and scallions and stir-fry for a few seconds to flavor the oil. Add the snow peas, sliced bell pepper, mushrooms and water chestnuts and stir-fry for 3 minutes.

5 Add the bean sprouts and bok choy and stir-fry for 2 minutes.

6 Pour in the glaze mixture and cook, stirring, for about 1 minute, until the glaze thickens and coats the vegetables. Turn the vegetables onto a warmed serving plate and top with the omelet shreds. Serve immediately.

Broccoli in Oyster Sauce

The broccoli florets retain their vivid shade of green and crunchy texture, as well as much of their vitamin and mineral content, when given this wok treatment. Vegetarians may prefer to substitute light soy sauce for the oyster sauce.

Ingredients

Serves 4

1 large bunch broccoli
3–4 tablespoons vegetable oil
½ teaspoon salt
½ teaspoon light brown sugar
2–3 tablespoons vegetable stock
   or water
2 tablespoons oyster sauce or light
   soy sauce

1 Cut the broccoli heads into small florets. Remove the rough skin from the stalks and cut them into even-size chunks.

2 Heat the oil in a preheated wok and add the salt, then stir-fry the broccoli for about 2 minutes. Add the sugar and stock or water, and continue stirring for 1 minute. Add the oyster or soy sauce, blend well and serve.

Cook's Tip

Always choose healthy-looking broccoli with firm stems that are neither woody nor wrinkled. Look for tightly packed, nicely colored flower heads with no signs of yellowing. Broccoli is best eaten on the day it is purchased or, better still, picked. It deteriorates rapidly in storage and loses many of the vitamins for which it is especially valued, as well as its crispness.

Deep-fried Onions

Known as *bawang goreng*, these are a traditional accompaniment and garnish to many Indonesian dishes. Asian stores sell them ready-made, but it is simple to make them at home, using fresh onions. The small red onions that can be bought at Asian food stores are excellent when deep-fried, as they contain less water than most European varieties.

INGREDIENTS

Makes 1 pound
1 pound onions
oil, for deep-frying

1 Peel the onions and slice as evenly and finely as possible.

2 Spread out thinly on paper towels in an airy place and let dry for 30 minutes to 2 hours.

3 Heat the oil in a wok to 375°F. Deep-fry the onions in batches, turning them all the time, until they are crisp and golden. Drain well on paper towels and cool. Deep-fried Onions may be stored in an airtight container.

COOK'S TIP

Garlic can be prepared and cooked in the same way, or some can be fried with the last batch of onions. Deep-fried garlic gives an added dimension of flavor as a garnish for many dishes.

An even faster way to prepare homemade deep-fried onions is to use a 3-ounce package of quick-dried onions, which you can fry in about 1 cup sunflower oil. This gives you 4 ounces of fried onion flakes.

Bamboo Shoots and Chinese Mushrooms

Another name for this dish is "twin winter vegetables," because both bamboo shoots and mushrooms are at their best in winter. For that reason, try using canned winter bamboo shoots and extra "fat" mushrooms.

INGREDIENTS

Serves 4
½ cup dried Chinese mushrooms
10-ounce can winter bamboo shoots
3 tablespoons vegetable oil
1 scallion, cut into short sections
2 tablespoons light soy sauce or
    oyster sauce
1 tablespoon Chinese rice wine or
    dry sherry
½ teaspoon light brown sugar
2 teaspoons cornstarch paste
few drops of sesame oil

1 Soak the mushrooms in warm water for 30 minutes. Drain, squeeze dry and discard any hard stalks, reserving the water. Cut the mushrooms in half or in quarters if they are large—keep them whole if small.

2 Rinse and drain the bamboo shoots, then cut them into small, wedge-shaped pieces.

3 Heat the oil in a preheated wok and stir-fry the mushrooms and bamboo shoots for about 1 minute. Add the scallion, soy or oyster sauce, wine or sherry and the sugar with 2–3 tablespoons of the reserved mushroom liquid. Bring to a boil and braise for 1–2 minutes. Stir in the cornstarch paste to thicken, sprinkle with the sesame oil and serve.

Stir-fried Tomatoes, Cucumber and Eggs

The cucumber can be replaced by a green bell pepper or zucchini if you prefer.

INGREDIENTS

Serves 4
4 large firm tomatoes, skinned
½ cucumber, unpeeled
4 eggs
1 teaspoon salt
1 scallion, finely chopped
¼ cup vegetable oil
2 teaspoons Chinese rice wine or dry
    sherry (optional)

1 Cut the tomatoes and cucumber in half lengthwise, then cut horizontally into small wedges. In a bowl, beat the eggs with a pinch of salt and a few pieces of the chopped scallion.

2 Heat about half the oil in a preheated wok, then pour in the eggs and scramble lightly over medium heat until set but not too dry. Remove the scrambled egg from the wok and keep warm.

3 Add the remaining oil to the wok and heat over high heat. Add the vegetables and stir-fry for 1 minute. Add the remaining salt, then the scrambled eggs and wine or sherry, if using. Serve immediately.

Daikon, Beet and Carrot Stir-fry

This is a dazzlingly colorful dish with a crunchy texture and fragrant taste.

INGREDIENTS

Serves 4
¼ cup pine nuts
4 ounces daikon, peeled
4 ounces raw beet, peeled
2 medium carrots, peeled
1½ tablespoons vegetable oil
juice of 1 orange
2 tablespoons chopped fresh cilantro
salt and freshly ground black pepper

1 Place the pine nuts in a preheated wok and toss until golden brown. Remove and set aside.

2 Cut the daikon, beet and carrots into long, thin strips.

3 Heat the oil in a preheated wok. When the oil is hot, stir-fry the daikon, beet and carrots for 2–3 minutes. Remove and set aside.

4 Pour the orange juice into the wok and simmer for 2 minutes. Remove and keep warm.

5 Arrange the vegetables attractively on a warmed platter, sprinkle the cilantro on top, and season to taste with salt and pepper.

6 Drizzle with the orange juice, sprinkle with the pine nuts, and serve immediately.

Bok Choy with Lime Dressing

For this Thai recipe, the coconut dressing is traditionally made using fish sauce, but vegetarians could use mushroom sauce instead. Beware, the red chilies make this a fiery dish!

INGREDIENTS

Serves 4
6 scallions
2 bok choy
2 tablespoons oil
3 fresh red chilies, cut into thin strips
4 garlic cloves, thinly sliced
1 tablespoon crushed peanuts

For the dressing
1–2 tablespoons fish sauce
2 tablespoons lime juice
1 cup coconut milk

1 To make the dressing, blend together the fish sauce and lime juice, then stir in the coconut milk.

2 Trim the scallions, then cut diagonally into slices, including all but the very tips of the green parts, but keeping the green and white parts separate.

3 Using a large, sharp knife, cut the bok choy into very fine strips.

4 Heat the oil in a preheated wok and stir-fry the chilies for 2–3 minutes, or until crisp. Transfer to a plate using a slotted spoon. Stir-fry the garlic for 30–60 seconds, or until golden brown, and transfer to the plate with the chilies. Stir-fry the white parts of the scallions for about 2–3 minutes and then add the green parts and stir-fry for another minute. Add to the plate with the chilies and garlic.

5 Bring a large pan of salted water to a boil and add the bok choy. Stir twice and then drain immediately. Place the warmed bok choy in a large bowl, add the coconut dressing and stir well. Spoon into a large serving bowl and sprinkle with the crushed peanuts and the stir-fried chili mixture. Serve immediately.

Stir-fried Vegetables with Pasta

This colorful Chinese-style dish is easily prepared and, for a change, uses pasta instead of Chinese noodles.

INGREDIENTS

Serves 4
1 medium carrot
6 ounces small zucchini
6 ounces green beans
6 ounces baby corn
1 pound ribbon pasta, such as tagliatelle
2 tablespoons corn oil, plus extra for tossing the pasta
½-inch piece fresh ginger, finely chopped
2 garlic cloves, finely chopped
6 tablespoons yellow bean sauce
6 scallions, sliced into 1-inch lengths
2 tablespoons dry sherry
1 teaspoon toasted sesame seeds
salt

1 Slice the carrot and zucchini diagonally into chunks. Slice the green beans diagonally. Cut the baby corn diagonally in half.

2 Cook the pasta in plenty of boiling salted water according to the package instructions, drain, then rinse under hot water. Toss with a little oil to prevent sticking. Set aside.

3 Heat the 2 tablespoons of oil in a preheated wok or frying pan and add the ginger and garlic. Stir-fry for 30 seconds, then add the carrots, green beans, baby corn and zucchini.

4 Stir-fry for 3–4 minutes, then stir in the yellow bean sauce. Stir-fry for 2 minutes, add the scallions, dry sherry and pasta and stir-fry for another minute, until piping hot. Sprinkle with sesame seeds and serve immediately.

Chinese Vegetable Stir-fry

This is a typical stir-fried vegetable dish popular all over China. Chinese cabbage is like a cross between a cabbage and a crunchy lettuce, with a delicious peppery flavor.

INGREDIENTS

Serves 4

3 tablespoons sunflower oil

1 tablespoon sesame oil

1 garlic clove, chopped

8 ounces broccoli florets, cut into small pieces

4 ounces sugar snap peas

1 head Chinese cabbage, about 1 pound, or Savoy cabbage, sliced

4 scallions, finely chopped

2 tablespoons soy sauce

2 tablespoons Chinese rice wine or dry sherry

2–3 tablespoons water

1 tablespoon sesame seeds, lightly toasted

1 Heat the sunflower and sesame oils in a preheated wok or large frying pan, add the garlic and stir-fry for 30 seconds.

2 Add the broccoli florets and stir-fry for 3 minutes. Add the sugar snap peas and cook for 2 minutes, then toss in the Chinese or Savoy cabbage and the scallions and stir-fry for another 2 minutes.

3 Pour in the soy sauce, rice wine or dry sherry and water and stir-fry for another 4 minutes, or until the vegetables are just tender. Sprinkle with the toasted sesame seeds and serve hot.

Indonesian Potatoes with Onions and Chili Sauce

This adds another dimension to French fries, with the addition of crisply fried onions and a spicy soy sauce and chili dressing. Eat *Kentang Gula* hot, warm or cold, as a tasty snack.

INGREDIENTS

Serves 6
3 large potatoes, about 8 ounces each, peeled and cut for fries
sunflower or peanut oil for deep-frying
2 onions, finely sliced
salt

For the dressing
1–2 fresh red chilies, seeded and ground
3 tablespoons dark soy sauce

1 Rinse the potatoes and then thoroughly pat dry with paper towels. Heat the oil and deep-fry the potatoes, until they are golden brown in color and crisp.

2 Put the potatoes in a dish, sprinkle with salt and keep warm. Fry the onion slices in the hot oil until they are similarly crisp and golden brown. Drain well on paper towels and then add to the potatoes.

3 Combine the chilies with the soy sauce and heat gently.

4 Pour over the potato and onion mixture and serve as suggested.

VARIATION

Alternatively, boil the potatoes in their skins. Drain, cool, peel and slice them, then shallow-fry until golden. Cook the onions and pour over the dressing.

Zucchini with Noodles

Any zucchini or member of the squash family can be used in *Oseng Oseng,* which is reminiscent of a similar dish eaten in Malaysia, whose cuisine has strong links with Indonesia.

INGREDIENTS

Serves 4–6
1 pound zucchini, sliced
1 onion, finely sliced
1 garlic clove, finely chopped
2 tablespoons sunflower oil
½ teaspoon ground turmeric
2 tomatoes, chopped
3 tablespoons water
14 ounces cooked, peeled shrimp (optional)
1 ounce cellophane noodles
salt

1 Use a vegetable peeler to cut thin strips from the outside of each zucchini. Cut the strips in neat slices. Set the zucchini on one side. Fry the onion and garlic in hot oil; do not allow to brown.

2 Add the turmeric, zucchini slices, chopped tomatoes, water and shrimp, if using.

3 Put the noodles in a pan and pour over boiling water to cover, let stand for a minute and then drain. Cut the noodles in 2-inch lengths and add to the vegetables.

4 Cover with a lid and cook in their own steam for 2–3 minutes. Toss everything well together. Season with salt to taste and serve while still hot.

Eggplant with Sesame Chicken

Young vegetables are prized in Japan for their sweet, delicate flavor. Here, small eggplants are stuffed with seasoned chicken.

INGREDIENTS

Serves 4

6 ounces chicken breast or thighs, skinned
1 scallion, green part only, finely chopped
1 tablespoon dark soy sauce
1 tablespoon mirin or sweet sherry
½ teaspoon sesame oil
½ teaspoon salt
4 small eggplants, about 4 inches long
1 tablespoon sesame seeds
flour, for dusting
vegetable oil, for deep-frying

For the dipping sauce

4 tablespoons dark soy sauce
4 tablespoons dashi or vegetable broth
3 tablespoons mirin or sweet sherry

3 To make the dipping sauce, combine the soy sauce, dashi or broth and mirin or sherry. Pour into a shallow bowl and set aside.

4 Heat the vegetable oil in a wok or deep-fryer to 385°F. Fry the eggplants, two at a time, for 3–4 minutes. Lift out with chopsticks or a slotted spoon and drain on paper towels. Serve with the dipping sauce.

1 Remove the chicken meat from the bone and grind it finely in a food processor for 1–2 minutes. Add the scallion, soy sauce, mirin or sherry, sesame oil and salt.

2 Make four slits in each eggplant, so they remain joined at the stem. Spoon the ground chicken mixture into the eggplants, opening them slightly to accommodate it. Dip the fat end of each stuffed eggplant in the sesame seeds, then dust with flour. Set aside.

Chinese Potatoes with Chili Beans

East meets West. An American-style dish with a Chinese flavor—the sauce is particularly tasty. Try it as a supper dish when you're in the mood for a meal with a zing!

INGREDIENTS

Serves 4

4 medium potatoes, cut into thick chunks
2 tablespoons sunflower or peanut oil
3 scallions, sliced
1 large fresh red chili, seeded and sliced
2 garlic cloves, crushed
1 can (14 ounces) red kidney beans, drained
2 tablespoons soy sauce
1 tablespoon sesame oil
salt and freshly ground black pepper
1 tablespoon sesame seeds and chopped fresh cilantro or parsley, to garnish

1 Boil the potatoes until they are just tender. Take care not to overcook them. Drain and set aside.

2 Heat the sunflower or peanut oil in a preheated wok or large frying pan, stir-fry the scallions and chili for about 1 minute, then add the garlic and fry for a few seconds longer.

3 Add the potatoes, stirring well, then the beans and finally the soy sauce and sesame oil.

4 Season to taste and cook the vegetables until they are heated through. Sprinkle with sesame seeds and cilantro or parsley and serve.

Chinese Garlic Mushrooms

Tofu is high in protein and very low in fat, so it is an extremely useful and healthful food to keep handy for quick meals and snacks like this one.

INGREDIENTS

Serves 4

8 large, open mushrooms
3 scallions, sliced
1 garlic clove, crushed
2 tablespoons oyster sauce
10 ounces marinated firm tofu, cut into small dice
1 can (7 ounces) corn kernels, drained
2 teaspoons sesame oil
salt and freshly ground black pepper
1 scallion, cut into thin stips, to garnish

1 Finely chop the mushroom stalks and mix with the scallions, garlic and oyster sauce.

2 Stir in the diced, marinated tofu and the corn, season well with salt and pepper, then spoon the filling into the mushrooms.

3 Brush the edges of the mushrooms with the sesame oil. Arrange the stuffed mushrooms in a baking dish and bake in a preheated oven at 400°F for 12–15 minutes, or until the mushrooms are just tender, then serve at once, garnished with the scallion strips.

COOK'S TIP

If you prefer, omit the oyster sauce and use light soy sauce instead.

Stir-fried Mixed Vegetables

When selecting different items for a stir-fried dish, never mix the ingredients indiscriminately. The idea is to achieve a harmonious balance of color and texture.

INGREDIENTS

Serves 4
8 ounces Chinese cabbage
4 ounces baby corn
4 ounces broccoli
1 medium carrot
4 tablespoons vegetable oil
1 teaspoon salt
1 teaspoon light brown sugar
Basic Broth or water, if necessary
1 tablespoon light soy sauce
few drops of sesame oil (optional)

2 Heat the oil in a preheated wok and stir-fry the vegetables for about 2 minutes.

3 Add the salt and sugar and a little broth or water, if necessary, and continue stirring for another minute. Add the soy sauce and sesame oil, if using. Blend well and serve.

1 Cut the vegetables into roughly similar shapes and sizes.

Tofu and Green Bean Red Curry

This is another curry that is simple and quick to make. This recipe uses green beans, but you can use almost any kind of vegetable, such as eggplant, bamboo shoots or broccoli.

INGREDIENTS

Serves 4–6

2½ cups unsweetened coconut milk
1 tablespoon red curry paste
3 tablespoons fish sauce
2 teaspoons palm sugar
3½ cups button mushrooms
4 ounces green beans, trimmed
6 ounces tofu, rinsed and cut into
 ¾-inch cubes
4 kaffir lime leaves, torn
2 red chilies, sliced
cilantro leaves, to garnish

1 Put about one-third of the coconut milk in a wok or saucepan. Cook until it starts to separate and an oily sheen appears.

2 Add the red curry paste, fish sauce and sugar to the coconut milk. Mix together thoroughly.

3 Add the mushrooms. Stir and cook for 1 minute.

4 Stir in the rest of the coconut milk and bring back to a boil.

5 Add the green beans and cubes of tofu and simmer gently for another 4–5 minutes.

6 Stir in the kaffir lime leaves and chilies. Serve garnished with the cilantro leaves.

Chinese Cabbage and Daikon with Scallops

A speedy stir-fry made using Chinese cabbage, daikon and scallops. Both the Chinese cabbage and daikon have a pleasant crunchy "bite." You need to work quickly, so have everything prepared before you start cooking.

INGREDIENTS

Serves 4

10 large scallops
5 tablespoons vegetable oil
3 garlic cloves, finely chopped
½-inch piece fresh ginger, finely sliced
4–5 scallions, cut lengthwise into
   1-inch pieces
2 tablespoons Chinese rice wine or
   dry sherry
½ daikon, cut into ½-inch slices
1 Chinese cabbage, chopped lengthwise
   into thin strips
4 tablespoons water

For the marinade

1 teaspoon cornstarch
1 egg white, lightly beaten
pinch of white pepper

For the sauce

1 teaspoon cornstarch
4 tablespoons water
3 tablespoons oyster sauce

1 Rinse the scallops and separate the roes from the white meat. Cut each scallop into two pieces and slice the roes. Place them on two separate dishes. For the marinade, blend together the cornstarch, egg white and white pepper. Pour over the scallops. Set aside for 10 minutes.

2 To make the sauce, blend the cornstarch with the water and the oyster sauce and set aside.

3 Heat about 2 tablespoons of the oil in a preheated wok, add half the garlic and let it sizzle, then add half the ginger and half the scallions. Stir-fry for about 30 seconds, then stir in the scallops. Stir-fry for up to 1 minute, or until the scallops start to become opaque. Reduce the heat and add 1 tablespoon of the rice wine or dry sherry. Cook briefly, then spoon the scallops and the cooking liquid into a bowl and set aside.

4 Heat another 2 tablespoons of the oil in the wok, add the remaining garlic, ginger and scallions and stir-fry for 1 minute. Add the roes and the remaining rice wine or dry sherry, stir-fry briefly and transfer to a dish.

5 Heat the remaining oil and add the daikon. Stir-fry for about 30 seconds, then stir in the cabbage. Stir-fry for about 30 seconds and add the oyster sauce mixture and the water. Allow the cabbage to simmer briefly. Stir in the scallops and cooking liquid. Cook briefly to heat through.

Spiced Tofu Stir-fry

You could add any quickly cooked vegetable to this stir-fry—try snow peas, sugar snap peas, leeks or thin slices of carrot.

INGREDIENTS

Serves 4

2 teaspoons ground cumin
1 tablespoon paprika
1 teaspoon ground ginger
generous pinch of cayenne pepper
1 tablespoon superfine sugar
10 ounces firm tofu
oil, for frying
2 garlic cloves, crushed
1 bunch scallions, sliced
1 red bell pepper, seeded and sliced
1 yellow bell pepper, seeded and sliced
8 ounces button mushrooms, halved, or
    quartered if very large
1 large zucchini, sliced
4 ounces green beans, halved
½ cup pine nuts
1 tablespoon lime juice
1 tablespoon honey
salt and freshly ground black pepper

3 Add a little more oil to the wok or frying pan and stir-fry the garlic and scallions for 3 minutes. Add the remaining vegetables and stir-fry over medium heat for 6 minutes, or until they are beginning to soften and turn golden. Season well.

4 Return the tofu to the pan with the pine nuts, lime juice and honey. Heat through and serve.

1 Combine the cumin, paprika, ginger, cayenne and sugar with plenty of seasoning. Cut the tofu into cubes and coat them thoroughly in the spice mixture.

2 Heat some oil in a preheated wok or large frying pan. Cook the tofu over high heat for 3–4 minutes, turning occasionally. Take care not to break up the tofu too much. Remove with a slotted spoon. Wipe out the wok or pan with paper towels.

Chinese Sprouts

If you are bored with plain boiled Brussels sprouts, try pepping them up with this unusual stir-fried method, which uses a minimum of oil.

INGREDIENTS

Serves 4

1 pound Brussels sprouts
1 teaspoon sesame or sunflower oil
2 scallions, sliced
½ teaspoon Chinese five-spice powder
1 tablespoon light soy sauce

1 Trim the Brussels sprouts, then shred them finely using a large sharp knife. Alternatively, shred them in a food processor.

2 Heat the oil in a preheated wok or frying pan and add the sprouts and scallions, then stir-fry for 2 minutes, without browning.

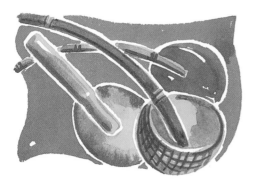

3 Stir in the five-spice powder and soy sauce, then cook, stirring, for another 2–3 minutes, or until just tender.

4 Serve hot, with grilled meat or fish or with Chinese dishes.

COOK'S TIP

Brussels sprouts are rich in vitamin C, and this is a good way to cook them to preserve the nutrients. Larger sprouts cook particularly well by this method; and cabbage can be cooked in the same way.

SALADS

There is much more to Asian salads than a few Chinese leaves and a bunch of bean sprouts. The superb collection of recipes here includes flamboyant combinations of raw fruit and vegetables, surprisingly refreshing warm salads, startling pairings of sweet and spicy ingredients, dramatic mixtures of crunchy and melt-in-the mouth textures and daring matching of flavors. Try Thai Fruit and Vegetable Salad, Warm Stir-fried Salad, Hot Coconut Shrimp and Papaya Salad, Sesame Noodle Salad with Hot Peanuts or Hot-and-sour Chicken Salad.

Bean Curd and Cucumber Salad

Tahu Goreng Ketjap is a nutritious and refreshing salad with a hot, sweet and sour dressing. It is ideal for buffets.

INGREDIENTS

Serves 4–6

1 small cucumber
oil for frying
1 square fresh or 4 ounces long-life
    bean curd
4 ounces bean sprouts, trimmed
    and rinsed
salt

For the dressing

1 small onion, grated
2 garlic cloves, crushed
½ teaspoon chili powder
2–3 tablespoons dark soy sauce
1–2 tablespoons rice-wine vinegar
2 teaspoon dark brown sugar
salt
celery leaves, to garnish

1 Trim the ends from the cucumber and then cut it in neat cubes. Sprinkle with salt and set aside, while preparing the remaining ingredients.

2 Heat a little oil in a pan and fry the bean curd on both sides until golden brown. Drain on paper towels and cut in cubes.

— COOK'S TIP —

Bean sprouts come from the mung bean and are easily grown at home on damp cotton or in a plastic bean sprouter. They must be eaten when absolutely fresh, so when buying from a shop check that they are crisp and are not beginning to go brown or soft. Eat within a day or two.

3 Prepare the dressing by blending together the onion, garlic and chili powder. Stir in the soy sauce, vinegar, sugar and salt to taste. You can do this in a screw-topped glass jar.

4 Just before serving, rinse the cucumber under cold running water. Drain and dry thoroughly. Toss the cucumber, bean curd and beans prouts together in a serving bowl and pour over the dressing. Garnish with the celery leaves and serve the salad at once.

Vegetable Salad with Hot Peanut Sauce

A wok is ideal for dry-frying as well as stir-frying, and here it is used to great effect in making this wonderful peanut sauce.

INGREDIENTS

Serves 4–6
2 potatoes, peeled
6 ounces green beans, trimmed

For the peanut sauce
³/₄ cup peanuts
1 tablespoon vegetable oil
2 shallots or 1 small onion,
    finely chopped
1 garlic clove, crushed
1–2 small fresh chilies, seeded and
    finely chopped
¹/₂-inch square shrimp paste, or
    1 tablespoon fish sauce (optional)
2 tablespoons tamarind sauce
¹/₂ cup canned coconut milk
1 tablespoon honey

For the salad
2 heads bok choy, shredded
1 head iceberg or Bibb lettuce,
    separated into leaves
1 cup bean sprouts, washed
¹/₂ cucumber, cut into fingers
5 ounces daikon, shredded
3 scallions, trimmed
8-ounce package fresh tofu, cut into
    large dice
3 hard-cooked eggs, quartered

1 Bring the potatoes to a boil in salted water and simmer for 20 minutes. Add the beans and cook for 3–4 minutes. Drain the potatoes and beans under cold running water.

2 For the peanut sauce, dry-fry the peanuts in a wok, or place under a medium broiler, tossing them constantly to prevent burning. Turn the peanuts onto a clean dish towel and rub vigorously to remove the papery skins. Place the peanuts in a food processor or blender and process for 2 minutes.

3 Heat the oil in a wok and soften the shallots or onion, garlic and chilies without letting them color. Add the shrimp paste or fish sauce, if using, together with the tamarind sauce, coconut milk and honey. Simmer briefly, add to the peanuts and process in a food processor to form a thick sauce.

4 Arrange the salad ingredients, potatoes and beans on a large platter and serve with a bowl of the peanut sauce.

Thai Seafood Salad

This seafood salad with chili, lemongrass and fish sauce is light and refreshing.

INGREDIENTS

Serves 4

8 ounces ready-prepared squid
8 ounces uncooked shrimp
8 scallops, shelled
8 ounces firm white fish
2–3 tablespoons olive oil
small mixed lettuce leaves and
   cilantro sprigs, to serve

For the dressing

2 small fresh red chilies, seeded and
   finely chopped
2-inch piece lemongrass, finely
   chopped
2 kaffir lime leaves, shredded
2 tablespoons fish sauce
2 shallots, thinly sliced
2 tablespoons lime juice
2 tablespoons rice vinegar
2 teaspoons superfine sugar

1 Prepare the seafood. Slit open the squid bodies. Score the flesh with a sharp knife, then cut into square pieces. Halve the tentacles, if necessary. Shell and devein the shrimp. Remove the dark beardlike fringe and tough muscle from the scallops. Cube the white fish.

— COOK'S TIP —

It is important to ensure that the shrimp are cooked properly, as undercooked shrimp can carry infection.

2 Heat a wok until hot. Add the oil and swirl it around, then add the shrimp and stir-fry for 2–3 minutes, until pink. Transfer to a large bowl. Stir-fry the squid and scallops for 1–2 minutes, until opaque. Remove and add to the shrimp. Stir-fry the white fish for 2–3 minutes. Remove and add to the cooked seafood. Reserve any juices.

3 Put all the dressing ingredients in a small bowl with the reserved juices from the wok; mix well.

4 Pour the dressing over the seafood and toss gently. Arrange the salad leaves and cilantro sprigs on four individual plates, then spoon the seafood on top. Serve immediately.

Cabbage Salad

A simple and delicious way of using cabbage. Other vegetables such as broccoli, cauliflower, beansprouts and Chinese cabbage can also be prepared this way.

INGREDIENTS

Serves 4–6

2 tablespoons fish sauce
grated rind of 1 lime
2 tablespoons lime juice
½ cup unsweetened coconut milk
2 tablespoons vegetable oil
2 large red chilies, seeded and finely cut into strips
6 garlic cloves, finely sliced
6 shallots, finely sliced
1 small cabbage, shredded
2 tablespoons coarsely chopped roasted peanuts, to serve

1 Make the dressing by combining the fish sauce, lime rind and juice and coconut milk. Set aside.

2 Heat the oil in a wok or frying pan. Stir-fry the chilies, garlic and shallots, until the shallots are brown and crisp. Remove and set aside.

3 Blanch the cabbage in boiling salted water for about 2–3 minutes, drain and put into a bowl.

4 Stir the dressing into the cabbage, toss and mix well. Transfer the salad to a serving dish. Sprinkle with the fried shallot mixture and the chopped roasted peanuts.

Hot-and-sour Chicken Salad

INGREDIENTS

Serves 4–6

2 boneless chicken breasts, skinned
1 small fresh red chili, seeded and
  finely chopped
½-inch piece fresh ginger, peeled
  and finely chopped
1 garlic clove, chopped
1 tablespoon crunchy peanut butter
2 tablespoons chopped fresh cilantro
1 teaspoon sugar
½ teaspoon salt
1 tablespoon rice vinegar or white
  wine vinegar
¼ cup vegetable oil
2 teaspoons fish sauce
  (optional)
½ cup bean sprouts
1 head bok choy, roughly shredded
2 medium carrots, cut into
  thin sticks
1 red onion, cut into fine rings
2 large gherkins, sliced

1 Slice the chicken thinly, place in a shallow bowl and set aside. Grind the chili, ginger and garlic in a mortar with a pestle. Add the peanut butter, cilantro, sugar and salt.

2 Add the vinegar, 2 tablespoons of the oil and the fish sauce, if using. Combine well. Cover the chicken with the spice mixture and let marinate for at least 2–3 hours.

3 Heat the remaining oil in a preheated wok. Add the chicken and cook for 10–12 minutes, turning the meat occasionally. Meanwhile, arrange the bean sprouts, bok choy, carrots, onion rings and gherkins decoratively on a serving platter. Serve the chicken arranged on the salad.

Alfalfa Crab Salad with Crispy Fried Noodles

INGREDIENTS

Serves 4–6

vegetable oil, for deep-frying
2 ounces Chinese rice noodles
5 ounces white crabmeat
½ cup alfalfa sprouts
1 small head iceberg lettuce
4 sprigs fresh cilantro, roughly chopped
1 tomato, skinned, seeded and diced
4 sprigs fresh mint, roughly chopped

For the sesame lime dressing

3 tablespoons vegetable oil
1 tablespoon sesame oil
½ fresh red chili, seeded and chopped
1 piece preserved ginger in syrup, cut
  into matchsticks
2 teaspoons preserved ginger syrup
2 teaspoons soy sauce
juice of ½ lime

1 To make the dressing, combine the vegetable and sesame oils in a bowl. Add the chili, ginger, ginger syrup and soy sauce with the lime juice.

2 Heat the oil in a preheated wok to 375°F. Deep-fry the noodles, one handful at a time, until crisp. Lift out and drain on paper towels.

3 Flake the crabmeat into a bowl and mix well with the alfalfa sprouts. Put the lettuce, cilantro, tomato and mint in a serving bowl, pour on the dressing and toss lightly. Place a nest of noodles on top and finally add the crab and alfalfa sprouts.

Egg Noodle Salad with Sesame Chicken

INGREDIENTS

Serves 4–6

14 ounces fresh, thin egg noodles
1 carrot, cut into long fine strips
2 ounces snow peas, ends removed, cut
    into fine strips and blanched
4 ounces bean sprouts, blanched
2 tablespoons olive oil
8 ounces skinless, boneless chicken
    breasts, finely sliced
2 tablespoons sesame seeds, toasted
2 scallions, finely sliced diagonally
    and cilantro leaves, to garnish

For the dressing

3 tablespoons sherry vinegar
5 tablespoons soy sauce
4 tablespoons sesame oil
6 tablespoons light olive oil
1 garlic clove, finely chopped
1 teaspoon grated fresh ginger
salt and freshly ground black pepper

1 To make the dressing, combine all the ingredients in a small bowl with a pinch of salt, and mix together well using a whisk or a fork.

2 Cook the noodles in a large saucepan of boiling water. Stir them occasionally to separate. They will only take a few minutes to cook: be careful not to overcook them. Drain, rinse under cold running water, and drain well. Turn into a bowl.

3 Add the vegetables to the noodles. Pour in about half the dressing, then toss the mixture well. Adjust the seasoning according to taste.

4 Heat the oil in a large frying pan. Add the chicken, and stir-fry for 3 minutes, or until cooked and golden. Remove from the heat. Add the sesame seeds, and drizzle in some of the remaining dressing.

5 Arrange the noodles on individual serving plates, making a nest on each plate. Spoon the chicken on top. Sprinkle with the sliced scallions and the cilantro leaves. Serve any remaining dressing separately.

Potato and Cellophane Noodle Salad

INGREDIENTS

Serves 4

2 potatoes, peeled and cut
   into eighths
6 ounces cellophane noodles, soaked in
   hot water until soft
4 tablespoons vegetable oil
1 onion, finely sliced
1 teaspoon ground turmeric
4 tablespoons gram flour
1 teaspoon grated lemon rind
4–5 tablespoons lemon juice
3 tablespoons fish sauce
4 scallions, finely sliced
salt and freshly ground black pepper

1 Place the potatoes in a saucepan.
Add water to cover, bring to a boil,
and cook for about 15 minutes until
tender but firm. Drain the potatoes,
then set them aside to cool.

2 Meanwhile, cook the drained
noodles in a saucepan of boiling
water for 3 minutes. Drain, and rinse
under cold running water. Drain well.

3 Heat the oil in a frying pan. Add
the onion and turmeric, and fry for
about 5 minutes until golden brown.
Drain the onion, reserving the oil.

4 Heat a small frying pan. Add the
gram flour, and stir constantly for
about 4 minutes until it turns light
golden brown in color.

5 Mix the potatoes, noodles and
fried onion in a large bowl. Add
the reserved oil and the toasted gram
flour with the lemon rind and juice,
fish sauce and scallions. Mix together
well, and adjust the seasoning to taste,
if necessary. Serve at once.

Curry Fried Pork and Rice Vermicelli Salad

Pork crackles add a delicious crunch to this popular salad.

INGREDIENTS

Serves 4
8 ounces lean pork
2 garlic cloves, finely chopped
2 slices fresh ginger, finely chopped
2–3 tablespoons rice wine
3 tablespoons vegetable oil
2 lemon grass stalks,
   finely chopped
2 teaspoons curry powder
6 ounces bean sprouts
8 ounces rice vermicelli, soaked in
   warm water until soft
½ lettuce, finely shredded
2 tablespoons mint leaves
lemon juice and fish sauce, to taste
salt and freshly ground black pepper
2 scallions, chopped, 2 tablespoons
   roasted peanuts, chopped, and pork
   crackles (optional), to garnish

1 Cut the pork into thin strips. Place in a shallow dish with half the garlic and ginger. Season with salt and pepper, pour over 2 tablespoons rice wine, and marinate for at least 1 hour.

2 Heat the oil in a frying pan. Add the remaining garlic and ginger, and fry for a few seconds until fragrant. Stir in the pork, with the marinade, and add the lemon grass and curry powder. Fry until the pork is golden and cooked through, adding more rice wine if the mixture seems too dry.

3 Place the bean sprouts in a strainer. Blanch them by lowering the strainer into a pan of boiling water for 1 minute, then drain and refresh under cold running water. Drain again. Using the same water, cook the drained rice vermicelli for 3–5 minutes until tender, drain, and rinse under cold running water. Drain well. Turn into a bowl.

4 Add the bean sprouts, shredded lettuce and mint leaves to the rice vermicelli. Season with the lemon juice and fish sauce. Toss lightly.

5 Divide the noodle mixture among individual serving plates, making a nest on each plate. Arrange the pork mixture on top. Garnish with the chopped scallions, roasted peanuts and pork crackles, if using.

Larp of Chiang Mai

Chiang Mai is a city in the north-east of Thailand. The city is culturally very close to Laos and famous for its chicken salad, which was originally called *Laap* or *Larp*. Duck, beef or pork can be used instead.

INGREDIENTS

Serves 4–6

1 pound ground chicken
1 lemongrass stalk, finely chopped
3 kaffir lime leaves, finely chopped
4 red chilies, seeded and chopped
4 tablespoons lime juice
2 tablespoons fish sauce
1 tablespoon roasted ground rice
2 scallions, chopped
2 tablespoons cilantro leaves
mixed salad leaves, cucumber and
    tomato slices, to serve
a few sprigs of mint, to garnish

1 Heat a large non-stick frying pan. Add the ground chicken and cook in a little water.

COOK'S TIP

Use sticky, or glutinous, rice to make roasted ground rice. Firstly put the rice in a frying pan and dry-roast it until golden brown. Remove and grind it to a powder in a mortar and pestle or in a food processor. Keep in a glass jar in a cool and dry place and use as required.

2 Stir constantly for about 7–10 minutes until cooked.

3 Transfer the cooked chicken to a large bowl and add the rest of the ingredients. Mix thoroughly.

4 Serve on a bed of mixed salad leaves, cucumber and tomato slices and garnish with sprigs of mint.

Chinese-style Chicken Salad

This delicious salad is a masterpiece of subtle flavors and contrasts in texture.

INGREDIENTS

Serves 4

4 boneless chicken breasts, about
  6 ounces each
4 tablespoons dark soy sauce
pinch of Chinese five-spice powder
generous squeeze of lemon juice
½ cucumber, peeled and cut into short
  thin sticks
1 teaspoon salt
3 tablespoons sunflower oil
2 tablespoons sesame oil
1 tablespoon sesame seeds
2 tablespoons Chinese rice wine or
  dry sherry
2 medium carrots, cut into short thin
  sticks
8 scallions, cut into fine strips
3 ounces bean sprouts

For the sauce

4 tablespoons crunchy peanut butter
2 teaspoons lemon juice
2 teaspoons sesame oil
¼ teaspoon hot chili powder
1 scallion, finely chopped

1 Put the chicken portions in a large pan and add just enough water to cover. Add 1 tablespoon of the soy sauce, the Chinese five-spice powder and the lemon juice, cover and bring to a boil, then simmer for about 20 minutes.

2 Meanwhile, place the cucumber sticks in a colander, sprinkle with the salt and cover with a plate with a weight on top. Let drain for 30 minutes—set the colander in a bowl to catch the liquid.

3 Lift out the poached chicken with a slotted spoon and let sit until cool enough to handle. Remove and discard the skin. Pound the chicken lightly with a rolling pin to loosen the fibers. Slice into thin strips and set aside.

4 Heat the sunflower and sesame oils in a preheated wok. Add the sesame seeds, fry for 30 seconds and then stir in the remaining soy sauce and the rice wine or dry sherry.

5 Add the carrots and stir-fry for 2–3 minutes, or until just tender. Remove from the heat and set aside.

6 Rinse the cucumber well, pat dry with paper towels and place in a bowl. Add the scallions, bean sprouts, cooked carrots, pan juices and shredded chicken and mix together. Transfer to a shallow dish. Cover and chill for about 1 hour, turning the mixture in the juices once or twice.

7 To make the sauce, cream the peanut butter with the lemon juice, sesame oil and chili powder, adding a little hot water to form a paste, then stir in the scallion. Arrange the chicken mixture on a serving dish and serve with the peanut sauce.

Shrimp Noodle Salad with Fragrant Herbs

A light, refreshing salad with all the tangy flavor of the sea. Instead of shrimp, try squid, scallops, mussels or crab.

INGREDIENTS

Serves 4

4 ounces cellophane noodles, soaked in hot water until soft
16 cooked shrimp, peeled
1 small green bell pepper, seeded and cut into strips
½ cucumber, cut into strips
1 tomato, cut into strips
2 shallots, finely sliced
salt and freshly ground black pepper
cilantro leaves, to garnish

For the dressing

1 tablespoon rice vinegar
2 tablespoons fish sauce
2 tablespoons fresh lime juice
pinch of salt
½ teaspoon grated fresh ginger
1 lemon grass stalk, finely chopped
1 red chili, seeded and finely sliced
2 tablespoons coarsely chopped mint
few sprigs tarragon, coarsely chopped
1 tablespoon snipped chives

1 Make the dressing by combining all the ingredients in a small bowl or cup. Whisk well.

2 Drain the noodles, then plunge them in a saucepan of boiling water for 1 minute. Drain, rinse under cold running water, and drain again well.

3 In a large bowl, combine the noodles with the shrimp, pepper, cucumber, tomato and shallots. Lightly season with salt and pepper, then toss with the dressing.

4 Spoon the noodles onto individual plates, arranging the shrimp on top. Garnish with a few cilantro leaves, and serve at once.

--- COOK'S TIP ---

Shrimp are available pre-cooked and often shelled. To cook shrimp, boil them for 5 minutes. Allow them to cool in the cooking liquid, then gently pull off the tail shell and twist off the head.

Warm Stir-fried Salad

Warm salads are becoming increasingly popular, because they are both delicious and nutritious. Arrange the salad greens on four individual plates so the hot stir-fry can quickly be served on them, ensuring that the greens remain crisp and the chicken warm.

INGREDIENTS

Serves 4

few large sprigs of fresh tarragon
2 skinless, boneless chicken breasts, about 8 ounces each
2-inch piece ginger, peeled and finely chopped
3 tablespoons light soy sauce
1 tablespoon sugar
1 tablespoon sunflower oil
1 Chinese lettuce
½ frisée head of lettuce, torn into bite-sized pieces
1 cup unsalted cashews
2 large carrots, cut into fine strips
salt and freshly ground black pepper

1 Strip the tarragon leaves from the stems and chop the leaves.

2 Cut the chicken into fine strips and place in a bowl.

3 To make the marinade, mix together in a bowl the tarragon, ginger, soy sauce, sugar and seasoning.

4 Pour the marinade over the chicken strips and marinate for 2–4 hours in a cool place.

5 Strain the chicken and reserve the marinade. Heat the oil in a preheated wok. When the oil is hot, stir-fry the chicken for 3 minutes, then add the marinade and allow to bubble for 2–3 minutes.

6 Slice the Chinese lettuce and arrange on a plate with the frisée. Toss the cashews and carrots together with the chicken, pile on top of the bed of lettuce and serve immediately.

Thai Beef Salad

A hearty salad of beef, laced with a chili and lime dressing.

INGREDIENTS

Serves 4

2 x 8-ounce sirloin steaks
1 red onion, finely sliced
½ cucumber, finely sliced into
   matchsticks
1 lemongrass stalk, finely chopped
juice of 2 limes
1–2 tablespoons fish sauce
2 tablespoons chopped scallions
2–4 red chilies, finely sliced, to garnish
fresh cilantro, Chinese mustard cress
   and mint leaves, to garnish

1 Pan-fry or broil the beef steaks to medium-rare. Allow to rest for 10–15 minutes.

2 When cool, thinly slice the beef and put the slices in a large bowl.

3 Add the sliced onion, cucumber matchsticks and lemongrass.

4 Add the scallions. Toss and season with lime juice and fish sauce. Serve at room temperature or chilled, garnished with the chilies, cilantro, Chinese mustard cress and mint.

Tangy Chicken Salad

This fresh and lively dish typifies the character of Thai cuisine. It is ideal for a snack or light lunch.

INGREDIENTS

Serves 4–6

4 skinned, boneless chicken breasts
2 garlic cloves, crushed and
　coarsely chopped
2 tablespoons soy sauce
2 tablespoons vegetable oil
½ cup coconut cream
2 tablespoons fish sauce
juice of 1 lime
2 tablespoons palm sugar
4 ounces water chestnuts, sliced
½ cup cashews, roasted
4 shallots, finely sliced
4 kaffir lime leaves, finely sliced
1 lemongrass stalk, finely sliced
1 teaspoon chopped galangal
1 large red chili, seeded and
　finely sliced
2 scallions, finely sliced
10–12 mint leaves, torn
1 head of lettuce, to serve
sprigs of cilantro and 2 green or red
　chilies, seeded and sliced, to garnish

1 Trim the chicken breasts of any excess fat and put them in a large dish. Rub with the garlic, soy sauce and 1 tablespoon of the oil. Allow to marinate for 1–2 hours.

2 Broil or pan-fry the chicken for 3–4 minutes on both sides or until cooked. Remove and set aside to cool.

3 In a small saucepan, heat the coconut cream, fish sauce, lime juice and palm sugar. Stir until all of the sugar has dissolved and then remove from the heat.

4 Cut the cooked chicken into strips and combine with the water chestnuts, cashews, shallots, kaffir lime leaves, lemongrass, galangal, red chili, scallions and mint leaves.

5 Pour the coconut dressing over the chicken, toss and mix well. Serve the chicken on a bed of lettuce leaves and garnish with sprigs of cilantro and sliced chilies.

Noodles with Pineapple, Ginger and Chilies

INGREDIENTS

Serves 4

10 ounces dried udon noodles
½ pineapple, peeled, cored and sliced
   into 1½-inch rings
3 tablespoons light brown sugar
4 tablespoons fresh lime juice
4 tablespoons coconut milk
2 tablespoons fish sauce
2 tablespoons finely grated fresh ginger
2 garlic cloves, finely chopped
1 ripe mango or 2 peaches,
   finely diced
freshly ground black pepper
2 scallions, finely sliced, 2 red chilies,
   seeded and finely shredded,
   plus mint leaves, to garnish

1 Cook the noodles in a large saucepan of boiling water until tender, following the directions on the package. Drain, refresh under cold water, and drain again.

2 Place the pineapple rings in a flameproof dish, sprinkle with 2 tablespoons of the sugar, and broil for 5 minutes or until golden brown. Cool slightly, and cut into small dice.

3 Mix the lime juice, coconut milk and fish sauce in a salad bowl. Add the remaining brown sugar, with the ginger and garlic, and whisk well. Add the noodles and pineapple.

4 Add the mango or peaches, and toss. Sprinkle over the scallions, chilies and mint leaves before serving.

Buckwheat Noodles with Smoked Salmon

Young pea sprouts are only available for a short time. You can substitute watercress, mustard cress, young leeks or your favorite green vegetable or herb in this dish.

INGREDIENTS

Serves 4

8 ounces buckwheat or soba noodles
1 tablespoon oyster sauce
juice of ½ lemon
2–3 tablespoons light olive oil
4 ounces smoked salmon, cut into
   fine strips
4 ounces young pea sprouts
2 ripe tomatoes, peeled, seeded and cut
   into strips
1 tablespoon snipped chives
salt and freshly ground black pepper

1 Cook the buckwheat or soba noodles in a large saucepan of boiling water, following the directions on the package. Drain, rinse under cold running water, and drain again.

2 Turn the noodles into a large bowl. Add the oyster sauce and lemon juice, and season with pepper to taste. Moisten with the olive oil.

3 Add the smoked salmon, pea sprouts, tomatoes and chives. Mix well, and serve at once.

Sesame Duck and Noodle Salad

This salad is complete in itself and makes a lovely summer lunch. The marinade is a marvelous blend of spices.

INGREDIENTS

Serves 4

2 duck breasts
1 tablespoon vegetable oil
2 medium carrots, cut into 3-inch sticks
5 ounces sugar snap peas
8 ounces medium egg noodles
6 scallions, sliced
salt
fresh cilantro leaves, to garnish

For the marinade

1 tablespoon sesame oil
1 teaspoon ground coriander
1 teaspoon Chinese five-spice powder

For the dressing

1 tablespoon garlic vinegar
1 teaspoon light brown sugar
1 teaspoon soy sauce
1 tablespoon toasted sesame seeds
freshly ground black pepper
3 tablespoons sunflower oil
2 tablespoons sesame oil

1 Slice the duck breasts thinly crosswise and place them in a shallow dish. Combine the ingredients for the marinade, pour over the duck and mix well to coat thoroughly. Cover and let sit in a cool place for 30 minutes.

2 Heat the oil in a preheated wok or frying pan, add the slices of duck breast and stir-fry for 3–4 minutes, or until cooked. Set aside.

3 Bring a saucepan of lightly salted water to a boil. Place the carrots and sugar snap peas in a steamer that will fit on top of the pan. When the water boils, add the noodles, place the steamer on top and steam the vegetables while cooking the noodles for the time suggested on the package. Set the steamed vegetables aside. Drain the noodles, refresh them under cold running water and drain again. Place them in a large serving bowl.

4 To make the dressing, mix the vinegar, sugar, soy sauce and sesame seeds in a bowl. Season well with black pepper, then whisk in the sunflower and sesame oils.

5 Pour the dressing over the noodles and mix well. Add the sugar snap peas, carrots, scallions and duck slices and toss to combine. Scatter the cilantro leaves on top and serve.

Duck, Avocado and Raspberry Salad

Rich duck breasts are roasted
until crisp with a honey and
soy glaze to serve warm with
fresh raspberries and avocado.
A delicious raspberry and red
currant dressing adds a wonderful
sweet-and-sour flavor.

INGREDIENTS

Serves 4

4 small or 2 large duck breasts, halved
  if large
1 tablespoon honey
1 tablespoon dark soy sauce
4 tablespoons olive oil
1 tablespoon raspberry vinegar
1 tablespoon red currant jelly
selection of salad greens, such as lamb's
  lettuce, red chicory and frisée
2 avocados, pitted, peeled and cut
  into chunks
4 ounces raspberries
salt and freshly ground black pepper

1 Prick the skin of each duck breast
with a fork. Blend the honey and
soy sauce together in a small bowl, then
brush all over the skin.

2 Place the duck breasts on a rack set
over a roasting pan and season with
salt and pepper. Roast in a preheated
oven at 425°F for 15–20 minutes, or
until the skin is crisp and the meat
is cooked.

3 Meanwhile, to make the dressing,
put the oil, vinegar, red currant
jelly and seasoning in a small bowl and
whisk well until evenly blended.

4 Slice the duck breasts diagonally
and arrange on individual plates
with the salad greens, avocado chunks
and raspberries. Spoon the dressing on
top and serve immediately.

Spicy Szechuan Noodles

INGREDIENTS

Serves 4

12 ounces thick noodles
6 ounces cooked chicken, shredded
2 ounces roasted cashews

For the dressing
4 scallions, chopped
2 tablespoons chopped cilantro
2 garlic cloves, chopped
2 tablespoons smooth peanut butter
2 tablespoons sweet chili sauce
1 tablespoon soy sauce
1 tablespoon sherry vinegar
1 tablespoon sesame oil
2 tablespoons olive oil
2 tablespoons chicken broth or water
10 toasted Szechuan peppercorns,
 ground

1 Cook the noodles in a saucepan of boiling water until just tender, following the directions on the package. Drain, rinse under cold running water, and drain well.

2 While the noodles are cooking, combine all the ingredients for the dressing in a large bowl. Whisk together well.

3 Add the noodles, shredded chicken and cashews to the dressing, toss gently to coat, and adjust the seasoning to taste. Serve at once.

VARIATION

For a change, you could substitute cooked turkey or pork for the chicken.

Sesame Noodles with Scallions

This simple, but very tasty, warm salad can be prepared and cooked in just a few minutes.

INGREDIENTS

Serves 4

2 garlic cloves, coarsely chopped
2 tablespoons Chinese sesame paste
1 tablespoon dark sesame oil
2 tablespoons soy sauce
2 tablespoons rice wine
1 tablespoon honey
pinch of five-spice powder
12 ounces soba or buckwheat noodles
4 scallions, finely sliced diagonally
2 ounces bean sprouts
3-inch piece of cucumber, cut
 into matchsticks
toasted sesame seeds
salt and freshly ground black pepper

1 Process the garlic, sesame paste, oil, soy sauce, rice wine, honey and five-spice powder with a pinch each of salt and pepper in a blender or food processor until smooth.

2 Cook the noodles in a saucepan of boiling water until just tender, following the directions on the package. Drain the noodles, and turn them into a bowl.

3 Toss the hot noodles with the dressing and the scallions. Top with the bean sprouts, cucumber and sesame seeds, and serve.

COOK'S TIP

If you can't find Chinese sesame paste, then use either tahini or smooth peanut butter instead.

Sweet-and-Sour Fruit and Vegetable Salad

With its clean taste and bright, jewellike colors, *acar bening* makes a perfect accompaniment to many spicy dishes. Any leftover salad can be covered and stored in the refrigerator for up to two days. This is an ideal dish for buffets.

INGREDIENTS

Serves 8
1 small cucumber
salt
1 onion
1 small ripe pineapple or 1 can (15 ounces) pineapple rings
1 green bell pepper, thinly sliced
3 firm tomatoes, cut into wedges
3–4 tablespoons cider vinegar or white wine vinegar
½ cup water
1 ounce light brown sugar

1 Peel the cucumber and cut in half lengthwise. Remove the seeds with a small spoon. Cut the cucumber into even-sized pieces. Sprinkle with a little salt. Thinly slice the onion and sprinkle with a little salt as well. Let cucumber and onion sit for a few minutes, then rinse and pat dry, and mix them together in a bowl.

2 Peel the fresh pineapple, if using, removing all the "eyes." Slice the pineapple thinly, then core the slices and cut into neat pieces. If using canned pineapple, cut the rings into similar-sized pieces. Add them to the bowl, together with the green bell pepper slices and tomato wedges.

3 Heat the vinegar, water and sugar until the sugar dissolves. Remove from the heat and let cool. When cool, add salt to taste and then pour over the fruit and vegetables. Cover and chill until required.

Rice Vermicelli and Salad Spring Rolls

Goi Cuor is a hearty noodle salad wrapped in rice sheets. It makes a healthy change from a sandwich and is great for a picnic.

INGREDIENTS

Makes 8

2 ounces rice vermicelli, soaked in
   warm water until soft
1 large carrot, shredded
1 tablespoon sugar
1–2 tablespoons fish sauce
8 x 8-inch round rice sheets
8 large lettuce leaves, thick
   stalks removed
12 ounces Chinese roast pork, sliced
4 ounces bean sprouts
handful of mint leaves
8 cooked jumbo shrimp, peeled,
   deveined and halved
½ cucumber, cut into fine strips
cilantro leaves, to garnish

For the peanut sauce
1 tablespoon vegetable oil
3 garlic cloves, finely chopped
1–2 red chilies, finely chopped
1 teaspoon tomato paste
½ cup water
1 tablespoon smooth peanut butter
2 tablespoons hoisin sauce
½ teaspoon sugar
juice of 1 lime
½ cup roasted peanuts, ground

1 Drain the noodles. Cook in a saucepan of boiling water for about 2–3 minutes until tender. Drain, rinse under cold running water, and drain well. Turn into a bowl. Add the carrot. Season with the sugar and fish sauce.

2 Assemble the rolls, one at a time. Dip a rice sheet in a bowl of warm water, then lay it flat on a surface. Place 1 lettuce leaf, 1–2 scoops of the noodle mixture, a few slices of pork, some of the bean sprouts and several mint leaves on the rice sheet.

3 Start rolling up the rice sheet into a cylinder. When half the sheet has been rolled up, fold both sides of the sheet towards the center, and lay 2 pieces of shrimp along the crease.

4 Add a few of strips of cucumber and some of the cilantro leaves. Continue to roll up the sheet to make a tight package. Place the roll on a plate, and cover with a damp dish towel, so that it stays moist while you make the remaining rolls.

5 Make the peanut sauce. Heat the oil in a small saucepan, and fry the garlic, chilies and tomato paste for about 1 minute. Add the water, and bring to a boil, then stir in the peanut butter, hoisin sauce, sugar and lime juice. Mix well. Reduce the heat, and simmer for 3–4 minutes. Spoon the sauce into a bowl, add the ground peanuts, and cool to room temperature.

6 To serve, cut each roll in half. Add a spoonful of the peanut sauce.

Fruit and Raw Vegetable Gado-gado

A banana leaf, which can be bought from oriental stores, can be used to line the platter for a special occasion.

INGREDIENTS

Serves 6

2 unripe pears, peeled at the last moment, or 6-ounce wedge *bangkuang* (yambean), peeled and cut in matchsticks

1–2 eating apples

juice of ½ lemon

1 small, crisp lettuce, shredded

½ cucumber, seeded, sliced and salted, set aside for 15 minutes, then rinsed and drained

6 small tomatoes, cut in wedges

3 slices fresh pineapple, cored and cut in wedges

3 eggs or 12 quail's eggs, hard-boiled and shelled

6 ounces egg noodles, cooked, cooled and chopped

deep-fried onions, to garnish

For the peanut sauce

2–4 fresh red chilies, seeded and ground

1¼ cups coconut milk

12 ounces crunchy peanut butter

1 tablespoon dark soy sauce or dark brown sugar

1 teaspoon tamarind pulp, soaked in 3 tablespoons warm water, strained and juice reserved

coarsely crushed peanuts

salt

1 To make the Peanut Sauce, put the chilies and coconut milk in a pan. Add the peanut butter and heat gently, stirring, until no lumps of peanut butter remain.

2 Allow to simmer gently until the sauce thickens, then add the soy sauce or sugar and tamarind juice. Season with salt to taste. Pour into a bowl and sprinkle with a few coarsely crushed peanuts.

3 To make the salad, peel and core the pears or *bangkuang* and apples. Slice the apples and sprinkle with lemon juice. Arrange the salad and fruit attractively on a flat platter. The lettuce can be used, instead of a banana leaf, to form a bed for the salad.

4 Add the sliced or quartered hard-cooked eggs (leave quail's eggs whole), the chopped noodles and the deep-fried onions.

5 Serve at once, accompanied with a bowl of the Peanut Sauce.

Sesame Noodle Salad with Hot Peanuts

An Eastern-inspired salad with crunchy vegetables and a light soy dressing.

INGREDIENTS

Serves 4

12 ounces egg noodles
2 medium carrots, cut into fine
  julienne strips
½ cucumber, peeled, seeded and cut
  into ½-inch cubes
4 ounces celery root, peeled and cut
  into fine julienne strips
6 scallions, finely sliced
8 canned water chestnuts, drained and
  finely sliced
6 ounces bean sprouts
1 small fresh green chili, seeded and
  finely chopped
2 tablespoons sesame seeds and 1 cup
  peanuts, to serve

For the dressing

1 tablespoon dark soy sauce
1 tablespoon light soy sauce
1 tablespoon clear honey
1 tablespoon Chinese rice wine or
  dry sherry
1 tablespoon sesame oil

1 Cook the egg noodles in boiling water, following the instructions on the package.

2 Drain the noodles, refresh in cold water, then drain again. Mix the noodles together with all of the prepared vegetables.

3 Combine the dressing ingredients in a small bowl, then toss into the noodle and vegetable mixture. Divide the salad among four plates.

4 Place the sesame seeds and peanuts on separate baking sheets and place in a preheated oven at 400°F. Take the sesame seeds out after 5 minutes and continue to cook the peanuts for another 5 minutes, or until evenly browned.

5 Sprinkle the sesame seeds and peanuts evenly over each salad portion and serve immediately.

Thai Fruit and Vegetable Salad

This fruit salad is typically presented with the main course and serves as a cooler to counteract the heat of Thai curry.

INGREDIENTS

Serves 4–6

1 small pineapple
1 small mango, peeled, pitted
  and sliced
1 green apple, cored and sliced
6 ramboutans or lychees, peeled
  and pitted
4 ounces green beans, halved
1 medium red onion, sliced
1 small cucumber, cut into short sticks
4 ounces bean sprouts
2 scallions, sliced
1 ripe tomato, quartered
8 ounces romaine, Bibb or iceberg
  lettuce leaves, torn into pieces
salt

For the coconut dipping sauce
6 tablespoons coconut cream
2 tablespoons sugar
5 tablespoons boiling water
¼ teaspoon chili sauce
1 tablespoon fish sauce
juice of 1 lime

1 To make the dipping sauce, place the coconut cream, sugar and boiling water in a screw-top jar. Add the chili sauce, fish sauce and lime juice and shake to mix. Set aside.

2 Trim both ends of the pineapple with a serrated knife, then cut away the skin. Remove the central core with an apple corer, or cut the pineapple into four pieces down the middle and remove the core with a knife. Roughly chop the pineapple and set aside with the other fruits.

3 Bring a small saucepan of lightly salted water to a boil and cook the beans for 3–4 minutes. Refresh under cold running water and set aside. To serve, arrange the fruits, vegetables and lettuce leaves in individual heaps in a serving bowl. Serve the dipping sauce separately.

--- COOK'S TIP ---

The ramboutan or rambutan, cousin to the lychee, originated in Malaysia but is now cultivated in much of Southeast Asia and the US. It has a dark reddish-brown, hairy skin with sweet, translucent flesh and an inedible pit. It is about two inches in diameter.

Bamboo Shoot Salad

This salad, which has a hot and sharp flavor, originated in northeast Thailand. Use fresh young bamboo shoots when you can find them, otherwise substitute canned bamboo shoots.

INGREDIENTS

Serves 4

14-ounce can whole bamboo shoots
1 ounce glutinous (sticky) rice
2 tablespoons chopped shallots
1 tablespoon chopped garlic
3 tablespoons chopped scallions
2 tablespoons fish sauce
2 tablespoons lime juice
1 teaspoon sugar
½ teaspoon dried flaked chilies
20–25 small mint leaves
1 tablespoon toasted sesame seeds

3 Turn the rice into a bowl, add the shallots, garlic, scallions, fish sauce, lime juice, sugar, chilies and half the mint leaves.

4 Mix thoroughly, then pour over the bamboo shoots and toss together. Serve sprinkled with sesame seeds and the remaining mint leaves.

1 Rinse and drain the bamboo shoots, finely slice and set aside.

2 Dry-roast the rice in a frying pan until it is golden brown. Remove and grind to fine crumbs with a mortar and pestle.

Egg Pancake Salad Wrappers

One of Indonesia's favorite snack foods, pancakes are assembled according to taste and dipped in various sauces.

INGREDIENTS

Makes 12

2 eggs
½ teaspoon salt
1 teaspoon vegetable oil, plus extra
    for frying
1 cup flour
1¼ cups water
shredded lettuce leaves, bean sprouts,
    cucumber wedges, shredded scallions,
    cooked peeled shrimp and cilantro
    sprigs, to serve

For the filling

3 tablespoons vegetable oil
½-inch piece fresh ginger, chopped
1 garlic clove, crushed
1 small red fresh chili, seeded and finely
    chopped
1 tablespoon rice vinegar or white
    wine vinegar
2 teaspoons sugar
4 ounces daikon, grated
1 medium carrot, grated
4 ounces Chinese cabbage, shredded
2 shallots or 1 small red onion,
    thinly sliced

1 Break the eggs into a bowl and stir in the salt, vegetable oil and flour until smooth; do not overmix. Add the water, a little at a time, and strain into a pitcher. Allow the batter to stand for 15–20 minutes before use.

2 Moisten a small, nonstick frying pan with vegetable oil and heat. Pour in enough batter just to cover the base of the pan and cook for 30 seconds. Turn over and cook the other side briefly. Stack the pancakes on a plate, cover and keep warm.

3 To make the filling, heat the oil in a preheated wok, add the ginger, garlic and chili and stir-fry for 1–2 minutes. Add the vinegar, sugar, daikon, carrot, Chinese cabbage and shallots or onion. Cook for 3–4 minutes. Serve with the pancakes, shrimp and salad ingredients.

Green Vegetable Salad with Coconut Mint Dip

This dish is usually served as an accompaniment to Singapore and Malaysian meat dishes.

INGREDIENTS

Serves 4–6

4 ounces snow peas, halved
4 ounces green beans, halved
½ cucumber, peeled, halved and sliced
4 ounces Chinese cabbage, roughly
  shredded
4 ounces bean sprouts
salt
lettuce leaves, to serve

For the dressing

1 garlic clove, crushed
1 small fresh green chili, seeded and
  finely chopped
2 teaspoons sugar
3 tablespoons creamed coconut
5 tablespoons boiling water
2 teaspoons fish sauce
3 tablespoons vegetable oil
juice of 1 lime
2 tablespoons chopped fresh mint

2 To make the dressing, pound the garlic, chili and sugar together in a mortar with a pestle. Add the coconut, boiling water, fish sauce, vegetable oil, lime juice and mint. Stir well.

3 Arrange the blanched vegetables, Chinese cabbage and bean sprouts on a bed of lettuce in a basket, pour the dressing into a shallow bowl and serve.

1 Bring a saucepan of lightly salted water to a boil. Blanch the snow peas, green beans and cucumber for 4 minutes. Drain and refresh under cold running water. Drain and set aside.

Eggplant Salad with Dried Shrimp and Egg

An appetizing and unusual salad that you will find yourself making over and over again.

INGREDIENTS

Serves 4–6

2 eggplant
1 tablespoon oil
2 tablespoons dried shrimp, soaked
    and drained
1 tablespoon coarsely chopped garlic
2 tablespoons fresh lime juice
1 teaspoon palm sugar
2 tablespoons fish sauce
1 hard-cooked egg, shelled and
    chopped
4 shallots, finely sliced into rings
cilantro leaves, to garnish
2 red chilies, seeded and sliced,
    to garnish

COOK'S TIP

For an interesting variation, try using salted
duck or quail eggs, cut in halves.

1 Broil or roast the eggplant until charred and tender.

2 When cool enough to handle, peel away the skin and slice the flesh.

3 Heat the oil in a small frying pan, add the drained shrimp and garlic and fry until golden. Remove from the pan and set aside.

4 To make the dressing, put the lime juice, palm sugar and fish sauce in a small bowl and whisk together.

5 To serve, arrange the eggplant on a serving dish. Top with the egg, shallots and dried shrimp mixture. Drizzle over the dressing and garnish with cilantro and red chilies.

Hot Coconut Shrimp and Papaya Salad

This Thai dish may be served as an accompaniment to beef and chicken dishes or on its own as a light lunch in the summer.

INGREDIENTS

Serves 4–6

8 ounces jumbo shrimp, raw or cooked, peeled and deveined
2 ripe papayas
8 ounces mixed salad greens, such as romaine, iceberg or Bibb lettuce, Chinese cabbage or young spinach
1 firm tomato, seeded and roughly chopped
3 scallions, cut into fine strips

For the dressing

1 tablespoon creamed coconut
2 tablespoons boiling water
6 tablespoons vegetable oil
juice of 1 lime
½ teaspoon hot chili sauce
2 teaspoons fish sauce (optional)
1 teaspoon sugar
1 small bunch fresh cilantro, roughly chopped

1 First make the dressing: place the creamed coconut in a screw-top jar and add the boiling water. Add the vegetable oil, lime juice, chili sauce, fish sauce, if using, sugar and cilantro. Shake well and set aside, but do not refrigerate.

2 If using raw shrimp, place them in a saucepan and cover with water. Bring to a boil and simmer for 2 minutes. Drain and set aside.

3 To prepare the papaya, cut each in half from top to bottom and remove the black seeds with a teaspoon. Peel away the outer skin and cut the flesh into even-sized pieces. Wash the salad greens and toss in a bowl. Add the other ingredients, pour the dressing on top and serve.

Seafood Salad with Fragrant Herbs

INGREDIENTS

Serves 4–6
1 cup fish stock or water
12 ounces squid, cut into rings
12 uncooked jumbo shrimp, shelled
12 scallops
2 ounces bean thread noodles, soaked
  in warm water for 30 minutes
½ cucumber, cut into thin sticks
1 lemongrass stalk, finely chopped
2 kaffir lime leaves, finely shredded
2 shallots, finely sliced
juice of 1–2 limes
2 tablespoons fish sauce
2 tablespoons chopped scallions
2 tablespoons cilantro leaves
12–15 mint leaves, coarsely torn
4 red chilies, sliced
sprigs of cilantro, to garnish

1 Pour the stock or water into a medium-size saucepan, set over high heat and bring to a boil.

2 Cook each type of seafood separately in the stock for a few minutes. Remove and set aside.

3 Drain the bean thread noodles and cut them into short lengths, about 2 inches long. Combine the noodles with the cooked seafood.

4 Add all the remaining ingredients, mix together well and serve garnished with the cilantro sprigs.

Pomelo Salad

Pomelo is a large fruit that resembles a grapefruit. It has a much sturdier and drier flesh.

INGREDIENTS

Serves 4–6
For the dressing
2 tablespoons fish sauce
1 tablespoon palm sugar
2 tablespoons lime juice

For the salad
2 tablespoons vegetable oil
4 shallots, finely sliced
2 garlic cloves, finely sliced
1 large pomelo
4 ounces cooked, shelled shrimp
4 ounces cooked crab meat
1 tablespoon roasted peanuts
10–12 small mint leaves, chopped
2 scallions, finely sliced, 2 red chilies,
  seeded and finely sliced, cilantro
  leaves and shredded fresh coconut
  (optional), to garnish

1 Whisk together the fish sauce, palm sugar and lime juice and set aside.

2 Heat the oil in a small frying pan, add the shallots and garlic and fry until they are golden. Remove from the pan and set aside.

3 Peel the pomelo and break the flesh into small pieces, taking care to remove any membranes.

4 Coarsely grind the peanuts, then combine with the pomelo flesh, shrimp, crab meat, mint leaves and the fried shallot mixture. Toss in the dressing and serve sprinkled with the scallions, red chilies, cilantro leaves and shredded coconut, if using.

NOODLES

Noodles are the original "fast food" in Asia and are eaten on almost every possible occasion, from weddings to funerals. There are numerous varieties and they are served both hot and cold, cooked in combination with vegetables, meat, poultry and seafood. They can be braised, deep-fried and stir-fried, as well as made into nests and cakes. Noodles may be served as a complete meal or simply as a side dish. Recipes here include Singapore Noodles, Special Chow Mein, Vegetarian Fried Noodles and Crisp Pork Meatballs Laced with Noodles.

Asian Vegetable Noodles

Thin Italian egg pasta is a good alternative to Asian egg noodles; use it fresh or dried.

INGREDIENTS

Serves 6

1¼ pounds thin tagliarini
4 ounces shiitake mushrooms
1 red onion
3 tablespoons sesame oil
3 tablespoons dark soy sauce
1 tablespoon balsamic vinegar
2 teaspoons superfine sugar
salt
celery leaves, to garnish

1 Cook the tagliarini in a large pan of salted boiling water, following the instructions on the package.

2 Thinly slice the mushrooms and the red onion, using a sharp knife.

3 Heat 1 tablespoon of the sesame oil in a preheated wok. When the oil is hot, stir-fry the onion and mushrooms for 2 minutes.

4 Drain the tagliarini, then add to the wok with the soy sauce, balsamic vinegar, sugar and salt to taste. Stir-fry for 1 minute, then add the remaining sesame oil and serve garnished with celery leaves.

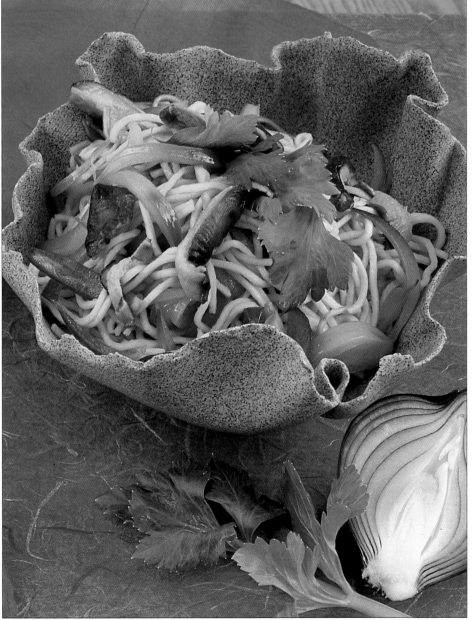

Peanut Noodles

Add any of your favorite vegetables to this recipe to make a great, quick midweek supper—and increase the chili, if you can take the heat!

INGREDIENTS

Serves 4

7 ounces medium egg noodles
2 tablespoons olive oil
2 garlic cloves, crushed
1 large onion, roughly chopped
1 red bell pepper, seeded and roughly chopped
1 yellow bell pepper, seeded and roughly chopped
12 ounces zucchini, roughly chopped
1¼ cups roasted unsalted peanuts, roughly chopped

For the dressing
¼ cup olive oil
grated rind and juice of 1 lemon
1 fresh red chili, seeded and finely chopped
4 tablespoons chopped fresh chives
1–2 tablespoons balsamic vinegar
salt and freshly ground black pepper

2 Meanwhile, heat the oil in a preheated wok or very large frying pan and cook the garlic and onion for 3 minutes, or until beginning to soften. Add the bell peppers and zucchini and cook for another 15 minutes over medium heat, until beginning to soften and brown. Add the peanuts and cook for 1 minute more.

3 For the dressing, whisk together the olive oil, grated lemon rind and 3 tablespoons lemon juice, the chili, 3 tablespoons of the chives, plenty of seasoning and balsamic vinegar to taste.

4 Toss the noodles into the vegetables and stir-fry to heat through. Add the dressing, stir to coat and serve immediately, garnished with the remaining chopped fresh chives.

1 Cook the noodles according to the package instructions and drain well.

Soft Fried Noodles

This is a basic dish for serving as an accompaniment or for those occasions when you are feeling a little out of sorts and just want something simple. Break an egg into the noodles if you want to add protein. They are also good tossed with oyster sauce and a dollop of chili black bean sauce.

INGREDIENTS

Serves 4–6
12 ounces dried egg noodles
2 tablespoons vegetable oil
2 tablespoons finely chopped scallions
soy sauce, to taste
salt and freshly ground black pepper

1 Cook the noodles in a large saucepan of boiling water until just tender, following the directions on the package. Drain, rinse under cold running water, and drain again.

2 Heat the oil in a wok, and swirl it around. Add the scallions, and fry for 30 seconds. Add the noodles, stirring gently to separate the strands.

3 Reduce the heat, and fry the noodles until they are heated through, lightly browned and crisp on the outside, but still soft inside.

4 Season with soy sauce, salt and pepper. Serve at once.

Egg Fried Noodles

Yellow bean sauce gives these noodles a savory flavor.

INGREDIENTS

Serves 4–6
12 ounces medium-thick egg noodles
4 tablespoons vegetable oil
4 scallions, cut into ½-inch rounds
juice of 1 lime
1 tablespoon soy sauce
2 garlic cloves, finely chopped
6 ounces skinless, boneless chicken breast, sliced
6 ounces raw shrimp, peeled and deveined
6 ounces squid, cleaned and cut into rings
1 tablespoon yellow bean sauce
1 tablespoon fish sauce
1 tablespoon light brown sugar
2 eggs
cilantro leaves, to garnish

1 Cook the noodles in a saucepan of boiling water until just tender, then drain well. Set aside.

2 Heat half the oil in a wok or large frying pan. Add the scallions, stir-fry for 2 minutes, then add the noodles, lime juice and soy sauce. Stir-fry for 2–3 minutes. Transfer the mixture to a bowl, and keep warm.

3 Heat the remaining oil in the wok or pan. Add the garlic, chicken, shrimp and squid. Stir-fry over a high heat until cooked.

4 Stir in the yellow bean paste, fish sauce and sugar, then break the eggs into the mixture, stirring gently until they set.

5 Add the noodles, toss lightly to mix, and heat through. Serve garnished with cilantro leaves.

Lettuce Wraps with Sesame Noodles

INGREDIENTS

Serves 4

1 tablespoon vegetable oil
2 duck breasts, about 8 ounces
 .each, trimmed
4 tablespoons saké
4 tablespoons soy sauce
2 tablespoons mirin
1 tablespoon sugar
½ cucumber, halved, seeded and
 finely diced
2 tablespoons chopped red onion
2 red chilies, seeded and
 finely chopped
2 tablespoons rice vinegar
4 ounces rice vermicelli, soaked in
 warm water until soft
1 tablespoon dark sesame oil
1 tablespoon black sesame
 seeds, toasted
handful of cilantro leaves
12–16 large green or red
 lettuce leaves
handful of mint leaves
salt and freshly ground black pepper

1 Heat the oil in a large frying pan, add the duck breasts, skin side down, and fry until golden. Turn each breast and fry the other side briefly. Remove the duck, rinse under hot water to remove excess oil, then drain.

2 Combine the saké, soy sauce, mirin and sugar in a saucepan large enough to hold both duck breasts in a single layer. Bring to a boil, add the duck, skin side down, lower the heat, and simmer for 3–5 minutes, depending on the thickness of the duck. Remove the pan from the heat. Let the duck cool in the liquid.

3 Using a slotted spoon, transfer the duck to a board. Then slice thinly using a large, sharp knife. Return the pan to a low heat, and cook the sauce until it reduces and thickens slightly.

4 In a serving bowl, mix the diced cucumber with the red onion, chilies and rice vinegar. Set aside.

5 Cook the noodles in a saucepan of boiling water for about 3 minutes or until tender. Drain and rinse under cold running water. Drain again, then pour into a serving bowl. Toss lightly with the sesame oil and seeds. Season with salt and pepper.

6 Place the thickened sauce and cilantro leaves in separate serving bowls, alongside the bowls of noodles and the cucumber mixture. Arrange the lettuce leaves and sliced duck on individual serving plates.

7 To serve, place a few slices of duck, some noodles, cucumber, herbs and sauce inside a lettuce leaf. Wrap and eat.

Singapore Noodles

Dried Chinese mushrooms add an intense flavor to this lightly curried dish.

INGREDIENTS

Serves 4

¼ ounce dried Chinese mushrooms
8 ounces fine egg noodles
2 teaspoons sesame oil
3 tablespoons peanut oil
2 garlic cloves, crushed
1 small onion, chopped
1 fresh green chili, seeded and
    thinly sliced
2 teaspoons curry powder
4 ounces green beans, halved
4 ounces Chinese cabbage, thinly
    shredded
4 scallions, sliced
2 tablespoons soy sauce
4 ounces cooked jumbo shrimp, peeled
    and deveined
salt

1 Place the mushrooms in a bowl, cover with warm water and soak for 30 minutes. Drain, reserving 2 tablespoons of the soaking water, then slice.

2 Bring a saucepan of lightly salted water to a boil and cook the noodles according to the directions on the package. Drain, transfer to a bowl and toss with the sesame oil.

COOK'S TIP

This dish lends itself to a variety of vegetables. Try snow peas, broccoli, bell peppers or baby corn. The shrimp can be omitted or replaced with ham or chicken, if desired.

3 Heat the peanut oil in a preheated wok. When it is hot, stir-fry the garlic, onion and chili for 3 minutes. Stir in the curry powder and cook for 1 minute. Add the mushrooms, green beans, Chinese cabbage and scallions. Stir-fry for 3–4 minutes, or until the vegetables are tender but still crisp.

4 Add the noodles, soy sauce, reserved mushroom soaking water and shrimp. Toss over the heat for 2–3 minutes, or until the noodles and shrimp are heated through.

Chinese Mushrooms with Cellophane Noodles

Red fermented bean curd adds extra flavor to this hearty vegetarian dish. It is brick-red in color, with a very strong flavor of cheese, and is made by fermenting bean curd (tofu) with salt, red rice and rice wine. Look out for it in cans or jars at Chinese food markets.

INGREDIENTS

Serves 4

4 ounces dried Chinese mushrooms
1 ounce dried wood ears
4 ounces dried bean curd
2 tablespoons vegetable oil
2 garlic cloves, finely chopped
2 slices fresh ginger, finely chopped
10 Szechuan peppercorns, crushed
1 tablespoon red fermented bean curd
½ star anise
pinch of sugar
1–2 tablespoons soy sauce
2 ounces cellophane noodles, soaked in
   hot water until soft
salt

2 Strain the mushrooms, reserving the liquid. Squeeze as much liquid from the mushrooms as possible, then discard the mushroom stems. Cut the cups in half if they are large.

5 Add the reserved mushroom liquid to the pan, with sufficient water to cover the mushrooms completely. Add the star anise, sugar and soy sauce, then cover, and simmer for 30 minutes.

6 Add the chopped wood ears and reconstituted bean curd pieces to the pan. Cover, and cook for about 10 minutes.

7 Drain the cellophane noodles, add them to the mixture, and cook for 10 minutes more until tender, adding more liquid if necessary. Add salt to taste, and serve.

1 Soak the Chinese mushrooms and wood ears separately in bowls of hot water for 30 minutes. Break the dried bean curd into small pieces, and soak in water according to the instructions on the package.

3 The wood ears should swell to five times their original size. Drain, rinse thoroughly, and drain again. Cut off any gritty parts, and cut each wood ear into two or three pieces.

4 Heat the oil in a heavy-bottomed pan. Add the garlic, ginger and Szechuan peppercorns. Fry for a few seconds, then add the mushrooms and red fermented bean curd. Mix lightly, and fry for 5 minutes.

COOK'S TIP

If you can't find Szechuan peppercorns, then use ordinary black ones instead.

Thai Noodles with Chinese Chives

This recipe requires a little time for preparation but the cooking time is very fast. Everything is cooked speedily in a hot wok and should be eaten at once.

INGREDIENTS

Serves 4

12 ounces dried rice noodles
½-inch piece fresh ginger, grated
2 tablespoons light soy sauce
3 tablespoons vegetable oil
8 ounces firm tofu, cut into small cubes
2 garlic cloves, crushed
1 large onion, cut into thin wedges
4 ounces fried firm tofu, thinly sliced
1 fresh green chili, seeded and
    finely sliced
6 ounces bean sprouts
4 ounces Chinese chives, cut into
    2-inch lengths
2 ounces roasted peanuts, ground
2 tablespoons dark soy sauce
fresh cilantro leaves, to garnish

1 Place the noodles in a large bowl, cover with warm water and soak for 20–30 minutes, then drain. Blend together the ginger, light soy sauce and 1 tablespoon of the oil in a bowl. Stir in the tofu and set aside for 10 minutes. Drain, reserving the marinade.

2 Heat 1 tablespoon of the oil in a preheated wok or frying pan and fry the garlic for a few seconds. Add the tofu and stir-fry for 3–4 minutes. Transfer to a plate and set aside.

COOK'S TIP

Tofu makes this a vegetarian meal, but, thinly sliced pork or chicken could be used instead.

3 Heat the remaining oil in the wok or frying pan and stir-fry the onion for 3–4 minutes, or until softened and just beginning to color. Add the fried tofu and chili, stir-fry briefly, and then add the noodles. Stir-fry for 4–5 minutes.

4 Stir in the bean sprouts, Chinese chives and most of the ground peanuts, reserving a little for the garnish. Add the tofu, the dark soy sauce and the reserved marinade.

5 When hot, spoon onto serving plates and garnish with the remaining ground peanuts and cilantro leaves.

Udon Pot

INGREDIENTS

Serves 4

12 ounces dried udon noodles

1 large carrot, cut into bite-size chunks

8 ounces chicken breasts or thighs, skinned and cut into bite-size pieces

8 raw jumbo shrimp, peeled and deveined

4–6 Chinese cabbage leaves, cut into short strips

8 shiitake mushrooms, stems removed

2 ounces snow peas, ends removed

6¼ cups chicken broth or instant bonito broth (dashi)

2 tablespoons mirin

soy sauce, to taste

1 bunch scallions, finely chopped, 2 tablespoons grated fresh ginger, lemon wedges, and extra soy sauce, to serve

1 Cook the noodles until just tender, following the directions on the package. Drain, rinse under cold water, and drain again. Blanch the carrot in boiling water for 1 minute, then drain.

2 Spoon the noodles and carrot chunks into a large saucepan or flameproof casserole, and arrange the chicken breasts or thighs, shrimp, Chinese cabbage leaves, mushrooms and snow peas on top.

3 Bring the broth to a boil in a saucepan. Add the mirin and enough soy sauce to taste. Pour the broth over the noodles. Cover the pan or casserole, bring to a boil over a moderate heat, then simmer gently for 5–6 minutes until all the ingredients are cooked.

4 Serve with chopped scallions, grated ginger, lemon wedges and a little soy sauce.

Combination Chow Mein

INGREDIENTS

Serves 4–6

1 pound thick egg noodles

3 tablespoons vegetable oil

2 garlic cloves, chopped

2 scallions, cut into short lengths

2 ounces pork loin, sliced, or Chinese roast pork cut into short lengths

2 ounces pork liver, sliced

3 ounces raw shrimp, peeled and deveined

2 ounces prepared squid, sliced

2 ounces mussels

4 ounces watercress, leaves stripped from the stems

2 red chilies, seeded and finely sliced

2–3 tablespoons soy sauce

1 tablespoon sesame oil

salt and freshly ground black pepper

1 Cook the egg noodles in a large saucepan of boiling water until just tender. Drain thoroughly.

2 Heat the oil in a wok, and fry the garlic and scallions for 30 seconds. Add the pork loin, if using, with the liver, shrimp, squid and mussels. Stir-fry for 2 minutes over a high heat.

3 Add the watercress and chilies, and stir-fry for 3–4 minutes more until the meat is cooked.

4 Add the drained noodles, stirring constantly but gently. Toss in the Chinese roast pork, if using, and add the soy sauce with salt and pepper to taste. Cook until the noodles are thoroughly heated through. Stir in the sesame oil, mix well, and serve.

Cellophane Noodles with Pork

Unlike other types of noodles, cellophane noodles can be reheated successfully.

INGREDIENTS

Serves 3–4

4 ounces cellophane noodles
4 dried Chinese black mushrooms
8 ounces boneless lean pork
2 tablespoons dark soy sauce
2 tablespoons Chinese rice wine or
   dry sherry
2 garlic cloves, crushed
1 tablespoon grated fresh ginger
1 teaspoon chili oil
3 tablespoons peanut oil
4–6 scallions, chopped
1 teaspoon cornstarch blended with
   ¾ cup chicken broth or water
2 tablespoons chopped fresh cilantro
salt and freshly ground black pepper
fresh cilantro sprigs, to garnish

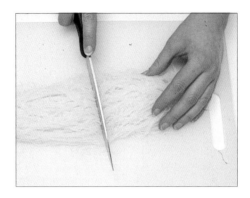

1 Put the noodles and mushrooms in separate bowls and pour in sufficient warm water to cover. Set aside to soak for 15–20 minutes, until soft. Drain well. Cut the noodles into 5-inch lengths using scissors or a knife. Squeeze out any excess water from the mushrooms, discard the stems and finely chop the caps.

2 Cut the pork into very small cubes and place them in a bowl. Add the soy sauce, rice wine or dry sherry, garlic, ginger and chili oil and mix well. Marinate for 15 minutes. Drain, reserving the marinade.

3 Heat the peanut oil in a preheated wok. Add the pork and mushrooms and stir-fry for 3 minutes. Add the scallions and stir-fry for 1 minute. Stir in the cornstarch mixture and reserved marinade and season to taste. Cook for 1 minute.

4 Add the noodles and stir-fry for about 2 minutes, until the noodles have absorbed most of the liquid and the pork is cooked through. Stir in the chopped cilantro. Serve immediately garnished with the cilantro sprigs.

Noodles with Chicken, Shrimp and Ham

Egg noodles can be cooked up to 24 hours in advance and kept in a bowl of cold water.

INGREDIENTS

Serves 4–6

10 ounces dried egg noodles
1 tablespoon vegetable oil
1 medium onion, chopped
1 garlic clove, crushed
1-inch piece fresh ginger, chopped
2 ounces canned water chestnuts, drained and sliced
1 tablespoon light soy sauce
2 tablespoons fish sauce or strong chicken broth
6 ounces cooked chicken breast, sliced
5 ounces cooked ham, thickly sliced and cut into short fingers
8 ounces cooked jumbo shrimp, peeled
6 ounces bean sprouts
7 ounces canned baby corn, drained
2 limes, cut into wedges, and 1 small bunch cilantro, chopped, to garnish

1 Cook the noodles according to the package instructions. Drain well and set aside.

2 Heat the oil in a preheated wok or frying pan. Fry the onion, garlic and ginger for 3 minutes, or until soft but not colored. Add the chestnuts, soy sauce, fish sauce or chicken broth, chicken breast, ham and shrimp.

3 Add the noodles, bean sprouts and baby corn and stir-fry for 6–8 minutes, until heated through. Transfer to a warmed serving dish, garnish with the lime wedges and chopped cilantro and serve immediately.

Seafood Chow Mein

This basic recipe can be adapted using different items for the "dressing."

Ingredients

Serves 4

3 ounces squid, cleaned
3 ounces jumbo shrimp
3–4 fresh scallops
½ egg white
1 tablespoon cornstarch paste
9 ounces egg noodles
5–6 tablespoons vegetable oil
2 ounces snow peas
½ teaspoon salt
½ teaspoon light brown sugar
1 tablespoon Chinese rice wine or
    dry sherry
2 tablespoons light soy sauce
2 scallions, cut into fine strips
Basic Broth, if necessary
few drops of sesame oil

1 Open up the squid and score the inside in a crisscross pattern with a sharp knife. Cut the squid into pieces, each about the size of a postage stamp. Soak the squid in a bowl of boiling water until all the pieces curl up. Rinse in cold water and drain.

2 Peel and devein the shrimp, then cut each in half lengthwise.

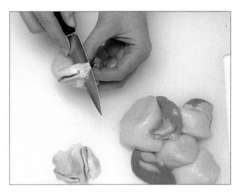

3 Prepare the scallops and cut into 3 or 4 slices. Combine the scallops, shrimp, egg white and cornstarch paste.

4 Cook the noodles in boiling water according to the package instructions. Drain and refresh under cold water. Mix with about 1 tablespoon of the oil.

5 Heat 2–3 tablespoons of the oil in a preheated wok. Stir-fry the snow peas, squid and shrimp mixture for about 2 minutes, then add the salt, sugar, rice wine or dry sherry, half the soy sauce and the scallions. Blend well and add a little broth, if necessary. Remove from the wok and keep warm.

6 Heat the remaining oil in the wok and stir-fry the noodles for 2–3 minutes with the remaining soy sauce. Place in a large serving dish, pour the "dressing" on top and sprinkle with a little sesame oil. Serve hot or cold.

Special Chow Mein

Lap cheong is a special air-dried Chinese sausage. It is available from most Chinese markets. If you cannot buy it, substitute with either diced ham, chorizo sausage or salami.

INGREDIENTS

Serves 4–6
3 tablespoons vegetable oil
2 garlic cloves, sliced
1 teaspoon chopped fresh ginger
2 red chilies, chopped
2 lap cheong, about 3 ounces, rinsed
  and sliced (optional)
1 boneless chicken breast, thinly sliced
16 uncooked jumbo shrimp, peeled,
  tails left intact, and deveined
1 cup green beans
1 cup bean sprouts
2 ounces garlic chives
1 pound egg noodles, cooked in
  boiling water until tender
2 tablespoons soy sauce
1 tablespoon oyster sauce
1 tablespoon sesame oil
salt and freshly ground black pepper
2 scallions, shredded, to garnish
1 tablespoon cilantro leaves,
  to garnish

2 Heat the rest of the oil in the same wok. Add the bean sprouts and garlic chives. Stir-fry for 1–2 minutes.

4 Return the shrimp mixture to the wok. Reheat and mix well with the noodles. Stir in the sesame oil. Serve garnished with scallions and cilantro leaves.

1 Heat 1 tablespoon of the oil in a wok or large frying pan and fry the garlic, ginger and chilies. Add the lap cheong, chicken, shrimp and beans. Stir-fry for about 2 minutes over high heat or until the chicken and shrimp are cooked. Transfer the mixture to a bowl and set aside.

3 Add the noodles and toss and stir to mix. Season with soy sauce, oyster sauce, salt and pepper.

Chicken Chow Mein

Chow Mein is arguably the best known Chinese noodle dish in the West. To make it, noodles are stir-fried with meat, seafood or vegetables.

INGREDIENTS

Serves 4

12 ounces noodles
8 ounces skinless, boneless chicken
  breasts
3 tablespoons soy sauce
1 tablespoon rice wine or dry sherry
1 tablespoon dark sesame oil
4 tablespoons vegetable oil
2 garlic cloves, finely chopped
2 ounces snow peas, ends removed
4 ounces bean sprouts
2 ounces ham, finely shredded
4 scallions, finely chopped
salt and freshly ground black pepper

1 Cook the noodles in a saucepan of boiling water until tender. Drain, rinse under cold water, and drain well.

2 Slice the chicken into fine, 2-inch shreds. Place in a bowl. Add 2 teaspoons of the soy sauce, the rice wine or sherry and sesame oil.

3 Heat half the vegetable oil in a wok or large frying pan over a high heat. When the oil starts smoking, add the chicken mixture. Stir-fry for about 2 minutes, then transfer the chicken to a plate, and keep it hot.

4 Wipe the wok clean, and heat the remaining oil. Stir in the garlic, snow peas, bean sprouts and ham, stir-fry for another minute or so, and add the noodles.

5 Continue to stir-fry until the noodles are heated through. Add the remaining soy sauce to taste, and season with salt and pepper. Return the chicken and any juices to the noodle mixture, add the scallions, and give the mixture a final stir. Serve at once.

Rice Noodles with Beef and Black Bean Sauce

This is an excellent combination – beef with a chili sauce tossed with silky, smooth rice noodles.

INGREDIENTS

Serves 4

1 pound fresh rice noodles
4 tablespoons vegetable oil
1 onion, finely sliced
2 garlic cloves, finely chopped
2 slices fresh ginger, finely chopped
8 ounces mixed bell peppers, seeded and cut into strips
12 ounces round steak, finely sliced against the grain
3 tablespoons fermented black beans, rinsed in warm water, drained and chopped
2 tablespoons soy sauce
2 tablespoons oyster sauce
1 tablespoon chili black bean sauce
1 tablespoon cornstarch
½ cup broth or water
2 scallions, finely chopped, and 2 red chilies, seeded and finely sliced, to garnish

1 Rinse the noodles under hot water. Drain well. Heat half the oil in a wok or large frying pan, swirling it around. Add the onion, garlic, ginger and mixed pepper strips. Stir-fry for 3–5 minutes, then remove with a slotted spoon, and keep hot.

2 Add the remaining oil to the wok. When hot, add the sliced beef and fermented black beans, and stir-fry over a high heat for 5 minutes or until they are cooked.

3 In a small bowl, blend the soy sauce, oyster sauce and chili black bean sauce with the cornstarch and broth or water until smooth. Add the mixture to the wok, then return the onion mixture to the wok and cook, stirring, for 1 minute.

4 Add the noodles, and mix lightly. Stir over a medium heat until the noodles are heated through. Adjust the seasoning, if necessary. Serve at once, garnished with the chopped scallions and chilies.

Straw Noodle Shrimp in a Sweet Ginger Dip

Shrimp are a popular feature in Japanese cooking. Rarely are they more delicious than when wrapped in crispy noodles.

INGREDIENTS

Serves 4–6

3 ounces somen noodles or vermicelli
3 sheets nori
12 large jumbo shrimp, peeled and deveined
vegetable oil, for deep-frying

For the dipping sauce

6 tablespoons soy sauce
2 tablespoons sugar
¼-inch piece fresh ginger, grated

1 Cover the somen noodles, if using, with boiling water and let soak for 1–2 minutes. Drain and dry thoroughly with paper towels. Cut the noodles into 3-inch lengths. If using vermicelli, cover with boiling water and let soak for 1–2 minutes to soften. Drain and set aside. Cut the nori into ½ x 2-inch strips and set aside.

2 To make the dipping sauce, bring the soy sauce to a boil in a small saucepan with the sugar, then add the ginger. Simmer for 2–3 minutes, strain and set aside to cool.

3 Line up the noodles or vermicelli on a wooden board. Straighten each shrimp by pushing a bamboo skewer through its length. Roll the shrimp in the noodles or vermicelli so that they adhere in neat strands.

4 Moisten one end of the nori strips and secure the noodles at the fat end of each shrimp. Set aside.

5 Heat the vegetable oil in a preheated wok with a wire draining rack or in a deep-fryer to 350°F. Fry the shrimp in the oil, two at a time, until the noodles or vermicelli are crisp and golden.

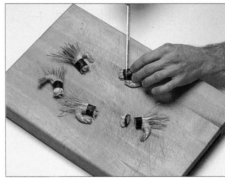

6 To finish, cut through the band of nori with a sharp knife, exposing a clean section of shrimp. Drain on paper towels and serve with the dipping sauce in a small dish.

Main Course Spicy Shrimp and Noodle Soup

This dish is served as a hot coconut broth with a separate platter of shrimp, fish and noodles. Diners are invited to add their own choice of accompaniment to the broth.

INGREDIENTS

Serves 4–6

¼ cup raw cashews
3 shallots or 1 medium onion, sliced
2-inch piece lemongrass, cut into strips
2 garlic cloves, crushed
5 ounces laksa noodles (spaghetti-sized rice noodles), soaked for 10 minutes before cooking
2 tablespoons vegetable oil
½-inch-square shrimp paste or 1 tablespoon fish sauce
1 tablespoon mild curry paste
1 can (14 ounces) coconut milk
½ chicken bouillon cube
3 curry leaves (optional)
1 pound white fish fillet, such as cod, haddock or whiting
8 ounces jumbo shrimp, raw or cooked, peeled
1 small head romaine lettuce, shredded
4 ounces bean sprouts
3 scallions, cut into fine strips
½ cucumber, sliced and cut into strips
shrimp crackers, to serve

1 Grind the cashews with the shallots or onion, lemongrass and garlic in a mortar with a pestle or in a food processor. Cook the noodles according to the instructions on the package.

2 Heat the oil in a large preheated wok or saucepan, add the cashew mixture and stir-fry for 1–2 minutes, or until the nuts are just beginning to brown.

3 Add the shrimp paste or fish sauce and curry paste, followed by the coconut milk, bouillon cube and curry leaves, if using. Simmer for 10 minutes.

4 Cut the white fish into bite-sized pieces. Add the fish and shrimp to the simmering coconut broth and cook for 3–4 minutes. Remove with a slotted spoon. Set aside.

5 To serve, line a large serving platter with the shredded lettuce leaves. Arrange the bean sprouts, scallions and cucumber in neat piles, together with the fish, shrimp and noodles. Serve the salad with a bowl of shrimp crackers and the broth in a closed-rim stoneware pot.

COOK'S TIP

When cooking the fish and shrimp, you may find it easier to put them in a large frying basket before immersing them in the coconut broth.

Special Fried Noodles

Perhaps the best-known dish of Singapore is *mee goreng.* It is prepared from a wide range of ingredients.

INGREDIENTS

Serves 4–6

10 ounces egg noodles
1 skinless, boneless chicken breast
4 ounces lean pork
2 tablespoons vegetable oil
6 ounces jumbo shrimp, raw or
   cooked, peeled
4 shallots or 1 medium onion, chopped
¾-inch piece fresh ginger, thinly sliced
2 garlic cloves, crushed
3 tablespoons light soy sauce
1-2 teaspoons chili sauce
1 tablespoon rice vinegar or white
   wine vinegar
1 teaspoon sugar
½ teaspoon salt
4 ounces Chinese cabbage, cut into strips
4 ounces spinach, cut into fine strips
3 scallions, cut into fine strips

1 Bring a large saucepan of lightly salted water to a boil and cook the noodles according to the instructions on the package. Drain and set aside. Place the chicken breast and pork in the freezer for 30 minutes to firm, but not freeze.

2 Slice the meat thinly against the grain. Heat the oil in a preheated wok and stir-fry the chicken, pork and shrimp for 2–3 minutes. Add the shallots or onion, ginger and garlic and stir-fry for 2–3 minutes, or until softened but not colored.

3 Add the soy sauce, chili sauce, vinegar, sugar and salt. Bring to a simmer. Add the Chinese cabbage, spinach and scallions, cover and cook for 3–4 minutes. Add the noodles, heat through and serve.

Crisp Pork Meatballs Laced with Noodles

These little meatballs, decoratively coated with a lacing of noodles, look very impressive but are actually extremely easy to make.

INGREDIENTS

Serves 4

14 ounces ground pork
2 garlic cloves, finely chopped
2 tablespoons chopped fresh cilantro
1 tablespoon oyster sauce
2 tablespoons fresh bread crumbs
1 egg, beaten
6 ounces fresh thin egg noodles
oil, for deep-frying
salt and freshly ground black pepper
fresh cilantro leaves, to garnish
spinach leaves and chili sauce or tomato
    sauce, to serve

1 Combine the pork, garlic, chopped cilantro, oyster sauce, bread crumbs and egg. Season with salt and pepper.

2 Knead the pork mixture until it is sticky, then form into balls each the size of a walnut.

3 Blanch the noodles in a saucepan of boiling water for 2–3 minutes. Drain, rinse under cold running water and drain well.

4 Wrap 3–5 strands of noodles securely around each meatball in a crisscross pattern.

5 Heat the oil in a deep-fryer or preheated wok. Deep-fry the meatballs in batches until golden brown and cooked through to the center. As each batch browns, remove with a slotted spoon and drain well on paper towels. Serve hot on a bed of spinach leaves, garnished with fresh cilantro leaves and with chili sauce or tomato sauce in a small dish on the side.

Noodles, Chicken and Shrimp in Coconut Broth

This typical Indonesian dish has several different components from which the diners may help themselves, making a complete meal in itself.

INGREDIENTS

Serves 8

2 onions, quartered
1-inch piece fresh ginger, sliced
2 garlic cloves
4 macadamia nuts or 8 almonds
1–2 fresh chilies, seeded and sliced
2 lemongrass stems, lower
  2 inches sliced
2-inch piece fresh turmeric, peeled and
  sliced, or 1 teaspoon ground turmeric
1 tablespoon coriander seeds, dry-fried
4 tablespoons sunflower oil
1 can (14 fluid ounces) coconut milk
6¼ cups chicken broth
12 ounces rice noodles, soaked in
  cold water
12 ounces cooked jumbo shrimp,
  peeled and deveined
salt and freshly ground black pepper

For the garnish

4 hard-cooked eggs, shelled and
  quartered
8 ounces cooked chicken, chopped
8 ounces bean sprouts
1 bunch scallions, cut into fine strips
1 onion, finely sliced and deep-fried

1 Place the quartered onions, ginger, garlic and nuts in a food processor with the chilies, lemongrass and turmeric. Process to a paste. Alternatively, pound all the ingredients in a mortar with a pestle. Grind the coriander seeds coarsely and add to the paste.

2 Heat the oil in a preheated wok or frying pan and fry the spice paste, without allowing it to color, to bring out the flavors. Add the coconut milk, broth and seasoning. Simmer for 5–10 minutes.

3 Meanwhile, drain the noodles and plunge them into a large pan of salted boiling water for 2 minutes. Remove from the heat and drain thoroughly. Rinse well with plenty of cold water. Add the jumbo shrimp to the soup just before serving and heat through for a minute or two.

4 Arrange the garnishes in separate bowls. Each person takes a helping of noodles, tops them with soup, eggs, chicken and bean sprouts, then scatters scallions and fried onion on top.

Noodles in Soup

In China, noodles in soup are far more popular than fried noodles. This is a basic recipe, which you can adapt by using different ingredients.

INGREDIENTS

Serves 4

8 ounces skinless, boneless chicken or
   pork loins
3–4 dried Chinese mushrooms, soaked
1 can (4 ounces) bamboo shoots, drained
4 ounces spinach leaves, lettuce hearts
   or Chinese cabbage
2 scallions
12 ounces dried egg noodles
2½ cups Basic Broth
2 tablespoons vegetable oil
1 teaspoon salt
½ teaspoon light brown sugar
1 tablespoon light soy sauce
2 teaspoons Chinese rice wine or
   dry sherry
few drops of sesame oil

1 Thinly slice the meat. Squeeze the mushrooms dry and discard any hard stalks. Thinly slice the mushroom caps, bamboo shoots, spinach, lettuce hearts or Chinese cabbage and the scallions. Keep the meat, the scallions and the other ingredients in three heaps.

2 Cook the noodles in boiling water according to the instructions on the package, then drain and rinse in cold water. Place in a serving bowl.

3 Bring the broth to a boil and pour over the noodles. Keep warm.

4 Heat the oil in a preheated wok, add the scallions and the meat and stir-fry for about 1 minute.

5 Add the mushrooms, bamboo shoots and spinach, lettuce or Chinese cabbage and stir-fry for 1 minute, or until the meat is cooked through. Add the salt, sugar, soy sauce, rice wine or dry sherry and sesame oil and blend well.

6 Pour the "dressing" over the noodles and serve.

Vegetable and Egg Noodle Ribbons

Serve this elegant, colorful dish with a tossed green salad as a light lunch or as an appetizer for six to eight people.

INGREDIENTS

Serves 4
1 large carrot, peeled
2 zucchini
4 tablespoons butter
1 tablespoon olive oil
6 fresh shiitake mushrooms, finely sliced
½ cup frozen peas, thawed
12 ounces broad egg noodle ribbons
2 teaspoons chopped mixed fresh herbs (such as marjoram, chives and basil)
salt and freshly ground black pepper
1 ounce Parmesan cheese, to serve (optional)

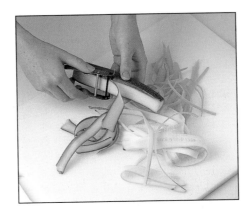

1 Using a vegetable peeler, carefully slice thin strips from the carrot and from the zucchini.

2 Heat the butter with the olive oil in a large frying pan. Stir in the carrots and shiitake mushrooms. Fry for 2 minutes. Add the zucchini and peas, and stir-fry until the zucchini are cooked, but still crisp. Season with salt and pepper.

3 Meanwhile, cook the noodles in a large saucepan of boiling water until just tender. Drain the noodles well, and turn them into a bowl. Add the vegetables, and toss to mix.

4 Sprinkle over the fresh herbs, and season to taste. If using the Parmesan cheese, grate or shave it over the top. Toss lightly, and serve.

Buckwheat Noodles with Goat Cheese

When you don't feel like doing a lot of cooking, try this good, fast supper dish. The earthy flavor of buckwheat goes well with the nutty, peppery taste of arugula leaves, offset by the deliciously creamy goat cheese.

INGREDIENTS

Serves 4
12 ounces buckwheat noodles
4 tablespoons butter
2 garlic cloves, finely chopped
4 shallots, sliced
½ cup hazelnuts, lightly roasted and coarsely chopped
large handful arugula leaves
6 ounces goat cheese
salt and freshly ground black pepper

1 Cook the noodles in a large saucepan of boiling water until just tender. Drain well.

2 Heat the butter in a large frying pan. Add the garlic and shallots, and cook for 2–3 minutes, stirring constantly, until the shallots are soft.

3 Add the hazelnuts, and fry for about 1 minute. Add the arugula leaves and, when they start to wilt, toss in the noodles, and heat through.

4 Season with salt and pepper. Crumble in the goat cheese, and serve immediately.

Shanghai Noodles with Lap Cheong

Lap cheong are firm, cured, waxy pork sausages, available in Chinese food markets. Sweet and savory, they can be steamed with rice, chicken or pork, added to an omelet or stir-fried with a variety of vegetables.

INGREDIENTS

Serves 4

2 tablespoons vegetable oil
4 ounces Canadian bacon, cut into bite-size pieces
2 lap cheong, rinsed in warm water, drained and finely sliced
2 garlic cloves, finely chopped
2 scallions, coarsely chopped
8 ounces chard or fresh spinach leaves, cut into 2-inch pieces
1 pound fresh Shanghai noodles
2 tablespoons oyster sauce
2 tablespoons soy sauce
freshly ground black pepper

1 Heat half the oil in a wok or large frying pan. Add the bacon and lap cheong with the garlic and scallions. Stir-fry for a few minutes until golden. Using a slotted spoon, remove the mixture from the wok or pan, and keep warm.

2 Add the remaining oil to the wok or pan. When hot, stir-fry the chard or spinach over a high heat for about 3 minutes until it starts to wilt.

3 Add the noodles, and return the lap cheong mixture to the wok or pan. Season with oyster sauce, soy sauce and pepper. Stir-fry until the noodles are heated through.

COOK'S TIP

There are many types of Chinese greens available. They include broccoli, rape and red and green chard.

Noodles with Tomatoes, Sardines and Mustard

Serve this simple dish hot or at room temperature.

INGREDIENTS

Serves 4

12 ounces broad egg noodles
4 tablespoons olive oil
2 tablespoons lemon juice
1 tablespoon whole-grain mustard
1 garlic clove, finely chopped
8 ounces ripe tomatoes, coarsely chopped
1 small red onion, finely chopped
1 green bell pepper, seeded and finely diced
4 tablespoons chopped parsley
8 ounces canned sardines, drained
salt and freshly ground black pepper
croûtons, made from 2 slices of bread, to serve (optional)

1 Cook the noodles in a large saucepan of boiling water for about 5–8 minutes until just tender.

2 Meanwhile, to make the dressing, whisk the oil, lemon juice, mustard and garlic in a small bowl with salt and pepper to taste.

3 Drain the noodles, turn them into a large bowl, and toss with the dressing. Add the tomatoes, onion, pepper, parsley and sardines, and toss lightly again. Season to taste, and serve with crisp croûtons, if using.

Vegetarian Fried Noodles

When making this dish for non-vegetarians, or for vegetarians who eat fish, add a piece of *blacan* (compressed shrimp paste). A small chunk about the size of a bouillon cube, mashed with the chili paste, will add a deliciously rich, aromatic flavor.

INGREDIENTS

Serves 4

2 eggs
1 teaspoon chili powder
1 teaspoon turmeric
4 tablespoons vegetable oil
1 large onion, finely sliced
2 red chilies, seeded and
  finely sliced
1 tablespoon soy sauce
2 large cooked potatoes, cut into
  small cubes
6 pieces fried bean curd (tofu), sliced
8 ounces bean sprouts
4 ounces green beans, blanched
12 ounces fresh thick egg noodles
salt and freshly ground black pepper
sliced scallions, to garnish

1 Beat the eggs lightly, then strain them into a bowl. Heat a lightly greased omelet pan. Pour in half of the egg to cover the bottom of the pan thinly. When the egg is just set, turn the omelet over, and fry the other side briefly. Slide onto a plate, blot with paper towels, roll up, and cut into narrow strips. Make a second omelet in the same way, and slice it. Set the omelet strips aside for the garnish.

COOK'S TIP

Fried bean curd can be found in the refrigerated section of most good Asian food markets. It will keep for several days after opening.

2 In a cup, mix together the chili powder and turmeric. Form a paste by stirring in a little water.

3 Heat the oil in a wok or large frying pan. Fry the onion until soft. Reduce the heat, and add the chili paste, sliced chilies and soy sauce. Fry for 2–3 minutes.

4 Add the potatoes, and fry for about 2 minutes, mixing well with the chilies. Add the bean curd, then the bean sprouts, green beans and noodles.

5 Gently stir-fry until the noodles are evenly coated and heated through. Take care not to break up the potatoes or the bean curd. Season with salt and pepper. Serve hot, garnished with the reserved omelet strips and scallion slices.

Fried Cellophane Noodles

INGREDIENTS

Serves 4

6 ounces cellophane noodles
3 tablespoons vegetable oil
3 garlic cloves, finely chopped
4 ounces cooked shrimp, peeled
2 lap cheong, rinsed, drained and
   finely diced
2 eggs
2 celery stalks, including leaves, diced
4 ounces bean sprouts
4 ounces spinach, cut into large pieces
2 scallions, chopped
1–2 tablespoons fish sauce
1 teaspoon sesame oil
1 tablespoon sesame seeds, toasted,
   to garnish

1 Soak the cellophane noodles in hot water for about 10 minutes or until soft. Drain, and cut the noodles into 4-inch lengths.

2 Heat the oil in a wok, add the garlic, and fry until golden brown. Add the shrimp and lap cheong. Stir-fry for 2–3 minutes. Stir in the noodles, and fry for 2 minutes more.

3 Make a well in the center of the shrimp mixture, break in the eggs, and slowly stir them until they are creamy and just set.

— COOK'S TIP —

This is a very versatile dish. Vary the vegetables if you wish, and substitute ham, chorizo or salami for the lap cheong.

4 Stir in the celery, bean sprouts, spinach and scallions. Season with fish sauce, and stir in the sesame oil. Continue to stir-fry until all the ingredients are cooked, mixing well.

5 Transfer to a serving dish. Sprinkle with sesame seeds to garnish.

Crispy Noodles with Mixed Vegetables

In this dish, rice vermicelli noodles are deep-fried until crisp, then tossed with a colorful selection of stir-fried vegetables.

INGREDIENTS

Serves 4

2 large carrots
2 zucchini
4 scallions
4 ounces yard-long beans or
  green beans
4 ounces dried rice vermicelli or
  cellophane noodles
peanut oil, for deep frying
1-inch piece fresh ginger, shredded
1 fresh red chili, sliced
¾ cup fresh shiitake or button
  mushrooms, thickly sliced
few bok choy leaves, roughly shredded
⅓ cup bean sprouts
2 tablespoons light soy sauce
2 tablespoons Chinese rice wine or
  dry sherry
1 teaspoon sugar
2 tablespoons roughly torn fresh
  cilantro leaves

— COOK'S TIP —

Vermicelli rice noodles, which are thin and brittle, look like a bundle of white hair. They cook almost instantly in hot liquid, provided they have been first soaked in warm water. Rice noodles can also be deep-fried. Cellophane noodles, which are made from ground mung beans, look a little like bundles of cotton candy. They are opaque white when dried, and expand and become translucent after soaking. Cellophane noodles are also known as bean thread, transparent or glass noodles. Dried noodles must be soaked for 5 minutes in hot water before cooking.

1 Cut the carrots and zucchini into fine sticks. Shred the scallions into similar-sized pieces. Trim the beans and cut them into short lengths.

2 Break the noodles into lengths of about 3 inches. Half-fill a wok with oil and heat it to 350°F. Deep-fry the raw noodles, a handful at a time, for 1–2 minutes, until puffed and crispy. Drain on paper towels. Pour off all but 2 tablespoons of the oil.

3 Reheat the oil in the wok. When hot, add the beans and stir-fry for 2–3 minutes.

4 Add the ginger, red chili, mushrooms, carrots and zucchini and stir-fry for 1–2 minutes. Add the bok choy, bean sprouts and scallions. Stir-fry for 1 minute, then add the soy sauce, rice wine or sherry and sugar. Cook, stirring, for about 30 seconds.

5 Add the noodles and cilantro and toss to mix, taking care not to crush the noodles too much. Serve immediately, piled on a plate.

Noodles with Meatballs

Mie Rebus is a one-pot meal, for which the East is renowned.

INGREDIENTS

Serves 6

1 pound Spicy Meatball mixture
12 ounces dried egg noodles
3 tablespoons sunflower oil
1 large onion, finely sliced
2 garlic cloves, crushed
1 inch fresh ginger root, peeled and cut
  in thin matchsticks
5 cups broth
2 tablespoons dark soy sauce
2 celery stalks, finely sliced,
  leaves reserved
6 Chinese cabbage leaves, cut in bite-
  size pieces
1 handful snow peas, cut in strips
salt and freshly ground black pepper

1 Prepare the meatballs, making them quite small. Set aside.

2 Add the noodles to a large pan of salted, boiling water and stir so that the noodles do not settle at the bottom. Simmer for 3–4 minutes, or until *al dente*. Drain in a colander and rinse with plenty of cold water. Set aside.

3 Heat the oil in a wide pan and fry the onion, garlic and ginger until soft but not browned. Add the broth and soy sauce and bring to a boil.

4 Add the meatballs, half-cover and allow to simmer until they are cooked, about 5–8 minutes depending on size. Just before serving, add the sliced celery and, after 2 minutes, add the Chinese cabbage and snow peas. Taste and adjust the seasoning.

5 Divide the noodles among soup bowls, add the meatballs and vegetables and pour the soup on top. Garnish with the reserved celery leaves.

Stir-fried Rice Noodles with Chicken and Shrimp

Shellfish have a natural affinity with both meat and poultry. This Thai-style recipe combines chicken with shrimp, and has the characteristic sweet, sour and salty flavor.

INGREDIENTS

Serves 4

8 ounces dried flat rice noodles
½ cup water
4 tablespoons fish sauce
1 tablespoon sugar
1 tablespoon fresh lime juice
1 teaspoon paprika
pinch of cayenne pepper
3 tablespoons oil
2 garlic cloves, finely chopped
1 skinless, boneless chicken breast, finely sliced
8 raw shrimp, peeled, deveined and cut in half
1 egg
½ cup roasted peanuts, coarsely crushed
3 scallions, cut into short lengths
6 ounces bean sprouts
cilantro leaves and 1 lime, cut into wedges, to garnish

1 Place the rice noodles in a large bowl, cover with warm water, and soak for 30 minutes until soft. Drain.

2 Combine the water, fish sauce, sugar, lime juice, paprika and cayenne in a small bowl. Set aside until required.

3 Heat the oil in a wok. Add the garlic, and fry for 30 seconds until it starts to brown. Add the chicken and shrimp, and stir-fry for 3–4 minutes until cooked.

4 Push the chicken and shrimp mixture in the wok out to the sides. Break the egg into the center, then quickly stir to break up the yolk. Cook over a medium heat until the egg is just lightly scrambled.

5 Add the drained noodles and the fish sauce mixture to the wok. Mix together well. Add half the crushed peanuts, and cook, stirring frequently, until the noodles are soft and most of the liquid has been absorbed.

6 Add the scallions and half of the bean sprouts. Cook, stirring, for 1 minute more. Spoon onto a platter. Sprinkle with the remaining peanuts and bean sprouts. Garnish with the cilantro and lime wedges, and serve.

Thai Fried Noodles

Phat Thai has a fascinating flavor and texture. It's made with fine rice noodles and is considered one of the national dishes of Thailand.

Ingredients

Serves 4–6

12 ounces rice noodles
3 tablespoons vegetable oil
1 tablespoon chopped garlic
16 uncooked jumbo shrimp, shelled, tails left intact, and deveined
2 eggs, lightly beaten
1 tablespoon dried shrimp, rinsed
2 tablespoons pickled white radish
2 ounces fried tofu, cut into small slivers
½ teaspoon dried chili flakes
4 ounces garlic chives, cut into 2-inch lengths
1 cup bean sprouts
½ cup roasted peanuts, coarsely ground
1 teaspoon sugar
1 tablespoon dark soy sauce
2 tablespoons fish sauce
2 tablespoons tamarind juice
2 tablespoons cilantro leaves and 1 kaffir lime, to garnish

1 Soak the noodles in warm water for 20–30 minutes, then drain.

2 Heat 1 tablespoon of the oil in a wok or large frying pan. Add the garlic and fry until golden. Stir in the shrimp and cook for about 1–2 minutes, until pink, tossing from time to time. Remove and set aside.

3 Heat another 1 tablespoon of oil in the wok. Add the eggs and tilt the wok to spread them into a thin sheet. Stir to scramble and break the eggs into small pieces. Remove from the wok and set aside with the shrimp.

4 Heat the remaining oil in the same wok. Add the dried shrimp, pickled radish, tofu and dried chilies. Stir briefly. Add the soaked noodles and stir-fry for 5 minutes.

5 Add the garlic chives, half the bean sprouts and half the peanuts. Season with the sugar, soy sauce, fish sauce and tamarind juice. Mix together well and cook until the noodles are completely heated through.

6 Return the shrimp and egg mixture to the wok and mix with the noodles. Serve garnished with the rest of the bean sprouts, peanuts, cilantro leaves and lime wedges.

Bamie Goreng

This fried noodle dish is wonderfully accommodating. To the basic recipe you can add other vegetables, such as mushrooms, tiny pieces of chayote, broccoli, leeks or beansprouts, if you prefer. As with fried rice, you can use whatever you have to hand, bearing in mind the need to achieve a balance of colors, flavors and textures.

INGREDIENTS

Serves 6–8
1 pound dried egg noodles
1 boneless, skinless chicken breast
4 ounces pork loin
4 ounces calves' liver (optional)
2 eggs, beaten
6 tablespoons oil
2 tablespoons butter or margarine
2 garlic cloves, crushed
4 ounces cooked, peeled shrimp
4 ounces spinach or Chinese cabbage
2 celery stalks, finely sliced
4 scallions, shredded
about 4 tablespoons chicken broth
dark soy sauce and light soy sauce
salt and freshly ground black pepper
Deep-fried Onions and celery leaves,
    to garnish
Sweet and Sour Fruit and Vegetable
    Salad, to serve (optional)

2 Finely slice the chicken, pork loin and calves' liver, if using.

4 Heat the remaining oil in a wok and fry the garlic with the chicken, pork and liver for 2–3 minutes, until they have changed color. Add the shrimp, spinach or Chinese cabbage, celery and scallions, tossing well.

5 Add the cooked and drained noodles and toss well again so that all the ingredients are well mixed. Add enough broth just to moisten and dark and light soy sauce to taste. Finally, stir in the scrambled eggs.

1 Cook the noodles in salted, boiling water for 3–4 minutes. Drain, rinse with cold water and drain again. Set aside until required.

3 Season the eggs. Heat 1 teaspoon oil with the butter or margarine in a small pan until melted and then stir in the eggs and keep stirring until scrambled. Set aside.

6 Garnish the dish with Deep-fried Onions and celery leaves. Serve with Sweet and Sour Fruit and Vegetable Salad, if using.

Somen Noodles with Zucchini

A colorful dish with lots of flavor. Patty pan squashes can be used as an alternative to zucchini.

INGREDIENTS

Serves 4

2 yellow zucchini or summer squash
2 green zucchini
4 tablespoons pine nuts
4 tablespoons extra virgin olive oil
2 shallots, finely chopped
2 garlic cloves, finely chopped
2 tablespoons capers, rinsed
4 sun-dried tomatoes in oil, drained and cut into strips
11 ounces somen noodles
4 tablespoons chopped mixed fresh herbs (such as chives, lemon thyme, and tarragon)
grated rind of 1 lemon
¾ cup finely grated Parmesan cheese
salt and freshly ground black pepper

1 Slice the zucchini diagonally into rounds the same thickness as the noodles. Cut the zucchini slices into matchsticks. Toast the pine nuts in an ungreased frying pan over a medium heat until golden in color.

2 Heat half the oil in a large frying pan. Add the shallots and garlic, and fry until fragrant. Push the shallot mixture to one side of the pan, add the remaining oil and, when hot, stir-fry the zucchini until soft.

3 Stir thoroughly to incorporate the shallot mixture, and add the capers, sun-dried tomatoes and pine nuts. Remove the pan from the heat.

4 Cook the noodles in a large saucepan of boiling, salted water until just tender, following the directions on the package. Drain well, and toss into the zucchini mixture, adding the herbs, lemon rind and Parmesan, with salt and pepper to taste. Serve at once.

Noodles Primavera

INGREDIENTS

Serves 4

8 ounces dried rice noodles
4 ounces broccoli florets
1 carrot, finely sliced
8 ounces asparagus, cut into 2-inch lengths
1 red or yellow bell pepper, seeded and cut into strips
2 ounces baby corn cobs
2 ounces sugar snap peas, ends removed
3 tablespoons olive oil
1 tablespoon chopped fresh ginger
2 garlic cloves, chopped
2 scallions, finely chopped
1 pound tomatoes, chopped
1 bunch arugula leaves
soy sauce, to taste
salt and freshly ground black pepper

1 Soak the noodles in hot water for about 30 minutes until soft. Drain.

2 Blanch the broccoli florets, sliced carrot, asparagus, pepper strips, baby corn and sugar snap peas separately in boiling, salted water. Drain them, rinse under cold water, then drain again. Set aside.

3 Heat the olive oil in a frying pan. Add the ginger, garlic and onions. Stir-fry for 30 seconds, then add the tomatoes, and stir-fry for 2–3 minutes.

4 Add the noodles, and stir-fry for 3 minutes. Toss in the blanched vegetables and arugula leaves. Season with soy sauce, salt and pepper, and cook until the vegetables are tender.

Egg Noodles with Tuna and Tomato Sauce

Raid the pantry, add a few fresh ingredients, and you can produce a scrumptious main meal in a matter of minutes.

INGREDIENTS

Serves 4

3 tablespoons olive oil
2 garlic cloves, finely chopped
2 dried red chilies, seeded
  and chopped
1 large red onion, finely sliced
6 ounces canned tuna, drained
1 cup pitted black olives
14-ounce can plum tomatoes, mashed,
  or 14-ounce can chopped tomatoes
2 tablespoons chopped parsley
12 ounces medium-thick
  egg noodles
salt and freshly ground black pepper

1 Heat the oil in a large frying pan. Add the garlic and chilies, and fry for a few seconds before adding the onion. Fry, stirring, for about 5 minutes until the onion softens.

2 Add the tuna and black olives to the pan, and stir until well mixed. Stir in the tomatoes and any juices. Bring to a boil, season with salt and pepper, add the parsley, then lower the heat and simmer gently.

3 Meanwhile, cook the noodles in boiling water until just tender, following the directions on the package. Drain well, toss the noodles with the sauce, and serve at once.

Stir-fried Noodles with Wild Mushrooms

The greater the variety of wild mushrooms you have available, the more interesting this dish will be. Of course, if you can't find wild mushrooms, then a mixture of cultivated mushrooms can be used instead.

INGREDIENTS

Serves 4

12 ounces broad flat egg noodles
3 tablespoons vegetable oil
4 ounces Canadian or lean bacon, cut
  into small pieces
8 ounces wild mushrooms, trimmed
  and cut in half
4 ounces garlic chives, snipped
8 ounces bean sprouts
1 tablespoon oyster sauce
1 tablespoon soy sauce
salt and freshly ground black pepper

1 Cook the noodles in a large saucepan of boiling water for about 3–4 minutes or until just tender. Drain, rinse under cold water, and drain well.

2 Heat 1 tablespoon of the oil in a wok or large frying pan. Add the bacon, and fry until golden.

3 Using a slotted spoon, transfer the cooked bacon to a small bowl. Set aside until needed.

4 Add the rest of the oil to the wok or pan. When hot, add the mushrooms, and fry for 3 minutes. Add the garlic chives and bean sprouts to the wok. Fry for 3 minutes, then add the drained noodles.

5 Season with salt, pepper, oyster sauce and soy sauce. Continue to stir-fry until the noodles are heated through. Sprinkle the crispy bits of bacon on top, and serve.

Noodles with Sun-dried Tomatoes and Shrimp

INGREDIENTS

Serves 4

12 ounces somen noodles
3 tablespoons olive oil
20 uncooked jumbo shrimp, peeled
  and deveined
2 garlic cloves, finely chopped
3–4 tablespoons sun-dried tomato paste
salt and freshly ground black pepper

For the garnish
handful of basil leaves
2 tablespoons sun-dried tomatoes in
  oil, drained and cut into strips

--- COOK'S TIP ---

Pre-made sun-dried tomato paste is often available, however you can make your own simply by processing bottled or canned sun-dried tomatoes with their oil. You could also add a couple of anchovy fillets and some capers, if you like.

1 Cook the noodles in a large saucepan of boiling water until tender, following the directions on the package. Drain.

2 Heat half the oil in a large frying pan. Add the shrimp and garlic, and fry them over a medium heat for 3–5 minutes, until the shrimp turn pink and are firm to the touch.

3 Stir in 1 tablespoon of the sun-dried tomato paste, and mix well. Using a slotted spoon, transfer the shrimp to a bowl, and keep hot.

4 Reheat the oil remaining in the pan. Stir in the rest of the oil with the remaining sun-dried tomato paste. You may need to add a spoonful of water if the mixture is very thick.

5 When the mixture starts to sizzle, toss in the noodles. Add salt and pepper to taste, and mix well.

6 Return the shrimp to the pan, and toss to combine. Serve at once garnished with the basil and strips of sun-dried tomatoes.

Mixed Rice Noodles

A delicious noodle dish made extra special by adding avocado and garnishing with shrimp.

INGREDIENTS

Serves 4

1 tablespoon sunflower oil
1-inch piece fresh ginger, peeled and grated
2 garlic cloves, crushed
3 tablespoons dark soy sauce
1 cup green peas, thawed if frozen
1 pound rice noodles
1 pound spinach, stalks removed
2 tablespoons smooth peanut butter
2 tablespoons tahini
$^2/_3$ cup milk
1 ripe avocado, peeled and pitted
roasted peanuts and shelled, cooked shrimp, to garnish

1 Heat a wok, then add the oil. When the oil is hot, stir-fry the ginger and garlic for 30 seconds. Add 1 tablespoon of the soy sauce and $^2/_3$ cup boiling water.

COOK'S TIP

Do not peel, pit or slice the avocado much in advance of using, as the flesh quickly discolors. Sprinkling with a little lemon or lime juice helps prevent this.

2 Add the peas and noodles, then cook for 3 minutes. Stir in the spinach. Remove the vegetables and noodles, drain and keep warm.

3 Stir the peanut butter, remaining soy sauce, tahini and milk together in the wok, and simmer for 1 minute.

4 Add the vegetables and noodles, slice in the avocado and toss together. Serve piled on individual plates. Spoon some sauce over each portion and garnish with roasted peanuts and shrimp.

Noodles with Asparagus and Saffron Sauce

A rather elegant, summery dish with fragrant saffron cream.

INGREDIENTS

Serves 4

1 pound young asparagus
pinch of saffron threads
1 ounce butter
2 shallots, finely chopped
2 tablespoons white wine
1 cup heavy cream
grated rind and juice of ½ lemon
4 ounces peas
12 ounces somen noodles
½ bunch chervil, coarsely chopped
salt and freshly ground black pepper
grated Parmesan cheese (optional)

1 Cut off the asparagus tips (about 2 inches in length), then slice the remaining spears into short rounds. Steep the saffron in 2 tablespoons boiling water in a cup.

2 Melt the butter in a saucepan, add the shallots, and cook over a low heat for 3 minutes until soft. Add the white wine, cream and saffron infusion. Bring to a boil, reduce the heat, and simmer gently for 5 minutes or until the sauce thickens to a coating consistency. Add the grated lemon rind and juice, with salt and pepper to taste.

3 Bring a large saucepan of lightly salted water to a boil. Blanch the asparagus tips, scoop them out, and add them to the sauce, then cook the peas and short asparagus rounds in the boiling water until just tender. Scoop them out, and add to the sauce.

4 Cook the somen noodles in the same water until just tender, following the directions on the package. Drain, place in a wide pan, and pour the sauce over the top.

5 Toss the noodles with the sauce and vegetables, adding the chervil and more salt and pepper, if needed. Finally, sprinkle with the grated Parmesan, if using, and serve hot.

Fried Noodles with Bean Sprouts and Asparagus

Soft-fried noodles contrast beautifully with crisp bean sprouts and asparagus.

INGREDIENTS

Serves 4

4 ounces dried egg noodles
¼ cup vegetable oil
1 small onion, chopped
1-inch piece fresh ginger, peeled and grated
2 garlic cloves, crushed
6 ounces young asparagus spears, trimmed
1 cup bean sprouts
4 scallions, sliced
3 tablespoons soy sauce
salt and ground black pepper

1 Bring a pan of salted water to a boil. Add the noodles and cook for 2–3 minutes, until tender. Drain and toss them in 2 tablespoons of the oil.

2 Heat the remaining oil in a preheated wok until very hot. Add the onion, ginger and garlic and stir-fry for 2–3 minutes. Add the asparagus and stir-fry for 2–3 more minutes.

3 Add the noodles and bean sprouts and stir-fry for 2 minutes.

4 Stir in the scallions and soy sauce. Season to taste, adding salt sparingly, as the soy sauce will add quite a salty flavor. Stir-fry for 1 minute, then serve immediately.

Noodles with Ginger and Cilantro

Here is a simple noodle dish that goes well with most Asian dishes. It can also be served as a snack for two or three people.

INGREDIENTS

Serves 4–6
handful of fresh cilantro sprigs
8 ounces dried egg noodles
3 tablespoons peanut oil
2-inch piece fresh ginger, finely
    shredded
6–8 scallions, shredded
2 tablespoons light soy sauce
salt and ground black pepper

— COOK'S TIP —

Many of the dried egg noodles available are sold packed in layers. As a guide, allow 1 layer of noodles per person as an average portion for a main dish.

1 Strip the leaves from the cilantro sprigs. Pile them on a cutting board and chop them roughly, using a cleaver or large, sharp knife.

2 Cook the noodles according to the package instructions. Rinse under cold water and drain well. Toss them in 1 tablespoon of the oil.

3 Heat a wok until hot, add the remaining oil and swirl it around. Add the ginger and stir-fry for a few seconds, then add the noodles and scallions. Stir-fry for 3–4 minutes, until hot.

4 Sprinkle with the soy sauce, cilantro and seasoning. Toss well, then serve immediately.

Stir-fried Tofu and Bean Sprouts with Noodles

This is a satisfying dish, that is both tasty and easy to make.

INGREDIENTS

Serves 4

8-ounce package fresh firm tofu
peanut oil, for deep-frying
6 ounces medium egg noodles
1 tablespoon sesame oil
1 teaspoon cornstarch
2 teaspoons dark soy sauce
2 tablespoons Chinese rice wine or
   dry sherry
1 teaspoon sugar
6–8 scallions, cut diagonally into
   1-inch lengths
3 garlic cloves, sliced
1 fresh green chili, seeded and sliced
1 head bok choy, roughly shredded
¼ cup bean sprouts
¼ cup toasted cashews, to garnish

1 Drain the tofu and pat dry with paper towels. Cut the tofu into 1-inch cubes. Half-fill a wok with peanut oil and heat to 350°F. Deep-fry the tofu in batches for 1–2 minutes, until golden and crisp. Drain on paper towels. Carefully pour all but 2 tablespoons of the oil from the wok.

2 Cook the noodles. Rinse them thoroughly under cold water and drain well. Toss them in 2 teaspoons of the sesame oil and set aside. In a bowl, combine the cornstarch, soy sauce, rice wine or sherry, sugar and remaining sesame oil.

3 Reheat the 2 tablespoons of peanut oil and, when hot, add the scallions, garlic, chili, bok choy and bean sprouts. Stir-fry for 1–2 minutes.

4 Add the tofu with the noodles and sauce. Cook, stirring, for about 1 minute, until well mixed. Sprinkle the cashews on top. Serve immediately.

Tossed Noodles with Seafood

INGREDIENTS

Serves 4–6

12 ounces thick egg noodles
4 tablespoons vegetable oil
3 slices fresh ginger, grated
2 garlic cloves, finely chopped
8 ounces mussels or clams
8 ounces raw shrimp, peeled
8 ounces squid, cut into rings
4 ounces oriental fish cake, sliced
1 red bell pepper, seeded and cut
    into rings
2 ounces sugar snap peas, ends
    removed
2 tablespoons soy sauce
1/2 teaspoon sugar
1/2 cup broth or water
1 tablespoon cornstarch
1–2 teaspoons sesame oil
salt and freshly ground black pepper
2 scallions, chopped, and 2 red chilies,
    seeded and chopped, to garnish

1 Cook the noodles in a large saucepan of boiling water until just tender. Drain, rinse under cold water, and drain well.

2 Heat the oil in a wok or large frying pan. Fry the ginger and garlic for 30 seconds. Add the mussels or clams, shrimp and squid, and stir-fry for about 4–5 minutes until the seafood changes color. Add the fish cake slices, bell pepper rings and sugar snap peas, and stir well.

3 In a bowl, mix the soy sauce, sugar, broth or water and cornstarch. Stir into the seafood, and bring to a boil. Add the noodles, and cook until they are heated through.

4 Add the sesame oil to the wok or pan, and season with salt and pepper to taste. Serve at once, garnished with the chopped scallions and red chilies.

Noodles with Spicy Meat Sauce

INGREDIENTS

Serves 4–6

2 tablespoons vegetable oil
2 dried red chilies, chopped
1 teaspoon grated fresh ginger
2 garlic cloves, finely chopped
1 tablespoon chili black bean paste
1 pound minced pork or beef
1 pound broad flat egg noodles
1 tablespoon sesame oil
2 scallions, chopped, to garnish

For the sauce

1/4 teaspoon salt
1 teaspoon sugar
1 tablespoon soy sauce
1 teaspoon mushroom ketchup
1 tablespoon cornstarch
1 cup chicken broth
1 teaspoon Shaohsing wine or
    dry sherry

1 Heat the vegetable oil in a large saucepan. Add the dried chilies, ginger and garlic. Fry until the garlic starts to color, then gradually stir in the chili black bean paste.

2 Add the minced pork or beef, breaking it up with a spatula or wooden spoon. Cook over a high heat until the minced meat changes color and any liquid has evaporated.

3 Mix all the sauce ingredients in a cup. Make a well in the center of the pork mixture. Pour in the sauce mixture, and stir together. Simmer for 10–15 minutes until tender.

4 Meanwhile, cook the noodles in a large saucepan of boiling water for 5–7 minutes until just tender. Drain well, and toss with the sesame oil. Serve, topped with the meat sauce and garnished with the scallions.

Tomato Noodles with Fried Egg

INGREDIENTS

Serves 4

12 ounces medium-thick
   dried noodles
4 tablespoons vegetable oil
2 garlic cloves, very finely chopped
4 shallots, chopped
½ teaspoon chili powder
1 teaspoon paprika
2 carrots, finely diced
4 ounces button mushrooms,
   quartered
2 ounces peas
1 tablespoon tomato ketchup
2 teaspoons tomato paste
salt and freshly ground black pepper
butter for frying
4 eggs

1 Cook the noodles in a saucepan
   of boiling water until just tender.
Drain, rinse under cold running water,
and drain well.

2 Heat the oil in a wok or large
   frying pan. Add the garlic, shallots,
chili powder and paprika. Stir-fry for
about 1 minute, then add the carrots,
mushrooms and peas. Continue to
stir-fry until the vegetables are cooked.

3 Stir the tomato ketchup and paste
   into the vegetable mixture. Add
the noodles, and cook over a medium
heat until the noodles are heated
through and have taken on the reddish
tinge of the paprika and tomato.

4 Meanwhile, melt the butter in a
   frying pan, and fry the eggs. Season
the noodle mixture, divide it among
four serving plates, and top each
portion with a fried egg.

Curry Fried Noodles

On its own, bean curd (tofu) has
a fairly bland flavor, but it takes
on the flavor of the curry spices
wonderfully.

INGREDIENTS

Serves 4

4 tablespoons vegetable oil
2–3 tablespoons curry paste
8 ounces smoked bean curd, cut into
   1-inch cubes
8 ounces green beans, cut into
   1-inch lengths
1 red bell pepper, seeded and cut into
   fine strips
12 ounces rice vermicelli, soaked in
   warm water until soft
1 tablespoon soy sauce
salt and freshly ground black pepper
2 scallions, finely sliced, 2 red chilies,
   seeded and chopped, and 1 lime, cut
   into wedges, to garnish

1 Heat half the oil in a wok or large
   frying pan. Add the curry paste,
and stir-fry for a few minutes, then add
the bean curd. Continue to fry until
golden brown. Using a slotted spoon,
remove the cubes from the pan. Set
aside until required.

2 Add the remaining oil to the wok
   or pan. When hot, add the green
beans and red pepper. Stir-fry until the
vegetables are cooked. You may need
to moisten them with a little water.

3 Drain the noodles, and add them
   to the wok or frying pan. Continue
to stir-fry until the noodles are heated
through, then return the curried bean
curd to the wok. Season with soy
sauce, salt and pepper.

4 Transfer the mixture to a serving
   dish. Sprinkle with the scallions
and chilies, and serve the lime wedges
on the side.

RICE

*Rice is a staple food throughout much of
China and Asia. While plain boiled
rice is a useful accompaniment that goes
well with a wide variety of dishes, it is
easy to combine rice with vegetables,
eggs and a range of flavorings and
spices to create a rather more special
meal. Rice dishes from each country
and region have their own unique
flavors. Try Chinese Special Fried Rice,
Sushi from Japan, Thai Coconut Rice
or Rice Porridge with Chicken
from Indonesia. Don't overlook
Coconut Rice Fritters, a sweet snack
from the Philippines.*

Plain Rice

Use long-grain or *patna* rice, or fragrant rice from Thailand. Allow two ounces raw rice per person. If you use fragrant Thai rice, omit the salt.

INGREDIENTS

Serves 4
generous 1 cup rice
about 1 cup water
pinch of salt
½ teaspoon vegetable oil

1 Wash and rinse the rice. Place the rice in a saucepan and add the water. There should be no more than ¾ inch of water above the surface of the rice.

2 Bring to a boil, add the salt and oil, then stir to prevent the rice from sticking to the bottom of the pan. Reduce the heat to very, very low, cover and cook for 15–20 minutes.

3 Remove from the heat and let stand, still covered, for 10 minutes. Fluff up the rice with a fork or spoon just before serving.

Egg-fried Rice

Use rice with a fairly firm texture. Ideally, the raw rice should be soaked in water for a short time before cooking.

INGREDIENTS

Serves 4
3 eggs
1 teaspoon salt
2 scallions, finely chopped
2–3 tablespoons vegetable oil
1 pound cooked rice
4 ounces frozen peas

1 In a bowl, lightly beat the eggs with a pinch of the salt and a few pieces of scallion.

2 Heat the oil in a preheated wok, and lightly scramble the eggs.

3 Add the cooked rice and stir to make sure that each grain of rice is separated. Add the remaining salt and scallions and the peas. Blend well, allow to heat through and serve.

Chinese Special Fried Rice

This recipe combines a tasty mixture of chicken, shrimp and vegetables with fried rice.

INGREDIENTS

Serves 4

scant 1 cup long-grain white rice
3 tablespoons peanut oil
1½ cups water
1 garlic clove, crushed
4 scallions, finely chopped
4 ounces cooked chicken, diced
4 ounces cooked jumbo shrimp, peeled
2 ounces frozen peas
1 egg, lightly beaten
2 ounces lettuce, shredded
2 tablespoons light soy sauce
pinch of superfine sugar
salt and freshly ground black pepper
1 tablespoon chopped roasted cashews,
    to garnish

1 Rinse the rice in two to three changes of warm water to wash away some of the starch. Drain well.

2 Put the rice in a saucepan and add 1 tablespoon of the oil and the water. Cover and bring to a boil, stir once, then cover and simmer for 12–15 minutes, until nearly all the water has been absorbed. Turn off the heat and cover; let stand for 10 minutes. Fluff up with a fork and let cool.

3 Heat the remaining oil in a preheated wok or frying pan, add the garlic and scallions and stir-fry for 30 seconds.

4 Add the chicken, shrimp and peas and stir-fry for 1–2 minutes, then add the cooked rice and stir-fry for another 2 minutes. Pour in the egg and stir-fry until just set. Stir in the lettuce, soy sauce, sugar and seasoning.

5 Transfer to a warmed serving bowl, sprinkle with the chopped cashews and serve immediately.

Egg Foo Yung

A great way of turning a bowl of leftover cooked rice into a meal for four, this dish is tasty and full of texture.

INGREDIENTS

Serves 4
3 eggs, beaten
pinch of Chinese five-spice
   powder (optional)
3 tablespoons peanut or
   sunflower oil
4 scallions, sliced
1 garlic clove, crushed
1 small green bell pepper, seeded and
   chopped
4 ounces bean sprouts
generous 1 cup white rice, cooked
3 tablespoons light soy sauce
1 tablespoon sesame oil
salt and freshly ground black pepper

1 Season the eggs with salt and pepper to taste and beat in the five-spice powder, if using.

2 Heat 1 tablespoon of the oil in a preheated wok or large frying pan and, when quite hot, pour in the eggs. Cook rather like an omelet, pulling the mixture away from the sides and allowing the rest to slip underneath.

3 Cook the egg until firm, then slide out. Chop the omelet into small strips and set aside.

4 Heat the remaining oil and stir-fry the scallions, garlic, green bell pepper and bean sprouts for about 2 minutes, stirring and tossing continuously.

5 Combine the cooked rice and heat thoroughly, stirring well. Add the soy sauce and sesame oil, then return the egg strips to the pan and mix in well. Serve immediately, piping hot.

Malacca Fried Rice

There are many versions of this dish throughout the East, all of which make use of leftover rice. Ingredients vary according to what is available, but shrimp are a popular addition.

INGREDIENTS

Serves 4–6

2 eggs

3 tablespoons vegetable oil

4 shallots or 1 medium onion, finely chopped

1 teaspoon finely chopped fresh ginger

1 garlic clove, crushed

8 ounces jumbo shrimp, raw or cooked, peeled and deveined

1–2 teaspoon chili sauce (optional)

3 scallions, green parts only, roughly chopped

8 ounces frozen peas

8 ounces thickly sliced roast pork, diced

3 tablespoons light soy sauce

1⅔ cups long-grain rice, cooked

salt and freshly ground black pepper

2 Heat the remaining oil in a large preheated wok, add the shallots or onion, ginger, garlic and shrimp and cook for 1–2 minutes, making sure that the garlic does not burn.

3 Add the chili sauce, scallions, peas, pork and soy sauce. Stir to heat through, then add the cooked rice. Fry the rice over moderate heat for 6–8 minutes. Transfer to a dish and decorate with the egg strips.

1 In a bowl, beat the eggs well and season to taste with salt and pepper. Heat 1 tablespoon of the oil in a large, nonstick frying pan, pour in the eggs and cook for about 30 seconds, without stirring, until set. Roll up the omelet, cut into thin strips and set aside.

Asian Fried Rice

This is a great way to use leftover cooked rice. Make sure the rice is very cold before attempting to fry it, as warm rice will become soggy. Some supermarkets sell frozen cooked rice.

INGREDIENTS

Serves 4–6

5 tablespoons oil
4 ounces shallots, halved and thinly sliced
3 garlic cloves, crushed
1 red chili, seeded and finely chopped
6 scallions, finely chopped
1 red bell pepper, seeded and finely chopped
8 ounces white cabbage, finely shredded
6 ounces cucumber, finely chopped
2 ounces frozen peas, thawed
3 eggs, beaten
1 teaspoon tomato paste
2 tablespoons lime juice
¼ teaspoon Tabasco sauce
1½ pounds cooked white rice, cooled
1 cup cashews, roughly chopped
2 tablespoons chopped fresh cilantro, plus extra to garnish
salt and freshly ground black pepper

1 Heat the oil in a large preheated wok or nonstick frying pan and cook the shallots until very crisp and golden. Remove with a slotted spoon and drain on paper towels.

2 Add the garlic and chili and cook for 1 minute. Add the scallions and red bell pepper and cook for 3–4 minutes, or until the scallions are beginning to soften.

3 Add the cabbage, cucumber and peas and cook for another 2 minutes.

4 Make a gap in the ingredients in the wok or frying pan and add the beaten eggs. Scramble the eggs, stirring occasionally, and then stir them into the vegetables.

5 Add the tomato paste, lime juice and Tabasco sauce and stir well to combine.

6 Increase the heat and add the cooked rice, cashews, cilantro and plenty of seasoning. Stir-fry for 3–4 minutes, until piping hot. Serve garnished with the crisp shallots and extra fresh cilantro, if desired.

COOK'S TIP

1½ pounds cooked rice is equivalent to 8 ounces raw weight.

Sushi

INGREDIENTS

Makes 8–10
For the tuna sushi
3 sheets nori (paper-thin seaweed)
5 ounces very-fresh tuna fillet, cut
  into strips
1 teaspoon wasabi paste
6 young carrots, blanched
6 cups cooked Japanese rice

For the salmon sushi
2 eggs
½ teaspoon salt
2 teaspoons sugar
5 sheets nori
6 cups cooked Japanese rice
5 ounces very-fresh salmon fillet, cut
  into fingers
1 teaspoon wasabi paste
½ small cucumber, cut into strips

1 To make the tuna sushi, spread half a sheet of nori onto a bamboo mat, lay strips of tuna across the full length and season with the thinned wasabi. Place a line of blanched carrot next to the tuna and roll tightly. Moisten the edge with water and seal.

2 Place a square of damp waxed paper on the bamboo mat, then spread evenly with sushi rice. Place the nori-wrapped tuna along the center and wrap tightly, enclosing the nori completely. Remove the paper and cut into neat rounds with a wet knife.

3 To make the salmon sushi, make a simple flat omelette by beating together the eggs, salt and sugar. Heat a large non-stick pan, pour in the egg mixture, stir briefly and allow to set. Transfer to a clean dish towel and cool.

4 Place the nori on a bamboo mat, cover with the omelette and trim to size. Spread a layer of rice over the omelette, then lay strips of salmon across the width. Season the salmon with the thinned wasabi, then place a strip of cucumber next to the salmon. Fold the bamboo mat in half. Cut into neat rounds with a wet knife.

Shiitake Fried Rice

Shiitake mushrooms have a strong, meaty aroma and flavor. This is a very easy recipe to make, and although it is a side dish, it can almost be a meal in itself.

INGREDIENTS

Serves 4
2 eggs
1 tablespoon water
3 tablespoons vegetable oil
12 ounces shiitake mushrooms
8 scallions, sliced diagonally
1 garlic clove, crushed
½ green bell pepper, seeded and
  chopped
2 tablespoons butter
about 1 cup long-grain rice, cooked
1 tablespoon medium-dry sherry
2 tablespoons dark soy sauce
1 tablespoon chopped fresh cilantro
salt

1 Beat the eggs with the water and season with a little salt.

2 Heat 1 tablespoon of the oil in a preheated wok or large frying pan, pour in the eggs and cook to make a large omelet. Lift the sides of the omelet and tilt the wok so that the uncooked egg can run underneath and be cooked. Roll up the omelet and slice thinly.

3 Remove and discard the mushroom stalks, if they are tough. Slice the caps thinly, halving them if they are large.

4 Heat 1 tablespoon of the oil in the wok and stir-fry the scallions and garlic for 3–4 minutes, until softened but not brown. Transfer them to a plate using a slotted spoon and set aside.

5 Add the green bell pepper and stir-fry for about 2–3 minutes, then add the butter and the remaining oil. As the butter begins to sizzle, add the mushrooms and stir-fry over moderate heat for 3–4 minutes, or until both vegetables are soft.

6 Loosen the rice grains as much as possible. Pour the sherry over the mushrooms and then stir in the rice.

7 Heat the rice over moderate heat, stirring all the time to prevent it from sticking. If the rice seems very dry, add a little more oil. Stir in the cooked scallions, garlic and omelet slices, the soy sauce and the chopped cilantro. Cook for a few minutes, until heated through, and serve.

Coconut Rice Fritters

These delicious fritters from the Philippines can be served at any time and go especially well with coffee or hot chocolate.

INGREDIENTS

Makes 28
⅔ cup long-grain rice, cooked
2 tablespoons coconut milk powder
3 tablespoons sugar
2 egg yolks
juice of ½ lemon
3 ounces shredded coconut
oil, for deep-frying
confectioners' sugar, for dusting

1 Place ⅓ cup of the cooked rice in a mortar and pound with a pestle until smooth and sticky. Alternatively, process in a food processor. Transfer to a bowl and mix in the remaining rice, the coconut milk powder, sugar, egg yolks and lemon juice.

2 Spread out the shredded coconut on a baking sheet or plate. With wet hands, divide the rice mixture into thumb-sized pieces and roll them in the coconut to make neat balls.

3 Heat the oil in a wok or deep-fryer to 350°F. Fry the coconut rice balls, three or four at a time, for 1–2 minutes, until the coconut is evenly browned. Transfer to a plate and dust with confectioners' sugar. Place a wooden skewer in each fritter and serve in the traditional way, as an afternoon snack.

COOK'S TIP

In the Philippines, hot chocolate is made by preparing a syrup with 2 tablespoons sugar and ½ cup water and then melting 4 ounces pieces of best-quality plain chocolate in it. Finally, a scant 1 cup evaporated milk is whisked in over low heat. This luxurious drink serves two.

Rice Porridge with Chicken

This dish is often served as sustaining breakfast fare. It can be served simply, with just the chicken stirred into it. Hearty eaters will relish helpings of porridge drizzled with a little soy sauce, with strips of chicken, shrimp, garlic and strips of fresh chili, topped with a lightly fried egg and garnished with celery leaves and fried onion.

INGREDIENTS

Serves 6

2¼ pounds chicken, cut into 4 pieces, or 4 chicken quarters
7½ cups water
1 large onion, quartered
1-inch piece fresh ginger, halved and bruised
12 ounces Thai fragrant rice, rinsed
salt and freshly ground black pepper
cooked peeled shrimp, strips of fresh chili, deep-fried onion and celery leaves, to garnish (optional)

1 Place the chicken pieces in a large saucepan with the water, onion and ginger. Season with salt and pepper, bring to a boil and simmer for 45–50 minutes, until the chicken is tender. Remove the chicken from the pan and reserve the broth. Remove the skin from the chicken pieces. Cut the meat from the bones and then into bite-sized pieces.

2 Strain and measure the reserved chicken broth. Increase the quantity to 7½ cups with water and transfer to a clean saucepan.

3 Add the rice to the broth and bring to a boil, stirring constantly. Lower the heat and simmer gently for 20 minutes. Stir, cover and cook for another 20 minutes, stirring from time to time, until the rice is soft.

4 Stir the chicken pieces into the porridge and heat through for 5 minutes. Serve as it is or with any of the garnishes suggested.

Coconut Rice

This rich dish is usually served with a tangy papaya salad.

INGREDIENTS

Serves 4–6
2 cups jasmine rice
1 cup water
2 cups unsweetened coconut milk
½ teaspoon salt
2 tablespoons sugar
fresh shredded coconut, to garnish
   (optional)

1 Wash the rice in several changes of cold water until it runs clear. Place the water, coconut milk, salt and sugar in a heavy-bottomed saucepan.

2 Add the rice, cover, and bring to a boil. Reduce the heat to low and simmer for about 15–20 minutes, or until the rice is tender to the bite and cooked through.

3 Turn off the heat and allow the rice to rest in the saucepan for about 5–10 minutes.

4 Fluff up the rice with chopsticks before serving.

Pineapple Fried Rice

This dish is ideal to prepare for a special occasion meal. Served in the pineapple skin shells, it is certain to be the talking point of the dinner.

INGREDIENTS

Serves 4–6
1 pineapple
2 tablespoons vegetable oil
1 small onion, finely chopped
2 green chilies, seeded and chopped
8 ounces lean pork, cut into
   small dice
4 ounces cooked shelled shrimp
3–4 cups cooked cold rice
½ cup roasted cashews
2 scallions, chopped
2 tablespoons fish sauce
1 tablespoon soy sauce
10–12 mint leaves, 2 red chilies, sliced,
   and 1 green chili, sliced, to garnish

1 Cut the pineapple in half lengthwise and remove the flesh from both halves by cutting around inside the skin. Reserve the skin shells. You need 4 ounces of fruit, chopped finely (keep the rest for a dessert).

--- COOK'S TIP ---

When buying a pineapple, look for a sweet-smelling fruit with an even brownish-yellow skin. To test for ripeness, tap the base – a dull sound indicates that the fruit is ripe. The flesh should also give slightly when pressed.

2 Heat the oil in a wok or large frying pan. Add the onion and chilies and fry for about 3–5 minutes, until softened. Add the pork and cook until it is brown on all sides.

3 Stir in the shrimp and rice and toss well together. Continue to stir-fry until the rice is thoroughly heated.

4 Add the chopped pineapple, cashews and scallions. Season with fish sauce and soy sauce.

5 Spoon into the pineapple skin shells. Garnish with shredded mint leaves and red and green chilies.

Thai Rice with Bean Sprouts

Thai rice has a delicate fragrance that is delicious hot or cold.

INGREDIENTS

Serves 6

1 cup Thai fragrant rice
2 tablespoons sesame oil
2 tablespoons fresh lime juice
1 small red chili pepper, seeded and chopped
1 garlic clove, crushed
2 teaspoons grated fresh ginger
2 tablespoons light soy sauce
1 teaspoon honey
3 tablespoons pineapple juice
1 tablespoon wine vinegar
2 green onions, sliced
2 canned pineapple rings, chopped
1¼ cups sprouted lentils or beansprouts
1 small red bell pepper, sliced
1 stalk celery, sliced
½ cup cashew nuts, chopped
2 tablespoons toasted sesame seeds
salt and freshly ground black pepper

1 Soak the Thai fragrant rice for 20 minutes, then rinse in several changes of water. Drain, then boil in salted water for 10–12 minutes until tender. Drain and set aside.

2 In a large bowl, whisk together the sesame oil, lime juice, chili, garlic, ginger, soy sauce, honey, pineapple juice and vinegar. Stir in the rice.

3 Add the green onions, pineapple rings, sprouted lentils or beansprouts, red pepper, celery, cashew nuts and the toasted sesame seeds and mix well. If the rice grains stick together while cooling, simply stir them with a metal spoon. This dish can be served warm or lightly chilled and is a good accompaniment to grilled or barbecued meats and fish.

--- COOK'S TIP ---

Sesame oil has a strong, nutty flavor and is good·for seasoning, marinating or flavoring rather than for cooking. Because the taste is so distinctive, sesame oil can be mixed with grapeseed or other light-flavored oils.

Spicy Peanut Rice Cakes

Serve these spicy Indonesian rice cakes with a crisp green salad and a dipping sauce, such as Hot Tomato Sambal.

INGREDIENTS

Makes 16

1 garlic clove, crushed
½-inch piece fresh ginger, finely chopped
¼ teaspoon ground turmeric
1 teaspoon sugar
½ teaspoon salt
1 teaspoon chili sauce
2 teaspoons fish sauce or soy sauce
2 tablespoons chopped fresh cilantro
juice of ½ lime
generous ½ cup long-grain rice, cooked
¾ cup raw peanuts, chopped
vegetable oil, for deep-frying

1 Pound together the garlic, ginger and turmeric in a mortar with a pestle or in a food processor. Add the sugar, salt, chili sauce, fish or soy sauce, cilantro and lime juice.

2 Add about ¼ cup of the cooked rice and pound until smooth and sticky. Stir the mixture into the remaining rice and mix well. With wet hands, shape 16 thumb-sized balls.

3 Spread the chopped peanuts out on a plate and roll the balls in them to coat evenly. Set aside.

4 Heat the oil in a preheated wok or deep frying pan. Deep-fry the rice cakes, three at a time, until crisp and golden. Remove and drain on paper towels. Serve immediately.

Rice with Seeds and Spices

This dish provides a change from plain boiled rice, and is a colorful accompaniment to serve with curries or grilled meats.

INGREDIENTS

Serves 4

1 teaspoon sunflower oil
½ teaspoon ground turmeric
6 green cardamom pods,
  lightly crushed
1 teaspoon coriander seeds,
  lightly crushed
1 garlic clove, crushed
1 cup basmati rice
1²/₃ cups vegetable stock
½ cup plain yogurt
1 tablespoon toasted sunflower seeds
1 tablespoon toasted sesame seeds
salt and freshly ground black pepper
fresh cilantro leaves, to garnish

1 Heat the oil in a non-stick frying pan and fry the spices and garlic for 1 minute, stirring constantly.

2 Add the rice and stock, bring to a boil, then cover and simmer for 15 minutes or until just tender.

3 Stir in the yogurt and the toasted sunflower and sesame seeds. Adjust the seasoning and serve the rice hot, garnished with cilantro leaves.

Nasi Goreng

One of the most familiar and well-known Indonesian dishes. This is a marvelous way to use up leftover rice, chicken and meats such as pork. It is important that the rice is really cold and the grains separate before adding the other ingredients, so it's best to cook the rice the day before.

INGREDIENTS

Serves 4–6

1⅞ cup long grain rice, such as basmati, cooked and allowed to become completely cold
2 eggs
2 tablespoons water
7 tablespoons oil
8 ounces pork loin or tenderloin of beef
4 ounces cooked, peeled shrimp
6–8 ounces cooked chicken, chopped
2–3 fresh red chilies, seeded and sliced
½ teaspoon shrimp paste
2 garlic cloves, crushed
1 onion, sliced
2 tablespoons dark soy sauce or 3–4 tablespoons tomato ketchup
salt and freshly ground black pepper
celery leaves, Deep-fried Onions and cilantro sprigs, to garnish

1 Once the rice is cooked and cooled, fork it through to separate the grains and keep it in a covered pan or dish until required.

2 Beat the eggs with seasoning and the water and make two or three omelets in a frying pan, with a minimum of oil. Roll up each omelet and cut in strips when cold. Set aside.

3 Cut the pork or beef into neat strips and put the meat, shrimp and chicken pieces in separate bowls. Shred one of the chilies and reserve it.

4 Put the shrimp paste, with the remaining chili, garlic and onion, in a food processor and grind to a fine paste. Alternatively, pound together using a mortar and pestle.

5 Fry the paste in the remaining hot oil, without browning, until it gives off a rich, spicy aroma. Add the pork or beef, tossing the meat constantly, to seal in the juices. Cook for 2 minutes, stirring constantly. Add the shrimp, cook for 2 minutes and then stir in the chicken, cold rice, dark soy sauce or ketchup and seasoning to taste. Stir constantly to prevent the rice from sticking.

6 Turn onto a hot platter and garnish with the omelet strips, celery leaves, onions, reserved shredded chili and the cilantro sprigs.

Thai Fried Rice

This hot and spicy dish is easy to prepare and makes a complete meal in itself.

INGREDIENTS

Serves 4

1¹/₂ cups Thai fragrant rice
3 tablespoons vegetable oil
1 onion, chopped
1 small red bell pepper, seeded and cut
 into ³/₄-inch squares
2 boneless chicken breasts (12 ounces
 total), skinned and cubed
1 garlic clove, crushed
1 tablespoon mild curry paste
¹/₂ teaspoon paprika
¹/₂ teaspoon ground turmeric
2 tablespoons fish sauce
2 eggs, beaten
salt and ground black pepper
fried basil leaves, to garnish

1 Put the rice in a sieve and wash well under cold running water. Put the rice in a heavy pan with 6 cups boiling water. Return to a boil, then simmer, uncovered, for 8–10 minutes; drain well. Spread out the grains on a tray and let cool.

2 Heat a wok until hot, add 2 tablespoons of the oil and swirl it around. Add the onion and red bell pepper and stir-fry for 1 minute.

3 Add the chicken cubes, garlic, curry paste and spices and stir-fry for 2–3 minutes.

4 Reduce the heat to medium, add the cooled rice, fish sauce and seasoning. Stir-fry for 2–3 minutes, until the rice is very hot.

5 Make a well in the center of the rice and add the remaining oil. When hot, add the beaten eggs, let cook for about 2 minutes, until lightly set, then stir into the rice.

6 Scatter the fried basil leaves on top and serve immediately.

COOK'S TIP

Among the various types of rice available, Thai fragrant rice is one of the more popular, especially in Thai, Vietnamese and some other Southeast Asian recipes. It does, in fact, have a particularly special fragrance and is generally served on feast days and other important occasions.

Chinese Jeweled Rice

This rice dish, with its many different, interesting ingredients, is practically a meal in itself.

INGREDIENTS

Serves 4

1½ cups long-grain rice
3 tablespoons vegetable oil
1 onion, roughly chopped
4 ounces cooked ham, diced
6-ounce can white crabmeat
½ cup water chestnuts, drained and cut into cubes
4 dried black Chinese mushrooms, soaked, drained and diced
½ cup green peas, thawed if frozen
2 tablespoons oyster sauce
1 teaspoon sugar
salt

1 Rinse the rice, then cook for 10–12 minutes in 3–3¾ cups salted water in a saucepan with a tight-fitting lid. When cooked, refresh under cold water. Heat half the oil in a preheated wok, then stir-fry the rice for 3 minutes. Remove and set aside.

2 Add the remaining oil to the wok. When the oil is hot, cook the onion until softened but not colored.

3 Add all the remaining ingredients and stir-fry for 2 minutes.

4 Return the rice to the wok and stir-fry for 3 minutes, then serve.

Indonesian Fried Rice

This fried rice dish makes an ideal supper on its own or as an accompaniment to another dish.

INGREDIENTS

Serves 4–6

4 shallots, roughly chopped
1 fresh red chili, seeded and chopped
1 garlic clove, chopped
thin sliver of dried shrimp paste
3 tablespoons vegetable oil
8 ounces boneless lean pork, cut into fine strips
1 cup long-grain white rice, cooked and cooled
3–4 scallions, thinly sliced
4 ounces shelled cooked shrimp
2 tablespoons sweet soy sauce
chopped fresh cilantro and fine cucumber shreds, to garnish

1 In a mortar pound the shallots, chili, garlic and shrimp paste with a pestle until they form a paste.

COOK'S TIP

Shrimp paste, sometimes called dried shrimp paste, is a strong-smelling and flavorful paste made from fermented shrimp that is used extensively in many Asian cuisines. Always use sparingly. It is available at most Asian food stores.

2 Heat a wok until hot, add 2 tablespoons of the oil and swirl it around. Add the pork and stir-fry for 2–3 minutes. Remove the pork from the wok, set aside and keep warm.

3 Add the remaining oil to the wok. When hot, add the spiced shallot paste and stir-fry for about 30 seconds.

4 Reduce the heat. Add the rice, sliced scallions and shrimp. Stir-fry for 2–3 minutes. Add the pork and sprinkle with the soy sauce. Stir-fry for 1 minute. Serve immediately, garnished with chopped fresh cilantro and cucumber shreds.

Festive Rice

Nasi Kuning is served at special events – weddings, birthdays or farewell parties.

INGREDIENTS

Serves 8

1 pound Thai fragrant rice
4 tablespoons oil
2 garlic cloves, crushed
2 onions, finely sliced
2 inches fresh turmeric, peeled
  and crushed
3 cups water
14-fluid ounce can coconut milk
1–2 lemon grass stems, bruised
1–2 *pandan* leaves (optional)
salt

For the accompaniments

omelet strips
2 fresh red chilies, shredded
cucumber chunks
tomato wedges
Deep-fried Onions
Coconut and Peanut Relish (optional)
Shrimp Crackers

1 Wash the rice in several changes of water. Drain well.

2 Heat the oil in a wok and gently fry the crushed garlic, the finely sliced onions and the crushed fresh turmeric for a few minutes until soft but not browned.

COOK'S TIP

It is the custom to shape the rice into a cone (to represent a volcano) and then surround with the accompaniments. Shape with oiled hands or use a conical strainer.

3 Add the rice and and stir well so that each grain is thoroughly coated. Pour in the water and coconut milk and add the lemon grass, *pandan* leaves, if using, and salt.

4 Bring to a boil, stirring well. Cover and cook gently for about 15–20 minutes, until all of the liquid has been absorbed.

5 Remove from the heat. Cover with a dish towel, put on the lid and let stand in a warm place for 15 minutes. Remove the lemon grass and *pandan* leaves.

6 Turn onto a serving platter and garnish with the accompaniments.

Special Fried Rice

Special Fried Rice is so substantial and tasty that it is another rice dish that is almost a meal in itself.

INGREDIENTS

Serves 4

8 medium cooked shrimp, shelled
1 thick slice cooked ham
½ cup green peas
3 eggs
1 teaspoon salt
2 scallions, finely chopped
¼ cup vegetable oil
1 tablespoon light soy sauce
1 tablespoon Chinese rice wine or
   dry sherry
1 pound cooked rice

1 Pat dry the shrimp with paper towels. Cut the ham into small dice about the same size as the peas.

2 In a bowl, lightly beat the eggs with a pinch of the salt and a few pieces of the scallions.

3 Heat about half of the oil in a preheated wok, stir-fry the peas, shrimp and ham for 1 minute, then add the soy sauce and rice wine or sherry. Remove and keep warm.

4 Heat the remaining oil in the wok and lightly scramble the eggs. Add the rice and stir to make sure that each grain of rice is separated. Add the remaining salt and scallions and the shrimp, ham and peas. Mix well and serve either hot or cold.

Jasmine Rice

A naturally aromatic, long-grain white rice, jasmine rice is the staple of most Thai meals. If you eat rice regularly, you might invest in an electric rice cooker.

INGREDIENTS

Serves 4–6
2 cups jasmine rice
3 cups cold water

COOK'S TIP

An electric rice cooker cooks the rice and keeps it warm. Different sizes and models of rice cookers are available. The top of the range is a nonstick version, which is expensive, but well worth the money.

1 Rinse the rice thoroughly, at least three times, in cold water until the water runs clear.

2 Put the rice in a heavy-bottomed saucepan and add the water. Bring the rice to a vigorous boil, uncovered, over high heat.

3 Stir and reduce the heat to low. Cover and simmer for up to 20 minutes, or until all the water has been absorbed. Remove from the heat and allow to stand for 10 minutes.

4 Remove the lid and stir the rice gently with a rice paddle or a pair of wooden chopsticks, to fluff up and separate the grains.

Fried Jasmine Rice with Shrimp and Thai Basil

Thai basil (*bai grapao*), also known as Holy basil, has a unique, pungent flavor that is both spicy and sharp. It can be found in most Asian food markets.

INGREDIENTS

Serves 4–6
3 tablespoons vegetable oil
1 egg, beaten
1 onion, chopped
1 tablespoon chopped garlic
1 tablespoon shrimp paste
4 cups cooked jasmine rice
12 ounces cooked shelled shrimp
½ cup thawed frozen peas
oyster sauce, to taste
2 scallions, chopped
15–20 Thai basil leaves, coarsely chopped, plus an extra sprig, to garnish

1 Heat 1 tablespoon of the oil in a wok or frying pan. Add the beaten egg and swirl it around the pan to set like a thin pancake.

2 Cook until golden, slide out on to a board, roll up and cut into thin strips. Set aside.

3 Heat the remaining oil in the wok, add the onion and garlic and fry for 2–3 minutes. Stir in the shrimp paste and mix thoroughly.

4 Add the rice, shrimp and peas and toss together until everything is heated through.

5 Season with oyster sauce to taste, taking great care as the shrimp paste is salty. Add the scallions and basil leaves. Transfer to a serving dish and serve topped with the strips of egg pancake. Garnish with a sprig of basil.

Fried Rice with Pork

If you like, garnish with strips of omelet, as in Fried Jasmine Rice with Shrimp and Thai Basil.

INGREDIENTS

Serves 4–6

3 tablespoons vegetable oil
1 onion, chopped
1 tablespoon chopped garlic
4 ounces pork, cut into small cubes
2 eggs, beaten
4 cups cooked rice
2 tablespoons fish sauce
1 tablespoon dark soy sauce
½ teaspoon superfine sugar
4 scallions, finely sliced, to garnish
2 red chilies, sliced, to garnish
1 lime, cut into wedges and egg omelet, to garnish (optional)

1 Heat the oil in a wok or large frying pan. Add the onion and garlic and cook for about 2 minutes, until softened.

2 Add the pork to the softened onion and garlic. Stir-fry until the pork changes color and is cooked.

3 Add the eggs and cook until scrambled into small lumps.

4 Add the rice and continue to stir and toss, to coat it with the oil and prevent it from sticking.

5 Add the fish sauce, soy sauce and sugar and mix well. Continue to fry until the rice is thoroughly heated. Garnish with sliced scallions, red chilies and lime wedges. If you like, top with a few strips of egg omelet.

Red Fried Rice

This vibrant rice dish owes its appeal as much to the bright colors of red onion, red bell pepper and cherry tomatoes as it does to their distinctive flavors.

INGREDIENTS

Serves 2

½ cup basmati rice
2 tablespoons peanut oil
1 small red onion, chopped
1 red bell pepper, seeded and chopped
8 ounces cherry tomatoes, halved
2 eggs, beaten
salt and ground black pepper

1 Wash the rice several times under cold running water. Drain well. Bring a large pan of salted water to a boil, add the rice and cook for 10–12 minutes, until tender.

2 Meanwhile, heat the oil in a wok until very hot. Add the onion and bell pepper and stir-fry for 2–3 minutes. Add the cherry tomatoes and stir-fry for another 2 minutes.

3 Pour in the beaten eggs all at once. Cook for 30 seconds without stirring, then stir to break up the egg as it sets.

4 Drain the cooked rice thoroughly, add to the wok and toss it over the heat with the vegetable and egg mixture for 3 minutes. Season the fried rice with salt and pepper to taste.

Spicy Fried Rice Sticks with Shrimp

This well-known recipe is based on the classic Thai noodle dish called *pad Thai*. Popular all over Thailand, it is enjoyed morning, noon and night.

INGREDIENTS

Serves 4

2 tablespoons dried shrimp
1 tablespoon tamarind pulp
3 tablespoons fish sauce
1 tablespoon sugar
2 garlic cloves, chopped
2 fresh red chilies, seeded and chopped
3 tablespoons peanut oil
2 eggs, beaten
8 ounces dried rice sticks, soaked in warm water for 30 minutes, refreshed under cold running water and drained
8 ounces cooked jumbo shrimp, shelled
3 scallions, cut into 1-inch lengths
½ cup bean sprouts
2 tablespoons roughly chopped roasted unsalted peanuts
2 tablespoons chopped fresh cilantro
lime slices, to garnish

1 Put the dried shrimp in a small bowl and pour in enough warm water to cover them. Let soak for 30 minutes, until soft, then drain.

2 Put the tamarind pulp in a bowl with ¼ cup hot water. Blend together, then press through a strainer to extract 2 tablespoons thick tamarind water. Mix the tamarind water with the fish sauce and sugar.

3 Using a mortar and pestle, pound the garlic and chilies to form a paste. Heat a wok over medium heat, add 1 tablespoon of the oil, then add the beaten eggs and stir for 1–2 minutes, until the eggs are scrambled. Remove and set aside. Wipe the wok clean.

--- COOK'S TIP ---

For a vegetarian dish, omit the dried shrimp and replace the jumbo shrimp with cubes of deep-fried tofu.

4 Reheat the wok until hot and add the remaining oil, then the chili paste and dried shrimp and stir-fry for 1 minute. Add the rice sticks and tamarind mixture and stir-fry for 3–4 minutes.

5 Add the scrambled eggs, shrimp, scallions, bean sprouts, peanuts and cilantro, then stir-fry for 2 minutes, until well mixed. Serve immediately, garnishing each portion with lime slices.

Fried Rice with Spices

This dish is mildly spiced, and is suitable as an accompaniment to any curried dish. The whole spices—cloves, cardamom, bay leaf, cinnamon, peppercorns and cumin—are not intended to be eaten.

INGREDIENTS

Serves 3–4

¾ cup basmati rice
½ teaspoon salt
1 tablespoon ghee or butter
8 whole cloves
4 green cardamom pods, bruised
1 bay leaf
3-inch piece cinnamon stick
1 teaspoon black peppercorns
1 teaspoon cumin seeds

1 Put the rice in a colander and wash under cold running water until the water runs clear. Put in a bowl and pour 2½ cups fresh water over the rice. Let the rice soak for 30 minutes, then drain thoroughly.

COOK'S TIP

You could add ½ teaspoon ground turmeric to the rice in step 2 of the recipe to color it yellow.

2 Put the basmati rice, salt and 2½ cups water in a large, heavy pan. Bring to a boil, then cover and simmer for about 10 minutes. The rice should be just cooked, with a little bite to it. Drain off any excess water, fluff up the grains with a fork, then spread the rice out on a tray and set aside to cool.

3 Heat the ghee or butter in a wok until foaming, add the spices and stir-fry for 1 minute.

4 Add the cooled rice and stir-fry for 3–4 minutes, until warmed through. Serve immediately.

Nutty Rice and Mushroom Stir-fry

This delicious and substantial supper dish can be eaten hot or cold with salads.

INGREDIENTS

Serves 4–6
1½ cups long-grain rice, preferably basmati
3 tablespoons sunflower oil
1 small onion or shallot, roughly chopped
2 cups wild mushrooms, sliced
½ cup hazelnuts, roughly chopped
½ cup pecans, roughly chopped
½ cup almonds, roughly chopped
¼ cup fresh parsley, chopped
salt and ground black pepper

1 Rinse the rice, then cook for 10–12 minutes in 3–3¾ cups salted water in a saucepan with a tight-fitting lid. When cooked, refresh under cold water. Heat a wok, then add half the oil. Stir-fry the rice for 2–3 minutes. Remove and set aside.

— COOK'S TIP —

Of all the types of long-grain rice, basmati is undoubtedly the king. This long, aromatic grain grows in India, where its name means "fragrant." Basmati rice benefits from being rinsed with plenty of cold water and soaked for 10 minutes before it is cooked.

2 Add the remaining oil and stir-fry the onion or shallot for 2 minutes, until softened but not colored. Mix in the wild mushrooms and stir-fry for 2 minutes.

3 Add all the nuts and stir-fry for 1 minute. Return the rice to the wok and stir-fry for 3 minutes. Season with salt and pepper. Stir in the parsley and serve immediately.

DESSERTS

*Surprise the family with something
completely different with these melt-in-
the-mouth dessert recipes collected from
all over China and Asia. Exotic Fruit
Salad from Vietnam tastes just as
wonderful – and tropical – as it looks.
Old or young, few can resist the
delicious little Japanese Sweet Potato
and Chestnut Candies. Thailand offers
an intriguing variation on an
international favorite with Steamed
Coconut Custard, and the combination
of crisp batter and soft, warm fruit in
Indonesian Deep-fried Bananas is quite
simply magical.*

Chinese Fruit Salad

For an unusual fruit salad with an Asian flavor, try this mixture of fruits in a tangy lime and lychee syrup, topped with a light sprinkling of toasted sesame seeds.

INGREDIENTS

Serves 4
½ cup superfine sugar
1¼ cups water
thinly pared rind and juice of 1 lime
1 can (14 ounces) lychees in syrup
1 ripe mango, peeled, pitted and sliced
1 eating apple, cored and sliced
2 bananas, chopped
1 star fruit, sliced (optional)
1 teaspoon sesame seeds, toasted

1 Place the sugar in a saucepan with the water and the lime rind. Heat gently until the sugar dissolves, then increase the heat and boil gently for about 7–8 minutes. Remove from the heat and set aside to cool.

2 Drain the lychees and reserve the juice. Pour the juice into the cooled lime syrup with the lime juice. Place all the prepared fruit in a bowl and pour the lime and lychee syrup over it. Chill for about 1 hour. Just before serving, sprinkle with toasted sesame seeds.

COOK'S TIP

To prepare a mango, cut through the fruit lengthwise, about ½ inch either side of the center. Then, using a sharp knife, cut the flesh from the central piece from the pit. Make even crisscross cuts in the flesh of both side pieces. Hold one side piece in both hands, bend it almost inside out and remove the cubes of flesh with a spoon. Repeat with the other side piece.

Date and Walnut Crisps

Try this sweet version of fried wontons; they make a truly scrumptious snack or dessert.

INGREDIENTS

Makes 15
25–30 dried dates, pitted
½ cup walnuts
2 tablespoons light brown sugar
pinch of ground cinnamon
30 wonton wrappers
1 egg, beaten
oil, for deep-frying
fresh mint sprigs, to decorate
confectioners' sugar, for dusting

1 Chop the dates and walnuts roughly. Place them in a bowl and add the sugar and cinnamon. Mix well.

2 Lay a wonton wrapper on a flat surface. Center a spoonful of the filling on the wrapper, brush the edges with beaten egg and cover with a second wrapper. Lightly press the edges together to seal. Make more filled wontons in the same way.

3 Heat the oil to 350°F in a wok or deep-fryer. Deep-fry the wontons, a few at a time, until golden. Do not crowd the pan. Remove the crisps with a slotted spoon and drain on paper towels. Serve warm, decorated with mint and dusted with confectioners' sugar.

Thin Pancakes

Thin pancakes are not too difficult to make, but quite a lot of practice and patience are needed to achieve the perfect result. Nowadays, even restaurants buy frozen, ready-made ones from Chinese supermarkets. If you decide to use ready-made pancakes, or are reheating home-made ones, steam them for about five minutes, or microwave on high for one to two minutes.

INGREDIENTS

Makes 24–30
4 cups all-purpose flour, plus extra for
   dusting
about 1¼ cups boiling water
1 teaspoon vegetable oil

1 Sift the flour into a mixing bowl, then pour in the boiling water very gently, stirring as you pour. Mix with the oil and knead the mixture into a firm dough. Cover with a damp cloth and let stand for about 30 minutes.

2 Lightly dust a work surface with flour. Knead the dough for 5–8 minutes, or until smooth, then divide it into three equal portions. Roll out each portion into a long "sausage," cut each into eight to ten pieces and roll each into a ball. Using the palm of your hand, press each piece into a flat pancake. With a rolling pin, gently roll each into a 6-inch circle.

3 Heat an ungreased frying pan until hot, then reduce the heat to low and place the pancakes, one at a time, in the pan. Remove the pancakes when small brown spots appear on the underside. Keep under a damp cloth until all the pancakes are cooked.

Red Bean Paste Pancakes

If you are unable to find red bean paste, sweetened chestnut purée or mashed dates are possible substitutes.

INGREDIENTS

Serves 4
about 8 tablespoons sweetened red
   bean paste
8 Thin Pancakes
2–3 tablespoons vegetable oil
granulated or superfine sugar, to serve

1 Spread about 1 tablespoon of the red bean paste over about three-quarters of each pancake, then roll the pancake over three or four times.

2 Heat the oil in a preheated wok or frying pan and fry the pancake rolls until golden brown, turning once.

3 Cut each pancake roll into three or four pieces and sprinkle with sugar to serve.

Almond Curd Junket

Also known as almond float, this dessert is usually made with agar or isinglass, although gelatin can also be used.

INGREDIENTS

Serves 4–6
¼ ounce agar or 1 ounce gelatin
   powder
about 2½ cups water
4 tablespoons superfine sugar
1¼ cups milk
1 teaspoon almond extract
fresh or canned mixed fruit salad with
   syrup, to serve

1 In a saucepan, dissolve the agar in about half the water over gentle heat. This will take at least 10 minutes. (If using gelatin, follow the package instructions.)

2 In a separate saucepan, dissolve the sugar in the remaining water over medium heat. Add the milk and the almond extract, blending well. Do not allow the mixture to boil.

3 Mix the milk and sugar with the agar or gelatin mixture in a serving bowl. When cool, place in the refrigerator for 2–3 hours to set.

4 To serve, cut the junket into small cubes and spoon into a serving dish or into individual bowls. Pour the fruit salad, with the syrup, over the junket and serve.

Stewed Pumpkin in Coconut Cream

Stewed fruit is a popular dessert in Thailand. Use the firm-textured Japanese kabocha pumpkin for this dish, if you can. Bananas and melons can also be prepared in this way and you can even stew corn kernels or dried beans, such as mung beans and black beans, in coconut milk.

INGREDIENTS

Serves 4–6
2¼ pounds kabocha pumpkin
3 cups unsweetened coconut milk
scant 1 cup sugar
pinch of salt
pumpkin seed kernels, toasted, and
 mint sprigs, to decorate

1 Wash the pumpkin skin and cut off most of it. Scoop out the seeds.

COOK'S TIP

Any pumpkin can be used for this dessert, as long as it has a firm texture. Jamaican or New Zealand varieties both make good alternatives to kabocha pumpkin.

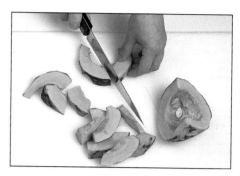

2 Using a sharp knife cut the flesh into pieces about 2 inches long and ¼ inch thick.

3 In a saucepan, bring the coconut milk, sugar and salt to a boil.

4 Add the pumpkin and simmer for 10–15 minutes, until the pumpkin is tender. Serve warm. Decorate each serving with a mint sprig and a few toasted pumpkin seed kernels

Celebration Cake

This mouthwatering cake is made from fragrant Thai rice covered with a tangy cream. Top with fresh berries or pipe on a greeting in melted chocolate.

INGREDIENTS

Serves 8–10

generous 1 cup Thai fragrant or jasmine rice
4 cups milk
generous ½ cup superfine sugar
2 bay leaves
6 cardamom pods, crushed open
1¼ cups heavy cream
6 eggs, separated

For the topping

1¼ cups heavy cream
scant 1 cup quark
1 teaspoon vanilla extract
grated rind of 1 lemon
soft berries and sliced star or kiwi fruits, to decorate

1 Grease and line a deep 10-inch round cake pan. Boil the rice in unsalted water for 3 minutes, then drain well.

2 Return the rice to the pan with the milk, a generous ½ cup of the sugar, the bay leaves and the cardamom. Bring to a boil, then lower the heat and simmer the mixture for 20 minutes, stirring occasionally.

3 Allow the mixture to cool, then remove the bay leaves and any cardamom husks. Transfer to a large bowl. Beat in the cream and then the egg yolks.

4 Whisk the egg whites until they form soft peaks and fold into the rice mixture. Spoon into the prepared pan and bake in a preheated oven at 350°F for 45–50 minutes, until risen and golden brown. The center should be slightly wobbly—it will firm up as it cools.

5 Chill overnight in the pan. Turn out onto a large serving plate. Whip the heavy cream until stiff, then mix in the quark, vanilla extract, lemon rind and remaining sugar.

6 Cover the top and sides of the cake with the cream, swirling it attractively. Decorate with soft berries and sliced star or kiwi fruits.

Steamed Coconut Custard

Srikaya is a very popular dessert that turns up all over South-east Asia, rather as crème caramel is found all over Europe and the Americas.

INGREDIENTS

Serves 8

14-fluid ounce can coconut milk
5 tablespoons water
1 ounce sugar
3 eggs, beaten
1 ounce cellophane noodles, soaked in warm water for 5 minutes
4 ripe bananas or plantains, peeled and cut in small pieces
salt
vanilla ice cream, to serve (optional)

1 Stir the coconut milk, water and sugar into the beaten eggs and whisk well together.

2 Strain into a 7½-cup heatproof soufflé dish.

3 Drain the noodles well and cut them into small pieces with scissors. Stir the noodles into the coconut milk mixture, together with the chopped bananas or plantains. Stir in a pinch of salt.

4 Cover the dish with foil and place in a steamer for about 1 hour, or until set. Test by inserting a thin, small knife or skewer into the center. Serve hot or cold, on its own or topped with vanilla ice cream.

Sweet Potato and Chestnut Candies

It is customary in Japan to offer special bean-paste candies with tea. The candies tend to be very sweet by themselves, but contrast well with Japanese green tea. They also make an unusual dessert at the end of a special evening meal.

INGREDIENTS

Makes 18

1 pound sweet potatoes, chopped
¼ teaspoon salt
2 egg yolks
1 cup sugar
4 tablespoons water
5 tablespoons rice flour or
   all-purpose flour
1 teaspoon orange-flower or rose water
   (optional)
1 can (7 ounces) chestnuts in heavy
   syrup, drained
superfine sugar, for dusting
2 strips candied angelica
2 teaspoons plum or apricot preserves
3–4 drops red food coloring

1 Place the sweet potatoes in a heavy saucepan, cover with cold water and add the salt. Bring to a boil and simmer for 20–25 minutes, until the sweet potatoes are tender. Drain and return to the pan. Mash until smooth or rub through a wire sieve. Place the egg yolks, sugar and water in a bowl, then mix in the flour and orange-flower or rose water, if using. Add the sweet potato purée and stir over a pan of simmering water for 3–4 minutes. Transfer the paste to a tray and let cool.

2 To shape the paste, place 2 teaspoons of the mixture in the center of a wet cotton napkin. Enclose the paste in the napkin and twist into a nut shape. Repeat. Make sure the napkin is wet, or the mixture will stick to it.

3 To prepare the chestnuts, rinse off the syrup and dry well. Roll the chestnuts in superfine sugar and decorate with strips of angelica. To finish the sweet potato candies, color the plum or apricot preserves with red food coloring and decorate each candy with a spot of color.

COOK'S TIP

Sugar-coated chestnuts will keep for up to five days in a sealed container at room temperature. Store sweet potato candies in a sealed container in the refrigerator.

Baked Rice Pudding, Thai-style

Black glutinous rice, also known as black sticky rice, has long black grains and a nutty taste similar to wild rice. This baked pudding has a distinct character and flavor all of its own.

INGREDIENTS

Serves 4–6
6 ounces white or black glutinous (sticky) rice
2 tablespoons light brown sugar
2 cups unsweetened coconut milk
1 cup water
3 eggs
2 tablespoons sugar

1 Combine the glutinous rice, brown sugar, half the coconut milk and all the water in a saucepan.

2 Bring to a boil and simmer for about 15–20 minutes, or until the rice has absorbed most of the liquid, stirring from time to time. Preheat the oven to 300°F.

3 Transfer the rice to one large ovenproof dish or divide it between individual ramekins. Mix together the eggs, remaining coconut milk and sugar in a bowl.

4 Strain and pour the mixture evenly over the par-cooked rice.

5 Place the dish in a baking pan. Pour in enough boiling water to come halfway up the sides of the dish.

6 Cover the dish with a piece of foil and bake in the oven for about 35 minutes to 1 hour, or until the custard is set. Serve warm or cold.

Mango with Sticky Rice

Everyone's favorite dessert. Mangoes, with their delicate fragrance, sweet and sour flavor and velvety flesh, blend especially well with coconut sticky rice. You need to start preparing this dish the day before.

INGREDIENTS

Serves 4
4 ounces glutinous (sticky) white rice
¾ cup thick unsweetened coconut milk
3 tablespoons sugar
pinch of salt
2 ripe mangoes
strips of lime rind, to decorate

1 Rinse the glutinous rice thoroughly in several changes of cold water, then let soak overnight in a bowl of fresh cold water.

2 Drain and spread the rice in an even layer in a steamer lined with cheesecloth. Cover and steam for about 20 minutes, or until the grains of rice are tender.

3 Meanwhile, reserve 3 tablespoons of the top of the coconut milk and combine the rest with the sugar and salt in a saucepan. Bring to a boil, stirring until the sugar dissolves, then pour into a bowl and let cool a little.

4 Turn the rice into a bowl and pour over the coconut mixture. Stir, then let stand for about 10–15 minutes.

5 Peel the mangoes and cut the flesh into slices. Place on top of the rice and drizzle over the reserved coconut milk. Decorate with strips of lime rind.

Sugar Bread Rolls

These delicious sweet rolls reveal the influence of Spain on the cooking of the Philippines. They make an unusual end to a special meal.

INGREDIENTS

Makes 10

3 cups stone-ground flour
1 teaspoon salt
1 tablespoon superfine sugar
1 teaspoon dried yeast
⅔ cup hot water
3 egg yolks
4 tablespoons unsalted butter, softened
¾ cup Cheddar cheese, grated
2 tablespoons melted unsalted butter
generous ¼ cup sugar

1 Sift the flour, salt and superfine sugar into a food processor fitted with a dough blade or the bowl of an electric mixer fitted with a dough hook. Make a well in the center. Dissolve the yeast in the hot water and pour into the well. Add the egg yolks and let sit until bubbles appear on the surface of the liquid.

2 Mix the ingredients for 30–45 seconds to form a firm dough. Add the softened butter and knead for 2–3 minutes in a food processor, or for 4–5 minutes with an electric mixer, until smooth. Turn the dough out into a floured bowl, cover and leave in a warm place to rise until doubled in volume.

3 Turn the dough out onto a lightly floured surface and divide it into ten pieces. Spread the grated cheese over the surface. Roll each of the dough pieces into 5-inch lengths, incorporating the cheese as you do so. Coil into snail shapes and place on a lightly greased high-sided baking sheet measuring 12 x 8 inches.

4 Cover the sheet with a loose-fitting plastic bag and leave in a warm place for 45 minutes, or until the dough has doubled in volume. Bake in a preheated oven at 375°F for 20–25 minutes. Brush with the melted butter, sprinkle with the sugar and let cool. Separate the rolls before serving.

Exotic Fruit Salad

A variety of fruits can be used for this Vietnamese dessert, depending on what is available. Look for mandarin oranges, star fruit, papaya and passion fruit.

INGREDIENTS

Serves 4–6
scant ½ cup sugar
1¼ cups water
2 tablespoons Canton ginger syrup
2 pieces star anise
1-inch piece cinnamon stick
1 clove
juice of ½ lemon
2 fresh mint sprigs
1 mango
2 bananas, sliced
8 fresh or canned lychees
8 ounces strawberries, hulled and
  halved
2 pieces Canton ginger, cut into sticks
1 medium pineapple

1 Put the sugar, water, ginger syrup, star anise, cinnamon, clove, lemon juice and mint in a saucepan. Bring to a boil and simmer for 3 minutes. Strain into a bowl and set aside to cool.

2 Remove the top and bottom from the mango, then remove the outer skin. Stand the mango on one end and remove the flesh in two pieces on either side of the flat pit. Slice evenly and add to the syrup. Add the bananas, lychees, strawberries and ginger.

3 Cut the pineapple in half down the center. Loosen the flesh with a small serrated knife and remove to form two boat shapes. Cut the flesh into chunks and place in the syrup.

4 Spoon some of the fruit salad into the pineapple halves and serve on a large dish. There will be sufficient fruit salad to refill the pineapple halves.

Black Glutinous Rice Pudding

This very unusual rice pudding, *Bubor Pulot Hitam,* which uses bruised fresh ginger root, is quite delicious. When cooked, black rice still retains its husk and has a nutty texture. Serve in small bowls, with a little coconut cream poured over each helping.

INGREDIENTS

Serves 6
4 ounces black glutinous rice
2 cups water
½ inch fresh ginger root, peeled
   and bruised
⅜ cup dark brown sugar
¼ cup superfine sugar
1¼ cups coconut milk
   or cream, to serve

1 Put the rice in a strainer and rinse well under cold running water. Drain and put in a large pan, with the water. Bring to a boil and stir to prevent the rice from settling on the bottom of the pan. Cover and cook for about 30 minutes.

2 Add the ginger and the brown and superfine sugars. Cook for about 15 minutes more, adding a little more water if necessary, until the rice is cooked and like porridge. Remove the ginger and serve warm, in bowls, topped with coconut milk or cream.

Deep-fried Bananas

Known as *Pisang Goreng,* these delicious deep-fried bananas should be cooked at the last minute, so that the outer crust of batter is crisp in texture and the banana is soft and warm inside.

INGREDIENTS

Serves 8
4 ounces self-rising flour
⅜ cup rice flour
½ teaspoon salt
1 cup water
finely grated lime rind (optional)
8 small bananas
oil for deep-frying
sugar and 1 lime, cut in wedges,
   to serve

1 Sift both the flours and the salt together into a bowl. Add just enough water to make a smooth, coating batter. Mix well, then add the lime rind, if using.

2 Peel the bananas and dip them into the batter two or three times.

3 Heat the oil to 375°F or when a cube of day-old bread browns in 30 seconds. Deep-fry the batter-coated bananas until crisp and golden. Drain and serve hot, dredged with sugar and with the lime wedges to squeeze over the bananas.

Thai Coconut Custard

This traditional dish can be baked or steamed, and is often served with sweet sticky rice and a selection of fruit, such as mango and persimmons.

INGREDIENTS

Serves 4–6

4 eggs
6 tablespoons light brown sugar
1 cup unsweetened coconut milk
1 teaspoon vanilla, rose or
 jasmine extract
mint leaves and confectioner's sugar,
 to decorate

1 Preheat the oven to 300°F. Whisk the eggs and sugar in a bowl until they are smooth. Add the coconut milk and vanilla or other extract and blend well together.

2 Strain the mixture and pour into individual ramekins or a cake pan.

3 Stand the ramekins or pan in a roasting pan. Carefully fill the roasting pan with hot water to reach halfway up the outsides of the ramekins or cake pan.

4 Bake for about 35–40 minutes, or until the custards are set. Test with a fine skewer or toothpick.

5 Remove from the oven and cool. Turn out on to a plate, and serve with sliced fruit. Decorate with mint leaves and confectioner's sugar.

Apples and Raspberries in Rose Pouchong Syrup

This delightfully fragrant and quick-to-prepare Asian dessert couples the subtle flavors of apples and raspberries, both of which belong to the rose family, within an infusion of rose-scented tea.

INGREDIENTS

Serves 4

1 teaspoon rose pouchong tea
1 teaspoon rose water (optional)
¼ cup sugar
1 teaspoon lemon juice
5 apples
1½ cups fresh raspberries

1 Warm a large teapot. Add the rose pouchong tea and 3¾ cups of boiling water together with the rose water, if using. Allow to stand and infuse for 4 minutes.

2 Measure the sugar and lemon juice into a stainless steel saucepan. Strain in the tea and stir to dissolve the sugar.

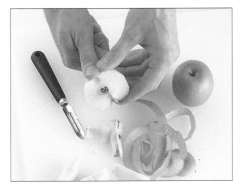

3 Peel and core the apples, then cut into quarters.

4 Poach the apples in the syrup for about 5 minutes.

5 Transfer the apples and syrup to a large metal baking sheet and let cool to room temperature.

6 Pour the cooled apples and syrup into a bowl, add the raspberries and mix to combine. Spoon into individual dishes or bowls and serve immediately.

Pancakes Filled with Sweet Coconut

Traditionally, the pale green color in the batter for *Dadar Gulung* was obtained from the juice squeezed from *pandan* leaves – a real labor of love. Green food coloring can be used as the modern alternative to this lengthy process.

INGREDIENTS

Makes 12–15 pancakes
¾ cup dark brown sugar
2 cups water
1 *pandan* leaf, stripped through with a fork and tied into a knot
6 ounces dried coconut
oil for frying
salt

For the pancake batter
8 ounces flour, sifted
2 eggs, beaten
2 drops edible green food coloring
few drops vanilla extract
scant 2 cups water
3 tablespoons peanut oil

1 Dissolve the sugar in the water with the *pandan* leaf, in a pan over gentle heat, stirring constantly. Increase the heat and allow to boil gently for 3–4 minutes, until the mixture just becomes syrupy. Do not let it caramelize.

2 Put the coconut into a wok with a pinch of salt. Pour over the prepared sugar syrup and cook over a very gentle heat, stirring from time to time, until the mixture becomes almost dry; this will take 5–10 minutes. Set aside until required.

3 To make the batter, blend together the flour, eggs, food coloring, vanilla extract, water and oil either by hand or in a food processor.

4 Brush a 7-inch frying pan with oil and cook 12–15 pancakes. Keep the pancakes warm. Fill each pancake with a generous spoonful of the coconut mixture, roll up and serve them immediately.

Toffee Apples

A variety of fruits, such as bananas and pineapple, can be prepared and cooked in this way.

INGREDIENTS

Serves 4
4 firm apples
1 cup all-purpose flour
about ½ cup water
1 egg, beaten
vegetable oil, for deep-frying, plus
   2 tablespoons for the toffee
¾ cup sugar

1 Peel and core each apple and cut into eight pieces. Dust each piece of apple with a little of the flour.

2 Sift the remaining flour into a mixing bowl, then slowly add the cold water and stir well to make a smooth batter. Add the beaten egg and blend well.

3 Heat the oil for deep-frying in a wok. Dip the apple pieces in the batter and deep-fry for about 3 minutes, or until golden. Remove and drain. Drain off the oil.

4 Heat the remaining oil in the wok, add the sugar and stir constantly until the sugar has caramelized. Quickly add the apple pieces and blend well so that each piece of apple is thoroughly coated with the toffee. Dip the apple pieces in cold water to harden before serving.

Mango and Coconut Stir-fry

Choose a ripe mango for this recipe. If you buy one that is a little underripe, let it sit in a warm place for a day or two before using.

INGREDIENTS

Serves 4
¼ coconut
1 large ripe mango
juice and finely grated zest of 2 limes
1 tablespoon sunflower oil
1 tablespoon butter
2 tablespoons honey
crème fraîche, to serve

1 Prepare the coconut flakes by draining the milk from the coconut and peeling the flesh with a vegetable peeler.

2 Peel the mango. Cut the pit out of the middle of the fruit. Cut each half of the mango into slices.

3 Place the mango slices in a bowl and pour the lime juice and zest over them, to marinate.

4 Meanwhile heat a wok, then add 2 teaspoons of the oil. When the oil is hot, add the butter. When the butter has melted, stir in the coconut flakes and stir-fry for 1–2 minutes, until the coconut is golden brown. Remove and drain on paper towels. Wipe out the wok. Strain the mango slices, reserving the juice.

5 Heat the wok and add the remaining oil. When the oil is hot, add the mango and stir-fry for 1–2 minutes, then add the juice and let bubble and reduce for 1 minute. Stir in the honey, sprinkle the coconut flakes on top and serve with crème fraîche.

COOK'S TIP

You can sometimes buy "fresh" coconut that has already been cracked open and is sold in pieces ready for use at supermarkets, but buying the whole nut ensures greater freshness. Choose one that is heavy for its size and shake it so that you can hear the milk sloshing around. A "dry" coconut will almost certainly have rancid flesh. You can simply crack the shell with a hammer, preferably with the nut inside a plastic bag, but it may be better to pierce the two ends with a sharp nail or skewer first in order to collect and save the coconut milk. An alternative method is to drain the milk first and then heat the nut briefly in the oven until it cracks. Whichever method you choose, it is then fairly easy to extract the flesh and chop or shave it.

Wonton Twists

These little twists are perfect when you want a quick snack.

INGREDIENTS

Makes 24
12 wonton wrappers
1 egg, beaten
1 tablespoon black sesame seeds
oil for deep-frying
confectioner's sugar for
    dusting (optional)

1 Cut the wonton wrappers in half. Make a lengthwise slit in the center of each piece with a sharp knife.

2 Take one wonton at a time, and pull one end through the slit, stretching it a little as you go.

3 Brush each twist with a little beaten egg. Dip the wonton twists briefly in black sesame seeds to coat them lightly.

4 Heat the oil in a deep-fryer or large saucepan to 375°F. Add a few wonton twists at a time so they do not overcrowd the pan. Fry the twists for 1–2 minutes on each side until crisp and light golden brown. Remove each twist, and drain on paper towels. Dust with confectioner's sugar, if you like, and serve at once.

COOK'S TIP

Use ordinary sesame seeds in place of the black ones, if you prefer.

Fried Wontons and Ice Cream

Here is the Chinese equivalent of American cookies and ice cream. Serve it with fresh or poached fruits or fruit sauces for an impressive treat.

INGREDIENTS

Serves 4
oil for deep-frying
12 wonton wrappers
8 scoops of your favorite ice cream

COOK'S TIP

Try using two flavors of ice cream – chocolate and strawberry perhaps, or vanilla and coffee. For a sophisticated adults-only treat, drizzle over a spoonful of your favorite liqueur.

1 Heat the oil in a deep-fryer or large saucepan to 375°F.

3 Let the cooked wontons drain on paper towels.

2 Add a few wonton wrappers at a time so that they do not crowd the pan too much. Fry for 1–2 minutes on each side until the wrappers are crisp and light golden brown.

4 To serve, place one wonton on each plate. Place a scoop of ice cream on top of each wonton. Top with a second wonton, then add another scoop of ice cream, and finish with a final wonton. Serve at once.

Tapioca Pudding

This warm pudding, made from large pearl tapioca and coconut milk, is much lighter than the Western-style version. Serve with lychees or the smaller, similar-tasting longans – also known as "dragon's eyes."

INGREDIENTS

Serves 4

²/₃ cup tapioca
2 cups water
scant 1 cup sugar
pinch of salt
1 cup unsweetened coconut milk
9 ounces prepared tropical fruits
finely shredded rind of 1 lime and
 coconut shavings (optional),
 to decorate

1 Soak the tapioca in warm water for 1 hour so the grains swell. Drain.

2 Put the water in a saucepan and bring to a boil. Stir in the sugar and the salt.

3 Add the tapioca and coconut milk and simmer for 10 minutes, or until the tapioca turns transparent.

4 Serve warm with some tropical fruits and decorate with lime rind strips and coconut shavings, if using.

Fried Bananas

These delicious treats are a favorite among children and adults alike. They are sold as snacks throughout the day and night at roadside stalls and market places. Other fruits, such as pineapple and apple, will work just as well.

INGREDIENTS

Serves 4

1 cup all-purpose flour
½ teaspoon baking soda
pinch of salt
2 tablespoons sugar
1 egg
6 tablespoons water
2 tablespoons shredded coconut or
 1 tablespoon sesame seeds
4 firm bananas
oil for frying
2 tablespoons honey, to serve (optional)
sprigs of mint, to decorate

1 Sift the flour, baking soda and salt together into a bowl. Stir in the sugar. Whisk in the egg and add enough water to make the mixture into quite a thin batter.

2 Whisk in the shredded coconut or sesame seeds.

3 Peel the bananas. Carefully cut each one in half lengthwise, then in half crosswise.

4 Heat the oil in a wok or deep-frying pan. Dip the bananas in the batter, then gently drop a few into the oil. Fry until golden brown.

5 Remove from the oil and drain on paper towels. Serve immediately with honey, if using, and decorate with sprigs of mint.

SAUCES, SAMBALS AND ACCOMPANIMENTS

Dipping sauces are often served with spring rolls, meat, fish, salads and vegetables. Sometimes, they provide a cooling or creamy contrast to hot spiced dishes. More often, they add piquancy and may be very fiery. Sambals, pungent relishes that originated in southern India, are now served throughout South-east Asia and are often quite substantial, containing vegetables, poultry or seafood. Whether raw or cooked, they are invariably very hot. Finally, no Balti dish would be complete without freshly cooked bread and a spicy chutney.

Sambal Goreng

Traditional flavorings for this dish are fine strips of calves' liver, chicken livers, green beans or hard-boiled eggs. A westernized version is shown here.

INGREDIENTS

Makes 3¼ cups

1 teaspoon shrimp paste
2 onions, quartered
2 garlic cloves, crushed
1 inch fresh *laos*, peeled and sliced
2 teaspoons Chili Sambal or 2 fresh red chilies, seeded and sliced
¼ teaspoon salt
2 tablespoons oil
3 tablespoons tomato paste
2½ cups broth or water
4 tablespoons tamarind juice
pinch sugar
3 tablespoons coconut milk or cream

1 Grind the shrimp paste, with the onions and garlic, to a paste in a food processor or with a mortar and pestle. Add the *laos*, Chili Sambal or sliced chilies and salt. Process or pound to a fine paste.

2 Fry the paste in hot oil for 2 minutes, without browning, until the mixture gives off a rich aroma.

3 Add the tomato paste and the broth or water and cook for about 10 minutes. Add 12 ounces cooked chicken pieces and 2 ounces cooked and sliced French beans, or one of the flavoring variations below, to half the quantity of the sauce. Cook in the sauce for 3–4 minutes, then stir in the tamarind juice, sugar and coconut milk or cream at the last minute, before tasting and serving.

— VARIATIONS —

Tomato *Sambal Goreng* – Add 1 pound of peeled, seeded and coarsely chopped tomatoes, before the broth.

Shrimp *Sambal Goreng* – Add 12 ounces cooked, peeled shrimp and 1 green bell pepper, seeded and chopped.

Egg *Sambal Goreng* – Add 3 or 4 hard-boiled eggs, shelled and chopped, and 2 tomatoes, peeled, seeded and chopped.

Sweet-and-Sour Ginger Sambal

This sambal is especially delicious with fish, chicken or pork—but beware, it is extremely hot.

INGREDIENTS

Makes 6 tablespoons
4–5 small fresh red chilies, seeded and chopped
2 shallots or 1 small onion, chopped
2 garlic cloves
¾-inch fresh ginger
2 tablespoons sugar
¼ teaspoon salt
3 tablespoons rice vinegar or white wine vinegar

1 Pound together the chilies and shallots or onion in a mortar with a pestle. Alternatively, grind them in a food processor.

2 Add the garlic, ginger, sugar and salt and continue to pound or grind until smooth. Stir in the vinegar and mix well.

COOK'S TIP

This sambal can be stored for up to a week in a screw-top jar in the refrigerator.

Satay Sauce

There are many versions of this tasty peanut sauce. This one is very speedy and it tastes delicious drizzled over grilled or barbecued skewers of chicken. For parties, spear chunks of chicken with toothpicks and arrange around a bowl of warm satay sauce.

INGREDIENTS

Serves 4
scant 1 cup coconut cream
4 tablespoons crunchy peanut butter
1 teaspoon Worcestershire sauce
few drops of Tabasco sauce
fresh coconut, to garnish (optional)

1 Pour the coconut cream into a small saucepan and heat it gently over low heat for about 2 minutes.

2 Add the peanut butter and stir vigorously until the mixture is thoroughly blended. Continue to heat, but do not allow to boil.

3 Add the Worcestershire sauce and Tabasco sauce to taste. Pour into a serving bowl.

4 Use a potato peeler to shave thin strips from a piece of fresh coconut, if using. Scatter the coconut over the sauce and serve immediately.

Vietnamese Dipping Sauce

Serve this dip in a small bowl as an accompaniment to spring rolls or meat dishes.

INGREDIENTS

Makes ²/₃ cup
1–2 small fresh red chilies, seeded and
    finely chopped
1 garlic clove, crushed
1 tablespoon roasted peanuts
4 tablespoons coconut milk
2 tablespoons fish sauce
juice of 1 lime
2 teaspoons sugar
1 teaspoon chopped fresh cilantro

1 Pound the chili or chilies with the garlic in a mortar with a pestle.

2 Add the peanuts and pound until crushed. Add the coconut milk, fish sauce, lime juice, sugar and cilantro. Mix well.

Thai Dipping Sauce

Nam prik is the most common dipping sauce in Thailand. It has a fiery strength, so use it with caution.

INGREDIENTS

Makes ¹/₂ cup
1 tablespoon vegetable oil
½-inch square shrimp paste or
    1 tablespoon fish sauce
2 garlic cloves, finely sliced
¾-inch piece fresh ginger, finely
    chopped
3 small fresh red chilies, seeded
    and chopped
1 tablespoon finely chopped cilantro
    root or stem
4 teaspoons sugar
3 tablespoons dark soy sauce
juice of ½ lime

1 Heat the vegetable oil in a preheated wok. Add the shrimp paste or fish sauce, garlic, ginger and chilies and stir-fry for 1–2 minutes, until softened, but not colored.

2 Remove from the heat and add the chopped cilantro, sugar, soy sauce and lime juice.

COOK'S TIP

Thai Dipping Sauce will keep for up to 10 days in a screw-top jar in the refrigerator.

Hoisin Dip

This speedy dip needs no cooking and can be made in just a few minutes—it tastes great with Mini Spring Rolls or shrimp crackers.

INGREDIENTS

Serves 4
4 scallions
1½-inch piece fresh ginger
2 fresh red chilies
2 garlic cloves
4 tablespoons hoisin sauce
½ cup tomato paste
1 teaspoon sesame oil (optional)

1 Trim off and discard the green ends of the scallions. Slice the white parts very thinly.

3 Halve and seed the chilies. Slice finely. Finely chop the garlic.

2 Peel and finely chop the ginger.

4 Stir together the hoisin sauce, tomato paste, scallions, ginger, chilies, garlic and sesame oil, if using. Serve within 1 hour.

Cucumber Sambal

This sauce has a piquant flavor and does not have the heat of chilies found in other sambals.

INGREDIENTS

Makes ⅔ cup
1 garlic clove, crushed
1 teaspoon fennel seeds
2 teaspoons sugar
½ teaspoon salt
2 shallots or 1 small onion, finely sliced
½ cup rice or white wine vinegar
¼ cucumber, finely diced

1 Pound together the garlic, fennel seeds, sugar and salt in a mortar with a pestle. Alternatively, grind them together in a food processor.

2 Stir in the shallots or onion, vinegar and cucumber and set aside for at least 6 hours to allow the flavors to combine.

Tomato Sambal

Sambal Tomaat, from Surabaya, can be used as a dip to eat with fritters and snack foods.

INGREDIENTS

Makes about 1¼ cups
2 large beefsteak tomatoes, about
  14 ounces in all, peeled if liked
1 fresh red chili, seeded, or
  ½ teaspoon chili powder
2–3 garlic cloves
4 tablespoons dark brown sugar
3 tablespoons sunflower oil
1 tablespoon lime or lemon juice
salt

1 Cut the tomatoes in quarters and remove the cores. Place in a food processor with the chili or chili powder, garlic, sugar and salt to taste. Process to a purée.

2 Fry the tomato pureé in hot oil, stirring all the time, until the mixture thickens and has lost its raw taste. Add the lime or lemon juice. Cool, then season. Serve warm or cold.

Carrot and Apple Salad

Known as *Selada Bortel*, this simple, crunchy salad is always a perfect accompaniment to spicy Indonesian food. It's best to grate the apple at the last minute and sprinkle it liberally with lemon juice to prevent discoloration. Cover the salad with plastic wrap and store in the fridge until needed.

INGREDIENTS

Serves 6
3 large carrots
1 green apple
juice of 1 lemon
3 tablespoons sunflower oil
1 teaspoon sugar
salt and freshly ground black pepper

1 Coarsely grate the carrot and set aside. Grate the apple, including the skin, and drizzle it with the lemon juice to prevent discoloration. Mix gently with your hand to evenly coat the apple with the lemon juice.

2 Add the sunflower oil and sugar to the apple mixture. Season to taste with salt and black pepper, then stir in the grated carrot.

3 Cover the salad with plastic wrap and chill in the fridge for a short time, until required.

---- VARIATION ----

For a tangy flavor, add lime juice and a little grated lime rind to the apple.

Apricot Chutney

Chutneys can add zest to most meals, and cooks in Pakistan often serve a choice of different kinds in tiny bowls.

INGREDIENTS

Makes about 450g/1lb

450g/1lb dried apricots, finely diced
5ml/1 tsp garam masala
275g/10oz/1¼ cups brown sugar
450ml/¾ pint/scant 2 cups malt vinegar
5ml/1 tsp ginger pulp
5ml/1 tsp salt
75g/3oz/½ cup golden raisins
450ml/¾ pint/scant 2 cups water

1 Put all the ingredients into a medium saucepan and mix together thoroughly.

2 Bring to a boil, then lower the heat and simmer gently for 30–35 minutes, stirring occasionally.

3 When the chutney has thickened to a fairly stiff consistency, transfer into 2–3 warm, clean jars and set aside to cool completely. Cover and store in the fridge.

Tasty Toasts

These crunchy toasts are excellent served as part of a weekend brunch. They are especially delicious served with broiled tomatoes.

INGREDIENTS

Makes 8

4 eggs
300ml/½ pint/1¼ cups milk
2 fresh green chilies, finely chopped
30ml/2 tbsp chopped fresh cilantro
75g/3oz Cheddar or mozzarella cheese, grated
4 slices bread
salt and freshly ground black pepper
corn oil, for frying

1 Break the eggs into a medium bowl and whisk together. Slowly add the milk and whisk again. Add the chilies, chopped cilantro and cheese and season with salt and pepper.

2 Cut the bread slices in half diagonally and soak them, one at a time, in the egg mixture.

3 Heat the oil in a frying pan and fry the bread triangles over medium heat, turning them once or twice, until they are golden brown.

4 Drain off any excess oil as you remove the toasts from the pan and serve immediately.

Paratha

Paratha is an unleavened bread with rich, flaky layers. The preparation time is quite lengthy and, as the parathas are best served fresh from the pan, you will need to plan your menu well ahead. They can be served as an accompaniment to almost any Balti dish.

INGREDIENTS

Makes about 8

225g/8oz/2 cups chapati flour or whole wheat flour, plus extra for dusting
2.5ml/½ tsp salt
200ml/7fl oz/scant 1 cup water
115g/4oz vegetable ghee, melted

1 Put the flour and salt into a large mixing bowl. Make a well in the center and add the water, a little at a time, to make a soft, but pliable, dough. Knead well for a few minutes, then cover and allow to rest for about 1 hour.

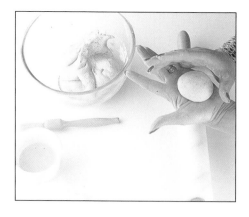

2 Divide the dough into 8 even portions. Roll each one out on a lightly floured surface into a circle about 10cm/4in in diameter. Brush the middle of each with about 2.5ml/½ tsp vegetable ghee.

3 Fold each circle in half and roll up into a tube.

4 Flatten slightly between your palms, then roll around your finger to form a coil. Roll out again into a circle about 18cm/7in in diameter, dusting with extra flour as necessary.

5 Heat a heavy-based frying pan and slap a paratha on to it. Move it gently around the pan to make sure that it is evenly exposed to the heat. Turn it over and brush with about 5ml/1 tsp of the ghee.

6 Cook for about 1 minute, then turn it over again and cook for about 30 seconds, moving it constantly.

7 Remove from the pan and wrap in foil to keep warm. Fry the remaining parathas in the same way. Serve warm.

Index

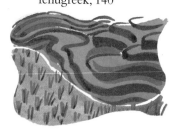

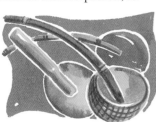